ON BEING A
PSYCHOTHERAPIST

Commentary

"This book is a gem and bound to become a widely read classic among burgeoning and master psychotherapists. The book's compelling content, organization, concise writing style, and optimal blend of case notes, references, and insightful reflections on Goldberg's own clinical practice make this volume highly respectable. One can easily infer that Goldberg is not only a seasoned practitioner in his own right, but he also possesses a talent for being able to portray the conflicts and struggles of psychotherapists at large."

—William Alexy

"This book by Goldberg is unique among the hundreds of books published on the practice of psychotherapy. It is not a how-to manual on methodology, techniques, theories, rationales of any one of the myriad schools of psychotherapy. Rather it is an attempt to explore the sources of the basic motivations of those who ultimately select the practice of psychotherapy as their professional goal. It is must reading for all students contemplating psychotherapy as their professional goal and for all therapists now in practice. It is critical that each of us knows the self and recognizes how the nuclear family impacted us toward our professional goal, if we are to succeed as psychotherapists."

—Leah Gold Fein, Ph.D.

"Goldberg has written a book that is both scholarly and clinically right about the inside world of the psychotherapists. The topics covered range from the abstract and philosophical to the concrete and practical. He discusses the inner struggles that lead many people to become psychotherapists and the ongoing courage required to deal with the personal demands and threats involved in this profession. The themes of courage and intimacy are the underpinnings of the book—courage, first, to risk knowing oneself and, then, to risk self-exposure in order to achieve intimacy with the client. Goldberg writes about the importance of the personal journey (i.e., the inward path to self-understanding) both to the therapist and to the client."

—Stephanie Adler, M.D.

ON BEING A PSYCHOTHERAPIST

by CARL GOLDBERG, Ph.D.

Foreword by James S. Grotstein, M.D.

JASON ARONSON INC.
Northvale, New Jersey
London

Library of Congress Cataloging-in-Publication Data

Goldberg, Carl.
　　On being a psychotherapist / Carl Goldberg.
　　　p. cm.
　　Reprint. Originally published: New York : Gardner Press, c1986.
　　Includes bibliographical references.
　　Includes indexes.
　　ISBN 0-87668-885-7   (previously 0-89876-112-3)
　　1. Psychotherapy — Practice — Psychological aspects.
　2. Psychotherapist and patient. 3. Intimacy (Psychology)
　4. Psychotherapists — Psychology. I. Title
　　[DNLM: 1. Professional-Patient Relations. 2. Professional
　Practice. 3. Psychotherapy. WM 21 G618o 1986a]
　RC465.5.G65   1990
　616.89′0097 — dc20
　DNLM/DLC
　for Library of Congress　　　　　　　　　　　　　　　　90-14498

Manufactured in the United States of America. Jason Aronson Inc. offers books and cassettes. For information and catalog write to Jason Aronson Inc., 230 Livingston Street, Northvale, New Jersey 07647.

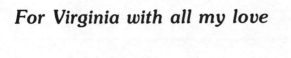
For Virginia with all my love

Contents

FOREWORD BY JAMES S. GROTSTEIN, M.D.   xiii
PREFACE   xix
     The Impossible Profession   xxiii
     Readership of This Book   xxv
     Author's Point of View   xxvii
     Notes   xxvii

PART ONE: BECOMING A HEALER

Chapter 1: **The Personal Journey of the Healer**   3
     The Practitioner's Journey in Search of Self   4
     The Age-old Journey of the Shaman   6
     Notes   14

Chapter 2: **The Role of Intimacy in the Personal Journey**   15
     The Nature of Intimacy   19
     Clinical Case   21
     Clinical Impression   23
     How Intimacy Develops   23
     Roger's History   25
     Notes   33

Chapter 3: **The Public's View of the Psychotherapist**   34
     The Spreading Influence of Psychotherapy   36
     Psychological Explanation   38
     Notes   45

Chapter 4: **Becoming a Psychotherapist**   47
     The Therapist's Identity   47

Psychotherapy as a Calling   48
The Backgrounds of Psychotherapists   52
The Therapist-to-be in the Family of Origin   54
The Psychic Vulnerabilities of the Psychotherapist   62
Notes   65

Chapter 5: **The Satisfactions of Practice**   67
The Practitioner's Inner Life   67
Unconscious Satisfactions   73
The Career of a Psychotherapist   75

Chapter 6: **The Hazards of Practice**   78
The Promise and Realities of Practice   79
Normal Stress of Practice   81
The Lure of Being a Psychotherapist   84
Identification Denial   84
The "As If" Practitioner   85
The Danger of Superiority   86
The Life-style of the Practitioner   88
Secrets and Shame   89
The Practitioner's vs. the Public's View of the Good
   Life   90
Psychology as a Guideline for Living   91
The World of the Practitioner   92
Psychotherapy as an Inexact Science   93
The Quest for Reason   95
Therapeutic Struggle with Clients   97
Intimacy and Relatedness   101
Responsibility and Illusion   102
Working with Undesirable Clients   103
What Can the Psychotherapist Actually Promise?   105
Notes   109

Chapter 7: **The Qualities of the Practitioner**   111
The Motivations of Those Drawn to Practice
   Psychotherapy   111
The Scholarly Motive   113
The Ethical Motive   115
The Creative Motive   117
The Qualities of the Practitioner   120
Education   124
The Apprenticeship of the Practitioner   127
Supervision   128

Experiential Training 129
Personal Psychotherapy for Practitioners 129
Notes 132

PART TWO: THE PRACTICE OF BEING A HEALER

Chapter 8: **Starting a Private Practice** 137
    Reasons for a Career in Institutional Settings 139
    Private Practice 140
    Ways Private Practice Differs from Institutional
      Practice 141
    Evaluating the Risks and Rewards of Private
      Practice 142
    Part-time or Full-time Practice 143
    Business Aspects of Practice 144
    Promoting One's Practice 146
    Public Appearances 146
    Getting Referrals 147
    The Impact of Geography on Technique and
      Approach 148
    Fees 149
    Interdisciplinary Work 152
    Professional Identity 153
    Group Practice 153
    Individual vs. Group/Family Psychotherapy 154
    Collaborative Therapy 155
    Time Management 156
    Flexibility of Scheduling 156
    The Office 157
    Practicing: Home vs. Office 158
    Answering the Phone 159
    Clinical Impact of the Work Setting 160
    Clients Who Don't Pay Bills 161
    Clients Terminating Treatment 161
    Management of Crisis 162
    Notes 164

Chapter 9: **Structuring the Personal Journey in
Psychotherapy** 165
    Modification of the Once Exclusive Therapeutic
      Relationship 166

Political and Societal Implications of Psychotherapy   169
A Frame of Reference for Psychotherapy   171
Contractual Psychotherapy   175
Relationship as Contract in Psychotherapy   177
Other Alternatives to Probing Psychotherapy   180
The Contractual Phase in Psychotherapy   181
Elements of a Contract   182
Outline for Establishing a Therapeutic Contract   184
Contract Negotiation Between Therapist and Client   190
Equity and Balance   191
Their Implications for Interpersonal Relations   192
A Contractual Approach for Difficult Clients   194
The Unspoken Dimension of Power in
    Psychotherapy   195
Power and Suicide Threat   198
Therapist's Relationship with a Client   203
Notes   206

Chapter 10: **The Role of Intimacy in Psychotherapy**   207
Human Suffering   207
Suffering as Learned   210
The Neglect of Courage in the Behavioral Sciences   214
The Contemporary View of Narcissism   215
The Changing Role: Psychotherapist as Affective
    Agent   216
The Role of Intimacy in Psychotherapy   217
The Struggle in Psychotherapy   224
Realizing That Human Relationships Are Destined
    to Fail   225
The Therapeutic Search for Truth   226
Ultimate Goal in Psychotherapy   227
The Personal Journey in Psychotherapy   227
Abuses of Therapeutic Intimacy   230
The Double as Soulmate   232
Notes   235

Chapter 11: **Developing Intimacy**   237
Basic Emotional Communication: 25 Principles   238
Notes   247

Chapter 12: **Dealing with Difficult Clients**   248
Negative Therapeutic Reaction   250

The Psychoanalytic Tradition 252
Fostering a Therapeutic Alliance 254
    Values 254
    Transference-Countertransference Interface 257
    Technique 264
Conclusion 277
Notes 278

Chapter 13: **A Prospectus for Dealing with the Concerns of Practice** 281
Tailoring Professional Objectives to the Practitioner's Personality 281
The Practitioner's Life Plan and Goals 282
Expanding One's Clinical Perspective 283
The Problem of Countertransference 284
Personal Experience, Research, or Authority? 286
Voyeurism vs. Active Participation in Life 287
When Personal and Social Needs Are Not Met 288
Private Practice as a Way of Life 288
Loneliness and Boredom in Practice 289
Impact on One's Family 290
Personal Involvements with Clients 290
When Sexual Problems Arise 290
Sexual Attraction in Psychotherapy 291
Being Real as a Psychotherapist 292
The Egalitarian Partnership in Psychotherapy 293
The Fear of Compassion 294
The Therapist as Role Model 295
The Therapist's Existential Choice 297
The Limits to Involvement with Clients 299
Psychotherapy as a System of Knowledge 300
Eastern and Western Thought Contrasted 302

Chapter 14: **The Practitioner's Continuing Personal and Professional Growth** 308
The Personal Concerns of the Practitioner 309
The Concerns of the Beginner 310
The Concerns of the Journeyman Practitioner 310
Addressing the Growing Concerns of the Seasoned Practitioner 311
    Private Supervision 311
    Growth by Collaborative Endeavors 315

Review of the Literature 316
Advantages and Limitations of Co-therapy 318
A Model for Co-therapy 320
Co-therapy as Personal Psychotherapy 324
Conjoint Consultation with Clients and
Colleagues 325
Consultation to Assess Progress and
Impasse 326
Peer Supervision Groups 328
Why Peer Groups Are Formed 329
Hidden Agendas That Impede Productive
Peer Supervision 329
Guidelines for Forming and Maintaining a
Peer Supervision Group 330
Peer/Colleague Support 345
Support from Family and Friends 346
Other Considerations 347
Taking Time Off 347
Time Management 347
Scheduling Sessions 348
Handling Between-session Time 349
Combining Professional Activities 350
The Question of Publication 350
Need for Additional Training 352
Notes 355

PART THREE: EPILOGUE

Chapter 15: **Careers After Practice** 359

Conclusion 363

Selected Bibliography 365

References 371

Author Index 385

Subject Index 389

Foreword

by James S. Grotstein, M.D.

Carl Goldberg's contribution is more than a welcome addition to the already burgeoning literature on psychotherapy. It is the first time, I believe, that anyone has dealt seriously, methodically, and in depth with the problems of being a psychotherapist. When a young medical school graduate enters internship, and later residency, at his/her fingertips are a *House Officer's Manual* and a concise, handy *Merck Manual*. The former is a compendium of virtually all the immediate information about blood levels of electrolytes, emergency procedures, and so forth, and the latter is a comprehensive review of virtually all human illnesses, and how to treat them. With these handbooks serving as talismans, the insecure intern or resident gains a sense of courage during the otherwise frightening journey toward responsibility for human life.

The need for a manual for the welfare of the psychotherapist has generally been ignored, both in training and in the literature; if the subject is addressed, it seems to be perfunctorily relegated to the confines of training analysis or reanalysis. The act of being a psychotherapist puts one at risk for subtle but powerful occupational hazards that transcend terms such as countertransference. The isolation and loneliness that the discipline of performing this job imposes are well known. What has received less attention is the wear and tear on our morale as we too suffer the pain of these strangers whom we admit into our own private worlds. Further, as we learn more about the failed responsibilities of parenthood, we too feel our client's newfound sense of enraged entitlement. As we grow to understand the failures of our own attunement with them in the here and now, we en-

dure an even more profound pain. We must suffer through the
rigors of a most unusual kind of relationship, which is, paradoxically, only unilaterally mutual. This gap in the relationship pin-
points our vulnerability to *being* "battered therapists," not just
batter*ing* therapists, as Dr. Goldberg so cogently reveals.

Why has there been no such handbook for psychotherapists
until now? The reasons, although complex, may be reduced to
such factors as a greater disorder in the conceptualization of psychopathological theories than is true in medical pathology and
disagreement about the efficacy of therapeutic methods in a field
where the "tissue" is invisible and, consequently, harder to stan-
dardize. Further, physicians of the body can, by mutual consent,
agree that the pathology with which they deal lies within the patient and therefore is separate from them; the patient is a speci-
men. Psychoanalysis, the main source for today's variegated
theories of psychotherapies, has long promulgated this Cartesian
notion of the separation between the observer and the observed
and its consequence, a hierarchical system between the observer
and the pitiable observed. Classical psychoanalysts are still
rigorously trained to comport themselves almost as insouciant,
implacable, Edwardians whose emotional noninteraction with
the patient serves to protect the analytic field from unwarranted
contamination. This method of analytic observation has been
subjected to scrutiny by Heinz Kohut, who labeled this technique "experience distant," in contrast to the technique he ad-
vocated, that of "empathic observation" (which is "experience
near" vis-à-vis the patient).

The field of humanistic-existential psychology has had an independent history, with one of its main emphases being that of
the therapist–client interaction. This emphasis, which long an-
tedated the contributions of Kohut and his school, is important
for at least two reasons—an emphasis on the *client*, as opposed
to the patient, and an emphasis on the interaction between therapist and client. The term "client" signifies a status of equality
between the observer and the observed and, to encompass the
second category, seems to signify that each is the observer and
the observed. A therapeutic class system consequently disap-
pears. At long last, these two main streams of psychotherapeutic traditions seem to be converging into the stream of interac-
tionism and/or intersubjectivity. This focus on the mutuality of
influence is also being paralleled in the field of infant development with the awareness of the mother–infant "reciprocity
dance," "mutual eye gaze," and the like. Robert Langs has

created a new school of psychoanalytic theory and therapy based upon the concept of a communicative field and emphasizes the danger in the therapist's capacity to injure the patient-client. The capacity of the patient-client to injure the psychotherapist is a theme that has been less rigorously studied except in the literature on countertransference. Yet we were made aware of it by F. Scott Fitzgerald's *Tender Is the Night* and got hints of it from the Kleinian conception of projective identification and counteridentification.

Dr. Goldberg's text fills this gap by systematically helping the would-be therapist, the new therapist, the experienced therapist, and the retiring therapist find their place in their professional life cycle. How and why does one choose psychotherapy as a career? Should one choose or not choose it? Why do therapists become disillusioned and experience "burn-out"? What is the relationship between being a "healer" and being a "therapist"? These are but a few of the profound questions Dr. Goldberg confronts in this work. There is a need for us to appreciate what we actually do, he states, and how what we are as personalities (in terms of our individual temperaments and character) impacts on our patients-clients, but *therapeutically*, not only harmfully, as is usually emphasized. In eschewing the experience-distant model of therapeutic intervention, Dr. Goldberg emphasizes that the therapist brings to the treatment situation the positive benefit of the values gleaned from the therapists' own background that comprise the central core of his/her authentic being. From this subjective base, the therapist responds to his/her patient-client, not emotionally, but from his/her emotions in a way that demonstrates the therapist's *emotional participation* as an observer rather than as a referee or an umpire calling the shots of a game with unilateral detachment. What we have been (and with whom we have been) is, in no small measure, what we are today. Our authentic appreciation of our backgrounds helps us existentially to compare our own experiences with what we hear expressed by our patients-clients so that, eventually, a concensus takes place—which we call "understanding."

At the same time, therapy is a two-way street, as Dr. Goldberg stresses. It was Harold Searles who reminded us that patients seem to be intuitive about psychopathology in the therapists as they had to be about it in their parents when they were children. Kohut, likewise, tells us that many patients have had to be self objects to their parents rather than the reverse, and

Robert Langs corroborates this from the point of view of the communicative field. What seems to be happening, consequently, is that there is a new focus in psychotherapy that emphasizes a mutual interaction between therapist and client in which each impacts on the other, both beneficially and harmfully, as the therapist must be more on guard than ever—and yet, paradoxically, less on guard in terms of being free enough emotionally to interact with the patient in such a way so as to be existentially honest and be present at the moment of impact in the therapeutic hour as him- or herself.

Dr. Goldberg states that practitioners, in pursuing their personal journey, utilize their own life experiences as the major source of their expertise. This statement is so obvious that one can agree with it and pass on without reflection if one is not careful. Just as the method actor must find within him/herself that memory of a life experience that corresponds to the *requisite* role he or she is now required to perform, a psychotherapist must also allow him/herself to resonate the impact of the patient's-client's feelings by allowing the emotional memory banks to be accessed so that the therapist can achieve a semblance of affective or experiential empathy of a highly personal kind, not merely the observational empathy suggested by Kohut and his followers. In fact, there is a danger in the therapist's denying personal values while functioning as a therapist, the author maintains, warning the therapist, thereby, of the pitfalls of martyr-like selflessness, which is the breakdown of mutuality and of interaction.

Dr. Goldberg emphasizes the importance of the therapist's mental health, the hazards of practice, the realization in mid-life of being unfitted for the profession, and a host of other dark considerations that will strike every reader who has been a therapist with a sense of sad familiarity.

The range of Dr. Goldberg's perspective is awesome. He introduces the beginning therapist to the mundane but necessary details of training, among which are getting a supervisor, getting treatment, setting up a practice, choosing a financial advisor, and facing the hazards of practice. He then goes on to demonstrate the connection between the shaman and the therapist, integrate the Eastern experience of psychotherapy in contrast with the Western, and deal with a host of practical, aesthetic, metapsychological, and philosophical aspects of therapy in between those extremes.

I found his concept of the double self of particular interest. Dr. Goldberg conceives of the double self as being that split-off aspect of ourselves that was not enfranchised or permitted to be a person. In that regard, it is not unlike Winnicott's "true self." The difference between them is that Dr. Goldberg's second self continues to exert a powerful, negative, magical influence over the compliant, "false self," the personality we are conscious of so that the therapist's awareness of his or her own double self facilitates the recovery of the patient-client. Conversely, if the therapist fails to comprehend his/her own double self, then this failure may result in an eclipse of the patient's attempt to make this integration. What is unique about this is that it seems to unite Freud's instinctual drives and repressed memories, Winnicott's "false self," Klein's internal object, and Jacobson's part object into a meaningful, personified entity that seems to have an alternate life within the self. This second self exerts a numinous personal power that appears to be negative or attacking, like a conscience, but actually compels the patient-client to muster the courage to reintegrate it, toward which end the therapeutic courage of the therapist is necessary. Dr. Goldberg movingly states that "Each partner can enable the other to be more fully present by enabling the other to experience what aspect of the partner is missing, denied, or underpresented in their dialogue."

Dr. Goldberg suggests that the existence of the repressed double self denies us access to an aspect of ourselves that is needed for our integration. As a consequence, each of us seeks this double self externally in terms of recognizing a strange–familiar, missing aspect of ourselves. "Suffering comes from lack of self-integration," he writes. "It is derived from the feeling that part of oneself, which is contained in another, is necessary for completion." And suffering is derived from desiring our other half.

Perhaps the Ariadne's thread running through this notable work is the experience of courage, the courage to be, the courage to confront, the courage to make oneself known. "There is always a struggle in psychotherapy about how each shall make himself known to the other," we are told. This courage is basic to the whole psychotherapeutic endeavor and fundamentally constitutes the modeling the therapist-healer conveys to his/her patient-client. The corollary to courage is the therapist's capacity to experience risk-taking on the therapeutic journey, where risk involves the jeopardy of exposure in the act of daring to experience.

Dr. Goldberg conceives of a basic form of therapeutic dialogue, which he terms "basic emotional communication." He likens it to keeping a ping-pong ball in motion on a table through the continuing strokes of each of the two players. This concept is one of Dr. Goldberg's methods of demonstrating his respect for dialectics. Dialectics is a philosophical concept popularized by Hegel, but derives from the attempts of the ancient Greek philosophers, particularly Plato and Socrates, to understand paradoxes in human communication and thinking. Freud never fully subscribed to the theory of dialectics, although the very concept of psychoanalysis is itself implicitly dialectical. Dr. Goldberg seeks to explicate the dialectics of therapy: "Each alternating statement [between therapist and patient-client] must reflect the same basic theme the speaker has presupposed and, until that moment, not consciously realized." The essence of his dialectical thesis is a series of 25 principles that comprise the therapeutic rules for courageous interaction and risk response, each to the other so that, as the metaphorical ping-pong ball goes back and forth, newer and more elaborate meaning is generated from the mutual confrontation.

I wish that I had had Dr. Goldberg's contribution as my own personal handbook when I was an intern and resident, let alone psychoanalytic candidate, to say nothing of a beginning psychotherapist in private practice. In stating that wish, I am not unlike the patient-client who, after eagerly benefiting from the interpretation's clarification, cannot help regretting that (s)he did not have access to this illumination earlier so as to have benefitted from it. Perhaps a corollary to the capacity to have courage and to take risks might be the ability to absorb regret—without envy toward the past—so as to continue to start again, and again. This is ultimately the hope with which Dr. Goldberg's contribution left me.

Preface

Each vocational career has its limitations and its own particular perils. There are, however, some careers which are, at times, downright dangerous. The practice of psychotherapy is one. The type of work in which we, as psychotherapists, are involved has a profound effect upon our health and well-being. The vast volume of material examining clinical practice focuses almost exclusively on understanding the client.[1] In contrast, there are few works which address both the personal and professional effect of the therapeutic endeavor on the practitioner. I find it rather ironic that, in discussing the most human of sciences, authors have largely ignored an extremely significant component of this process—the practitioner.[2] It would appear that those who write on the subjects of psychoanalysis and psychotherapy have made the assumption that once the practitioner acquires clinical skills, he or she should be able to maintain them over a lifetime.[3] Those who make this assumption poorly serve their readers. We can no longer disregard the process of disillusionment that comes through aging and maturation, a disillusionment that has seriously afflicted a considerable number of practitioners, if not every practitioner at some point in a full-time career. Clearly, serious work dissatisfactions will reduce clinical effectiveness. But no less significantly, it will, concomitantly, jeopardize the clinician's physical and emotional well-being.

These hazards are similar for all types of practitioners. For the most part, I do not make distinctions in this volume between analysts and other types of psychotherapists. Of course, theory and technique do have a differential impact upon the experience of the practitioner. One could argue that the disillusionment about being able to help clients is greater for the traditional analyst than for an active, pragmatic practitioner who is more "directly" involved in doing something for the client. Analytic

psychotherapy is slower and its aims are generally more ambitious. Yet, this feeling of helplessness in trying to work with
some analysands may be balanced or canceled out by rationalizations about the characterological unsuitability of the analysand for psychoanalysis. I believe, however, the impact of theory and technique of the practitioner is less telling than is
his/her temperament and character—whether or not the practitioner is an analyst or an active psychotherapist. As I will seek
to show, the differential impact of practice resides essentially in
how the practitioner uses his/her own vulnerability and sensitivity to intimacy in guiding the client's personal journey in
search of self.

Each profession has its own guiding needs. Above all, I believe that, like any other service profession, we require reassurance that we are involved in a significant human endeavor. The
mass media, among many other powerful voices in contemporary society, such as influential practitioners like Hans Ey-
senck and Thomas Szasz, have called into question whether
psychotherapists have any more healing power than does a
friendly bartender or an inquisitive hairdresser. On the other
hand, practitioners and writers supportive of the ameliorative effects of the therapeutic endeavor have failed to provide succor.
Perhaps this is because it seems obvious to them that psychotherapists carry out a vital human service and/or because it
sounds patronizing to reassure professionals of their value.

Obviously, practitioners are especially sensitive to the criticism of their willingness and ability to heal. After all, the calling of our profession is forged to this propensity. There seems
to be considerable evidence, to be discussed later, that many
people are drawn to the profession of psychotherapy from a need
to heal others, but, at the same time, neglect their own psychic
pain. Indeed, one of the theses of this book is that practitioners
frequently experience the deleterious effects of practice, because
their sensitive empathy and insight is directed toward their
clients' needs exclusively. The practitioner's character, because
it gives his life purpose and direction, has been forged from a
need to care for others, and at the same time, from a feeling of
shame for addressing his/her own immediate and long term
needs. The very significant rates of "burn-out," deep depression,
broken relationships, and suicide among psychotherapists attest
to the ambivalence many have about their own well-being.

The reader may question whether practitioners actually feel

shameful about attending to their own needs. My thesis is that practitioners in Western society often deny in themselves the very issues they are concerned with in their clients. Certainly, this is an issue for the neophyte practitioner during the initial years of practice. However, the young practitioner is more likely than the seasoned therapist to be in his/her own therapy or in close supervision. A competent training therapist or supervisor will quickly spot this issue and help the neophyte effectively examine it. On the other hand, the senior practitioner who still suffers from a need to be available to those with whom he/she works at a cost to the practitioner's well-being is less likely to be in treatment and may be ashamed to seek supervision for such an issue.

In examining the malaise being addressed here we should not lose sight of the realization that psychotherapeutic work is a very significant human service. I have written this volume in the belief that there is no longer a question but that a skillful practitioner helps those who are psychically suffering. Consequently, there is a need for us to appreciate what we actually do, what we are attempting to do, and, no less importantly, what we can reasonably expect of ourselves and others of us as practitioners; and what, on the other hand, it is unreasonable to expect.

This volume is intended as a practical guide for people doing psychological work with other people. It is not another ponderous textbook. I trust that any practitioner who reads this book shares with me a lack of confidence in artless advice that oversimplifies what we, as practitioners, have learned from our own experience and that of our colleagues. I will not offer formulas, techniques, or shortcuts for understanding our work, the effects that work has upon our person or for handling the distress that results from our work. Instead I will try, as comprehensively in a single volume as I can to examine these issues. To do this, I will examine the nature of our work, the basis of what we do and, as important, why we have been drawn into the field. I propose to do this by examining where we have come from; this is to say, what our families were like; what our personal development consisted of; how we seem to view the world; and what we believe human existence is all about.

One might point out that family background affects why bankers became bankers and tailors went into tailoring as much as why therapists pursued a service profession. Argumentatively, this may be correct. There simply is too little data to definitively answer this question. I believe, however, on the basis of evidence now available that the dynamics and the circumstances in the family backgrounds of psychotherapists is quite significant as I will seek to demonstrate in Chapter 4. As I seek to make statements about a large number of practitioners, I offer characterizations and descriptions that, for any one reader, may be, in part or whole, unfamiliar and invalid. However, there are a sufficient number of common denominators in the background of practitioners, which available research suggests are present, in order dynamically to relate practitioners' backgrounds to the career that they have chosen.

In this manner we can address the reasons we have been drawn into practice and why we continue, despite hazards and dissatisfactions. Unless we know what the satisfactions are that we seek and how to reasonably achieve them, our practice is strewn with peril, and our health, well-being and perhaps our very lives are in danger.

The hazards of practice can not be relegated to simple disappointment. These hazards induce anguish central to the identity of the practitioner. Moreover, to reiterate, because of the practitioner's need to deny his/her own anguish, therapists often take better care of their clients than themselves. If you believe that I am overdramatizing the situation, then consider the nature of our work which deals directly with questions of health, well-being and perils of existence. We, as practitioners, are no less susceptible to the dilemmas of these issues than are our clients. Once having carefully examined the sources of our intended satisfactions and the impediments inherent in many of the ways we pursue these ends, we can, hopefully, arrive at a more functional and satisfying means of achieving these goals. If this hope is well-founded, then the book will have aptly served its intention.

As a frame of reference for support and constructive self-examination, I have written the kind of book I would have liked to have had available when I began my psychotherapy career and at various difficult times in its development. Correspondingly, this guide is also the kind of book that practitioners I have supervised and trained have requested. The material discussed in this book is derived from my colleagues' experiences, as well as my own. These are issues I, too, have struggled with and I suspect, will continue to struggle with as long as I practice and train others. For the past 20 years I have trained mental health practitioners on the firing lines and taught in medical schools, graduate and undergraduate psychology programs and in professional institutes. Throughout these endeavors I have been concerned about the dearth of texts that relate the therapist's struggle with his/her own humanity to sound conceptualizations of psychotherapy, personality development and psychosocial education.

The major theme of this volume is that since the person and the practice of the psychotherapist are inexorably related, wise and effective practice requires deep personal satisfaction in one's personal life and in one's practice. This becomes more apparent as we immerse ourselves, over time, in our work. The stresses from the serious responsibilities of practicing psychotherapy usually militate against a career which is sedate and harmonious. It is not that there are not those in our ranks who practice psychotherapy the way others sell cars, process customer complaints or practice constitutional law. They may be quite friendly, readily informative and responsible to the ethical standards of the profession. But they clearly see their work as a rather circumscribed job and find effective means for avoiding more complications and difficulties than are necessary to make their practice a convenient, profitable and time-limited endeavor. Work issues and concerns are left at the office when they leave for the day. They are rarely bothered by telephone calls from clients at night who threaten suicide or other difficulties that cannot be safely contained within the regular therapeutic session. They may well be able to practice in a nine-to-five framework. Such practitioners generally refer the less affluent, more demanding and difficult prospective clients to other practitioners, or request that these people contact public agency clinics.

THE IMPOSSIBLE PROFESSION

This book is not written for the practitioners described above, who would have absolutely no use for it. It is, rather, written for those who realize the extraordinary difficulties that seem inherent in the practice of psychotherapy. Many of these are issues that have not adequately been addressed in training or supervision and cannot simply be relegated to concerns that will be

worked out by additional personal psychotherapy. A meaningful career decision to practice psychotherapy requires knowledge
of the hazards of practice, which cannot be reduced to the misunderstanding and mishandling of transference and countertransference, despite what most textbooks on psychotherapy
claim. Freud himself seemed to hold a pessimistic view regarding the avoidance of pitfalls in practice. He sympathetically
wrote, late in his career:

> "Here let us pause for a moment to assure the analyst that he
> has our sincere sympathy in the very exacting requirements he
> is expected to fulfil. It almost looks as if analysis were the third
> of those "impossible" professions in which one can be quite sure
> of unsatisfying results. The other two, much older-established,
> are the bringing-up of children and the government of nations.
> Obviously, we cannot demand that the prospective analyst be
> a perfect human being before he takes up analysis, and that only
> persons of this rare and exalted perfection should enter the
> profession. (Freud, 1937, p. 352)

If the practice of psychotherapy is not the impossible profession Freud suggests, then it is an extremely demanding one, at
best, for those of us who are not willing to relegate our commitment to the examined life to a comfortable and convenient business. There are factors inherent in the work we do, as well, as
qualities of those who experience a calling to the profession,
which transcends a conscious, vocational choice.

In short, there are particular mitigating factors that create
the inevitable pitfalls for the practitioner. Alan Wheelis maintains that the vocation of psychotherapy[4] misleads those who
wish to pursue it as a career. According to Wheelis (1956), psychotherapy is experienced quite differently by the practitioner
than by the outsider. Psychotherapy has certain qualities which
cannot properly be communicated in words. It can only be found
by experiencing it. Therefore, the neophyte practitioner can only
realize by gradual steps what is required of him as a practitioner
and the effect it will have upon his inner resources and his own
vulnerabilities. A Jungian analyst, Groesbeck (1975), states the
case for the danger in practicing psychotherapy even more
caustically than does Wheelis. He points out that risky occupa-
tions, such as fire-fighting, clearly warn their recruits and neophyte apprentices of the inherent dangers of the work. But no

such warning is given to psychotherapy practitioners. This is unfortunate because a considerable period of one's life may have elapsed before the practitioner learns whether or not he/she is in the right profession. Such a long time, says Wheelis, may elapse that in fact, "he may no longer be a young man, but at the midpoint of life and deeply committed. Indeed, he may never realize his mistake, for there are powerful forces opposed to such awareness."

If this picture is accurate, and I believe it is, then it would appear that psychotherapists have not devoted adequate time and attention to understanding the stress inherent in their work. To get some idea of this problem, consider first that, according to recent actuaries, the rate of suicide among physicians in the U.S. is more than the combined figures for fatal accidents, drownings and homicide among physicians. Suicide among physicians generally is high everywhere in the world. However, the current rate among American physicians removes from society a number roughly equivalent to that of the average medical school graduating class.

Now consider that suicides among psychiatrists are even higher than among physicians in general. The rate for the fifth profession[5] as a group approximates that for psychiatrists alone. These figures suggest that although the process of psychotherapy induces powerful effects in both therapists and clients, many practitioners apparently have considerable difficulty seeking assistance for their own suffering.

READERSHIP OF THIS BOOK

Let me be specific about the prospective readership of this book. It has been written as a guide for practitioners with varying degrees of experience. First, its aim is for seasoned practitioners to reflect upon their experience in its entirety. In reviewing their experience, to enable practitioners to look at aspects of their person that have been pushed aside and neglected because of concerns with client issues. We will examine the things they aspire to in being a practitioner. We will explore the effect—the anguish—that ensues when their aspirations are not met and the numerous other ways the experience of being a psychotherapy practitioner produces noxious and toxic effects on practitioners' well-being.

I don't have to convince the seasoned practitioner of the perils of the therapeutic practice by telling vivid horror stories. Practitioners know them too well! I am concerned, instead, with the reasons for these perils and how to handle them.

For the practitioner who is running into certain kinds of patterns of conflict, I have made suggestions for examining and dealing with these issues. My hope is that in gaining a new perspective on these conflictual concerns the practitioner may invigorate his/her practice. I will also address the satisfactions, if not the joys, of psychotherapeutic practice. If the satisfactions of practice do not sufficiently exceed the anguish, then the practitioner must seriously consider why he/she continues to practice.

Second, this guide may be useful to the beginning therapist who has been in the field only a few years and is currently working in a hospital, mental hygiene clinic, counseling center or some other institutional center prior to entering private practice. In forecasting and anticipating obstacles he/she will encounter as a private practitioner the psychotherapist will be better prepared to head them off or deal with them when entering independent practice.

Third, the student in graduate training in psychology, social work, nursing, pastoral counseling and residency training in psychiatry may profit from this volume. Because future practice has numerous perils, it is advisable for students to appreciate the phenomenological experience of practitioners in order to make a prudent decision about the work they are choosing to commit themselves to. Especially for the student, this book contains an annotated summary of references for exploring the issues discussed in this volume from the perspective of practitioners and theorists other than myself.

Fourth, this book may be of use to various clients of psychotherapy in reflecting upon their experience inside the therapeutic hour. It may help them understand how their therapist experiences him/herself and how this effects their work together. Finally, this book may be of interest to those who are simply curious about who the therapist is, aside from the professional role. These may be readers who have never been in analysis or psychotherapy. It may include all those who refer clients to psychotherapists, and/or work with or consult with psychotherapists in their own professional or paraprofessional capacities.

AUTHOR'S POINT OF VIEW

I will relate to the issues raised in this book with a discernible point of view in regard to the function and meaning of human interaction. Without a point of view this book would simply be a travelog. Most psychotherapy volumes are heavily directed to a single academic perspective. The field is laden with conflicting doctrines and systems of theory and technique, each of which holds itself to be the only true torch of enlightenment. I offer no such oracle! I will examine the issues affecting the practitioner as informally and nontheoretically as seems reasonable—cutting across schools of thought in an attempt to address the core elements common in the practice of psychotherapy.

This volume is intended primarily for the experienced practitioner and secondarily for the beginner. In instances in which the level of sophistication is not balanced for both levels of practitioner, the guide will veer to the side of the more experienced psychotherapist.

In conclusion, this book is not written for those who feel that what is important about psychotherapy cannot be put into a book, nor, in contrast, is it written for those who feel that everything important about psychotherapy has already been written. Rather, it is addressed to the growing concerns of the practitioner and his/her need for personal and professional growth.

NOTES

1. It is hard to believe that few have written to provide *support* for the practitioner that therapy is a significant endeavor! Nevertheless, this seems to be the case. The annotated summaries in the Appendix is a compilation of the best of the scant literature on the subject.

2. The classic statement of this view of the practitioner as a mechanical component of the therapeutic hour who requires no exploration of his person can be found in the psychoanalytic literature. One such statement can be found in R. Fliess (1944), *The Metapsychology of the Analyst*. The paper begins:

Of the two persons involved in the analytic situation, the one customarily not considered a problem is the object of this brief metapsychologic study. While in the course of the analytic procedure the patient gradually moves towards becoming truly an individual, the analyst remains from beginning to end what he always is while at work: essentially a 'categorical person.'

3. In one of the better works on the training of the psychotherapist, *To Be a Therapist*, J. M. Lewis (1978) indicates that:

> as a group, we, the teachers of psychotherapy, do an inadequate job of starting trainees on the road to competence. We throw them in the deep water of treating troubled patients at a tender age and help them, only in retrospect, to learn from their errors. We know so much more than what we teach beginners that it is tempting to think that we are caught up in a not-too-subtle initiation process.

4. Wheelis' article was published in a psychoanalytic journal, *International Journal of Psychoanalysis*, and, as such, discussed the dangers of practice in terms of psychoanalysis. What Wheelis has to say in this superb article speaks to all psychotherapists, not only to analysts.

5. The term "the fifth profession" is used by Henry and his associates (1975) to refer to those clinicians among the four mental health disciplines—psychoanalysis, psychology, psychiatry, and social work—whose primary professional interest is the practice of psychotherapy.

—C.G.

PART I

Becoming
A Healer

Chapter 1
The Personal Journey of the Healer

For this is the journey that men make: to find
themselves. If they fail in this, it doesn't matter
much what else they find.

—*James Michener*

This chapter is concerned with the theme of the journey of the healer. It interprets the requirements and risks of this journey in light of modern-day practice.

I will set the stage for examining this quest by relating a parable. The tale concerns a young man who believed that he wished to devote his life to the search for truth. The route he chose was that of a psychotherapist. After completing his graduate training in one of the mental health disciplines, he entered with great eagerness a psychotherapy training institute. He anticipated that after several years of course work, intensive supervision, and personal psychotherapy he would be a polished practitioner. However, after several years of training he realized that his apprenticeship as a practitioner had barely begun. He felt dismayed because he believed that, without some idea of when his training would be completed, he could not properly plan a future for himself. Wrestling with this concern, he awoke startled one night from having had the following dream:

He and two companions were climbing Mount Sinai. On reaching the summit they spied a column of white smoke. They continued in the direction of the smoke and came upon a burning bush. A voice called from the bush, "Approach, and question from thy heart's desire! For I am thy Lord and God."

Somewhat timidly, the first companion, wearing cowboy boots and a Western hat, approached and requested, "When will our national budget ever be balanced?"

"In the year 2,000," the voice answered.

"Unfortunately, not in my administration," replied Ronald Reagan.

The second companion, garbed in a majestic robe, approached the bush with a firm step and bold voice. He was obviously experienced speaking with the Lord. He asked, "When will there be world peace?"

"In the year 2,010," answered the Lord.

"It's a pity this will not be in my administration!" exclaimed Pope John.

Finally the young psychotherapist stepped in front of the bush. Scratching his beard, he asked, "When will my apprenticeship as a psychotherapist be completed?"

"Alas, not in my administration!" answered the Lord.

The parable above can be taken to suggest that complex monetary issues and international strife are less difficult to resolve than the creative development required of the healer.

THE PRACTITIONER'S JOURNEY
IN SEARCH OF SELF

The contention that apprenticeship is perpetual is based on the realization that the journey into self is a bottomless realm. One of the early psychoanalytic masters, Hans Sachs, is reported by Edward Glover (1937) to have said that the most thorough analysis is little more than scratching the earth's surface with a trowel. Potentially, the healer is available for new realizations and transformation, not only from growing confluence of clinical experience but, more significantly, from an ongoing dialectical experience within the practitioner's self that working with another's journey serves to restimulate. This point of view is consistent with the observation that the process of life involves each of us in an endless series of developmental challenges and frequent crises. The people who petition us with their suffering have, according to Kovacs (1976), "lost heart for that journey" somewhere along the road. Hopefully, the psychotherapist will not!

Those who are called to the profession of healing generally do so with an intense interest in learning about themselves. They find a career that will support their life style (or to which they aspire), while, at the same time allow them the opportunity to amelioratively touch others, as well as provide a continuous means for examining their own lives. Practitioners who feel that they know themselves well enough from their personal therapy and introspection will find their work as practitioners rather dull and mechanical. Unless practitioners are *still* interested in examining their own lives after completing personal treatment, they will feel restless and bored. Contrastingly, the practitioners who are available for further personal growth will be curious about the inner happenings of clients in terms of what they can learn about themselves. The interpolation of another's experience with one's own leads to a conscious examination of the nature of the human condition. This is especially true about the meaning of suffering in one's self and others. On the other hand, the person who does not recognize his or her own suffering cannot be responsive to the suffering of others. The mandate of understanding the sufferer's problems from the healer's insight into his or her own is a basic tenet of the healing tradition. From the earliest times practitioners have created healing systems for those they treated in terms of the meaning they have made of their own suffering and life crises. These are meanings they have come upon in their own personal journey.

The theme of personal journey provides the crucible for the essential developmental process of healing from its earliest roots. It captures both the shaman wisdom through the millennia and that of efficacious modern psychotherapy.

In short the journey of the healer seems a consonant metaphor for the apprenticeship of those who seek to heal. It implies that the healer does not work in a mechanical or strictly scientific and impersonal way, applying an infallible body of knowledge and methodology to a disease entity. Instead, the theme of personal journey suggests that effective practitioners utilize their own life experiences as the major source of their expertise. In a word, the practitioner uses his/her own journey to guide others in their requisite voyages.

The journey into self requires the presence of another. We come to know ourselves through the other. The journey in quest of meaning is, in my view, most productive in a setting in which each agent seeks an increased awareness of his/her own identity (Goldberg, 1976). Parenthetically, the habit of denying one's own values while functioning as a therapist becomes resistently entrenched in many practitioners. They have been led to believe, from their training and from reports in the literature of other practitioners, that the responsible practitioner should not want anything for him/herself other than to be fairly remunerated. The practitioner should be there only to deal with how the client wishes to be. For many, the exploration of the being-in-the world of the practitioner within the therapeutic encounter is an unconscionable endeavor, as if the practitioner were without anxiety and personal concern, which might be decisively shaping the encounter. I hope to show later both the illusion and the lack of usefulness of this belief.

THE AGE-OLD JOURNEY OF THE SHAMAN

The careers of all healers emanate from a common societal need. The practices of the healer are as spontaneous to daily life as individuals coming together with others to soothe their suffering; to attend their emotional, social, and curiosity interests; and —in so doing—to examine the fabric that holds people together in human company. Because people have always lived in close connection with others, their concerns have been affected by their common social weal—their well-being depending on one another. Over time, each society and culture has designated a certain person by virtue of special gifts, to be its shaman,[1] that is to say, to combine the roles of spiritual leader, wise person, and healer. In these roles shamans concerned themselves with the alienation of the sufferer from others in the social clan.

The presence of the shaman has persisted through millennia and is found, with some striking and unexplained similarities, among peoples living geographically far apart (Rogers, 1982). According to a medical anthropologist of shaman practices, Joan Halifax (1979), the term "shaman" is derived from *Sram* from the Vedic language. *Sram* means "to heal oneself or practice austerities." Halifax maintains, however, that the origins of shamanism are more archaic than the paleo-oriental influences suggested by the derivation of the word, shamanism probably having been a part of the prehistoric cultures of Siberian hunters, as well as found among peoples of preliterate history in all parts of the world. A historian of psychiatric practices, Walter Bromberg (1975), indicates that shaman practices can be dated to even Neanderthal times. He tells us that paleontologists studying the remnants of the Stone Age have come across bits of bone, vertebrae of snakes, and teeth of animals in amulet sacks. These artifacts, according to Bromberg, were used to contribute to psychic amelioration by practitioners who attempted to petition supernatural forces. Together with their attempts to gain magical powers in their healing endeavors, shamans also used dream prophecy and interpretation, repetition rituals, and controlled breathing.

To harness magical powers, the practitioner needed, of course, to know where to find them. According to Bromberg, early human beings borrowed from the world around them the notion of an external, all powerful force, which could be utilized to help kindred in their pain and suffering. An ancient word for the force that appears to reside beyond the observable world and that supposedly grows crops, subdues enemies, and heals the sufferer from illness is "mana," a term found among various peoples the world over. Shamans combined shrewd knowledge of their kindred, together with an understanding of the spiritual world "to heal the sick, divine the weather, and undo mischief; [in so doing, the shaman became] an all-purpose expert in human relations" (Bromberg, 1975, p. 3).

Most anthropologists regard the shaman as a constructive leader in society, who practices mysteries beyond the understanding of most members of the community. They point to the indispensable role the shaman plays in primitive societies in liberating the sufferer from physical, psychological, and spiritual disease. In these functions, anthropologists generally regard the shaman as a skillful therapist, who utilizes principles and methods which are basic to the practice of psychotherapy.

Moreover, the shaman was not only the sole professional— probably the first professional in the development of human society—in the community, but frequently, as well, the composite of tribal wisdom and knowledge. In this capacity, the shaman perpetuates the traditional values of the society (Rogers, 1982).

Even without the scientific methodology and knowledge of

the Western mind, shaman cures were often effective. There seems to be a consensus among anthropologists that shaman healing throughout the millennia has been no less effective than that of our own modern psychotherapy. In order to understand how the shaman's healing techniques relieved the suffering of those who depended upon the shaman as their sole source of deliverance from suffering, we must understand the epigenetic role of the personal journey for *all* who seek to become healers.

We may begin to unravel the conditions that have fueled the age-old journey in search for self by questioning why no other species of being but humans appears in need of a personal journey. In an epigenetic sense, the limits of development and maturation are set at birth for all species except humans. Joseph Campbell (1968) tells us that myths from earliest times reveal that, unlike other creatures, humans are born too soon—they are unfinished and unprepared to deal alone with the world. The infant, still to be shaped and directed, is cast into the world in concert with a nurturing other. This is to say, the infant encounters the external world as part of a dual physical and psychological unit with the mother. This union continues many months after birth in face of countless catastrophic dangers, any of which could instantly annihilate the neophyte if the infant were not protected. The susceptibility to danger without the protection of a caring other is the human creature's initial source of vulnerability. It is, at the same time, the source of human creative potential. Early inability to be separate and autonomous in ourselves mandates protection for us from caretakers against external danger. This external custody, when caringly provided, gives us the freedom to explore unhampered our own psyches and to develop and shape our own destinies.

The potential for creative development, of course, is not unlimited and undemanding. There are inherent strictures which must be attended in order for creative growth to ensue. Chief among these is the requirement of finding a path and choosing a direction to pursue along the journey. Myth and legend from antiquity reveal that, although each person's personal journey is somewhat unique, each journey, if dutifully pursued, is also a rediscovery of what countless other travelers have found before (Campbell, 1968). These rediscovered factors provide a pathway for the traveler to venture forth and study how others before have interpreted the universal conditions of the human psyche.

We see, then, that intimate bonding with the mother provides the individual with the initial sanctuary to develop curiosity about the psyche. But, as I have already indicated, although all of us begin our personal journeys, few of us relentlessly continue the search of self-discovery. Something more than a capacity for growth and development, which is inherent in the human condition, is required. Alfred, Lord Tennyson, in *Ulysses* reveals to us poetically this necessity when, Odysseus, after 20 years of separation, tells his son, Telemachus, "I am the father whom your boyhood lacked."

Tennyson is speaking here of a *mentor* and guide. Myths and folk legends from earliest times describe the journey of the apprentice accompanied by a wise man/woman through perilous ordeals in order to become purified, transformed, and integrated with the apprentice's higher attributes, human nobility, and spirituality. The role of mentorship is highly crucial and well-articulated, although often metaphorical in these mythical accounts. Carlos Castaneda's (1976) tutor, Don Juan, in this regard, tells him that the world is full of inexplicable and uncontrollable forces. Consequently, the path of knowledge is a difficult one. Only a "crackpot" would undertake the task of becoming a man of knowledge of his own accord. A "soberheaded" man has to be encouraged and taught; often he has to be tricked into staying with a difficult and perilous journey.

Regardless of the methods they use, mentors play a vital role in normal human development. Adolescence and young adulthood, particularly, are marked by a search for an inspiring person wiser than one's self, who can help one with difficult life situations and what we call "identity crises," in such a way as to avoid what the young person experiences as the uncertainties and tribulations of ordinary ways of dealing with these situations. In this role, the mentor serves as a psychological teacher in examining and searching the human psyche for ways to live one's life with purpose. To do this efficaciously, the mentor requires a theory of human development and some idea of the tasks required to meet these developmental needs. These ideas generally come from his/her own life experiences. They are expressed indirectly by way of metaphor, parable, and personal example. Freud, in this respect, wrote of the analyst as a teacher and a better superego-parent (Freud, 1937).

Supporting this notable view of mentors, I would add that the autobiographies of numerous and creative people evince that at crucial periods in their lives a mentor appeared who effected a vital transformation in their lives (Burton, 1977). Generally, the mentor influenced a new perspective by offering the disciple a socially useful and creative solution for the young person's teeming energies and ambitions—by providing a role model and active tutoring and encouragement. Without this relationship, the young person might have turned with unconstructive rebellion against those elders whose power controlled those areas of life toward which the individual aspired (Levinson, 1978).

Finding a suitable mentor is not a matter of happenstance. The tragic manifold of destructive charismatic leaders[2] makes it evident that it is easy to fall prey to false messiahs (Goldberg, 1983b). To find a suitable mentor, the journeyer requires several essential characteristics. One of the most important of these is the willingness to postpone gratification in order to acquire more durable satisfactions in the future. This endurance makes possible a serious commitment to undergo ordeals. The personal journey, among other things, is a creative venture. In this endeavor one's whole identity may be forged on the basis of the task at hand. The journeyer may hold the sentiment that without being able to experience the world in a different and significant way than ordinary experience offers, he or she would rather not continue to exist; that is, amassing material goods and financial fortune, knowing famous and influential people, and visiting exotic lands are not of interest. During periods of the journey, the traveler is willing to push away the mundane and commonplace—including friendships, and responsibilities to family, even neglecting to take care of personal health—in pursuing the journey.

The journeyer's pursuit of self-discovery, because it is susceptible to an obsessive fervor, needs to be sobered by common sense. The traveler needs the strength that comes from critical intelligence to be able to identify and resist false mentors. These are mentors who promise all boons, requiring no effort on an apprentice's part, except homage to the master. These mentors take over and provide all the steps for the apprentice. More prudent mentors give the power for self-discovery to the journeyer by permitting the apprentice to become transformed through ordeal.

In that the journeyer cannot rely solely on the protection and wisdom of the mentor, the apprentice must secure other means of guidance for finding the path to an enlightened existence through ordeal. It has always been the prime function of *myth* and *rite* to supply the direction and intentionality that carry the human spirit forward in constructive ways (Campbell, 1968). Since empirically we can not acquire absolute truth, we attempt through myth and metaphor, to create reliable guides for living. They serve the purpose of telling us how things became as they are. The poet Stanley Kunitz has said, "Old myths, old gods, old heroes have never died. They are only sleeping at the bottom of our mind, waiting for our call. We need them. They represent the wisdom of our race."[3]

The myth-symbolizing process is at the heart of endeavors that make us human. Susan Langer (1957) has indicated that there is a human tendency to envision stories with the images we see. This tendency to create narrative from minimal-sense data forms the basis of all creative, artistic, and inventive accomplishments. The apprentice who wishes to become a healer must rediscover and assimilate precisely those basic "archetypical imagos," as Jung (1968) called them, contained in universal myths. These symbols have inspired people throughout the millennia to face the longings and the suffering of the human psyche with courage, compassion, and vision. These symbols are the rediscovered wisdom of the healer. A considerable part of the healer's wisdom throughout the ages, as Kopp (1976) has indicated, came from the healer's ability to speak "the forgotten language of prophecy, the poetic language of the myth and of the dream" (p.12). Examining the obstacles in the journeyer's path in terms of the symbolic meaning of enduring myths provides viable options for understanding human experience, while, at the same time, sharing the spiritual tradition with those kindred who have preceded the journeyer. Once he or she starts a personal journey, the traveler begins a trek as venerable as human existence.

All mentors routinely share their symbols and their prophecy with their apprentices. The wise mentor, however, encourages the apprentice to find or reshape his/her own. The requirement of finding one's own symbols necessitates a separation from the mentor. Longfellow in *The Secret of the Sea* tells us poetically,
"Wouldst thou"—So the helmsman answered,
learn the secret of the sea?
Only those who brave its danger comprehend its mystery!"

The message conveyed by the millennia of countless shamans is that wisdom is to be found only beyond the abodes of humankind, out in the great solitude. Moreover, they have emphatically insisted that only *privation* and *suffering* can open the mind of the healer to mysteries hidden from the more trepid (Halifax, 1979). The most important of these, in regard to healing, concerns the concept of the *wounded healer.*

In the oldest myths of healing, it is precisely because healers were vulnerable to wound and suffering that they had the power to heal (Groesbeck & Taylor, 1977). Heraclitus tells us that "conflict is the source of all things." The capacity to heal others comes from confronting our own adversity. The psychological implication of the "myth of Asclepius" is that the sufferer has a healer within. Each agent in the healing encounter must accommodate his unconscious projection to the needs of the other if meaningful healing is to take place (Groesbeck & Taylor, 1977). Shamans know that we heal ourselves through healing others. To do this, the practitioner needs to be prepared to have his/her own inner wounds activated by healing practices. Shaman healing, in this sense, imposes a paradox, which lies at the heart of all healing: Those who cure may remain eternally ill or wounded themselves (Groesbeck & Taylor, 1977).

Don Juan, the shaman in the Carlos Castaneda (1976) stories, speaks to the double-edged boon of being a healer: A shaman "is only slightly better off than the average man. Sorcery does not help him to live a better life . . . [in fact] sorcery hinders him . . . By opening himself to knowledge—[he] becomes more vulnerable" (p.214).

It is highly significant that most shaman practitioners have had near-death experiences, usually as a result of an accident or serious physical (or mental) illness. Many have experienced what, from a Western perspective, clearly appears to have been psychotic decompensation and subsequent extraordinary psychic reconstitution.

A major selective criterion for acceptance as a shaman healer is the incident of serious illness and recovery. In the shaman tradition only a person who has healed him/herself is regarded as a practitioner, as only such a person truly knows the dark secrets of the psyche. The wounded healer's illness is usually due to a combination of physical and conflictual psychological tensions. During the course of the illness the wounded healer struggles, dramatically and valiantly, against powerful forces, which have persistently afflicted his life. The ways which the wounded healer finds effective in combating these forces guide him or her in future encounters with suffering on behalf of others who are ill. Thus, according to Halifax (1979), "the shaman's ability to subdue, control, appease, and direct spirits separates him or her from ordinary individuals, who are victims of these powerful forces" (p. 11).

Acquaintance with the dark secrets of the psyche, which comes from bouts with illness and the possession of venerable symbols from myth and rite, provides the wounded healer with a visionary wisdom. The vision is not only representative of the struggles of the present society, but an articulation of ancient truths by means of which society is perpetually reborn and reformed (Campbell, 1968). Jung (1968) has said that the major problems of our lives are never fully overcome. However, by having struggled with them and having subdued them for the moment, we are enabled to continue our development of sensitivity toward, and empathy and concern for others. In a word, the traveler who has suffered deeply and recovered can boldly face other sufferers' deepest feelings about mortality.

In short, the crisis of a powerful illness offers a crucible for the mysteries of life. It involves an encounter with forces that decay and destroy, together with those that resuscitate and inspire. Illness can, thus, become a vehicle for attaining a higher level of consciousness (Halifax, 1979), if the traveler has kept his inner fires ignited and utilized them as a means to direct his life. These inner fires, originating from the fierce passion of combat with illness, may be employed to inspire others, as well.

Having overcome serious illness, the apprentice must, as the next step, teach others, by powerful example, that illness can be a passageway in which one's real powers can transcend a given state of affairs. The mentor demonstrates that his/her power to heal comes from the transformation of vulnerability into sensitivity, vision, and compassion. In reality, what the mentor offers is guidance toward accepting the imperfections of a temporary existence in an ultimately unmanageable world (Kopp, 1976). Mentors as healers, whether shamans of old or modern psychotherapists, may appear to be ideal bearers of truth but, as Kopp wisely indicates, in reality, they are simply the most extraordinary human members of their community. This is to say, they can be of assistance to others only to the extent that they are fellow travelers.

I have emphasized the personal journey in tracing the age-old saga of healing, because I believe that it reveals what has been lost in the careers of many modern practitioners. They have forgotten what has brought them into the field of healing in the first place, or have dropped out, or have taken impossible and hazardous paths because they lacked a proper guide. By focusing on the personal journey and its requisite steps, I hope to give a direction to the practitioner's life and work, and not only show the common dangers and fears in working with clients, but provide, as well, a sense of community with other healers who, despite variations in scientific knowledge and practice, have dealt with similar human concerns since the dawn of time. In dealing with these concerns, the modern psychotherapist represents the wise old man of myth and folk legend, whose words assist other travelers through the trials and terrors of fantastic adventure and opportunity (Campbell, 1968).

NOTES

1. For the sake of convenience, I will call the healers from many disparate places "shamans" in this chapter.

2. I have examined this issue in considerable detail in the chapter, "Courage and fanaticism: The charismatic leader and modern religious cults" in D. A. Halperin (Ed.), *Psychodynamic perspectives on religion: Sect and cult.* Boston: John Wright, 1983.

3. The statement by Stanley Kunitz was made during a conference of writers, artists, and scholars on "The Presence of Myth in Contemporary Life" in New York City, October 1984. The conference was entitled, "The Presence of Myth in Contemporary Life" and was held at the New School for Social Research and Cooper Union.

Chapter 2
The Role of Intimacy in the Personal Journey

We know truth, not by reason, but by the heart.
—Blaise Pascal

The unfinished crucible of the mother-child bonding, as I discussed in the last chapter, sets the stage for the personal journey. How courageously the journeyer is able to face the ordeals encountered in the quest for psychic development depends upon early intimate bonding. Stated succinctly, this means that aspects of the personal journey are necessarily struggled with and experienced in solitude. The ability to withstand aloneness, however, is dependent upon prior satisfying experiences in intimate relatedness with others. As intentional beings, directed toward social relations with intimate others, our human needs are unfulfilled without close relatedness. In the absence of the succor of early satisfying intimate bonding, the frustrated longing for intimacy is made intolerable during periods of separation and privation from other people. This speaks both to normal development and to the therapeutic relationship.

A theory about how intimacy develops in the mother-child bonding and its relationship to therapeutic work is required for the practitioner in influencing the client's personal journey. The person who petitions the psychotherapist may be seen from the

15

vantage of voyage, as one who has not had sufficiently "good enough" mothering and guidance, which, in large measure, involves a caring encouragement of the other's personal journey.

Both client and therapist share the epigenetic unfinished quality of self. What differentiates them—hopefully, only initially—is the active curiosity and passion for life discovery of the practitioner, the same curiosity and passion that has been thwarted in the client's early bonding relationship. This is, however, only an ideal. Practitioners struggle with the same needs for integration of self as do their clients. When they are unsuccessful at integration, not only will their clinical work suffer, but so will their willingness to continue to practice.

For a number of years I experienced increasing feelings of isolation and existential exhaustion in both my professional and personal life. These feelings developed into the sense of being burnt out—evoking a disillusionment about my work as a psychotherapist and a writer, about the importance of this work and its impact on others. I experienced little or no meaning in my life for a number of years as I practiced psychotherapy. I sensed that I was dying—far faster than I wished, slower than I cared. I found my life almost entirely involved with my work as a psychotherapist, theoretician, and educator. I realized that I spent more time with my clients and students than I did with others. I experienced myself more as a concerned therapist than I was a caring person outside of therapy with friends or toward myself. I felt little satisfaction in my marriage and my social life. My wife was also a therapist. This was a cause of considerable friction between us. Most of the satisfaction in my life came from my clinical work. I recognized in myself, with no easy conscience, the manifestations of a deep distress of self-esteem, suffocating feelings of inner emptiness, apathy of personal concern in most areas other than intellectual endeavor, lack of initiative, and frequently a sheer refusal to function socially. I recoiled in horror, seeing in myself the identical malady with which I had so arduously tried to enable my clients to come to terms—their narcissistic disturbance. It was not that I had been unaware of my narcissism before. But rather than regarding my narcissism as *my affliction*, I had viewed it simply as another of my personal traits, like my vertebrate stubbornness. Once I seized upon an idea or a venture, it took considerable argument or consequence to dissuade me from its pursuit. I recall that when in my early twenties, while in psychotherapy with a rather well-known New

York analyst, I had vigorously argued and tried to convince him that suffering was necessary for creative endeavor, that no truly creative person could escape emotional pain as a mainspring of his existential struggle. I am reminded now of a character in Pirandello's *Six Characters in Search of an Author* (1952):

> For man never reasons so much and becomes so introspective as when he suffers; since he is anxious to get at the cause of his suffering, to learn who has produced them, and whether it is just or unjust that he would have to bear them. On the other hand, when he is happy, he takes his happiness as it comes and doesn't analyze it, just as if happiness were his right . . . (p.267)

My analyst remained unconvinced of my argument. As I worked as a therapist myself over the years, I modified my viewpoint about the neurotic elements in suffering; yet I remained as ardent in my willingness to forge my art with the anguish of my personal struggles. During periods of self-doubt, however, a certain uneasiness gnawed in me. I had to seriously question whether my depression was simply a masochistic stance, the only way I would permit myself in the dark hours of my life to create and sustain meaning for my existence.

Having questioned my depression, I had to, concomitantly, question my courage and honesty. This was a far more anguished introspection for me than most other sorts of self-inquiry. If I found my courage and my honesty illusory, then I would be left empty. For these attributes have been my existential anchorages—the self-reported reasons for enduring emotional pain. I have always claimed that I had to be more honest and more courageous than others. I had chosen these attributes as my uniqueness. But what if my purported self-honesty and courage were merely masochistic ploys to cover and protect myself from more painful truths about myself? Was I honest and courageous enough to pursue this potential deception and follow it to its burning core?

A friend and colleague jolted me with the statement that my defiance, periods of aloofness, and willingness to undergo my difficult struggles alone, were, ironically, attempts to deny my very deep need to please others. Her statement had considerable impact on me. She was, I thought, probably quite right. But how could I be certain? What were my credentials for assuming that I could come to terms with my own struggles? I came to realize that my professional credentials were insufficient alone to qualify me as my own healer. For, indeed, part of the cost of gaining these credentials was neglecting to attend to my need to develop an inner core of security and self-esteem that traditionally derives from pursuing mutually gratifying and caring relationships with others. I realized that instead of relationships, I was programmed for productivity and, as creatively as I was allowed to express myself, I did not have permission for enjoyment. Whatever I produced wasn't good enough or was simply not enough. So I strove for greater and greater proficiency—first as an athlete when I entered college. But because whatever I did had to be the best, giving the endeavor my entire body and soul, I could not devote sufficient energies to athletics, schoolwork, and the other areas of my life. Because I could not sufficiently care for myself, implying perhaps that I did not know how, I invested more in my image than in trying to fill the emptiness within. I chose to devote the energies I spent in athletics to scholarship instead, and after graduate school, to writing and professional psychotherapeutic skill proficiency.

The examination of my ideas and sentiments in trying to write about them and experience them in the struggles of my clients evoked considerable perturbation and self-consciousness in me. The more I learned about myself and those with whom I worked, the more I was forced to ask myself, "What is it all about? What is my existence all about?" The more I learned about myself and others, the more I realized and became concerned by the increasing awareness of all I had successfully avoided.

To hide and divert the emotional impotence and pain I experienced, I kept working and producing. But, finally, I found that I could not continue as a therapist, because I realized that I was a hypocrite. I was not dealing with the very issues that I expected my clients to confront and work through. I could tolerate almost any other form of weakness in myself—but not hypocrisy. It was too allied with my need to see myself as courageous and honest. Oh, what stirring reverberations I experienced with the character of Dysart when I first saw *Equus* on Broadway! I experienced critical attacks on the integrity of Dysart's struggles in the play as personal attacks on my own integrity.

During these struggles I asked myself, "What more is there for me as a therapist?" I could not answer this question at the time of my disillusionment. However, what became clear over time was that I could not be the kind of therapist I had in mind when I made a decision to become a therapist, nor could I, for that matter, be the kind of therapist I had actually become. It is not that I regretted that I became a psychologist and a therapist. Even were I to choose again, I could choose nothing in such congruence with what my needs have been. Nor is it that when I practiced I wasn't a useful and effective therapist. This was simply not the issue! The question for me was: "What am I to become as a person?" I had to become a healer to myself, but I realized that this task could not be borne alone. The journey into self requires the presence of another. The last few years have been an attempt on my part to engage friends and those whom I encounter in my journeys to explore myself as openly as possible. I have utilized the skills I acquired in my practice to face up to the issues and concerns I had previously avoided by becoming a practitioner. I have been particularly interested in looking at ways that bring myself and others into experiencing and utilizing parts of ourselves that we have heretofore avoided experiencing. It is the great deal of soul-searching that these issues aroused in me that has, in large part, generated the writing of this book.

THE NATURE OF INTIMACY

It seems to me that the issues I had been struggling with turned on the nature of human intimacy and the value I placed on it, not only in the healing of emotional wounds in my clinical practice, but also in my own development as a person. Intimacy is the vehicle for the development of all human endeavor. It is the aim of all our interpersonal striving. It brings into play the full range of human emotion and complexity. As a crucible of intricate interpersonal experiences and desires, striving for intimacy vivifies that range of fertile emotions which foster our humaneness. However, whereas intimate encounter and commitment is the singular human experience most desired, it is, at the same time, the most feared. We often experience the achievement of intimacy with others as elusive to our efforts. The difficulty of establishing intimate bonds speaks to the impoverishment of contemporary life.

The perplexities in obtaining satisfactory intimate relations have led countless denizens in modern society to examine their experiences in psychotherapy. Indeed, the experience of shared intimacy between therapist and client may be a key to, although certainly not the only condition for, successful psychotherapeutic experience. This is to say, without the advent of intimacy, psychotherapeutic endeavors may pursue worthwhile goals, but the scope and meaningfulness of these goals will be limited.

Comparatively little has been written on the subject of intimacy in the therapeutic situation (Goldberg & Simon, 1982). A few professional papers have dealt with the significance of therapeutic relatedness. Other papers and, most notably, trade books, have focused on the therapist's betrayal of the therapeutic alliance by means of sexual abuse and other forms of personal exploitation of the patient. The emphasis on the misadventures of therapeutic intimacy together with the paucity of discussion of the conditions that foster therapeutic intimacy suggest that, in general, practitioners do not understand those conditions that provide for meaningful intimacy. The impression, it is hoped, is misleading.

There are a small number of consistent and closely related principles and concepts in human development that effectively explain both creative and constructive human growth and those regarded as psychopathological. These principles touch on the most basic human emotions and desires. The sources for the development of intimacy, courage, and caring are worth exploring, for difficulties in the normal development of these basic needs results in a division of the self from itself; and human plights, such as the manifestations of suffering, result directly from conflicts and difficulties with intimacy.

My thesis is that human development is predicated upon the early intimate bonding between mother and child. In this relationship the mother serves as a mirror and representation of how the larger world will respond to the child. Courage and nonintrusive caring are essential attributes in the development of meaningful intimacy. When the mother is not straightforward and tries to hide her fears and limitations, she is more wont to relate to her child by controlling its responsiveness to her. The child who is denied an open, inner being of the mother for identification of its own psychic experience will be in search of external mirrors—other people and objective "reflections." The child uses these mirrors to reveal its own psyche and, at the same time, paradoxically, tries to control the information these mirrors render, so that it conforms to the "acceptable" self demanded of it in its early bonding relationships.

The unacceptable parts of self of the children of controlling mothers are forced to be disavowed. Collectively, over time, they are sensed as a magical or second (double) self. I will refer to this sense of self as "the magical self" in this book. The individual who is troubled by manifestations of his/her self may be distressed at being told such observations as "there seem to be two people in you." This is because people continually seek a sense of integration through interpersonal and creative endeavors. To the extent that the individual is unable to achieve integration —not experiencing a sense of wholeness and well-being in a caring relationship, he/she will utilize cajoling, manipulating, and coercive strategies to gain the power over and respect of others which he/she hopes will lead to feeling complete. These illusory integrative ploys failing, he/she will utilize despair and "illness" roles to force fusion and dependency integration on others, in order to assuage his/her loneliness and feelings of disintegration of self.

Here I will attempt to provide a paradigm for the interrelated acts of courage and intimacy by examining my work with a rather difficult and fascinating client. To do this, I will require a certain degree of poetic license. At this stage of our understanding of the development of intimacy, both in its natural setting in the mother-child bonding and in the therapeutic setting, scientific parlance will unduly restrict the meaningfulness of the experience I will be delineating. Consequently, my descriptions at times may sound metaphorical rather than scientific. I hope, however, that these descriptions will help elucidate the interrelated roles of intimacy and courage when I examine the therapeutic situation in Chapter 10.

CLINICAL CASE

The client I will describe in some detail I will call Roger. Roger was referred to a colleague by his dance teacher after he requested the name of a therapist. The colleague referred him to me after an initial interview. The precipitating event for his coming to therapy was the departure of his male lover. He stated that coming to therapy was very different from his usual way of handling difficulties in his life. Previously, he simply traveled from one city or country to another to evade uncomfortable situations. His dance teacher had labeled his behavior as problematic since he could not expect to have a dance career if he could not remain long enough to study on a continuous basis.

Roger says he hasn't had much experience with the practical situations in life. His independent wealth seemed to support his vagrant life style, since he did not have to concern himself with the realities of earning a living. He has turned to dance only because he cannot think of anything else he'd like to do. In his adolescence he took acting lessons with children several years older and felt he could not keep up with their pace. Roger continually struggles with whether he wishes to stay alive. His first of approximately eight suicide attempts within the two and one-half years before entering therapy occurred following the breakup of a love relationship. He went to bed with a friend of his male lover and claimed that he was totally unaware his actions would even precipitate a disturbance, let alone the termination of the relationship. He took an overdose of sleeping pills and Valium intending to end his life. He awoke in the hospital after nearly succeeding. Returning home to his parents, he made another suicide attempt. A third occurred after his return to New York following an experience with a tarot card reader, who, Roger claimed, called in a black witch as a consultant. The black witch proceeded to play tricks on him. Although she was in New Mexico at the time, he asserted that she threw a glass of wine in his face, then set down the empty, intact glass on the floor. A friend supposedly witnessed this incident. Roger was rather concerned that I, and the psychiatrist colleague who initially interviewed him, would not believe him. He told each of us in separate interviews that he was totally convinced that the situation happened as he reported it, and he wanted us to be convinced as well.

Roger also reported that he has paranormal or supernatural powers. After recovering from his suicide attempt, he managed to rid himself of the black witch by writing her name on a piece of paper, dropping it in a glass of water, and freezing the water, thus immobilizing and controlling the witch. He said this method was successful, and he was able to remove the glass from the freezer several months later.

Roger visualized death in two contradictory ways. He stated he thought he would just go to sleep "for a very long time." When confronted with his view of death as a long sleep, he denied it, saying, "Oh, no, I believe in reincarnation, and suicide is the worst thing I can do for my Karma."

Several other suicide attempts and gestures followed relatively small disappointments by friends, such as last-minute cancellations of social plans.

Roger also abused drugs and alcohol. The drugs included Valium; an English drug, Mandrax; placidyl; cocaine; and LSD. He drank to relax and go to sleep, but lost track of how much he had drunk and was unaware of how little control he had over his actions. It had been at least five or six years since he slept without alcohol and/or pills.

CLINICAL IMPRESSION

Roger is an attractive, dark-haired, slender though muscular man, appearing older than his stated age of 23 years, with delicate features and a mildly effeminate manner. He is articulate, though he intersperses his seemingly insightful comments with raucous laughter indicating extreme anxiety. On the other hand, affects besides anxiety and occasional outbursts of rage are camouflaged. His impulsiveness and the degree to which he is able and willing to take responsibility for his life-threatening actions fluctuate rapidly during the course of a single session—as did his desire to deal with his alcoholism and drug-abuse problems. He reported that his behavior was unpredictable. He admitted that, at times, he would like to have more control over it, but, simultaneously, he indicated pride in his impulsiveness, saying he is known for his staccato-like moods among his friends.

The reactions evoked in my colleague and me in our separate interviews ranged from being charmed and seduced to feeling enraged, hopeless and helpless about being able to reach this young man.

I will relate this clinical picture to some theoretical notions.

HOW INTIMACY DEVELOPS

The earliest and most basic aim of social behavior is the striving for intimate relations with a caring other. Important socio-emotional needs are served in this manner. Intimate connectedness is a mechanism of survival. The infant who is able to appropriately respond to what the mother wants and requires of the child is more adaptive in pleasing the mother and more likely to be rewarded by her. The quality of the early bonding relationship between mother and child mirrors and models how the child will subsequently relate to others. It is the bonding relationship that gives the child a sense of self. Developmental studies suggest that a rather important phase of the child's development of a sense of self, referred to as the *mirror phase* of personality development, occurs between the child's sixth and eighteenth month.

The "mirror phase," according to the French psychoanalyst Jacques Lacan (1977), is a period in the development of the child in which it becomes unusually excited, even "ecstatic," upon witnessing its image in a mirror. This is, perhaps, understandable, in that the child sees its body reflected in the mirror as a whole, a single integrated entity. This reflection is in sharp contrast to its actual physical sense of lacking coordination and control and experiencing "organic disturbances and discord," such that it feels it to be "in bits and pieces." The infant's mirror image, consequently, has "the prestige of stature, the impressiveness of statues," says Lacan, and the infant joyfully identifies with it. In so doing, the infant is identifying with something outside itself, something which it experiences as very different from how it feels inside of itself. The child psychoanalyst Paulina Kernberg[2] indicates that what the child experiences in the mirror at this stage is a condensed configuration of self and mother. This is to say, when the child glances into the mirror even when alone, it probably sees a configuration of itself and its mother. I emphasize this particular phase of the development of intimacy in the bonding relationship because of its relevance to the development of my theory about the magical self (to be discussed presently). Particularly, in the mirror phase, the child needs to be looked at, smiled at, and approved of by an active, loving, and supportive person. Without this emotional nurturance the child experiences the world as persecutory and regards parts of itself as unacceptable. In a word, a person subjected in childhood to an unresponsive or distorted mirroring relationship will be handicapped to a greater or lesser degree in his or her capacity to accurately mirror another person and, as a consequence, to empathically respond to the other and experience what the other person may be feeling.

I have now come to the place in which I can be more specific about what I mean by "intimacy." Intimacy is a uniquely personal experience. I will operationally define intimacy in this book as the experience of being recognized and emotionally touched in the way the self wishes, such that self experiences the other as accurately and satisfactorily mirroring its desires for caring and closeness. The other in the intimate encounter is the medium for how the self wishes to be related and regarded. Therefore, unlike its often associated state—privacy—intimacy always involves the real or imagined presence of the other. Moreover, unlike privacy, which is the reaction of the other's encroachment upon the self's experience of space and time, the experience of intimacy has no sense of time. It is experienced as a flow of tactile sensation. Intimacy is grounded in the immediacy of the present moment. The present moment is experienced as located in space, not time. Only the past and future are associated with time. Intimacy leads to an accentuation of how each partner uses the space between them. Anxieties in intimate relating are experienced as going out of space and are projected to moments in the future. Intimacy, then, is a moment that the self experiences as if time stopped and stood on end. The self's intention in the throes of intimacy is that this moment go on forever. Nietzsche wrote that every pleasure wants eternity—deep, deep eternity. This intent has a definitive body locus—even when there is no actual physical contact occurring between self and other. The experience is analogous to the reception of evocative music in which the vibrations of the distal stimulus (the musical instruments) touch the proximal stimulus (sense receptors) causing bodily sensation, which is neurologically transformed into deeply experienced emotion.

Developmental and clinical evidence suggests that intimate strivings have to do with an attempt to recreate the events of the tender, caring touch experienced in the early mother-child bonding. Consequently, the hunger and potency for this striving have to do with frustrations that occurred in this early relationship, whereas fears about intimate coupling involve the import of painful rejection and exclusion from these intimate relations.

ROGER'S HISTORY

Roger was adopted shortly after birth by a couple in their thirties who already had one adopted daughter, thirteen years

Roger's senior. Later, they adopted a second daughter, when Roger was five years old.

The (adoptive) mother came from a wealthy family in the Southwest. She is described as "hard as nails," who thinks "people should be strong," though she changed slightly after the (adoptive) father's death a year before Roger entered psychotherapy. Roger's father had developed a successful advertising business. A major theme in Roger's contrasting of his parents seemed to revolve around his father's acceptance of his homosexuality and his mother's strong disapproval.

Roger's education includes one year of college. He left college, giving up plans for a career for several years in order to travel, and then became involved in a long-term romantic relationship in Europe. He became concerned again about a career upon his return to the United States.

At the time of my inception of therapy with Roger, he had never been employed except for a very brief period in his teens.

As stated in the previous section, and according to the late psychoanalyst Heinz Kohut (1977), the capacity for intimacy develops in the infant by means of the mother's mirroring function. The mother's role in the child's development of intimacy is to serve as a supportive self-object for the child's curiosity about self and other. Roger was restricted in his curiosity about his own and his mother's body. He could remember no instance in which his mother actually held him, although he indicated in his theatrical intonation that she must have, when he was very young. On the other hand, he does remember some touching with his father in taking showers together and expressions of good feelings with his father.

The event of intimacy requires a bond between persons in which each "feels into" the other, as well as an openness with oneself which permits the other to connect with typically hidden aspects of oneself (Szalita, 1981). What does this mean in terms of the bonding relationship between mother and child? Basically, the mother gives the child one of two very different and crucial options in the child's response to the mother. In a bonding relationship with the mother the child may be given tacit permission by the mother to look *into* her depths and, metaphorically, into her mystery, or he may be given the constraint of merely looking at her and his own reflection in her eyes. Intimacy between mother and child in the early bonding relationship involves the mother's willingness to be intimate with her own self. It requires courage on the part of the mother in order to struggle with or, at least, be comfortable with her own uncertainties.

Roger's mother appears to have been an extremely repressed, action-oriented woman who was more concerned with deeds rather than feelings. She appears to have had no strong sexual interest of her own. We suspect that there may not even have been a sexual relationship between Roger's parents.

The role of courage in pain and suffering has serious implications for the role of courage in the healing process. Therefore, significant in intimate bonding with the mother is the child's witnessing the mother's willingness to bear pain and suffering in her creative functions. For example, in the acts of bearing children, the mother demonstrates her unwillingness to abort her pain and suffering in order that she may produce hope and possibility. The experimental work of the Stanford University psychologist, David Rosenman, has demonstrated that the individual's pattern of altruism is deeply influenced by parental models in regard to handling issues requiring persistence and fortitude (Rosenman, Karylowski, & Hargis, 1981). Thus, the child's witness to the mother's relationship with her own depths allows him to have a relationship with the mystery of another self. On the other hand, narcissistic or repressive mothers will not allow their child to probe their fears and uncertainties. She will restrict him to the image reflected upon her face and will not allow him to search her own depths or to have his own mystery. In short, the two basic options the mother in the bonding relationship may offer her child are: (a) sharing her mystery and uncertainties; or (b) restricting the child to relate to her in terms of how she wishes him to see himself as reflected on her face.

The child in the former relationship is allowed to find beauty and contentment within himself. He is allowed to take in and hold onto the inchoate, unfinished aspects of himself, cogitate with them, play with them in fantasy and action and, if he wishes, share them with others. Without restriction on his inner being, he feels no compulsion or haste to immediately share his inner being or the products of his imagination. He experiences permission to do so in his own time. Exploring his thoughts and feelings becomes a regular dimension in his ongoing development as a person. It does not require abrupt separation and withdrawal from other people.

On the other hand, the child who is denied the mystery of his mother's inner being becomes uncomfortable with his own psyche and its mysteries. He feels unsettled and perturbed inside.

He is continually on a search to find something or someone in the external environment to relieve urgent promptings within his psyche, which he has not been allowed to explore. Most particularly, he searches for the opportunity to find other people who will mirror acceptable parts of himself, thereby validating his existence.

My colleague, Dr. Jane Simon, and I (Goldberg & Simon, 1982) have found that in those clients toward whom parental dictates emphasized "doing" rather than "being," internal experiences that were inconsistent with the kind of person demanded by the parent, contributed to a tenuous sense of self in the child. In contrast, where parents emphasized "being" rather than "doing," self feelings of any kind are implicitly allowed. In these cases the parent is most concerned with regulating only the child's overt behavior. This kind of concern allows the child the freedom of his own thoughts and feelings. In contrast, there are parents who cannot tolerate that their child has thoughts and feelings of his own. The self feelings of these children, which are discordant with the parent's image of what is acceptable, are denied validity and implicitly or even directly, negatively sanctioned. The parents' unwillingness to "feel into" their child leads to an inability on the child's part to feel for other people.

The inability or unwillingness to psychologically take the place of the other—to take into consideration how the other feels—seems to lead to the tendency to treat the other as an object rather than as a person who has feelings like one's self. Clinical studies have demonstrated that when a person experiences parts of him/or herself as unacceptable because these attributes do not accord with how the person wishes to be seen, these parts of self tend to be attributed to other people rather than recognized as aspects of one's self. The greater the need of the attributor to rid him/or herself of unacceptable aspects of self by attributing them to another person, the more likely is the attributor to attempt to psychologically express unconsciously or even consciously experienced self-hatred in "uncontrollable" behavior; that is to say, behavior that results in expression of forceful dominance, aggression, and violence. My clinical studies suggest that the inability or unwillingness to be empathic is derived from the individual's early experience of suffering. (Suffering is a topic which I examine more closely in later chapters.)

I have found that in the presence of one's own suffering, in which no empathic bonds are established with another person, a false self is attributed to the other person and the other is treated as an object without feeling or the feelings that are inferred in the other person are regarded as being of no consequence to oneself.

This consideration is telling in Roger's development. Roger told us that he had been effeminate since he was rather young. He was frequently teased about it by his classmates. But whereas he reported that his mother became sick and vomited when she learned of his affair with a male teacher in high school, nonetheless, his mother apparently enjoyed his witty, charming behavior as a child who felt quite at home with her women friends at bridge games and social gatherings. She apparently did not realize that her fear and disdain of a masculine personality in her child restricted him from exploring those attributes as a part of his personal development. Understandably, he was frightened but nevertheless fascinated by the clandestine explorations of his own body and his budding sexuality by two men who seduced him on separate occasions in his latency years.

The child learns to recognize himself in the eyes and facial expressions of the mother. The child of narcissistic and repressive mothers will be restricted to superficial reflection—that is, literal image (such as in the mirror) for self-evaluation and esteem. Kohut and Wolf (1978) have referred to people who crave approval and confirmation to forage their impoverished self as "mirror-hungry personalities":

> They are impelled to display themselves and to evoke the attention of others, trying to counteract, however fleetingly, their inner sense of worthlessness and lack of self-esteem. Some of them are able to establish relationships with reliably mirroring others that will sustain them for long periods. But most of them will not be nourished for long, even by genuinely accepting responses. Thus, despite their discomfort about their need to display themselves and their sometimes severe stage fright and shame, they must go on trying to find new self objects whose attention and recognition they seek to induce." (Kohut & Wolf, 1978)

The two people who were curious and interested in Roger's body and sexuality in the incidents mentioned above emphasized his appearance, but had little or no concern for his feelings. They were also men with apparently sadistic tendencies who alternated between intimacy and rejection. This had contributed to Roger's difficulties with caring in intimacy. Without conflict and without being forcefully put in his place (although, generally, being rejected psychologically), Roger found his romantic relationships boring and searched for more excitement elsewhere.

I have spoken about the mother's role in the child's development of intimacy but not yet of the father. What part does the father play in the child's striving for intimacy? In general, we know very little about the father's role in the child's development of a capacity for intimacy. We do know that the father in the consanguine family of Western society cuts the cord (Meerloo, 1948). This is to say, the father forces the child out of the timeless space of intense, intimate bonding with the mother. Of course, other siblings and external situations may do so, as well. However, in the early triangular family relationship, this appears to be one of the father's major functions in terms of his child.

According to psychoanalytic theory, the mother, as an object for relating, is experienced by the infant as coming from within the self of the infant. The father, in contrast, exists only as an external figure, as part of a gradual process in which the figure of the mother becomes experienced as outside of the child. In fact, it is the relationship of the parents which helps the child differentiate what is inside and what is outside of himself (Gaddini, 1976). By keeping the mother-child relationship from becoming too exclusive, the father serves as a representative of space and time and of the larger society. The father's presence between child and mother enables the child to experience sufficient frustration from the absence of unlimited intimacy with the mother to feel induced to seek intimate relations with peers and parental surrogates. Without the structure of time and space created by the father the child would stay magically in symbiotic fusion with the mother.

In Roger's case, because he never actually received the tender bonding relationship with his (adoptive) mother, he had remained magically fused with his unknown natural mother. The yearning for intimacy with his natural mother was a wish that he had tenaciously kept out of awareness. On the basis of other clients who have had greater access to early memories than did Roger, I can speculate about the compelling forces underlying Roger's amnesia toward his early experience. I believe that the potent force with which he acted out his ravenous need for external stimulation is a compromised means of distracting Roger from his once very painful feelings of desertion by his consciously forgotten natural mother. I would further speculate that he has projected his longing for union with his natural mother into magical objects, which he split off into good and bad witches, whom he entreated to fight for possession of him in a similar way as he manipulated potential lovers. When he could not obtain the desired union with a love object, he joined with the other side—the ultimate embrace—signifying his ambivalence toward life and death, and said, "I just wish I could go to sleep and never awaken."

The role played by Roger's father is not as clear as that played by his mother. But it would appear to us that his role saved Roger from even greater psychopathology. He served Roger in the *idealized* parental role described so cogently by Kohut (1977). Roger described his father as patiently understanding and approachable. "He was," said Roger, "the best man I've known." He was "a real happy guy," who had done some modeling and acting, but stopped because he was "too good-looking" and was approached (the implication was by men, perhaps, as well as women). Apparently, Roger's father encouraged and supported his exhibitionism and his becoming a dancer and socialite. Roger had remarked that at times when he felt desperate and in the need of support he wished his father were still alive. Yet, paradoxically, in talking about his father's death, he reported it matter-of-factly.

How do we make sense of the difficulty such clients as Roger experience in securing intimate relations? Psychoanalytic theory does not appear to offer us a viable direction. Little more work has been done in explaining difficulties with intimacy than Freud's own explanation in *Group Psychology and the Analysis of the Ego* (1921) that the transition from a male's intimacy with the mother to coupling with other women effects a separation between the feelings of affection and sexuality. Freud seems to suggest, but not quite explicitly state, that a man can never be as intimate with another woman as he once was with his mother. He says:

> ...the prohibition of any sexual relation with those women [mother and sisters] of the family who had been tenderly loved since childhood [creates] a wedge—between a man's affectionate and sensual feelings...As a result of this exogamy the sensual needs of men [have] to be satisfied with strange and unloved women. (p. 94)

Quite obviously, this poetic passage is misleading in explaining clients like Roger. Roger did not feel tenderly loved in his bonded relationship with his mother. Her inability to share her depths with him made meaningful intimacy impossible. Those attributes which she felt threatened by and denied in her self, she denied to her child. The mother teaches the child not only how to love or to be intimate with another person, but, as importantly, how to love and be intimate with oneself. As I have stated, the attributes and potentials of self disavowed in the child by their threat to the mother create a magical self. I should, however, indicate that it is my observation that the origins of the magical self actually have several potential sources. The most apparent are: (a) the denied attributes that the narcissistic or repressive mother doesn't allow; (b) the attributes of mother or father that are denied to the child by the forbidden nature of the parents' seclusive coupling; and (c) certain attributes, assigned to other siblings or family intimates, that are denied to the child.

These rejected feelings are disassociated from the child's experience of himself. However, because they relate to once deeply felt experiences of the inchoate self, they are dynamically retained, but as shrouded images resembling that primal self, now with obliviscence and, when ascendant, sensed as external, hostile, and elusive. These images were accessible to Roger only in dreams and hypnagogic experiences. Whether these images were due to a psychedelic state induced by drugs, or an altered state of consciousness stimulated by the dynamic tensions of painful memories partially repressed, was not clear.

The images Roger reported are similar to the fearful symbols referred to as the *shadow*, which is found in myth and ritual in many cultures. In the psychological theories of Carl Jung, the shadow is conceptualized as externalized self-hatred, playing a significant role in Jungian therapeutics. As the missing, hidden and secret part of the self, the shadow must be "owned" for harmonious existence. In Karen Horney's theory, the shadow is referred to as "alienation from self"—a coterie of despised selves which must be integrated with the idealized selves to create a unified, holistic, real self. In Heinz Kohut's theory, the missing aspects of the self are those that have gone unmirrored by the narcissistic mother who possesses her own agenda and is not sufficiently empathic with her child (Simon & Goldberg, 1984).

In summary, I believe that we cannot understand the nature of intimacy if we view the self as a solitary and complete entity. In the act of intimacy the self tries to transcend itself and to reach out and rescue its disavowed and denied aspects. It is the pursuit of the disavowed aspects of self in the desire to feel whole that draws people to psychological services.

We will return to Roger frequently throughout this book to illustrate the developmental considerations in developing the capacity for intimacy.

NOTES

1. The capacity for intimacy, caring, courage, and creativity are regarded as the most significant, positive human attributes. However, clear delineation as to how these capacities become developed has not yet been presented by behavioral scientists. They have turned their attention more exclusively than seems warranted to examining and accounting for human ills and misfortunes, as if we could foster constructive attributes by examining misfortune exclusively. As a result, we lack a personality theory that explains how constructive human expression is derived. One of the few exceptions is the theoretical position of the British developmental behavior psychologist, R. A. Hinde (1978). For the past 25 years, he has been working on a science of interpersonal relationships within the context of social-bond theory. Intimacy is a dimension of interpersonal bonding to which he gives significant emphasis. Erik Erikson and Harry Stack Sullivan also emphasize the importance of intimacy in their influential theories. Unfortunately, none of these theories delineate clearly how intimacy develops.

As a psychologist, social theorist, and psychotherapy practitioner, I have been searching for a foundation for social theory that is not reductionistic. I have not been satisfied with theoretical positions that attempt to explain human endeavors in terms of one or two determinants, especially, if in so doing, they do not convincingly explain both the ills that befall humans, as well as account for their highest and most notable achievements. Something important is absent when we account for human behavior in terms of drives, for example, rather than human purpose.

2. Presentation, Grand Rounds, Department of Psychiatry, Roosevelt-St. Luke's Hospitals, New York City, Spring 1983.

Chapter 3
The Public's View
of the
Psychotherapist

The correct perception of any matter and a
complete misunderstanding of the matter do not
wholly exclude one another
—Franz Kafka

Psychoanalysis and other types of psychotherapy are as ubiquitously discussed a subject as any topic of conversation in modern society. Ironically, the personal reactions of practitioners to their work are, for most lay people, obscured by considerable secrecy, mystification, and cliché, such as found in *New Yorker* magazine cartoons and other media caricatures. Most important, appropriate information about the psychotherapist's practice is often difficult to obtain. The Health Research Group in Washington, D.C., a consumer advocacy organization sponsored by Ralph Nader, has reported an extraordinary amount of resistance from professional mental health societies toward those collecting data on the practices of their constituents (Adams &, Orgel, 1975). This evidence underlines Torrey's complaint (1974) that it is easier to obtain information about the qualifications of a plumber than of a psychotherapist.

Psychotherapists have maintained a pattern of aloofness, with considerable consequence. Too many people decide to enter psychotherapy treatment without giving due consideration to the complex concerns this important decision raises. Selecting an appropriate therapist is one of the most crucial dimensions in therapeutic outcome. Practitioners vary considerably in their training, expertise, styles of practice, fees, and so forth. It is essential that the prospective client be aware of these differences in order to select an appropriate therapist. Although mental health practitioners may be certified or licensed,[1] they are essentially unregulated in terms of the fees they charge and the quality and style of their practice (Goldberg, 1977).

Practitioners themselves realize that there is considerable variation in therapeutic approaches and in the quality of available practitioners. For a prospective client, however, any port in the storm may appear more secure than the crisis and confusion he/she is experiencing in his/her search for psychological assistance. Clients, as a consequence, quite frequently select practitioners who are expensive and subject themselves to treatment programs that are psychologically (and sometimes physically) risky, without realizing or carefully considering the options available to them.[2] Sharland Trotter (1975), in a report to the members of the American Psychological Association, has summarized a number of salient concerns encountered by prospective clients in selecting practitioners and treatment programs:

> The current psychotherapy scene is, for most of the lay public, a jumble of conflicting schools, theories, methods, and techniques. Anyone seeking professional help is confronted with a confusing smorgasbord of therapies ranging from orthodox psychoanalysis to drug therapy; from client-centered, existential, humanistic, gestalt, rational-emotive or family therapy, to biofeedback, hypnosis, megavitamin therapy, or transactional analysis—or some combination of these. Requesting a referral from professional associations will usually net one a list of therapists' names and addresses—but to avoid possible bias, information about the kind, quality, or price of treatment is scrupulously not included. These things the consumer must find out the hard way—by costly and time-consuming trial and error.

Friedson (1976) has argued from his study of doctor-patient relationships that the patient's reluctance to question the doctor's judgment and his/her subsequent acceptance of poor quality and ill-conceived treatment is due to certain "myths of the medical mystique." Patients tacitly assume that: (1) doctors must tailor to each patient such complicated judgments that no one except another doctor who has gone through the case step by step can judge the validity of the diagnosis and treatment rendered by his/her doctor; (2) the quality of medical care is assured by the long and rigorous course of training a doctor must undergo to secure his/her degree and pass the licensing examination; and (3) doctors are always responsible professionals who are dedicated to the welfare of the patients they treat and the public they serve. Friedson and others seriously question the validity of these assumptions. I submit that these assumptions hold true for nonmedical healing arts practitioners, as well.

Let us look at some of the reasons why society in general has accepted this view.

THE SPREADING INFLUENCE
OF PSYCHOTHERAPY

At one time, psychotherapy was a specialized medical technique for only a narrow and circumscribed patient population; it is now considered to be the *sine qua non* application in all matters in which human suffering is involved (Small, 1971). The craft of psychotherapy is now expected to provide answers to questions about "malfunctions" in all areas of human endeavor. The twentieth century has awakened to a fervent exploration of the human psyche in all of its irrational depths. The reader need only glance at current periodicals or view cinema or television dramas to appreciate readily that most complex human problems and concerns are typically reduced to the level of psychological explanation. The ideas of Freud and his followers, though they may seem somewhat less impressive than they did four decades ago, nevertheless remain as influential in modern thought and living as the ideas of any personalities who have lived in the last century (Goldberg, 1977).

The public tempts the mental health practitioner in becoming an authority in too many areas outside his/her own field of expertise and as a result the practitioner has often overstated his/her abilities (Henry, Sims, & Spray, 1973). Much of what the practitioner achieves is a matter of art, the exercise of intuition and craft in a way no other form of ameliorative endeavor can achieve. Vivified by breakthroughs in reaching seriously disturbed people in the 1930s, 1940s, and 1950s, together with the public acceptance that came with sensational successes reported in books and magazines, and depicted in dramatic films, psychotherapists became overconfident and have claimed too much.

In short, psychology has imposed an impossible task upon itself. It has allowed the public to believe that it can deal with all the dark secrets of the mind. For every disturbing societal event the psychologist can offer a psychological cause and a plausible explanation. The public has become increasingly attracted to these explanations. They offer the public some semblance of order and meaning in an otherwise inexplicable world. In the past, the public was offered theological and, later natural science explanations of the human condition. This is vividly exemplified in the ever-proliferating phenomenon of media psychology. Some professionals regard these media personalities, such as radio and television psychologists, as offering public education and lessening the mystification of the therapist's way of seeing the world. Others are alarmed by the pop-psychology entertainment image the media psychologist casts. It has been pointed out that in order "to score high in the ratings, the hosts of these psychology oriented shows are frequently pressed to take as many calls as possible and to issue quick, often spectacular judgments" (Sobel, 1980).

The image of practitioner as a public entertainer and informant may take ludicrous forms. In New York City, at one of the famous disco studios, a former counterculture figure from the 1960s held business network parties. Two or three nights a month, under the flashing lights, the flow of drinks, and amid the punk-dressed crowd, mental health professionals were invited up on a rotating stage to tell their names, give their office addresses, and demonstrate what they do in practice. The simulated demonstrations, attempted in three to five minutes, were a sorry sight. Standing and watching them, I felt quite embarrassed *for* my colleagues, who were so eager for acceptance and hire that they allowed themselves to reduce psychotherapy to an entertainment routine.

I believe that the pervasive influence of psychological explanation of societal concerns deserves serious examination. It appears that there is always at least one psychotherapy practitioner who is eager and willing to demonstrate that he/she can explain anything that is of concern to the public. Psychologists, psychiatrists, and the techniques of both are involved in virtually every facet of society. Psychologists reportedly have helped to win several important jury trials (e.g., the Mitchell-Stans trial, the Joanne Little trial, and the Wounded Knee Indian trial) by enabling defense attorneys to select jurors most psychologically responsive to their clients' situation.

In addition, drivers in Venezuela need to convince a psychiatrist that their aggressive propensities are within acceptable limits in order to gain a license to drive an automobile; bartenders in Racine, Wisconsin, are being taught by psychologists and hairdressers in Miami, Florida, are being taught by psychiatrists to improve their ability to listen empathetically to their customers. A successful tennis instructor in Maryland has described his approach as a method of psychological counseling that deals with students "where they're at," using meditation and body exercises to help them overcome the neurotic cycles they are locked into. Edifices that exude a "therapeutic environment" are being created by an interdisciplinary team of Yale University psychologists and psychiatrists in collaboration with architects, administrators, and interior designers. But whereas thousands of books and tens of thousands of professional articles, reports, and papers have been written on the craft of psychotherapy and its applications to everyday life, few practitioners have deemed it necessary to explore the personal world of the psychotherapist and how it affects his/her work. This has had an unfortunate consequence. In overextending ourselves we have helped to create an overideal image of ourselves, which we can not adequately fulfill. In not revealing our own personal world we have set ourselves open to being misunderstood. As I shall show in Chapter 6, the personal world of the practitioner integrally influences the tools of his/her trade, most notable, psychological explanation.

PSYCHOLOGICAL EXPLANATION

It may be useful to give some attention to the importance of psychological theory and explanation. It is generally agreed that psychological theory rose to prominence in the second half of the nineteenth century. The view that prevailed in the nineteenth century prior to Freud was that the criminal and the mentally ill possessed a malignant, inscrutable disease that prevented them from behaving as rational human beings. This pessimistic view stemmed from a world sobered by scientific nihilism based on unswaying determinism, reinforced by witness to revolutionary and devastating war. Theological and scientific explanations had failed to offer resolute life strategies for dealing with personal dissatisfaction. They were equally unsuccessful in resolving societal conflict.

Psychoanalysis was a double protest against the prevailing concept of the nature of man. Freud rejected the view that mental disturbance was due to disease or to the genetic make-up of the individual. He protested no less vehemently against the doctrine of free will that held that a human being could make conscious choices between good and evil in selecting a course of action. The idea of free will persisted in the theology and in much of the philosophy of Freud's day despite the nihilism of science. Freud believed that behavior was determined by unconscious strivings. The mentally disturbed adult behaves irrationally because of childhood experiences that operate unconsciously upon her. Freud claimed a clinician is able to understand a disturbed person's actions by being able to discern the unconscious forces behind her behavior. More important, if the clinician is able to induce the patient to bring her childhood experiences and fantasies into consciousness, the insight the patient gains into her own disturbances makes it possible for her to deal rationally with her situation. Hence, in Freud's view, mental illness was determined, comprehensible, and subject to therapeutic correction.

The psychological revolution was the third of four world ideological revolutions. The First World War ended, for all practical purposes, the rule of monarchical government by the will of God and Church. The Second World War demonstrated the inability of the scientific knowledge of industrial nations to control each other's destructive power. The Vietnam war was, for the United States, a fourth revolution. It was an individualistic and existential struggle in the sense that the collective beliefs in patriotism and governmental authority gradually eroded during the dragged-out course of the war. Citizens increasingly held their leaders personally accountable for their behavior, while at the same time demanding a shared responsibility for the conduct of government. Young people in considerable numbers altered life-styles, many gave up their United States citizenship, in a desperate striving for an authenticity of purpose and personal commitment to try to live harmoniously with others.

The striving for authenticity has had a pervasive influence on the current practices of psychotherapy. The search for authenticity has become for increasing numbers of practitioners the driving force of their personal and professional endeavors. In reaction to what many practitioners regarded as an overemphasis on rationality in the practice of psychotherapy in the past there is today a deep respect for personal commitment and authenticity in the way the practitioner relates to his/her client and, correspondingly, what the practitioner implicitly regards as the highest values for the client. This is not to suggest that the therapeutic stances formulated in one era are necessarily obsolete in the next. Many of the basic concerns therapists and clients are struggling with have plagued the therapeutic relationship since the dawn of the healing practices. Nonetheless, how these concerns are expressed and dealt with is determined by the particular resources and conditions in any particular period in history (Goldberg, 1977).

Let us look at how the profession of psychotherapy is viewed by the general public today. The mystification of the psychotherapist imbues him/her with considerable influence. Due to this mystification there is little or no appreciation of the personal struggle of the therapist. Generally, presenting him/herself to the best light, the practitioner—the public assumes—came by psychotherapeutic skill without effort or personal risk. Studies of charismatic people, as well as those investigations that have examined the roles of projection and projective identification in ambiguous situations, demonstrate that a great deal of power and influence is attributed to those who are ascribed leaders in situations that are not clearly defined. In particular, the psychoanalytically oriented anthropologist, Weston La Barre (1980), in examining charisma has found it to consist of the projection of the populace's childhood hopes and fears onto a leader.

Similarly to the physician, the psychotherapist has been viewed very differently from other professions—certainly, from business people. We give a great deal of power to the psychotherapist in private practice, which we would not normally ascribe to any businessperson, because we assume, as a service professional, that the practitioner acts in accordance with the ethical and professional standards of the profession. In this restraint the practitioner will not take advantage of others because of their emotional or financial vulnerability. Indeed, the public assumes that the psychotherapist is subservient to a code which requires him/her even to take care of those who cannot afford the practitioner's services. Thus, while the layperson may be hesitant to ask a businessperson to give goods and services without remuneration, clients may not hesitate to ask the private practitioner to give services when they don't have the money or when they have other large bills that they believe have to be paid first. In a word, due to the mystification of psychotherapy there is often an accompanying denigration of the business and financial interests of the practitioner. It was as if, by romanticizing professional regulation, some of the public believe that the practitioner should be giving services without expecting profitable remuneration.

Because psychotherapists are particularly susceptible to mythologizing in their theories, practices, and personal manners, the powers and responsibilities of psychotherapists are frequently not tested by reality.[3] The public has, because of a lack of intimate understanding of psychotherapy, unrealistically high expectations of the practitioner. If we know someone as a person, we'll generally see the person as having the same human frailties and limitations that we have. We cannot, then, realistically, expect magical cure and omniscient understanding from a therapist.

The mystification of the psychotherapist is, of course, doubleedged. The work of Jerome Frank, comparing psychotherapy with the native healing of the shaman has shown that the religio-magical methods of behavior change have considerable similarity with what we regard as the modern practice of scientific psychotherapy. The influence system of the healer, faith in his/her knowledge and skills, hope, suggestion, and a wish to be cared for, taken together create a powerful field of affect in which the so-called scientific practices of psychotherapy occur (Frank, 1961). In fact, Frank's work seems to indicate that the nonspecific factors—both the practitioner's real attributes and those transferentially bestowed upon the psychotherapist—are much more significant in successful treatment than are the specific factors of therapeutic methods, such as interpretation and insight strategies.

Accompanying magic, there are, of course, lurking fears. Recently, the media gave considerable attention to a major league baseball player named Jim Eisenreich. According to a story by Ira Berkow in *The New York Times* (April 19, 1984). Eisenreich had made several attempts to play major league baseball. Ap-

parently, there was no question of his skill and physical attributes, nor were his problems with the opposing ballplayers. The
Times tells us that

> he took himself out of the lineup, unable to continue the season.
> He was suffering from a nervous disorder and hyperventilating
> and twitching on the field. (According to his father, Cliff, the
> team he plays for, the Twins) spent about $50,000 in trying to
> identify and do something about his problems.
> "They've tried biofeedback, hypnosis, drugs on the kid," Cliff
> Eisenreich said. "Everything but psychotherapy. A lot of people
> think that's like witchcraft."

In another recent event, a Minnesota State Senator abandoned the idea of hiring a psychiatrist to counsel the members
and staff of the Minnesota State Senate after receiving a large
score of negative letters and the appearance in newspapers of
"shrink" jokes. The Senator attributed the public reaction to a
misunderstanding and mistrust of psychiatry. He is reported,
nonetheless, to have said that he would hire a preacher instead.

The public's fear comes from the sense that the psychotherapist can read minds and see through people. As such, the practitioner can understand things, such as their dark secrets, that
other people cannot.[4] The label, "shrink," comes from the notion of the witchdoctor who can control us in fearful ways by
knowledge of our internal processes and our hidden recesses.
The psychotherapist is regarded by many as the possessor of the
"evil eye," the all-seeing father whom we fear will read our
thoughts. In former times evil and the evil eye were regarded
almost synonymously. Hart (1949) tells us that evil and evil eye
have been joined together since biblical times.

> No science, religon or law has been able to eradicate it. Incan-
> tations and reference to it go back to early records of Egyptian,
> Assyrian and Chaldean civilizations. The Persians believed that
> most diseases were due to it, and the Athenians and Etruscans
> were both susceptible to it.

According to this universal depiction of evil, certain persons
can cause injury or harm to people, animals or inanimate objects
by intentional stares or even an unwitting glance. This notion
is an interesting image of vision that confounds the eye as an object which is both window and searchlight. This is to say, the no-

tion of the evil eye regards the eye as both the object of active knowing and of passive disclosure. This notion is supported by Otto Fenichel (1937), who characterizes the eye as not only the organ that depicts our own search of other people but also exposes things we would rather hide than reveal within ourselves. In short, writers such as William Shakespeare, who ascribed to the evil eye notion, contend that eyes are not only for seeing, but also for telling and disclosing. The so-called evil eye is so regarded because it does not respect the image of the person as the person consciously presents him/herself to the world. Unlike normal eyes, the evil eye does not confine itself to the surface persona. It plunges into the dark secrets of the other's soul. In a word, the evil eye is feared because it supplements "objective reality" with the imposition of the other's internal base motives. No doubt, before the advent of the X-ray machine, the microscope and other diagnostic instruments, sensitive eyes often could see disease in a person, which normal vision did not. By extension, if an eye could see physical illness, people might have believed that it could also recognize maladies of the soul. Parenthetically, people have always feared physicians who probed their insides and could, therefore, come upon their conflictual hidden urges. It is no wonder then, that through projective mechanisms, physicians have been suspected of evil and depicted in such infamous forms as Dr. Frankenstein, Dr Jekyll-Mr. Hyde, the Mad Scientist, and so forth (Goldberg, 1985). This is in accord with Judd Marmor's view (1953) that psychotherapists are presented in extremes in our society as either Devil or Deity, rather than as persons with special training and ability who have, like everyone else, strengths and frailties.

The unrealistic view of the psychotherapist may be attributed, in part, to the role of the practitioner as a *healer of the last resort*. Most of the people the psychotherapist treats have reached the practitioner only after numerous unsuccessful attempts at help by others. In a typical case, family and friends have encouraged the sufferer to feel better, to be more active and enthusiastic, or made repeated efforts to dissuade the sufferer from acting in ways that are socially inappropriate and disturbing to others. These efforts have failed. The sufferer is sent to see still other helpers. These are people known to the family as wise and knowledgeable and possessing sound advice. But they, too, have been unable to reach the sufferer. The person we are discussing is then sent to professionals who deal with illness and health but who are not trained psychotherapists. For example, the unhappy child is sent to the school counselor, while the mother visits her internist. The physician gives her advice, tries to reassure her and, in instances where reassurance does not suffice, recommends, finally, that she and/or her child consult a specialist in emotional problems. In short, before visiting the psychotherapist, various other types of attention and treatment have been tried. They have all failed. Family and friends feel antagonized and emotionally drained by the sufferer. As such, the family implores the practitioner to either change the character of the sufferer to a more acceptable demeanor, or to get rid of the sufferer by custodial action. As odious as it may seem, in a real sense, the psychotherapist is asked to serve as a type of sanitation agent to the public in getting rid of human problems. Because of this, the sufferer feels shunned by those with whom the person has been the most intimate.

To serve this important and, often, unpleasant social function, the practitioner is given a great deal of power. This power is predicated on the psychotherapist's imputed ability to understand "craziness," that is, why people act in ways that are personally and socially destructive of the best interests of the person. The public also rewards the practitioner for his/her superior comprehension and the willingness to withstand behaviors that are intolerable to others. They render the psychotherapist status and high fees. The price for these rewards is that the practitioner deliver. Consequently, when a practitioner is unable to comprehend the reasons for a client's difficulties or unable to make any definitive change in the sufferer, there is often a great deal of disappointment and resentment toward the therapist. In short, in balancing the considerable amount of status, the psychotherapist is given because of his/her imputed skills, there is a comparable amount of disappointment if the practitioner doesn't deliver.

I would like to touch briefly upon one last point here. Despite the pervasive influence of the mental health practitioner in society today, a vital function in which the psychotherapist has expertise has been relatively untouched. Each society has myths about how things came to be as they are. As a modern shaman, I believe that we can help the public look at the myths society uses to guide their existential options. We need to help the public examine, in particular, those destructive myths that have created such situations as the nuclear dilemma of our age. In this process practitioners must delineate the effects myths have upon how we live our lives and we must vivify the possibilities we believe can exist. We also need to help the public examine myths about us as practitioners which impute inappropriate expectations of our skills and capabilities.

NOTES

1. Some professionals prefer to refer clients to practitioners who have attained some professional distinctions, such as board certification in psychiatry and neurology, or have become diplomats of the American Board of Professional Psychology. This is not always sound. These distinctions are indicative of knowledge of theoretical principles and of professional standards and practices, and as such, they evince diagnostic and teaching competence rather than the sensitivity, intuition, personal adaptability, and the meaningful life experiences required of an effective psychotherapist. Moreover, many well-trained mental health practitioners with many years in the field as diagnosticians and educators have had relatively little actual experience as psychotherapists. Most practitioners know that the taking and passing of a professional licensing examination is not significantly related to competence as a practitioner. Consequently, certification and licensure on the basis of such examination does not, in fact, verify that the practitioner is competent. On the other hand, the general public believes that when a medical board, a psychology board, or social work accrediting committee certifies a practitioner, the board is stating by its certification that the holder of certification is a competent practitioner. Why shouldn't the public believe this since not a single department of state education endorsing these boards has, to my awareness, done anything to inform the public of the actual significance of certification! Besides, the dubious status and prestige it has, certification, essentially, offers tangible financial reward and protection against competitors, but nothing more.

2. There is considerable confusion among the lay public about the distinctions between, and the specific merits of psychoanalysis and psychotherapy, to say nothing about distinctions among the other psychotherapies. The public may be getting fewer services (at least, limited services or inappropriate services) for a higher fee because of this lack of understanding.

3. Burton (1972) aptly summarizes the situation in indicating that

> society abets the passionate loneliness of the therapist by conferring specific privileges upon him, by raising him above the herd, and mystifying his messages. And by so doing it marks him somewhat untouchable .... The total effect is to thrust the therapist deeper into himself, his family, and the therapeutic ghetto.

4. Of course, when we speak about the public we are referring to a rather heterogeneous admixture of people. In actuality, psychotherapists serve different functions depending upon the specific vector of society requiring psychological services.

Chapter 4
Becoming a Psychotherapist

Lives of great men all remind us
we can make our own lives sublime
and, departing, leave behind us
footprints in the sands of time.
—Henry Wadsworth Longfellow

THE THERAPIST'S IDENTITY

We will demonstrate in this chapter that the choice of career as a psychotherapist is shaped by the role provided for the psychotherapist-to-be in the family of origin. Responding to the calling of being a psychotherapist suggests that the role of being responsive to the emotional substratum of human experience is central to the identity of the practitioner. As such, the practitioner's identity is continually being defined by his or her clients. The ways clients respond to the practitioner's family role in regard to how the practitioner employs it in therapeutic relationships will effect the ongoing tempering of the practitioner's identity. The therapist whose identity is ill-defined and still tentative and whose self-esteem is contingent upon the momentary satisfactions and disappointments of how clients respond to the practitioner, will experience an identity crisis when the practitioner's family role is frustrated. Helm Stierlin, a German psychiatrist, speaks to this point when he examines how the practitioner's work with clients touch disassociated and unintegrated parts of his or her own self. The ability to enable clients to grow depends on the practitioner properly utilizing his/her own family role in enabling clients to differentiate their needs.

According to Stierlin (Burton, 1972),

> we can distinguish between repair needs and growth needs. Repair needs come into play when the therapist realizes he needs his patients in order that he can be confirmed as a therapist. He thus becomes aware that his self-esteem depends on his seeing his patients thrive . . . as a mother feels confirmed by seeing her child thrive. Winnicott has specifically made this point. He emphasized that a doctor usually embarks on a life-long career of doing repair work . . . because of his own psychological needs. Obviously, he could not do this repair work without recruiting a patient . . . . In addition to becoming confirmed as a parent and doctor, the therapist needs his patient in order to realize his growth potential. There growth needs, rather than repair needs, seem important. Thus, a deeply anxious schizophrenic patient may bring the therapist into closer touch with areas of disassociation, disintegrative anxiety which the therapist can now experience . . . and allow to contribute to his growth. Yet when we reflect . . . we find we have to steer a narrow and precarious path from which we can stray in either of two directions. Either we can need our patients too much, keeping them dependent and needy or we can need our patients too little and lack motivation for getting ourselves deeper into it. (p. 135)

Many of us who choose to become psychotherapists do so with the hopeful prospect that we can experience and be an ascendant agent in intimate relationships without some of the risks for hurt and disappointment that we experienced in our earlier attempts at love and friendship, particularly, within our own families. This conscious intention, wedded to a somewhat less conscious need to help and understand ourselves through others' plights and suffering, may create a tenacious gravitation toward the healing professions in ways we may have little understood when we entered the field. I will examine these contentions in terms of existing data in this chapter.

PSYCHOTHERAPY AS A CALLING

My thesis is that for many, if not most, practitioners deeply committed to meaningful therapeutic work, psychotherapy is

not a conscious and rational vocational choice. It may sound un-
scientific, but in many ways I believe that it is accurate to regard
the choice of practicing psychotherapy as a spiritual calling. As
a spiritual calling, it imposes certain concerns, problems and
hazards in the course of the practitioner's pursuit of a commitment to a way of life that transcends his/her professional hours.
The practice of psychotherapy has as a foundation and basic
tenet the pursuit of the examined life. For us, as practitioners,
in order to understand why we have been drawn to examine our
lives and the lives of others who petition us with their suffering
in the ways we do, we require some penetrating examination of
the backgrounds of those who practice psychotherapy. We need
to understand the kinds of families practitioners come from and
the roles they were cast into as children. Among other important considerations in this examination we should know the
values, satisfactions, and ways of responding to the world as derived from the practitioner's family of origin. Moreover, it also
would be useful to know whether there was someone in the family or in the psychotherapist's background who provided a role
model for being a healer. Also, we would like to know whether
there was a particular event or series of events that contributed
to the calling of the healer. And, perhaps, most importantly, we
would like to know how conflict was handled in the family. Without this examination we cannot sufficiently understand the
sources of concern and hazard in psychotherapeutic practice.

These considerations are more important for the development of the psychotherapist than in the development of a physician or an attorney. Unlike most other professionals, psychotherapy involves the totality of the practitioner's being. This
is because, unlike professional disciplines that treat circumscribed areas of human functioning, ideally psychotherapy
treats the whole person.

Of course, the personal journey in less complex societies may
more often achieve this ideal. An eminent anthropologist compared Shaman and Western healing in the following ways:

> In Shaman therapy, when an individual is sick he is not given
> treatment for his body in one way, for his mind in another, and
> for his soul in another—illness is something wrong with the en-
> tire being rather than with a particular part of it (p. 136).
>
> A highly important factor to be included in any evaluation
> of the Shaman's healing efforts is that he works within the pe-
> rimeter of the culture of his patients, which he well understands.

The modern Western psychiatrist may have difficulty in attaining a comparable degree of rapport and understanding (S. L. Rogers, 1982, p. 135).

A holistic understanding of our clients is essential. Difficulties in our own work arise from our inability to see the interrelations among the various spheres of the person's existence. (This point will be more fully examined in Chapter 13.) However, to encompass the whole of human functioning in all its complexities would require an encyclopedic knowledge and a vast diversity of skills few persons could ever achieve. The psychotherapist, therefore, must simplify his/her complex task by reducing all of a human being's concerns to the level of psychological functioning viewed in terms of a belief system the therapist has found to provide a plausible explanation for human behavior. Such a belief system is not objectively arrived at nor impersonally maintained. In his/her attachment to a professional belief system, the psychotherapist stands in sharp contrast to other helping professionals. The physician's hallmark is a proficiency in acquiring technical skill to diagnose and treat organ dysfunction. Rarely do physicians develop an emotional attachment to their professional technology as do psychotherapists. Similarly, whereas attorneys may develop a rather pronounced social and legal philosophy, unless they become active politically (which is, of course, usually outside their professional roles as attorneys), they are not generally known to become emotionally imbued disciples of a legal mentor. In contrast, the practice of psychotherapy issues more from the personality and temperament of the practitioner than from a body of ideas or technical procedures. In this respect, then the psychotherapist's practice is radically different from that of medical healing (Szasz, 1969) or legal counseling. I should make clear that I am not saying that most practitioners operate without a body of ideas and techniques; only that these are not objectively derived. Among the helping professionals, only the clergyman parallels the psychotherapist in an attempt to treat the whole person (Goldberg, 1977).

This all-encompassing psychological life can be so demanding as to insulate the practitioner from the "nonpsychological" world. Rogers (1982) indicates that

Western medicine is a subculture, an esoteric entity, usually detached from the lives of healthy persons. Physicians commonly form an elite enclave, quite apart from the lives of their patients. Quite often, there is a distrust of the institutions on the part of the sick person, and, in dire emergency, he may avoid doctors and hospitals—the physician-patient encounter is inherently conflictual. (p. 168)

A number of years ago I treated a clinical psychology graduate student whose father-in-law was a well-known training analyst. She described him as existing in a psychoanalytic ghetto. He analyzed the same seven or eight patients five or six times a week for several years. All of his "patients" were psychiatrists who were candidates at the analytic institute at which he taught. His social and personal life was also insulated from the nonanalytic world. At the theater or opera he was always in the company of other analysts and their spouses. This analytic ensemble would sit together, oblivious to what was going on around them. Parenthetically, quite obviously, cults are found not only among medically trained analysts, but in analytic and psychotherapy schools established by psychologists and social workers, as well.

Apparently, these analysts derive pleasure only from other analysts' company. This speaks to the demands of psychotherapeutic practice. Freud (1937) suggested that the demands of practice exceed those of satisfaction. He regarded psychoanalysis as being one of the three impossible professions. How valid is this view? If we are not masochists, then we have to disagree with Freud. The demands of practice need not exceed those of the satisfactions we derive. There are several important satisfactions in therapeutic practice in addition to the numerous concerns, stresses, and traumas of practice. To understand both satisfactions and concerns, we will now turn to why we are drawn into the profession in the first place.

I will approach this question from the point of view of practitioners and theorists such as Carl Jung, who contend that psychotherapists do not choose their profession by chance. Those drawn to psychotherapy are impelled by the instinctual disposition of their psyche, a psyche whose vulnerability has never fully healed. Until rather recently this point of view was speculative, since there were no comprehensive research studies of the origins and background of mental health practitioners. The lives of most psychotherapists were veiled in mystery as if concealing embarrassing secrets. About a decade and a half ago, three books that examined the lives of mental health practitioners were published. Two of these were by William Henry and his associates at the University of Chicago. These were based on an extensive in-depth survey of practitioners from the four mental health disciplines—psychoanalysis, psychiatry, psychology, and social work. The other book was edited by Arthur Burton. Burton's pioneer work, examining autobiographically the reasons people are drawn to practice psychotherapy, confirms the data found by Henry, in revealing quite baldly that psychotherapists are quite human and full of emotional concerns that one might not expect in highly skilled practitioners. Burton (1972), however, makes the point:

> To meliorate the distinctive problems of living, one has also to be human, and that means to have problems like everyone else. The distinction between client and therapist comes only in that the therapist works his problems through, recovers thereby a consistent and fulfilling philosophy of existence, and then offers it to others in a spirit of comradeship. We might say he shares his problems rather than broods on them. (p.x)

Where does this willingness and ability to understand and share one's personal concerns originate? And are the origins of the psychotherapist's character different from those of other professions? These are two questions which I will attempt to address in this chapter. My argument, posited earlier—that the choice of a psychotherapy practice as a career is integrally related to the practitioner's unmet psychic needs—suggests that to write a book that simply offers suggestions about how to deal with the concerns and hazards in the practice of psychotherapy cannot be any more than superficial, at best, and is, more likely, dangerously distracting to the deeper issues involved in therapeutic practice.

THE BACKGROUNDS OF PSYCHOTHERAPISTS

The research of Henry and his associates seems to readily demonstrate that people who go into the psychotherapy profession come from rather homogeneous backgrounds. They are highly overrepresentative by people from urban centers and from families from eastern European countries. Henry's research, confirmed by the autobiographical accounts in Burton's book, strongly suggests that in more personal terms these practitioners share common belief systems, as well.

> They tend to have rejected parental political belief systems in favor of more liberal positions. They are religious apostates. And they are socially mobile, a fact describing their occupation but also describing an additional aspect of the separation from the political and religious beliefs of their familes. (Henry et al., 1971, p. 8)

Not only are the characteristics mentioned above indicative of a considerable proportion of the mental health practitioners studied, but, even more significantly, they were more completely accurate of those surveyed who most claimed a devotion to practicing psychotherapy, regardless of the particular discipline in which they were originally trained[1] (Henry et al., 1971).

Let us purview the person who becomes a psychotherapist. He or she was undoubtedly one who, at an early age, became sensitized to the emotional substratum of human life with regard to how people interact and to how they may feel about themselves. He/she gave considerable thought as to why Uncle Harry acted so strangely and what Aunt Sarah was feeling in her attempts to control the family's affairs. Many who are drawn to the profession were, at an early age, more observers than active participants at home, in school, and in community life. This may have been due to chaotic family situations, in which they felt it unsafe to act openly and spontaneously. Psychotherapists are rarely people who have led armies, built bridges, or ran successfully for public office. On the other hand, they have great acuity in discerning the reasons others have for doing so. Therefore, even those who were encouraged to be active participants in the world are reflective, as well—wondering about other people's motives and their own. Some came from families that placed high imperatives on self-exploration and social perceptiveness, qualities that require a safe retreat into one's own self. Arthur Burton (1972) convincingly demonstrates: that therapists find the best consolation within their inner selves.[2] Apparently, this was especially true of Sigmund Freud and C. G. Jung. Similarly, in his autobiographical account, Carl Rogers tells us that during the first summer he left home to work he preferred to be by himself than to spend time with his fellow mill workers. In Rogers' words:

> I remember no social life at all. I was not too lonely, however, because I spent the long evenings with my new books—I realize that I lived in a world of my own, created by these books. (Burton, 1972, p. 35)

Burton posits the notion that psychotherapists are of a certain temperament such that long periods of solitude are not only tolerated but frequently sought. This solitude is instrumental in the practitioner's creative work. Burton writes:

> It is not that therapists are uncomfortable with the social scene but that their inner life is so much richer than the often ritualized allegro which passes for social life. The words introvertive or schizoid do not describe this creative state of being—these are pejorative terms—for it is voluntarily elected, and some people require more incubation of their creativity than do others. This inner dialogue with parts of the self, or with the self temporarily and spatially juxtaposed, satisfies the interpersonal Self-Other need but also provides an epiphenomenal feeling of being separated or special." (Burton, 1972, p. 11)

THE THERAPIST-TO-BE IN THE FAMILY OF ORIGIN

The solitary pursuits discussed in the previous section are not sufficient to account for why people from homogeneous backgrounds become psychotherapists rather than bench scientists, mathematicians, or poets—professions that also require considerable solitude and the cultivation of an inner life. There is, undoubtedly, something additionally significant in these backgrounds that impels some to become practitioners while others from similar backgrounds to follow quite different professions.[3] Examining psychotherapists' backgrounds suggests that the family roles were different for those who pursue different careers than for those who became professional healers. Burton's book *Twelve Psychotherapists* provides a connection between career and family roles—i.e., a career as a practitioner of psychotherapy and the need to cure one's own parents. In that

Burton found such a high incident of practitioners from Jewish backgrounds, he draws a parallel between traditional Jewish values and those of the practitioners whose lives he studied. He notes that Jews generally are known for not deserting their families in times of difficulty. They are regarded as people who hang in there and try to work things out. If they can't, then they try to make some sense of the misery they are suffering. Both the Jewish and Christian practitioners whose autobiographical accounts are found in Burton's book seem to share these same family values, insofar as none could easily leave their families, even those who had miserable childhoods.

An underlying principle in the field of psychology of work is that people tend to be drawn to vocational endeavors that are harmonious with their psychological needs. Ann Roe (1964) is a leading exponent of this notion. She maintains that the emotional quality of the parent-child relationship is a decisive factor in eventual occupational choice. Psychotherapists are people who have been cast at a young age into the role of helper or nurturer in their families. The various reports and impressionistic papers written by practitioners seem uniform in attributing a major determinant in the choice of psychotherapy as a profession to conflicts in the childhood of these persons. There seems to be several major sources of this overdetermined choice. The therapist-to-be may have been cast as a nurturer in the family because of a missing or psychologically unavailable parent. On the other hand, the choice may have been due to being among the offspring of a large family of origin in which he/she assumed a nurturing role. Or the therapists-to-be served early on as healers because of a psychologically disabled parent(s) by whom they were induced to try to heal and comfort as best they could at an age at which they had neither the maturity nor skill to do so effectively.

Henry's research, as well as that of Burton, indicates that the majority of healers come from families in which a serious problem existed. In some families this was a debilitating physical illness in one of the parents, but more frequently a serious psychological problem with a possible element of psychotic depression. The family relationships were, because of this and other reasons, in constant jeopardy and the majority of the family's problems seemed never finally resolved. A child in such a family is, in some way that we have not yet determined, selected to provide happiness for all; to him/her is given the role and responsibility of being a healer. Obviously, among families, the role of healing or nurturer is defined in different ways. A recent news story in New York City told of two brothers: one became a physician; the other was accused of slaying a young actress on an apartment building rooftop after an attempted rape and robbery. The physician explained the different paths he and his brother had taken as largely influenced by his mother's severe asthma. When he was growing up, his mother spent half her life in hospitals. "She regularly had severe asthma attacks, and as the eldest son in the family—he would call for ambulances or hail taxis to rush his mother to the hospital. [He adds that] his fierce ambition to become a doctor stemmed from [his] wanting to help, from seeing that doctors want to help."[4]

The autobiographical accounts in *Twelve Psychotherapists* provide various manifestations of the above theme. Reuben Fine tells us that before he was two years of age, his father left home, and his mother never remarried. Her dominant preoccupation was that of some day taking revenge on Fine's father whom she always referred to as "that bastard." Fine tells us that he gave considerable thought to ways of trying to reconcile the differences and the hurt experienced between his parents. Moreover, his mother, as the long-suffering, self-sacrificing Jewish mother, left him with an implicit dictate that he was to assume the responsibility of properly caring for her as soon as he was able to do so.[5] Steinzor, in the same book, tells of gaining his mother's appreciation for taking care of his younger brother. This enabled her to support the family by running a day care service during the Depression years. Polster's script was a sensitization to the vulnerability of women and the stoicism of men. His father, he tells us:

> was a self-possessed man who struggled to support us all and tightened every muscle to keep his body and soul together during the depression. He asked for no help, guidance, or sympathy from anyone and he never gave me any, either...My mother never had to venture into "America" as he did, nor did she ever try to...all she had to do was say my name and I could feel her love...My brother was a simple pleasure, always a luminous person...I never needed to "do" anything for him. My mother and sister, though, wanted something from me which I could not identify. I was affected by my own feeling that women had a

lousy fate in this world and I felt sorry for them. (Burton, 1972, pp. 149–150)

Of foremost relevance to our thesis, then, the therapist-to-be early in life becomes sensitized to the suffering and degradation of others.

Second, family position plays some part in the selection of family nurturer. Henry and his associates, in analyzing the data of their large survey, concluded that a considerable number of psychotherapists in their study described themselves as having been the dominant sibling. They maintain that this factor is consistent with our understanding of power relationships in general and of the specific "nurturance-succor relationship" which enables the practitioner to practice a healing art. However, personal compromise and social power through identification also seem to be a component of the family role. This is seen in the family role of "supporter" by a psychotherapist-to-be, who was the younger of two girls in a larger (mixed) Latin immigrant extended family household.[6] She and her sister were American-born. Her sister developed considerable self-assertion, together with artistic talent, and left home in her teens. The younger sister stayed home. There she served as the defender and supporter of her father, who was not able to defend himself against a more ambitious, aggressive, and articulate German-born wife. The younger daughter, who had blonde hair and blue eyes, in contrast to her dark-complexioned cousins, had readily assimilated American values, while her Latin-born cousins had not. She continually needed to be available to guide them in the American ways. She, then, as now, as a therapist, frequently felt drained of energy in having to be readily available to others.

Third, many of the practitioners-to-be showed distress in early life (Henry, 1966). According to *Twelve Psychotherapists*, early in life John Warkentin developed a serious physical ailment which afflicted him through life. This was similar to Albert Ellis. Helm Stierlin was afflicted with an illness as a child that kept him in bed for a year; Rudolph Ekstein, with a chronic ear condition, which later developed into partial deafness, and Arthur Burton, with pulmonary asthma. O. S. English also manifested the marked illness that characterizes the lives of so many psychotherapists. Less typically, his illness developed at a later period than most—during his medical internship. He went into psychiatry because he believed that he would have more control over his working hours in this subspecialty than in internal medicine. At the same time, he reports that he had no real sense of what psychiatry was all about. He was increasingly concerned:

> about myself because my adult life was just beginning and I had to think that I had been educated to the point of some usefulness to society; if I did not recover, all my preparation would have been wasted. (Burton, 1972, p. 92)

Fourth, long periods of loneliness to compound the sickness is evident in the lives of some psychotherapists as children. Ekstein tells us that in addition to his physical affliction he was lonely and frightened throughout childhood. He was brought up by a mother substitute, a kind, simple, Catholic mother who tried to make up for the loss of his own mother during the Holocaust in Europe. However, the reports of the therapists in Burton's book suggest that the periods of aloneness became transformed to positive experiences. As John Milton said in verse, "For solitude sometimes is best society."

Fifth, for many of the people we are discussing brooding and desperation are also present. Personal illness, loneliness, serious expectations about having to fulfill an adult role before maturity, and guilt for letting down family members weigh heavily upon the vulnerable psyche of the practitioner-to-be. But these factors also serve to foster an exquisite sense of the inner life of others, which becomes the hallmark of the therapist's calling.

In a word, a therapist is molded in childhood, whose early experiences left him/her with a certain residue of impotence in the face of human suffering. As an adult with mature life experiences the therapist-to-be is better equipped to carry out the practitioner's family script than he/she was as a child. The therapist-to-be, in the face of his/her frustration at fulfilling the family manifest as a healer, selects those educational and life experiences, often, largely unwittingly, that enable him/her to feel more adequate in dealing with human suffering. Thus, the young adult who, as a child, could not effectively or realistically fulfill the role in keeping his/her family from suffering may continue the mission by attending medical or graduate school. Burton describes this cogently in his own autobiographical account:

> My family left me with what I call a riddle-residue...I was im-
> printed with the responsibility for the psychological welfare of
> our family...to do this I had unconsciously to be a trained
> professional with deeper insight. (Burton, 1972, p. 194).

To this juncture there seems to be no satisfaction in the role
of nurturer, which seems to be compelled by guilt and compassion for others. Warkentin's autobiographical account is il-
luminating, therefore, because it suggests that the *unconscious
reversal* of therapist and patient roles are deeply rooted in childhood frustrations and role-modeling. Thus, part of the satisfaction of being a healer for these people is *vicarious.* Warkentin
tells us:

> Going through many years to my first interest in counseling, I
> find it began at age six for me. My father was a teacher...he
> brought a young boy to our house and to his bedroom where
> they talked. I was listening at the keyhole...I craved such an
> occasion for myself...which I never had...[my father's] last
> comment to me was "It's too bad that we never got acquainted."
> (Burton, 1972, p. 254)

The vicarious and reciprocal relation of the roles of nurturer
and of recipient of healing in his/her work as a practitioner and
in his/her own personal therapy draw the practitioner into a
highly circumscribed world and life-style. Carl Whitaker, the
highly innovative psychiatrist, sums up his philosophy of psychotherapy by indicating that:

> As a person, psychotherapy has been a tremendously exciting
> way to live. I often think of how boring my life might have been
> as a country practitioner...Through that availability of psy-
> chotherapists for me, I had the opportunity to link up with col-
> leagues whose lovingness made the stress growthful. I doubt
> these would have been available to me in any other professional
> setting. As John Warkentin used to say, "Imagine spending
> fulltime at your own self-development. It's kind of like spending
> your lifetime as a patient or like raising children. We just face
> the pain and the joy of significant others day after day."
> (Whitaker, 1973)

For many practitioners, their clients provide a psychological
route to their own family-of-origin riddle in ways that their mar-

riage and home do not. Henry and his associates tell us that their data reveal that, although the typical relationship of therapists to their spouses is generally positive and satisfying, it is, at the same time, emotionally more temperate than their clinical involvements. As such the typical mental-health practitioner's

> relationship with spouse and children stand in contrast to the more emotionally intense relationships of the practitioner's past . . . with parents and siblings—and to his professional present with patients. (Henry et al., 1973, p. 162)

A number of readers may recoil at the notion that psychotherapists are troubled people from conflictual backgrounds. They may claim that Henry's findings are dated, as are the impressionistic reports found in the literature. Disclaimers might point out that people today go into the practice of psychotherapy for somewhat different reasons than individuals did in the past. Psychotherapy today, for example, offers social workers easy access to independent practice. Second, it was one of the first professions to be open to women as co-equals with men. Quite evidently, prominent women practitioners and teachers have been readily accepted by the rank-and-file. This point may be related to a third factor that women are specifically better suited to a healing profession by virtue of their cultural training to be more nurturant than most men.

However, if these disclaimers are accurate and practitioners generally develop their psychological maturity without much struggle, then the practice of psychotherapy as a personal journey becomes suspect. Our thesis is that the need to struggle with suffering is a universal condition. The practitioner who denies his/her suffering poses a severe problem in the face of the client's need for a personal journey into his/her own suffering. Let me verify this! Several practitioners (Marston, 1984; Farber & Heifitz, 1982; Freudenberger & Robbins, 1979) have written about the "disillusionment effect," or, as it is known in the vernacular, "the burn-out" syndrome of psychotherapy endeavor and its effect on practitioners over time. This phenomenon is not, of course, confined to the healing arts. We know from our clinical work that craftspersons and professionals of all kinds suffer from similar symptoms. In the past we heard much less of this concern. Consequently, one wonders if people take the time these days developing and maturing their skills in the way craftspeople and practitioners did in the past. Today many therapists, reflecting society-at-large, seem more interested in methods, techniques, and maneuvers that get results and "solve" the clinical problem than in the struggle for meaning in psychotherapy, which cannot be reduced to a prescribed procedure. The inner emptiness and dissatisfaction of these practitioners are not apparent to them. Increasingly, I have heard practitioners speak at conferences and state in the professional literature that the practitioner's willingness to struggle with clients is masochistic.

I regard these kinds of statements as defensive and narrowly self-serving. I believe that personal struggle is required for the practitioner's growth as a therapist, as well as a direct resource for the client. As I have mentioned previously, many of those we treat have come to us as a last resort. No one else in his/her life has been either willing or able to struggle over the person's painful issues as we, as psychotherapists, should be professionally and personally prepared to do. If we fail to pursue this struggle then who is left for him/her?

The willingness to struggle with our clients is, of course, closely related to our own willingness to journey in search of ourselves. On the other hand, it may be asked that if psychotherapists bring unmet psychic needs to their work, why do they become therapists and not simply patients? And, for that matter, why don't all people with unmet needs (e.g., most of our clients) become therapists?

In fact, of course most psychotherapists have been patients and many continue to be (at least, intermittently) throughout their lives. However, for a person to wish to be a therapist and commit him- or herself to ameliorative work as I've indicated in previous chapters, the presence of unmet needs is not sufficient. Unless the individual has some confidence that these needs can be successfully handled by psychological or psychotherapeutic approaches, healing as a profession will not be a viable option. This explains some of the considerable ambivalence clients bring with them into treatment, i.e., doubts about whether opening their psychic wounds will result in more healing than pain. Moreover, once the client does experience the "success" of psychological treatment, it is my experience that a considerable number from all walks of life become interested in some kind of counseling career. However, it is the background variables found in this chapter and discussed in Chapter 6 that largely render this interest a viable option.

We may summarize our argument to this point with Burton's contention that the family demand remain

> a draft on the currency of the personality. How else do we explain the total acceptance of unbridled venom from some clients, the terrible vicissitudes of doing psychotherapy with chronic repressed schizophrenics, the endless complaints and victimization of the neurotic, the narcissism and infantality of the character disorder? On the face of it, no therapist would rationally submit to psychotherapy for any of the rewards now extant. (Burton, 1972, p. 10)

I propose that the same potent psychological forces that lead to the highest achievements of humankind are also the forces that cause human suffering. We need to see that the same fibers in all of us may branch out either in creative or misdirected ways. We may ask, for example, in this regard, if some of the impetus for Sigmund Freud's study of symbols of the unconscious may have come from the need to understand his own disturbing dreams; which aspects of Harry Stack Sullivan's interpersonal theory of personality came from suffering in his own personal life in which he had difficulty making close friendships; and how much of Jean Piaget's motivation to systematize the child's conceptions of reality was derived from his experience with an emotionally disturbed mother? I do not wish to reduce genius to simply the expression of deep suffering. Competence, will, and vision also need to be present. However, the sources of suffering may give genius a direction and a task to pursue. (Simon & Goldberg, 1984).

THE PSYCHIC VULNERABILITIES OF THE PSYCHOTHERAPIST

I have examined the lives of practitioners as inferred from the observations and generalizations noted in an extensive survey of practitioners and from the autobiographical account of twelve famous practitioners. These studies strongly suggest that practitioners bring unmet psychic needs to their work. We need to ask whether these psychic needs cause emotional difficulties that are specific to psychotherapists as compared with other service practitioners.

Unfortunately, there are very little empirical data which address this question. For the most part, impressionistic inferences have been drawn on the self-reports and general observations of practitioners themselves. These self-reports are rarely empirical. Fortunately, I have found one empirical self-report. The study was conducted by a San Francisco psychiatrist who surveyed 75 psychiatrists in the Bay area. The study strongly supports Henry's findings and the contentions in Burton's book. The investigator concluded from the responses to his questionnaire that psychiatrists do have special emotional difficulties that are specific to them and their work. It is of interest to summarize the findings. The questions and responses are as follows:

1.   "Do you think that psychiatrists have emotional difficulties that are special to them and their work as contrasted with nonpsychiatrists?" Sixty-eight of those questioned replied "yes," while seven answered "no." Those respondents who elaborated on their negative response indicated that they believe that psychiatrists have no more problems and the personal problems they have are not significantly different from other professional people, such as physicians in general. Some of the respondents indicated that psychiatric education and training were specifically designed to prepare a practitioner for dealing with the demands of the field. They believed that further experience and increased understanding of psychiatric work would eventually diminish most of the difficulties the practitioner experienced.

2.   "If you believe that psychiatrists have special emotional problems, do you believe that these problems come from the kind of person who went into the field or from the type of work itself?" Forty-five of the respondents indicated that they believed that the problems emanated from the personality of the psychiatrist. However, 15 of these respondents believed that these problems were compounded by the work psychiatrists were involved in. On the other hand, 60 of the psychiatrists reported

that the problems were largely an outgrowth of psychiatric work, but of these respondents 30 also believed that the personality of the practitioner contributed to the problems.[7]

3. "For those who believe that special problems do exist, exactly what do you think are the special difficulties?" The answers given are summarized by the author as follows:

Isolation was referred to by 38 people. Twenty-three of this group made special reference to the actual physical aloneness in the practice of psychiatry. One quoted the hole-in-one joke wherein God punishes the minister who plays golf on the Sabbath by giving him a hole-in-one, the punishment being that he cannot tell anyone what he has accomplished. Six said that the need for intimacy was not satisfied in the office. Five felt that inability to communicate with others about patients because of the need to preserve confidentiality created a high degree of isolation. Four believed that personality problems interfered with the ability to achieve intimacy outside the office.

The need to control emotions was regarded as a burden by 21. The feelings of the therapist were stimulated by patients. Several specified that these feelings were primitive in nature. Ten spoke directly of difficulties dealing with countertransference, and many others alluded to this problem using different terminology. Five specifically mentioned that the practice of psychiatry produced an increased awareness of deep emotional issues in oneself, and that this was a source of strain.

"*Omnipotent wishes and the frustration* thereof was listed by 17 respondents. Therapists often had a great need to help and rescue others. This was seen as concealing great wishes to receive love. When the need to be an all-powerful rescuer was thwarted, a sense of helplessness was felt. Six referred to a high ego ideal and exaggerated demands upon the psychiatrist's performance, with consequent guilt when unable to meet such standards. Although these respondents appeared to be related more to matters of conscience and guilt, the sense of mission and rescuing self-image related to the omnipotent theme.

Ambiguity in the field itself was listed as a major source of distress by 16 psychiatrists. Nine mentioned ambiguity specifically, and seven mentioned the impossibility of validation of results. Some felt ambiguity of the field was more an issue for residents in training, and others observed the problem of validation more as an issue in the midlife crisis years. (Bermak, 1977)

The above-mentioned hazards will be further examined in Chapter 6.

NOTES

1. Henry and his associates indicate that professionals across disciplines who define themselves as psychotherapists more closely resemble one another in background than they do fellow professionals in their own discipline who specialize and define themselves as administrators, researchers, teachers, and so forth. Not only are their social and cultural backgrounds similar, but although they have taken different career routes, they have in fact made "individual choices of learning experiences that appear to parallel the choices made by their colleagues in the other systems" (Henry et al., 1971, p. x). Of the four early professional routes which may go in different directions, based upon field of specialty, for populations of students entering their eventual careers at different ages and from somewhat different socioeconomic status, there emerges, at the completion of professional training, what Henry calls a "fifth profession." This collective name for professionals from four different mental health fields reflects a highly similar selection of course work and professional clinical training experience. It also represents common motifs of personal beliefs about human existence and commitment to certain ways of expressing these beliefs in professional endeavor.

2. Several were themselves severely disabled early in life by physical illness. These problems led to prolonged periods of "quiet inaction and introspection, sometimes with a concomitant fear of death, and systematized fantasy rather than reality become the source of childhood gratifications . . . In some, handicap is followed by superordinate attempts to overcome and compensate for it . . . and the handicap becomes the human sensitivity and justification for unreasonable dedication and effort . . ." (Burton, 1972, p. 312).

3. There are, of course, sociological and political considerations in selecting a career. For example, some jobs are gender-coded; women have traditionally done secretarial work. Still others are ethnically stereotyped, e.g., blacks have been more readily accepted in athletics and entertainment careers than in

other work. These factors, however, do not detract from the thesis I am proposing in this chapter.

4. *The New York Times,* December 1984.

5. The practitioners in both Henry's and Burton's studies were highly critical of their mothers and much more praising of their fathers. Mothers, moreover, were seen by many of the therapists as interfering with the father's self-esteem and directly or indirectly separating the family from him. Burton's autobiographies of therapists reveal that the therapist-to-be in several instances resents being put in the father's abandoned role.

6. Henry's data suggest that practitioners come from families of origin smaller than average.

7. The overlapping of the figures beyond the total number of the sample is accounted for by the fact that various people weighted these factors differently, and this was taken into account in the rating of the answers (Bermak, 1977).

Chapter 5
The Satisfactions
Of Practice

If I am not for myself, who will be for me?
If I am for myself alone, what am I?
If not now, when?
—Rabbi Hillel

To continue to practice psychotherapy there have to be satisfactions to neutralize the distress. Like the pursuit of other service careers, I suspect the wish to provide a livelihood to support a lifestyle is rarely a primary motive in pursuing a therapeutic career. There are other more prominent satisfactions. In general, the satisfaction the practitioner derives from work consists of doing what the practitioner's life history and psychic disposition have impelled him/her toward—the exploration with others of the mysteries of human existence by means of a highly personal experience in which one's most intimate sentiments are exchanged. The satisfaction of this experience, depending upon the particular personality of the practitioner, has to do with some combination of successful endeavor in responding to the suffering of one's clients and in experiencing intellectual and emotional growth in oneself. I will attempt to express this more explicitly.

THE PRACTITIONER'S INNER LIFE

In discussing the qualifications of being a practitioner of psychotherapy in Chapter 7 I will talk about the practitioner's need

67

to have his/her own being self-accessible. This involves imagination and fantasy and how the practitioner utilizes them in understanding both client and self. The practitioner's utilization of
his/her own fantasy life is both a potent skill as well as a source
of personal satisfaction in practice. Its satisfaction is derived
from the congruence of how the practitioner wishes to be seen
and how he/she is responded to by his/her clients. For if the
satisfactions of the practitioner's creative imagination are not
paramount, the practitioner can be little more than a detached
observer or one whose fee is a primary satisfaction.

Not only do many of us who become practitioners anticipate
that being a psychotherapist will be a creative way of expressing ourselves but, as Freudenberger and Robbins indicate (1971).

> the profession also permits an expression of power of taking not
> only care but charge of a human being, who initially came in
> feeling in need and helpless. Through working with people's
> needs, the psychoanalyst can continually reaffirm or restore his
> own sense of being strong, healthy, and in control.

One practitioner spoke to me of his not having much self-
esteem or social confidence earlier in life. He had been an excellent athlete and recognized for his accomplishments in sports,
but this was one of the few areas in which he felt comfortable
in public. The feelings of reticence and lack of self-esteem
quickly changed during his clinical internship. He now felt he
understood people, and through his ability to convey his insight
into his work, he felt respected and appreciated by them. Power
is often regarded as a reproachable reference to the conduct of
psychotherapists (as we will discuss in Chapter 9). Nevertheless,
this young practitioner was comfortable in admitting that he experienced a social and personal power as a psychotherapist
which he had rarely experienced before, not even on the football
field.

Many professions do not have this same kind of opportunity.
An eminent analyst tells us that it is a great privilege being a
member of a small, select enclave who study the individual psyche in the only way that it can be probed in depth. He adds,
many more people study insects and many, many more
manufacture weapons of destruction (Spruiell, 1984). Psychotherapy is potentially the most human of sciences. The practitioner's consulting room is one of the few places in our world

where science, art, and intellectual pursuits come together creatively and with vast stores of potential energy. Greenson (1966)
reminds us that psychotherapists work with some of the most
interesting people in the world, probably the most creative, and
each offers a vast unexplored world to share. Many practitioners
regard the endless variation of themes produced in sessions as
psychotherapy's chief virtue. Each client, Greben (1975) indicates, presents familiar themes, but with unique differences.
There is always something new to be heard and something novel
to be understood.

There is also the humanitarian satisfaction of therapeutic
responsibility. Not only the happiness of individual clients but,
often, the well-being of entire families, whom the practitioner
may never directly encounter, depend upon the work the practitioner does with their family member. There are few professions that present the professional with so intriguing a series of
daily challenges. These are tasks that challenge all of his/her
faculties—intellectually, emotionally, and spiritually. Collectively, the practitioner is involved in a creative task.

Above all, the psychotherapist needs to feel that in some real
sense he/she is a necessary and responsive agent of healing for
those who petition the practitioner with their burdens of distress
and uncertainty. Long years of experience and proven expertise
generally do not blunt this deeply felt need. The practitioner gets
these satisfactions from such encounters as helping a person return to the vibrance of life after a long and painful depression;
seeing the smile of realization after an insightful and well-timed
interpretation; enabling distressed parents to learn to relate
more meaningfully to their children, and so forth.

On the other hand, the student therapist watches the clash
and interchange of the divergent and conflicting forces within
a therapeutic session transpiring between therapist and client
and marvels at the compatible and facilitating energies and behavioral modalities that frequently are their synthesis. Struggling with uncertainty as to whether he/she possesses the attributes to induce these enabling processes, the young practitioner,
of necessity, queries how these processes come about. Of course,
the endeavor is more than simply intellectual. Being intimately
involved in an ameliorative endeavor, with its heightened human drama, its challenges, its penetrating philosophical issues,
its tragedy and personal pathos, no less than its exalting moments, is comparable to being involved in the creation of the

world's greatest art (Goldberg, 1977). As such, Ella Sharpe pointed out there is "a fundamental pleasure in listening, for one who chooses this career, not essentially different from the plea-sure of those who enjoy music, in spite of the fact that the client's communications are generally tales of discord." (Sharpe, 1947). In short, in addition to his/her wish (need) to assist others, the psychotherapist is both personally and intellectually curious about the intricacies of the human drama. It is a most exciting, albeit often ungratifying, experience. Edith Weigert (1965) wrote: ". . .like Ferenczi, I don't count many completed analyses in a practice of some twenty years."

In a word, the human drama we work with is never finished. As such, it can be very frustrating. The psychotherapist is in-volved in the creation of some of the world's greatest drama, but unlike classical theatre or literary drama, because it is a continu-ous human journey, it is unfinished. Frequently, the psychother-apist is left with the feeling of incompletion. Not necessarily that the client has not been able finally to deal with issues and bring some closure to excruciating issues that he/she deals with; but often these gratifying experiences for the client are after leaving therapy. Thus, the therapist often does not see the result of his/her work. Very few of us are able to conduct a complete anal-ysis or psychotherapy; at least, I have experienced that, in con-firming Weigert's statement. Too often, circumstances—practi-cal matters at that—prevent this from happening. So we are regularly left with a sense of incompletion. This is the basis of some of the frustrations that occur in practice. We often see peo-ple who are at their worst. We are involved with them when they are suffering. But when they are able to deal with these issues, they often leave, because they do not want to go beyond assuag-ing pain and suffering. Consequently, the deeper joys come from working intimately with those who are willing to ask more from life than the commonplace. We may refer to these as *emotional* satisfactions—the opportunity to experience the whole range of human emotion, and to be responsive to and to be able to be in-fluential and even helpful in other people's growth. Being in-fluential in abetting others to creatively deal with their life sit-uation can, of course, be a very satisfying experience.

Interpersonal satisfactions are related here as well. The psy-chotherapist is able to interact in a more bald and unpretentious way than in most instances of interaction in the world in general. There are also *reference group* satisfactions in being a member of a profession where people are dealing with emotional issues, in a way that many other people would envy. The practice of psychotherapy may also serve some of the *intellectual* needs and satisfactions of the practitioner as well. The questions that the practitioner always wondered about—how other people think about things and how they struggle with their concerns—are part and parcel of his/her daily endeavor. The practitioner is able to be party and privy to the inner thoughts and secrets of others, which satisfactorily answers many of his/her questions that were only intellectually posed in what the practitioner read and heard from others.

The experienced therapist is often so busy facilitating the therapeutic process that he/she does not always have the opportunity to figure out why what happened in a particular session happened as it did. But as an inquiring and critical person, the practitioner, too, questions the marvelously complex and obscure process that is his/her daily professional endeavor. Successful as he/she may be, relative to colleagues, each practitioner is forced, nonetheless, to acknowledge resistance and befuddling failures in particular cases and, to a degree, with each client. Some experienced practitioners learn to balance their own frustrations about ungratifying aspects of therapeutic process against a satisfaction derived from their increasing understanding of their role in the process. Still others are not assuaged by past successes, requiring continual success and recognition. The former, in order to transmit to younger colleagues the essence of the procedures the practitioner has developed through the years, as well as to become more effective in what he/she does, draws generalizations from his/her large stock of "successes" and "failures." In this way the practitioner tries to sort out the specific processes and procedures that have contributed to particular therapeutic outcomes. He/she can never be certain that these generalizations are substantial and valid. In canvassing their therapeutic endeavor, practitioners are forced to admit that clinical procedures that lead to successful outcomes with some clients are the same procedures and conditions that seem to stultify and antagonize effective work with other clients. At this juncture the clinician may abandon objective assessment of his/her therapeutic procedures as fruitless labor replete with epiphenomenological implications and revert instead to introspection in search of subjective truth. In this endeavor creative satisfaction presents itself (Goldberg, 1977).

The *creative* satisfactions have to do with sublimating our animal instincts in conjunction with our spiritual needs for harmonious existence. Empathy and compassion are the latest developments in the cultivation of our instinctual human nature (Bernstein, 1972). Our human physical vulnerability to the dangers of the natural world has been largely eliminated; yet our psychic vulnerability remains. It is the analyst's unique task to help his/her fellow beings to blend both their animal and spiritual natures. The practitioner whose own psychic terror precludes a bridge to other people's fears ultimately must fail clients in this unique task. On the other hand, the psychotherapist who creates this bridge experiences a unique vantage of human existence.

Then, of course, there are the *status* satisfactions that I have already discussed and the *economic* satisfactions of being a practitioner. While I do not believe that status and financial fees are a primary part of the satisfaction of being a practitioner for most psychotherapists, nevertheless, a private practitioner's perceived importance of financial reward, as Freudenberger and Robbins (1979) suggest, "lies in being born into or adopting a certain kind of material value system that exists in our society." A practitioner can conduct a very profitable practice with very little overhead; just a room with two chairs is sufficient. He needs client referrals, of course; that is not too difficult, as we will explore in Chapter 8. "In the past it seemed that one entered private practice only after a good deal of experience and if one's credentials were beyond reproach. Times have changed, and it seems that the availability of third party insurance money has led to the change" (Meltzer, 1975).

In Washington, D.C., where I practiced for many years, and which probably has the highest concentration of mental health practitioners of all metropolitan areas in the country, young psychiatrists generally find that in six months beyond the completion of their residency in psychiatry they can fill up a private practice. Psychiatrists and clinical psychologists must, of course, first apprentice themselves for some rather extensive training, but practitioners without extensive formal training in mental health are, as well, ubiquitous these days.

These practitioners utilize sundry impressive titles, such as "psychotherapist," "family counselor," "analyst," or "communications specialist." Of course, some practitioners who employ these titles may be well-trained mental health practitioners or well-trained nonprofessionals, but it is just as likely that they have had little or no training. As long as they do not employ the legally protected titles of "psychiatrist," "psychologist," or "certified social worker," there are no laws barring their practice (Goldberg, 1977).

What I have written above is not to say that the private practice of psychotherapy is a thriving business for every practitioner. Particularly in the last few years, due to the economic conditions in this country, more than a few practitioners are hungrily looking for referrals. This is especially true for young practitioners, social workers, and those who have moved to new locations, without a network of referral sources. During economic depression, mental health services are one of the first expenses to be discarded both in the public and private domains. Nevertheless, for the established practitioner and those who have worked and trained in areas in which they have developed a strong referral network, it is, more or less, business as usual.

Finally, there are also *research* satisfactions for investigating certain issues that arise in practice and exploring how they may be generalized to other situations, as well as finding ways for resolution to problems that arise in therapy.

UNCONSCIOUS SATISFACTIONS

Covertly, all of the satisfactions discussed previously offer the practitioner a special kind of personal power, consisting of privileges not afforded other people (Weinberg, 1984). Holt (1981) tells us that the role of the practitioner of psychological services contains elements of voyeur, autocrat, and saint, which, in turn, induces feelings of anxiety and guilt, as well as the practitioner's own particular personal problems. To thwart these untoward feelings the practitioner may be tempted to become a "peeping Tom," "an authoritarian dictator," a "kind mother," or an "infallible and omniscient seer." In short, the practitioner may unconsciously attempt to accomplish through influencing clients' lives what the practitioner can not directly attain for him- or herself. Through mechanisms of voyeurism, manipulation, and projective identification the practitioner may act out his/her own impulses. For example, the unhappily married therapist may encourage clients with marital problems to separate—pushing them to enact what the therapist wants to do but is too afraid to attempt.

Weinberg (1984) indicates, that,

> as psychotherapists we have an almost unholy power during a session. We can ask our patient about any event or what it reminds him of. We can ask him how he acted in some situation, or why, and how he felt at the time. We can ask him what he thinks, or feels, about anything—including us. If he's quiet, we can ask, "What are you thinking right now?" No other professional, nor even the person's lover, has quite our privileges." (p. 71)

If we lack integrity, are unaware of or unable to handle our own unfinished business, these privileges may be misused and our clients exploited (see Chapter 10 for exploitation of clients).

On the other hand, if we are willing to face our own unfinished business courageously, then the most cogent satisfaction of all is the opportunity for personal journey that has been unfulfilled in any other way. I will describe this with a parable of my own:

> Young Coyote left the reservation in search of meaning. A sense of meaning, he had been told by those older and wiser than he, was the measure by which all people need to live. Young Coyote stopped each traveler he chanced to meet upon his journey, inquiring, "I am young and ignorant, not knowing the ways of the world. I seek meaning. Have you seen it? Can you tell me where to find it?" The bewildered travelers fled from young Coyote's naive and intrusive request, regarding him as a madman. Young Coyote abandoned the day's barren promise, traveling furtively by night. He scoured the sky seeking the brightest star of all, hoping that within might be meaning. Bright stars, he observed, faded with prolonged inspection. Young Coyote grew older and wearier in journey, but apparently not wiser. He obstinately continued his pilgrimage.
>
> By chance, he wandered into a university city on a dry, dusty plain. Meeting a bright-eyed scholar, he again posed his query. To young Coyote's plea, the scholar replied, "Truth is that which has meaning. All else is ignorance. Truth is an ode to him who plagiarizes experience—stealing it from the world, ripping it out of context and putting it into books!" Not understanding the scholar's sage words, young Coyote continued his journey. He encountered a gray-haired theologian in silent meditation and

repeated his now familiar query. He was told with earnest conviction that that which is truly meaningful is the Eternal Hand clinging to the heavens in unrest above the boiling sea of human chaos. Meaningful emotion is the everlasting Eye, lashing a Heavy Tear above the stagnant hearts of futility. Meaningful regard is the Heavenly Smile turning grotesque above the charred cities of unholiness. Being yet a simple man, young Coyote did not comprehend the theologian's references to ultimate concern.

Pushing on, he stopped by a grove of graceful willow trees where by moonlight sat a young man with the look of unrequited love still burning in his eyes. The meaningful moment, the young lover told him, is when the summer's palpitating passions turn to languish and the leaves begin to fall.

Thoroughly confused, having never experienced the magic of love, young Coyote dizzily wandered through the streets of delirium. He came upon a professional building from which a sad but thoughtful youth of his own age was emerging. In a weak but persistent voice, young Coyote uttered once more his obsessive inquiry. "You should make an appointment to see my doctor," he was told. Having been to other doctors, young Coyote was not convinced, until the other youth told him what his doctor had told him: "What would be meaningful for me would be to be there for you." His doctor was, of course, a psychotherapist.

THE CAREER OF A PSYCHOTHERAPIST

Who is young Coyote? I am young Coyote of course! So, for that matter, are most of the clients with whom I work in psychotherapy. Each of us initially sought the meaning of his/her existence through identification with the complacency and quasi-security of the values and proposed ways of being of the prefabricated world into which we were thrust. As we moved slowly and painfully into the world at large, we sought confirmation of these values in scholarship, religion, competition, love, and productivity. For many of us, none of these prescribed modes offered us a final or stable meaning for our being-in-the-world. We entered psychotherapy with considerable disillusionment, often as a last resort, to assume careers as patients and/or psychotherapy practitioners. As a result of psychotherapy being regarded as a last resort—the one short step before divorce; before the abandonment of family and family values; indeed for some, the pause prior to homicide or suicide—psychotherapy and its practitioners have obtained a unique place in modern society, rivaled only by the modern day priests and the shamans of the ancient world (Goldberg, 1977).

In his autobiography, Werner Mendel, a psychiatrist born in Germany of a prominent upper-middle-class Jewish family with the stability of many generations of all the male members being physicians, tells us of the startling disillusionment that drew him into psychiatry. The first 12 years of his life were in the midst of a conservative family that would not recognize a changing world. Most of them, according to Mendel, were, as a result of their unwillingness to adapt to the needs of the times, sent to the gas chambers of the Nazi concentration camps. Even when the family regrouped in Los Angeles in 1939, Mendel tells us, they continued to pretend that it was still 1928. This led him to realize that

> nothing is permanent, that nothing has real value, that all is changeable. The only value that one can depend on is one's own integrity and the ability to relate to people and time. [As a result] what I prized over anything else was my personal feeling of competence, my reliance upon myself, my mobility, and most importantly, my willingness to let go of acquired goods and titles and to go on to other things. (Burton, 1972, pp. 286–287)

Mendel's statement helps us recognize the close connection between the satisfactions and the perils of therapeutic practice. It may help us understand why we cannot simply separate these issues and defend ourselves against the hazards of practice. To become competent as a practitioner means to become increasingly aware of our own unfinished journey to work out issues of intimacy and caring with significant people in our own lives and how this unfinished business effects our availability to clients. If this is not apparent enough, let us look at the perspective of a young practitioner who has been struggling with conflicts about his own family. These feelings came to the surface in his work with a young female client only a few years younger than he. She grew up in the same city as he, and is of the same religion and of a similar socioeconomic background.

The client was seen twice a week during the practitioner's initial first years of private practice. The client brought up one Thursday about returning home that weekend to visit her parents. She launched into a litany of conflictual issues that she had not successfully broached with her family. This reluctance to deal directly with people was symptomatic of the way she fostered superficial relations with most other people to avoid others' expressing displeasure at her for not acting in the way they wanted. The therapist believed that by systematically returning to these family issues he had a frame of reference for addressing all her avoidance patterns. However, he soon realized that if he were to regularly bring up the client's avoidance of family issues he would be espousing a hypocrisy. He, too, was involved in some of the same issues as his client. He caught himself feeling quite hypocritical in the midst of a session with his client. He indicated this to her. He told her that he was asking her to do something which he needed to do as well. She seemed pleased to hear this and was not put off. Instead, she regularly brought up whether or not he had dealt with his own family at times when she was aware he had traveled to the city in which his family lived. This alliance seemed to foster a climate of joint journey, although the client did not attempt to deal with the therapist's issues with his own parents.

This therapeutic experience early in the practitioner's career enabled him vividly to realize that therapeutic work is an illusory palliative of superficial discourse unless the practitioner's unfinished journey is vivified in the process.

Chapter 6
The Hazards
of Practice

In much wisdom is much grief; and he that increaseth knowledge increaseth sorrow.
—Ecclesiastes 1:18

It is difficult to face, hour after hour, day after day, certain aspects of oneself which one has tried to distance oneself from and to deny. Yet, when we scrupulously examine the therapeutic situation without rationalization and altruistic bias, we are faced with the startling realization that psychotherapy practitioners may well be touching some of their own deepest vulnerabilities each day of their practice. A well-known, seasoned practitioner makes a clear statement of this position when he writes: "I am no longer willing to accept anyone as my patient to whose pain I do not feel vulnerable" (Kopp, 1976, pp. 23–24).

From this vantage we might regard the practitioner as a trapped masochist, while, at the same time, realizing the source of the psychotherapist's continuing concerns and apprehensions. Nonetheless, it is probably more valid to view the practice of psychotherapy as the practitioner's courageous endeavor to come to terms with his/her own demons—the denied and disintegrative aspects of self—than to understand it as a masochistic enterprise. This in no way suggests that the practice of psychotherapy is essentially a self-serving profession for the practitioner. As psychotherapists we realize, at least ideally, that by using a deeply subjective understanding of ourselves we have the most potent human instrument available for understanding and responding to the hurt and suffering of our fellow beings. This belief, I assume, is not contested. What is, however, is the required state of vulnerability of the practitioner's psyche in order to be maximally responsive to those with whom he/she works.

THE PROMISE AND REALITIES OF PRACTICE

The practice of psychotherapy isn't for everyone. It takes a special kind of person to be a psychotherapist. We should realize that although a person may be intelligent, insightful, interested in other people and concerned about their well-being, these factors alone are not sufficient for being a practitioner. Being a competent psychotherapist also involves the willingness to touch upon personal problem areas of the practitioner as clinical work absorbs the practitioner's entire being, often very deeply. Consequently, the person who practices psychotherapy has to very thoroughly examine his/her motives, interests, and expectations for practice. The practitioner has to ask him/herself why he/she is choosing this profession rather than some other. The practitioner needs to examine not only what he/she expects to get from it, but also what he/she needs to give in order to be successful and satisfied.

Again, I will say that monetary considerations are not sufficient. Of course, it is possible to make quite a good living as a practitioner in private practice. Nevertheless, treating people who are in severe conflict and agitated disturbance session after session, day after day, as many of us do, at least early in our careers, wears the practitioner down emotionally. People who are quite insightful, psychologically knowledgeable, and interested in studying people psychologically, but whose emotional vulnerabilities are overly compromised by working with those in suffering, may do better in some capacity other than psychotherapist. They may have contributions to make in teaching, research, consulting, writing, or even practicing counseling in nonclinical settings, such as in the educational, vocational, or industrial areas of psychology. People who have thoroughly examined their motives and expectations for being a psychotherapy practitioner need to decisively commit themselves to a willingness to touch the deeper recesses of themselves in the work.

Practitioners cannot allow themselves to become inordinately fearful of the people they work with or their own internal processes evoked by these therapeutic encounters.

There are specific stresses that are resistive to the practitioner's willingness to communicate and share his/her experiences with colleagues. These will be examined in the remainder of this chapter. Spensley and Blacker (1976), in an excellent short article in the *American Journal of Orthopsychiatry* a few years ago, cogently point to some of the inherent pitfalls that practicing psychotherapy typically imposes. Clinical situations that potentially hold the greatest stress for us are when clients come to us in acute suffering and despair. If we feel competent about our skills (or, for that matter, insensitive to our limitations) working with them feels challenging. However, if we are not able to offer palliatives and quick solutions, or if we question the impact of what we do, we frequently feel helpless to assuage the client's suffering. For the beginning practitioner, open-ended listening leads the practitioner to feelings of ignorance, confusion and impotence in face of the complexity of the material. The practitioner may feel the need to do something active in order to reassure him/herself and the client that the practitioner has the wisdom and the capacity to help. Even those of us who feel that we are effective practitioners may have to wait a long while to be able to ascertain that we have helped a particular client. There is something about being with someone in pain and not being able to do something actively at that distressing moment to alleviate the pain that is excruciating to the practitioner.

Compounding this stress, the practitioner, in trying to empathize and recognize within him/herself the experience of the client, is conflicted by the dilemma of trying to realize the impact of the client's feelings while, at the same time, expected by training and doctrine to avoid being adversely affected by them. These feelings are referred to in psychotherapy literature as "countertransference." The use of the term frequently has a pejorative implication, suggesting that the practitioner, in reacting intensely to what occurs in sessions, is somehow at fault in allowing clinical work to have a deep effect upon him/her. Traditionally, psychoanalytic theory has strongly stressed emotional neutrality. Theory has contended that countertransferential reactions could lead to a reduction in the practitioner's ability to understand and to communicate that understanding to the client. In recent years, some influential psychoanalytic practitioners have seriously questioned the negative connotation given to therapist affective reactions. They have maintained that it is necessary for the therapist to remain vulnerable—open to all feelings—in order to be most available and responsive to the client's communication. In a word, although countertransferential feelings (as I will discuss at length in Chapter 12) involve stress in the practitioner, they also serve a potentially invaluable therapeutic function.

It should also be pointed out that countertransference can be pleasurable, as Anthony Storr alludes to in his review of a book about the French psychoanalyst Marie Bonaparte.

> In 1925, when Marie Bonaparte consulted him, Freud was sixty-nine and already afflicted with the cancer that eventually killed him. They took to each other immediately. Freud, who was never good at following his own injunctions about how psychoanalysts should conduct themselves, told her about his illness and his financial difficulties and was delighted when she told him that she loved him. She soon replaced Lou Andreas-Salomé in Freud's affections and became so much his favorite analysand that he gave her two hours a day of his time. (Storr, 1983)

NORMAL STRESS OF PRACTICE

Countertransference is only part of the story. A second important point that Spensley and Blacker (1976) posit is that the typical stress in therapeutic work is not necessarily or always predicated upon the practitioner's existing vulnerabilities. The typical stress in therapeutic work may be inherent in the nature of the psychotherapeutic process itself. There is a "normal" stress which is not reducible to the countertransferential stress induced by the practitioner's unresolved conflicts and psychic vulnerability.

The very process of working intimately with human suffering presents the practitioner with real painful psychic discomfort. In few other situations in life is there a continual, direct onslaught of emotionally jarring communication as is experienced in the therapeutic relationship. Because psychotherapy is frequently an emotionally evocative encounter, strong affect—including hurt and anger—are more often demonstrated in the practitioner's consulting room than in most other professional offices. Effective therapeutic work, from a psychoanalytic point of view, can not be done unless the client transfers the resentments and hurts, including overwhelming rage experienced toward parental and other significant figures in the client's life, to the practitioner. The unconscious strategy of the client in this process is often to reverse the feelings of anger, helplessness, and fright felt in the presence of a hurtful authority figure in the past by inducing the therapist to feel as frightened and helpless as the client did in the past. In a real sense, there are professional dictates to encourage the reception and retention of emotions provoked by the affective interchange between the practitioner and his/her clients. This leaves the practitioner continually with a residue of powerful affect. In short, there are numerous typical situations that place considerable emotional stress on the practitioner. Spensley and Blacker (1976) give a number of examples, such as when a well-liked client previously very positive toward the therapist explodes with intense rage. And there is the termination of a therapeutic relationship with people the practitioner has worked with intimately for a number of years.

Of course, some types of stressful situations are more consistently recognized than others. Handling a client who is suicidal is a situation that would raise considerable anxiety for anyone. Also, there is the danger that a highly disturbed client might take physical action against the practitioner. Almost every practitioner encounters at least once in a career an agitated client who actually carries a weapon, threatens an assault, or expresses strong hostility toward the practitioner. If the therapist is not wary or is unlucky, one such incident may be sufficient to end a career, if not a life. Despite this ominous possibility there is very little discussion in the professional literature about the causes of these dangers and how to recognize them before an attack.

Practitioners with considerable expertise with violent patients, such as John Lion, caution the practitioner to properly monitor counter-transferential reactions to agitated patients. Practitioners who work in urban hospitals in large cities, which are magnets for highly disturbed people, face seriously agitated and violent patients regularly. This is particularly true of practitioners who work in crisis services and emergency rooms.

Many of the victims of attacks by agitated patients are younger practitioners who inevitably treat the most difficult clients.

Madden, Lion and Penna (1976) report a study of practitioners who were assaulted by patients. According to their findings, more than half of the assaulted practitioners had acted in a provocative manner toward the assaultive client prior to the attack. Lion indicates that many of these incidents can be related to the inexperience of the practitioner who was too *insistent* that a client deal squarely with upsetting material.

Even when no actual attack occurs, the fear and threat of not being able to manage agitated clients occupies the thoughts of many young therapists. The first psychotherapy patient I was assigned as a clinical intern in a large city hospital when I was in my twenties was a rather beautiful, sensual-looking black woman. She had been recently discharged from the in-patient unit of the hospital. I read in her clinic folder that her husband was a paranoid Black Muslim who had been recently released from prison for armed robbery with a rifle. He and the patient were separated. In the folder was a statement reputed to have been made by the husband that he would shoot anyone he found his wife with. The woman had come to the clinic for a prescription for medication. As a psychologist I could not, of course, prescribe medication. I was told by my supervisor to convince her that she needed psychotherapy on a weekly basis in the clinic. As she and I climbed three flights of steps of the 100-year-old clinic building to a small room on the fourth floor, I wondered about what I was going to tell her about why I was seeing her. At the same time, I had a fantasy of her husband charging up the stairs after us demanding to know what I was doing with his wife. As an inexperienced practitioner with my first psychotherapy case, I wasn't sure myself.

In short, I have tried to demonstrate that there is normal stress inherent in the process of psychotherapy, which is over and beyond the issues of countertransference and therapist psychopathology. The very process of psychotherapy induces real and distressful reactions in the practitioner. We may assume that the emotionally healthy practitioner can successfully and constructively handle the normal stress of psychotherapeutic work. But what of those practitioners we have referred to before who are especially vulnerable? We must inquire what effect these continual activities have on their psyches. Let us examine some of the issues on which the practitioner's vulnerability is predicated.

THE LURE OF BEING A PSYCHOTHERAPIST

The motives that have drawn a person to the process of psychotherapy influence the roles the practitioner takes with clients. For some practitioners—a small number, it is hoped—practicing psychotherapy is a means of denying their own conflictual issues. There are practitioners, according to Groesbeck and Taylor (1977), who have had serious illnesses of one sort or another in their lives but have never fully acknowledged that they were actually ill. In short, they have denied for themselves a need to be a patient and have not assimilated the archetype of the wounded healer. Nevertheless, they are fascinated by the patient role for others. Because of their own "identification denial" they cannot get very close emotionally to their clients. This issue may be a part of all of us who enter the profession and struggle with intimacy as the crucible of the personal journey in our search of self.

IDENTIFICATION DENIAL

Since we are so similar to the clients we select to work with, as Henry's (1973) research clearly indicates, it may not be clear why we have so much difficulty at certain times understanding and helping these clients. I will try to explain this. There is a natural tendency for us to identify with people with whom we are significantly emotionally involved. We may also overidentify—we may be more concerned with what the clients are doing destructively in their lives than the clients are themselves. When the therapist becomes more concerned than a client about the client's suffering, the client is prevented from examining adequately conflictual concerns.

In such situations, the therapist attempts to protect and do the work for the client. Or, on the other hand, the therapist may become threatened by a sense (usually not conscious) that he/she shares with the client certain traits and attitudes he/she finds unacceptable in him/herself. In short, there are threatening personal concerns of the practitioner that are touched on in encounters with clients who are struggling with similar issues. I refer to this kind of countertransference reaction as "identification denial," which I will examine clinically in Chapter 12. When either or both client and therapist deny their commonality with one another, magical rather than realistic expectations and demands are potentiated. The practitioner's unwitting need to gain distance from his/her own unacceptable attributes which he/she encounters without conscious awareness in the client makes therapeutic alliance unattainable. Ostensibly, the practitioner works arduously to develop a relationship with these threatening clients. Covertly, he/she resists this relationship. These incompatible aims inevitably foster conflict (Goldberg, 1983a).

THE "AS IF" PRACTITIONER

There is another class of practitioners who become psychotherapists from their intense identification with their own therapist. They have experienced considerable conflict in their own lives. They find personal psychotherapy so helpful that they may even regard it figuratively, if not actually, as having saved their lives. With gratitude for their own survival, they are willing to devote the rest of their lives to saving others. This is a commendable motive. However, some of these fervently dedicated practitioners have never resolved in their personal psychotherapy a pervasive denial of their feelings of unworthiness. They see themselves through the eyes of their therapist. In this light, they are appalled by their desperation, dependency, and deep oral craving. To deny this painful picture of themselves they have become "as if" people. They desperately try to convince themselves they "are" their therapist. This is to say, they are his/her strengths, wisdom, and interpersonal skill. In short, they have been able to partially disown their wretched feelings by projective identification with their own therapist.

To maintain this "as if salvation," they find practical ways to become psychotherapists themselves. Many of them, because they come upon this solution later in life (generally, midlife) feel they have little time left to gratify the "solution" they have found. They find the quickest route to practice, with or without sufficient training and supervision. The unconscious rationale they give themselves is that if other people come to them and regard them as helpful or, at least, as impressive, then, maybe, they are not really wretched after all. Under these circumstances they may deny their own dissatisfactions and conflictual issues. But what is harmful for both them and their clients is the therapist's desperate need for their clients' admiration. Their denial of wretched feelings is abetted by intellectual strivings. For them and many other kinds of practitioners, psychotherapy is the pinnacle of intellectual and psychological knowledge. The psychotherapist knows things that other people do not. The "emotional truth" with which the practitioner is conversant is not confined to cognitive knowledge. Thus, for many, being a psychotherapist is the highest achievement of intellectual and emotional development. For the "as if" practitioner these intellectual rationalizations prevent the person from fully recognizing and effectively resolving psychic suffering.

THE DANGER OF SUPERIORITY

Let us be frank with one another! Psychotherapists do not regard themselves as ordinary people. They believe that, in a number of particular ways, they are special. Generally, we seem to believe that we are more intelligent, more compassionate, and more perceptive than most people. We also believe that we are more willing to express our perceptiveness about others in caring and concerned ways. For some practitioners this constellation of beliefs about themselves may be more exaggerated than in other practitioners and result in what the British analyst and close ally of Freud, Ernest Jones, referred to as "the God complex." In discussing Jones's classic paper "The God Complex," Judd Marmor (1953) suggests that many who are drawn toward the professions of healing have disavowed their own sense of impotence through an identification with the Supreme Being. People with this type of character structure demonstrate intense scopophilia and curiosity about the private lives of others, together with a strong need to be recognized and admired for superior skills in helping others.

This air of superiority creates serious dangers for practitioners. If they are not ordinary people, then, they cannot allow themselves the same excuses and rationalizations that ordinary people use to defend themselves from their own fears. Consequently, many therapists appear to believe that they are not entitled to use the same methods of dealing with anxiety that other people use. Thus, by regarding themselves as being more than ordinary, practitioners force themselves to assume responsibility for living life more exceptionally than the ordinary person. In fairness to practitioners we should recognize that this attitude is not simply a product of defensive grandiosity. As I pointed out in a previous chapter, it is a part of a mutually induced relationship with the public.

Marmor (1953) indicates that one of the greatest strains for the practitioner occurs in mid-life when the practitioner measures him/herself in terms of the great emphasis placed in American culture on wealth, prestige, and power. However, much is expected of the psychotherapist from the very onset of his/her career as one who is an expert in examining the fears and rationalizations of ordinary people. The public assumes that the skills and knowledge of the trade will forge the way the practitioner lives life outside of the office as well as how the practitioner conducts him/herself as a practitioner during work time. Freudenberger and Robbins (1979) indicate that, while psychotherapists are experts about problems in living, they are not at the same time necessarily proficient in living their own lives. But the public won't accept this.

The public expects a certain kind of life-style from the psychotherapist. No other profession, it would seem, is on duty as constantly as psychotherapists in how they conduct their lives and comport themselves. Only people in the public eye (politicians, ministers, ministers' children, entertainers, and athletes) have this kind of exposure pressure. In the first few months of my private practice, a couple referred to me did not return after their initial session. The woman was kind enough to write me a note, which she thought might be helpful since it was apparent that, as a young doctor, I must be beginning my practice. The major reason they would not return, she reported, was that I was not professional enough. My office furniture confirmed this. (I held practice in my townhouse living room, beautifully decorated, or so other clients reported.) This client wrote that they had found a "real" professional at a local university (who happened to be an untrained psychologist). His furniture, she indicated, was leather and firm, as it should be in a professional office.

And yet the psychotherapist is given the mandate to "be yourself!" The quality of being oneself is continually under scrutiny unless the practitioner can retreat from the view of others.

One of the areas in which this issue has considerable bearing, as I suggested in an earlier chapter, is that of money. The psychotherapist is unlike other professionals—such as attorneys and physicians, whose avarice has now been firmly "accepted" by the public. Like the minister, the practitioner is viewed by the public as having a spiritual calling. As such, the practitioner is supposed to be caring and available at all times without considerations of fee or personal convenience. This causes many problems for the practitioner who feels guilty about business practices. One young practitioner was referred a client by a former client who was a business partner of the man he was referring. The new client, after a couple of months' excuses for not paying the bill, gave the therapist a large check, which was subsequently returned by the bank because of insufficient funds. The practitioner found out that the client had permanently left town. Nevertheless, he was reluctant to check on the whereabouts of the client by contacting his client's business associate. The practitioner felt checkmated both by concerns about confidentiality and by embarrassment about his lack of business acumen.

Many of us would like to practice in a kind of ivory tower, where the financial concerns are taken care of by someone else. The business concerns and the financial concerns of practice cannot be separated from the psychotherapeutic issues in most instances.

THE LIFE-STYLE OF THE PRACTITIONER

There are other important expectations of the psychotherapist. The public expects the practitioner to deal better with life's vicissitudes than do ordinary people. The practitioner has to be wiser, more temperate, kinder, and more considerate than others. Practitioners have to be able to go beyond the petty jealousies, angers, annoyances, and concerns to which other people fall prey. When they do have problems they are expected to work them out with greater magnanimity, yes, and even decorum, than do others. This is an unfair demand and a cause for an embarrassed retreat into secrecy whenever the practitioner's own problems show themselves. As we know, embarrassment and shame may lead to a vicious cycle of retreat and further shame.

SECRETS AND SHAME

The therapist is bound by confidentiality and privacy. The practitioner ethically cannot disclose the names, details, and sordid or interesting facts and events in client's lives. And yet, if the practitioner does not share his/her work with others, the practitioner feels contained, restricted, and frustrated. Silence can also lead to psychic pain. There is something unbalanced in the client being encouraged to tell the practitioner his/her secrets, frequently laden with upset and trauma, which the psychotherapist is sworn to contain in silence. This often noxious burden can readily be demonstrated. If a man saw someone jump off the roof of a building across the street, he would undoubtedly feel quite upset and agitated. If he could not talk to anyone about it, his feelings about the event would begin to fester in him. He becomes distressed from the horrible experience that he has to hold within himself. But if he has an opportunity to tell someone else, then he can get it off his chest and would undoubtedly feel better. Studies (Pennebaker & O'Heeron, 1984) have shown that those who are able to confide in other people about their distressed feelings, rather than to hold onto them, are less susceptible to illness.

Similarly, the person who hears the story will also feel bad. He probably will feel as the original viewer did and will have to pass it on to someone else to feel relieved. As Theodore Reik (1959) convincingly demonstrated, we all, to some degree, have a need to confess. I suppose that most practitioners share the tales that they have been told and that make them feel terrible with a spouse, a colleague, a personal therapist or a consultant. But frequently they don't. Considering the family script many carry around with them, any release of pain they harbor might be returned with an equal part of guilt for being unwilling to bear life's burdens alone.

When I lived in the South, I became friends with an elderly woman analyst. She had been trained by one of the famous psychoanalytic masters from Europe. She was regarded as the dean and chief spokesperson for psychoanalysis in this southern community. She had lost her husband a few years before and her children lived far away. Apparently her loneliness was such that her patients became her favorite topic of conversation. It was uncomfortable and embarrassing to hear intimate details about people I knew reported from their analytic sessions. In my presence and that of others, she freely discussed her patients by name as if she were gossiping about neighbors. When a colleague suggested that her behavior was inappropriate, she scoffed at the suggestion and indicated that many renowned analysts did the same.

This bears upon Freud's (1915) observation:

> Whoever is familiar with the nature of neurosis will not be astonished to hear that even a man who is very well able to carry out analysis upon others can behave like any other mortal and be capable of producing violent resistances as soon as he himself becomes the object of analytic investigation.

THE PRACTITIONER'S VS. THE PUBLIC'S VIEW OF THE GOOD LIFE

There is still another societal expectation of the psychotherapist that touches upon the issues of shame I have been discussing. Part of the conflict of practice is that we live in a culture and society which tell us that we should not live with pain, discomfort, or distress. In *The Lives of a Cell*, Lewis Thomas (1974) wrote that

> the great secret, known to internists and learned early in marriage by internists' wives, but still hidden from the general public, is that most things get better by themselves. Most things, in fact, are better by morning. (p. 85)

We have become accustomed to expecting, indeed demanding, instant relief from our ailments, our pains, our trepidations, and our doubts. Why wait until the morning when we have been repeatedly led to believe that prolonged suffering can generally be avoided (Goldberg, 1980)

Despite our knowing better, does not this cultural ethic intrude in our practice, as well? Don't we, as Burton (1972) suggests, attempt to make the psychotherapeutic situation as unstressful as possible and encourage the client to go away happy at closing time? When this does not happen as frequently as we would like, we may dutifully become overly concerned and distressed. This is problem enough for the typical practitioner. But what if the practitioner is unhappily living life with the strife and pain that society has condemned as unjustified? Will the practitioner, when problems begin to reveal themselves to clients, feel shameful and embarrassed? Will these untoward sentiments drive the practitioner into deeper retreat from clients, perhaps, even from continuing to practice? If so, we are faced with an ironic situation. More than any single volume, Sigmund Freud's *Psychopathology of Everyday Life* (1914), read by large segments of the public, helped to psychologize the meaning of illness, explaining why people's behavior may appear to defy common sense. It served also to detoxify private areas of the individual's life, which had been painful sources of shame and embarrassment. In psychologizing shame—this is to say, in demonstrating how many of the socially disproved actions by people were evoked by forces that they were neither conscious of nor able to control—Freud provided a path to the safe exploration of secrets in the consultation room. Typically, issues of shameful thoughts and deeds are the *sine qua non* of the therapeutic hour. Yet society denies the psychotherapist justification for even needing to have secrets! The public expects therapists to live idyllic lives. These considerations are closely related to the disillusionary effects of practice that have appeared so prominently among psychotherapists in recent years. In examining the lives of psychotherapists in the past, it is rare to learn of one who became so "burned out" by the demands of practice as to leave a psychotherapy career, particularly, as early in one's career as we are now witnessing.

PSYCHOLOGY AS A GUIDELINE FOR LIVING

Clearly what has changed in more recent decades is society's expectations of the psychotherapist. As I have pointed out in an earlier chapter, psychotherapy was in the past only a narrow and circumscribed set of procedures. It is now regarded as the primary perspective in all matters of human endeavor. In an age in which the old reliable guideposts of the past, religion and natural science, have been largely discarded by most of the Western world, people have come to look to psychotherapists as supposedly relentless pursuers of truth and providers of constant and reliable guidelines for living one's life.[1]

In the following sections I will examine the type of world view psychotherapists represent.

THE WORLD OF THE PRACTITIONER

The psychotherapist lives in a certain circumscribed world framed by basic themes and particular levels of focus and attention. Even though the psychotherapist is confronted with the entirety of the person he/she encounters in his/her consulting room—the whole person—the practitioner cannot realistically deal with this entire myriad of human issues and dimensions. For few individuals, psychotherapist or other, are expert and knowledgeable in all the arts and sciences. Consequently there is a need on the part of the psychotherapist, even without giving it much thought, to reduce human experience to a manageable form of inquiry. All professions specialize in one or a few dimensions of human experience. The psychotherapist focuses on the emotional substratum of experience. Human experience is relegated to what the client actually felt and the inferred motives impelling the client's experience. As important, as a corresponding focus, at least for practitioners working from psychodynamic orientations (but probably for all therapists), an examination of the emotional attitudes transacted between client and therapist is crucial to their work together.

For many, if not most, practitioners, the inexactness of practice is a constant stress factor. Emotions are, of course, a highly uncertain dimension of experience. We have no reliable, scientifically agreed upon method for assessing the validity of our inferences about the intricate interplay of emotions that are at work. This does not rest on idle curiosity. The well-being of our suffering clients, if not their very lives, may rest upon our ability to correctly sense their experience and respond appropriately. Psychotherapy is such a complex process that the clinician is never certain about the effect saying something—or saying nothing, for that matter—will have upon a client. The contrast between the world of the psychotherapist and physical medicine is cogently shown in the words of a psychiatric resident who revealed that

> When I was a [medical] intern . . . people felt I had saved their lives—and sometimes they were right. No way do you get that in psychiatry. You need a lot more internal strength, because you're not going to get a lot of external gratification. I came into psychiatry because it promised the chance to change people's lives . . . Well, it turns out it's easy to get the patients over the

acute event, but it's very difficult to get them to have insight. I often feel at odds with the patients. They don't see the need to change, and I do. You could say that psychiatry is a poor choice for me, because I have a low threshold of frustration. (Schwartz, 1984)

PSYCHOTHERAPY AS AN INEXACT SCIENCE

As I will show in the next chapter, there are different types of personalities drawn to practice psychotherapy. Those whose intellectual and scientific attitudes require certainty about what they are doing and why they are doing it are rarely satisfied with their own skills.[2] Insofar as their emotional character militates against their taking clinical risks, they are plagued by the unpredictability of their clients' behavior and the therapeutic methods available to guide their understanding. For example, an economic view of psychoanalysis as a system of allocating psychic energy between analyst and analysand, predicated upon the congruence between the analysand's behavior and the analyst's ability to understand these behaviors, suggests that those practitioners whose scientific orientation is highly operative in their work would prefer errors of omission to errors of commission. This is generally built into the training philosophy of psychoanalytically oriented programs. Young psychoanalysts are taught there that the best therapeutic attitude for an inexperienced therapist is to say as little as possible.

My psychoanalytic supervisor during my internship as a clinical psychologist required me to keep verbatim notes of both what the client and I said during the sessions. Since this compilation required so much attention I had little or no time to think about what to say. On the other hand, it did serve as an excellent vehicle for "fine point" supervision. An hour's supervision would be expended on only a few exchanges. Nonetheless, I quickly realized that the main function of the compulsive notetaking was to avoid errors of commission. I was uncomfortable being as inactive as this method of recording mandated. Therefore, I suggested to my supervisor that a tape recording would be far more accurate and efficient. His face turned white and he was speechless for quite a while. Nevertheless, he reluctantly allowed me to tape my sessions. In contrast to practitioners who fear errors of commission, therapists who more closely identify with their client's suffering than with a scientific framework for their work, find themselves thwarted by not being able to be helpful enough. Finding their theoretical formulations limited, as I did, they may become more active in trying to reach and gain the cooperation of their clients than their training orientation generally has recommended. Therefore, they are more likely to commit errors of commission than their more cautious and scientifically oriented colleagues.

I supervised an inexperienced practitioner who worked in a low-cost mental health clinic. Because he was being paid only 12 dollars per session, he saw about 15 clients a day, generally seven or eight in a row without a break. Most of the clients were severely impaired people who had been diagnosed as suffering from psychotic and borderline conditions. Many had several psychiatric hospitalizations, and some had made suicidal attempts in the past. In supervision the young practitioner indicated that the mother of a child he was treating had been recently hospitalized in a nonpsychiatric hospital after a suicide attempt. The family of the woman wanted her home and not sent to a psychiatric hospital. They had told the practitioner that they were willing to see him weekly if he would work with them as a family. The practitioner, although inexperienced with family therapy and having never before worked with a client who had made a recent suicide attempt, said he was eager to do anything to help the woman. He indicated to me that family therapy could get her over her difficulties. He said that he didn't believe inpatient treatment helped patients. I asked him if he had spoken with the hospitalized woman about treatment plans. He said that he had. The woman, he reported, was quite agitated and felt hopeless and trapped in her domestic and occupational situations. She expressed considerable anger that the emergency personnel of the hospital had resuscitated her. She promised to try to take her own life again. She also demanded to be taken out of the hospital. In return for her being taken out of the hospital she agreed to see the practitioner with her family.

I was concerned that the practitioner wasn't taking the woman seriously, nor was he recognizing and accepting his own therapeutic limitations. I pointed out that it was one thing to be unrealistic with what he could therapeutically do to help a person who had sufficient ego-strength to deal with his or her frustrations if therapy wasn't helpful. It was quite another matter to be unrealistic with a person who had made at least two suicidal attempts (according to a clinical report he had written less than a month before and had forgotten the contents of) and promised to do it again. He became quite defensive and plaintively indicated that if he recognized and accepted his present clinical limitations, then he couldn't continue to practice psychotherapy because all of his clients were psychodynamically similar to this woman. Apparently, therefore, he needed to deny his limitations by the sort of reaction formation in which he unrealistically assumes that with the blessing of providence he can help anyone, under any circumstances. His optimism would be commendable if amalgamated with comon sense and compassion for himself, as well as for his clients. But he set an impossible task for himself by assuming that he was not allowed to recognize and accept his own limitations as a practitioner and the inexact nature of the profession in which he practiced.

In short, many practitioners work hour after hour in a climate of uncertainty and, at the same time, intense emotional transaction. To the extent that their clients are not agitated they may feel safe and intellectually challenged by the transactional uncertainty. On the other hand, it may be a very different experience for the practitioner whose clients are highly agitated and the practitioner can find no effective means of reaching them.

THE QUEST FOR REASON

In our discussion of the frustrations and disillusionment inherent in the practice of psychotherapy, we should not lose sight of the fact that one of the cardinal principles of psychotherapy is based upon the precept of a working relationship in which therapist and client can reason together. There is, therefore, a kind of certainty which the practitioner, particularly if the practitioner is psychoanalytically oriented, struggles to find. The basic professional commitment of the practice of psychotherapy is to the assumption that each person we work with is capable of self-understanding, which will lead to self-modification and a sense of purpose in their lives.[3] Wheelis (1956) points out that

> For some persons the principle determinant of the vocational choice of psychoanalysis is to be found in the development of the capacity for insight and in the function of insight in the strug-

gle for self-mastery . . . It implies a belief that no inner danger is
so bad but that knowledge about it will be better than not knowing. It presupposes further an implicit faith in the adaptive potential of intelligence, and the wish to place at the disposal of intelligence all available information.

Kernberg (1968) adds to this:

If the clinician has no rational, scientific conviction about the
possibility of helping an individual through understanding he is
in danger of facing a professional identity crisis.

The problem with all of this emphasis on rationality, Wheelis
soberly indicates, is that the most common illusion of clients and
psychotherapists alike is the belief that insight actually helps.
Consequently, the most common disappointment in psychotherapy is that insight frequently does *not* lead to change. Wheelis
states the dilemma rather poetically: "Analysts are purveyors of
insight, patients are applicants for magic." What makes this situation inherently antagonistic, according to Wheelis, is that the
analyst by disposition and training is the least likely of all people to rely upon methods of reaching clients who eschew self-
examination. At the same time, the practitioner becomes "the
object for the most intense and continuous demand for magic
performance" (Wheelis, 1956).

Alan Wheelis indicates that the source of uncertainty of insight in psychoanalytic work rests upon the fact that even those
areas of human experience that are least accessible to scientific
investigation, e.g., unconscious thoughts and repressed motives,
are held by psychoanalytic theory to be as strictly determined
and fully subject to natural law as are the more accessible and
observable human phenomenon. It is those less accessible areas
of human functioning that are the analyst's chief bailiwick. To
do his/her job competently, the practitioner soon learns that
those theoretical formulations the practitioner has been taught
in training cannot be depended upon for accurate predictability
and insight as in other sciences. Wheelis indicates that the analyst is "forced to realize that insight is not for his patient the
edged tool that it is for him." Although the practitioner is expected to uphold the highest standards of scientific objectivity,
he/she observes that it is actually how effectively the practitioner
utilizes his/her personality that enables him to emotionally reach

and gain the therapeutic cooperation of analysands. In short, the success of therapeutic work actually rests upon the interpersonal skills of the practitioner.

The practitioner's success has to do with how skillfully his/her personality and temperament are forged to struggle with the inherent antagonism between therapist and client. In examining the major contemporary theories of psychotherapy, Lawrence Friedman (1975) concludes that the common problem in psychotherapy has to do with the conflict between therapist and client. All forms of psychotherapy, even psychoanalysis, contends Friedman, are a subtle but not unique form of coercion. All forms of interpersonal influence are susceptible to coercion strategies. What is this conflict that requires a struggle?

THERAPEUTIC STRUGGLE WITH CLIENTS

A major strain in Western thought is that happiness is the goal of living. A corollary to this thesis is that to harbor self-doubts and to engage in extensive self-examination prevents happiness. Not surprisingly, then, most people erect defenses to deny unpleasantness, dissatisfaction, and fear. These defenses collide jarringly with the contrasting belief system of the psychotherapist. The practitioner proclaims from the Socratic stance that life is meant to be examined because the unexamined life is not worth living. Moreover, it is enduring meaning, not momentary pleasure, that is the goal of life, according to the psychotherapist. But are all types of clients ready to accept the psychotherapist's value orientation?

The providers of mental health services are predominantly middle-class and college-educated. Their sociocultural backgrounds are highly similar to those of the clients they treat in private practice. Both come from a markedly circumscribed section of the social world, representing a high congruence of ethnic experience and religious, political, and philosophical values (Henry et al., 1971). They share an orientation toward resolution of problems by means of rational discussion and compromise, working within and accommodating to the established social order (Goldberg & Kane, 1974a; Goldberg & Kane, 1974b). It is small wonder, then, that the middle-class mental health professional's attitudes best prepare the practitioner to provide ameliorative modalities that are insight-oriented and to direct them toward clients who have a conscious philosophical stance toward life, who are capable of abstract and symbolic reasoning, and who have sufficiently conflict-free areas of psychological functioning to permit them to withstand day-to-day frustrations, tensions, and problems so that they can struggle with the meaning of their existence and develop a viable sense of identity (Goldberg & Kane, 1974b).

Unfortunately, a large proportion of the persons requiring psychological services, and certainly the most difficult cases, do not possess the required emotional and intellectual faculties necessary for traditional psychotherapy (Goldberg, 1973). Schofield (1964) and other investigators have documented that the younger, more attractive, better educated, and less severely agitated client is more likely to be seen in private psychotherapy.

When clients choose certain ways of handling their anxieties which run counter to therapists' belief systems, anxiety and security may become tripped off in both participants. To the extent that the idealized image of the practitioner is threatened, considerable stress may result in controlling and defensive behavior. One of the more serious of these is caring more for the client than the client does for him/herself. Overidentifying with clients is often a part of the therapeutic struggle and its negativity.

A clinical psychology intern was working with an extremely disturbed patient in a psychiatric hospital. The patient, whom I will refer to as "Mr. Webster," was referred for therapy due to his extreme isolation and autistic withdrawal from other patients. He had been unresponsive to the attention directed from ward personnel. Psychological tests suggested that he had mild mental retardation. The psychology intern who was selected as his therapist was a friendly, warm, and very conscientious young man. Mr. Webster told this therapist that his main problem was that he had swallowed too much saliva and would have to make it go away. For several months the therapist had considerable difficulty moving the therapeutic dialogue onto any other level than that of the patient attending sessions because of his saliva problem. But even this concern could not be consistently engaged in, as the patient continued his long silences and frequently left the room to wander in the hall and smoke. At other times, five or ten minutes into a session, he claimed that his mouth was dry and he could not swallow his saliva. He would then bolt up and leave the room to go down the hall to the water fountain. The therapist, conscientiously and passively, sat in his chair waiting for the patient to return. Over time it became clear that the therapist's conscientiousness militated against Mr. Webster actually experiencing either the consequences or the unreasonableness of his own dilemma. It was also leaving the therapist rather dismayed and doubting his ability to be an effective therapist. The psychological methods he had been taught in graduate school could not reach difficult clients like Mr. Webster.

The disillusionment of practice may stem from the ultimate failure of talk and reason. Many of us, as practitioners, have gone into the field because we have been led to believe from significant figures in our backgrounds and the ways we ourselves have tried to handle our conflicts that all problems can be resolved if only we face up to them and talk them out in a reasonable way, to someone else. As psychotherapists, I think we find, as Wheelis has suggested, that often this is not enough. All problems cannot be resolved by talk and reason. I believe that often in our therapeutic work we and our clients need to be willing to go beyond reasoning and talk and to take courageous action. I will illustrate this by returning to the therapeutic struggle with Mr. Webster.

The therapist working with Mr. Webster realized that his deadly seriousness about the session militated against Mr. Webster experiencing the unreasonableness of his own dilemma. I suggested that only to the extent that the therapist could let go of his seriousness and play with the patient's absurd resistive ploys could Mr. Webster get in touch with the meaning of his personal dilemma. I suggested a number of paradoxical maneuvers that would enable the therapist to engage Mr. Webster more than he could by reason and interpretation. (The reader who is interested in these therapeutic considerations can consult my book *In Defense of Narcissism*, 1980a.) The point I wish to draw is concerned with the need to engage Mr. Webster's courage. The utilization of several paradoxical interventions dissolved the various resistive ploys of the patient. In fact, after some months the therapist and Mr. Webster were speaking together in earnest. Interestingly, Mr. Webster no longer appeared retarded as he had during the early months of therapy. The constituents had reached what I regarded as a rather propitious moment in their therapeutic encounter. Unfortunately, in a few months the intern would be finishing his internship and leaving the hospital.

Practitioners are generally people with a deep caring concern for others, together with a desire to be close, but at the same time requiring a special structure in which to exercise closeness. Within the therapeutic enterprise, there are manifold illusory powers that come to the therapist by virtue of clients' transference distortions and magical hopes. For clients, the therapist becomes the most significant and powerful figure in their lives; the embodiment of every person they have ever known, cared for, feared, or hoped to encounter. To one who is uncomfortable with real power, the illusory power bestowed by clients is ideal. He/she can choose to nurture their sentiments as genuine when they are ego-syntonic or, on the other hand, to interpret and disarm them when threatened by the client's wish to act upon these sentiments in ways uncomfortable to the therapist.

RESPONSIBILITY AND ILLUSION

We have not addressed the most obvious source of the practitioner's stress—clinical responsibilities. The psychotherapist is a professional who is asked to help people, many of whom come to the practitioner after failing to find resolution with other helpers. In this endeavor, we are given a very heavy responsibility for other people's lives. In assuming this heavy responsibility we actually have very little power. Rarely, unless we work in a custodial institution, do we have real control over our clients' lives. Our power generally derives from transferential and magical attributes given to us by our clients. At best, we have some influence through reasoning and persuasion. But this rests upon an often fragile alliance. Moreover, unlike practitioners from other professions who deal with crisis and life threatening situations, e.g., the police officer, we don't have a codified standard of procedure and clear limitations of whether and how to deal with these dire situations. Nor do we have a clear idea how we will be supported or reacted to by our colleagues for our actions. This stands in sharp contrast to the law officer or the attorney who have codified standards of procedure which do not speak in broad vagaries as do the professional codes of the disciplines that comprise the mental health disciplines.

These considerations make quite clear the illusion of acting as if psychotherapy were a scientific and regulated profession. Because it isn't, we, as practitioners, are thrown back on our own resources to handle serious and critical situations as best we can. The need to find the means of sharing these concerns with our colleagues is heightened in clinical situations, in which formal procedures for handling these issues are vague and open to free interpretation. This is a consideration to which I will devote considerable discussion in the second half of this book.

We do not handle crises every day of our practice, of course, unless we specialize in this work. Nevertheless, our typical unmotivated client—the client who succeeds in threatening our imago as a concerned and competent practitioner—raises in subtler form issues in regard to our idealized image of ourselves as practitioners similar to those raised by the client in crisis.

Len Bergantino (1975), a California practitioner, relates failure in psychotherapy to the practitioner's inability or unwillingness to confront the client's magical expectations about psychotherapy.

> Patients come to psychotherapy seeking what they were not able to find in all of their other relationships. They seek a relationship with someone they expect to be warm, caring, loving, and all of the other things a perfect relationship might have. The expectations the client has of his therapist are the same ones he has of other people in his daily existence. He has met with failure in all his other attempts at attaining that type of relationship whereby the therapist cares more about the client's needs than he does about his own. How the therapist deals with this issue is critical. I have seen many therapists respond to their clients in a way that only perpetuates the delusion that the client may yet be able to attain the perfect relationship. Many therapists are unwilling to be a disappointment to their clients.

We will return to examining ways of handling these magical expectations in Part Two of this book.

WORKING WITH UNDESIRABLE CLIENTS

Certain types of clients cause special distress for practitioners. Aside from those usually regarded as difficult because of the severity of their psychopathology and propensity for acting out their pathology in ways harmful to themselves and others, there are a number of clients most abhorred by the private practitioner. According to an investigator who surveyed pri-

vate practitioners, there is general agreement about clients practitioners wish to avoid. To her surprise, there was considerable
consensus about who these clients were. The investigator
reports that

> It mattered little whether or not the therapist was male or fe-
> male, psychoanalyst, psychiatrist, or psychologist. Nor did the-
> oretical backgrounds make much difference: conservative Freu-
> dians, liberal humanists...and others in between all spoke in
> similar terms. Virtually all feelings expressed reflected one cen-
> tral theme: What your shrink really thinks about you depends
> largely on how you make him feel about himself. Shrinks, it
> seems, need attention and admiration, too. (Ames, 1980)

This is in accord with a statement made by the prominent
Philadelphia psychiatrist O. S. English, in selecting clients: "If
I have a personal demon it is my need (perhaps even lust) for ac-
knowledgement of *me*" (Burton, 1972, p. 99).

It is not surprising then that the "young, attractive, verbal,
intelligent and successful" client (the YAVIS), who is "well-
informed, knows what's going on in the news, is interested in
talking about his (or her) problems, and can verbalize a deeper
awareness about himself" and can, consequently, help the practitioner do his job well is highly desired as a client (Ames, 1980).
The less fortunate practitioner encounters those "obnoxious"
and "boring" clients, who, typically and sometimes skillfully,
deny the practitioner the recognition and admiration many of us
require to feel fulfilled in our work. Greenson (1966) referred to
these clients in a classic paper, "The Impossible Profession," in
the *International Journal of Psychoanalysis* as inspiring "a feeling of 'oi vay' in the analyst."

As a result of ungratifying efforts with our difficult clients we
may place ourselves in a position which Haveliwala and his associates (1979) have referred to as "whitemail." There are
clients who, due to physical and/or personality characteristics
or because of rapid improvement in therapy, readily reward us
for our time spent with them. For such clients there are countless ways the practitioner unwittingly may pay back the client
by providing special appointment, remaining overtime, or not
broaching embarrassing issues and other special considerations.
The problem presents itself when we catch ourselves doing these
"extras," try to stop doing them, and have these clients enraged
at our unwillingness to continually play Santa Claus. Some of

these clients may stop at nothing in order to resurrect the holiday spirit, not even at self-destructive threats and attempts.

We must face the serious nature of our work. Unless we select clients who wish only cosmetic touches and we choose to indulge them at a perfunctory level, we must accept the inevitable: Sooner or later we will have a client attempt suicide, become psychotically decompensated or regard our sincerest efforts as incompetent practice. How far will we go in trying to reach these clients? Bared to its core, the crucial issue that is involved in the hazards of practice may be examined by the answers to the following questions: How far should we go in trying to help others? What are the limits of our obligations? How far are we personally willing and able to go beyond these obligations?

How we address these questions has much to do with what hazards we experience in our work.

WHAT CAN THE PSYCHOTHERAPIST ACTUALLY PROMISE?

The practitioner cannot promise with any kind of scientific certainty that involvement with a client will result in any kind of definitive help. All the practitioner can really promise is that he/she will attempt to understand and to intervene as best as the practitioner knows how in order to favorably influence the person with whom the practitioner is working. To do this the practitioner can promise to look at issues that he/she believes are being denied or pushed away. This does not come without a cost. The practitioner should warn the client that to deal meaningfully with issues may often cause additional pain and suffering. It is analogous to the patient to having a painful wound. To get at the core of it may mean causing greater pain in lacerating the wound to rid its pernicious effect. Clearly, then, the practitioner cannot promise a magical cure—that he/she will take all the suffering and unhappiness away; or that, having a client in the practitioner's hands, he/she will deliver a reborn and fully functioning person. What the psychotherapist has to offer is based upon the reality in which that client lives. This depends upon how responsible family members and others in the community in which the client lives and works will be to accepting and integrating the person back into the community. The suffering that the client carries into interaction with the practitioner is predicated upon frustrations and limited opportunities with others. Unless family, friends, and colleagues respond favorably to the client's new endeavors at friendship and relationship, the reality of therapy may be limited. Modern healing, as with shaman practices in the past, depends upon factors other than simply the skill of the healer.

Shaman healers seem intuitively to realize that psychic disturbance may often be more accurately viewed as emotional impoverishment. The psychologically disturbed person has been deprived of meaningful and significant relationships with others in his/her community. Each of these relationships serves as a lifeline that sustains and maintains the individual, keeping him/her alive and well. The strength of the shaman's healing practices came not only from the interpersonal ties between the healer and the sufferer, but also from the reinforcing effect of the entire community presence. In this capacity, the shaman served a therapeutic function by inducing trances, prophesying from dreams and visions in such a way that the core beliefs of the community were confirmed and validated. By skillfully bringing in relatives and other significant community members in these clinical events, the shaman achieved a combination of psychological healing and community integration. In a word, the success of healing is never based simply on the practitioner's knowledge and skills, or even on the client's willingness to deal with these issues. What also is involved is what is possible within the community in which the sufferer lives.

In the last two chapters I have attempted to spell the specific satisfactions and hazards that I believe are central to the practice of psychotherapy. The reader may ask how well my contentions hold up against the empirical findings of satisfactions and stresses among practitioners. Until recently the few empirical studies of satisfaction and stress in therapeutic practice have been limited in scope, either focusing entirely on psychiatrists (Daniels, 1974; MaCiver & Redlich, 1959; Rogow, 1970) or restricted to examining only hazards (Daniels, 1974).

To rectify this lack, Farber and Heifetz (1981) systematically investigated the specific sources of stresses and satisfactions that existed among psychiatrists, psychologists, and social workers in a contemporary psychotherapeutic community of a Northeast metropolitan center of 350,000 people.[4]

Using factor analysis, the authors found

That for psychotherapists the most satisfying aspects of work include promoting growth and change in themselves as well as in
patients, becoming intimately and helpfully involved in the lives
of patients, and feeling proud and respected as competent professionals. Therapeutic work appears to be most satisfying when
therapists themselves can learn and grow and develop skills
while being helpful and involved with others."

The stresses of practice clustered around three areas:

negative "after hours" consequences of work, the demanding
and precarious equilibrium of intimacy and objectivity during
therapy, and problematic working conditions...These basic
sources of stress also suggest one way of looking at the phenomenon of burnout. When the baseline of expected difficulties is ex-
ceeded either by intolerable working conditions or by unusually
stressful therapeutic work—then personal pressures may intensify dramatically, stresses may appear disproportionate to satisfactions, and burnout may result.

In Farber and Heifetz's study, it appears that the core of the
problem for the psychotherapist is not unlike what other professionals in contemporary society require. Thus, a major conclusion may be drawn from the interrelationship of stress and satisfaction in improving psychological service and enabling
practitioners to feel gratified in their work. Marston (1984)
writes:

worker satisfaction requires a safe and pleasant workplace (physically and socially) and adequate compensation (monetary, social, and psychological) which reflects the quality (or quantity)
of the production. A combination of socioeconomic, professional,
and personal factors have tended to provide many therapists
with a workplace that is uncertain and/or unsatisfying.

Marston (1984) also draws special attention to what he
regards as the most important of the factors in the consortium
of variables found by Farber and Heifetz (1981). *Difficulty in
receiving adequate positive feedback* for competent work, Marston believes, is the practitioner's primary frustration. He indicates that although successful therapeutic work rests on a mixed
set of influences, the practitioner is more affected by failures

than by successes. In Marston's words: "Failures come back to haunt them, often under conditions which do not give another crack at the job—yet, if the patients succeed they more often than not are never heard from again."

In summary, the growing concerns of the practitioner relate to the origins of our interest in self-examination and understanding of others. To the extent that the practitioner understands self and clients, and to the extent that the practitioner is not dutifully recognized or rewarded for skills and compassion, the practitioner may begin seriously to reconsider a career as a healer.

There are, of course, many different ways practitioners may react to their growing concerns. They may rationalize their practice and relegate it to a business, concerning themselves rather exclusively with financial considerations. This is reinforced by the feeling that, because the practitioner has spent more years than most other professionals in training, the practitioner is now owed a good income. Or practitioners may join or initiate new theories, schools of thought, and psychological movements that offer new meaning to their work. On the other hand, they may gradually shift their time, energy, and interest to new pursuits or fields of interest, peripheral to clinical work, or simply devote more time to teaching, research, or supervision than they formerly did. Or, more unfortunately, they may become increasingly more iatrogenic for their clients. This is to say, they may deleteriously affect their clients because they are not aware of their own needs and how they use their clients to meet these needs. If they continue in this way they will sooner or later experience a "burnout."[5] Some of us forget too quickly that the source of our ability to touch others lies in our being human. We heal others by courageously heeding our own suffering. Clearly, the practitioner shares with clients the existential requirement to give some direction to his/her own existence. The therapist can enable a client to derive meaning from the client's struggles by offering the client the courage the practitioner has found and the values he/she has derived in experiencing his/her own world and in struggling with the forces pressing upon the practitioner's own human condition. This courage may be found in everyday and ostensibly indirect ways.

I have been told of a psychiatrist who took up gourmet cooking to relieve the stress of his therapeutic work. His *pièce de resistance* was cooking a meal for Craig Claiborne, the internationally known culinary expert and former food editor of *The New York Times*.

If the practitioner regards his/her own struggles, not as weakness and shame, but as the pangs of passion, caring, and concern, the practitioner is more likely to offer clients meaningful therapeutic experience than the scientifically objective practitioner (Goldberg, 1980a). Nietzsche told us as much: "Physician help yourself! Thus you help your patient, too. Let this be his best help that he may behold with his eyes the man who heals himself."

For the client to become a more responsible and effective person, the client needs to be given responsibility for collaborating in his/her own emotional growth. This endeavor requires a partnership between therapist and client. The practitioner serves as a role model. The client will be no more willing to struggle for meaning in his/her journey in Self than the client senses the practitioner is in his/her own personal and interpersonal journeys (Goldberg, 1980a). Guidelines for creating a partnership and therapeutic alliance with clients will be discussed in Chapter 9, but before we discuss therapeutic alliance we will examine in Chapter 7, the issues involved in becoming an independent practitioner.

NOTES

1. Rabbi Arthur Herzberg offered the opinion at the 1984 Conference of the American Academy of Psychoanalysis in New York City that Freud appeared to believe that he was the new Prometheus. He wished that others follow the hints and directions he was offering in order to build a radical new culture. According to Rabbi Herzberg, Freud saw himself in Jewish prophetic tradition as a leader who was dealing with the assimilation issue for Jews, as were his contemporaries Theodor Herzl and Franz Kafka. But Freud took a very different route than they did. Freud was attempting to assimilate the Jews by "dynamiting" existing Jewish culture through revealing its underlying psychological fallacies. He hoped this would leave the Jew with no other recourse than to meld with Christians into a new intellectual worldview.

2. Even experienced psychotherapists have difficulty differentiating psychotic patients from those who are not functional psychotics. A few years ago, David Rosenhan, a Stanford psychologist, planted eight volunteers, one a psychiatrist, in psychiatric wards of both public and private hospitals across the

United States. They were instructed to act normally. According to Rosenhan, many of the other patients quickly realized that the eight were not psychiatric patients. But the staff never did. Rosenhan writes that any diagnostic process which could be so prone to errors of this kind cannot be very reliable (Rosenhan, 1973). The novel and the film *One Flew Over the Cuckoo's Nest* vividly depict the arbitrariness of psychiatry.

3. Moreover, since medicine is no longer accessible only to the privileged, more people have the legitimate right to use it. Significant shifts have results in the *meaning of illness*. In brief, these meanings have come to regard psychology as the decipherer of illness.

4. In that I came across Farber and Heiftez's study after writing Chapters 5 and 6, I am gratified to find the considerable agreement between their findings and my own impressions, which were not contaminated by *ex post facto* reasoning.

5. Farber and Heifetz (1982) describe burned-out practitioners as "cynical toward their clients, blaming them for creating their own difficulties or labeling them in derogatory terms. To maintain a safe emotional distance from an unsettling client, professionals may increasingly resort to technical jargon and refer to clients in diagnostic terms. Furthermore, the emotional frustrations attendant to this phenomenon may lead to psychosomatic symptoms (e.g., exhaustion, insomnia, ulcers, headaches) as well as to increased family conflicts."

Chapter 7
The Qualities of the Practitioner

The Shaman's path is unending. I am an old
man and still a *manatsi* [baby] standing before
the mystery of the world, filled with awe.
—Statement of a Shaman of an Eskimo culture
as reported by Joan Halifax (1979)

THE MOTIVATIONS OF THOSE DRAWN
TO PRACTICE PSYCHOTHERAPY

It is the hope of many laypeople and practitioners alike that
the practice of psychotherapy will eventually become a legitimate scientific endeavor, with a verified body of principles, techniques, and methodologies. Under these conditions, we might be
able to predict with perhaps statistical significance those students, trainees, and candidates who will become successful practitioners and to know what training they will require. At that
time, standards of conduct might be sufficiently developed to insure the integrity of effective therapeutic work. But psychotherapy today is more of an intuitive art than a science (Goldberg,
1977). The relationship between psychotherapeutic skill and
personality attributes is, as Ralph Greenson (1966) has indicated, so complex that we have not yet defined those personal
qualifications of the practitioner that may be more influential in
the outcome of therapeutic work than are the quality and pre-
cision of the practitioner's methodology. Moreover, it is question-

able whether there is a single best type of therapist. Correspondingly, there is no single type of motivation, nor any unitary type of character that is drawn to the profession of psychotherapy. The motives vary from individual to individual. They are found in a combination of intellectual interests, unconscious wishes to address inner psychological conflicts of one's own, need to care for others, and prestige values fostered by the considerable status afforded psychotherapists by society.

However, having said this, I wish to emphasize that I do not believe that there are as wide a range of personalities among psychotherapists as there are in any professional group, as the eminent psychiatrist Judd Marmor (1953) and some other practitioners seem to believe. I have shown evidence in Chapter 4 that certain common background factors and early life experiences greatly limit the type of person who is drawn to practice psychotherapy. These commonalities in backgrounds foster certain specific traits and personality attributes which appear to draw people towards an interest in understanding and dealing with psychological problems. The sensitivity to unresolved conflict in the family served as the crucible to later career choice for the person. But this is true only to the extent that the therapist-to-be experienced, at least some *success* in supporting and nurturing others. If not, although the person may have been highly sensitized to unmet family needs, other career choices were probably sought.

There is reason to believe that there are specific types of people who are drawn to practice psychotherapy. Ella Sharpe (1947) long ago indicated that students gravitate toward psychoanalysis by two main routes. The first she called the *objective* (or scientific). Psychoanalysis offered these students a means of examining the obstinate problems of human existence. The second she referred to as the *subjective* (or emotional) route. This path to becoming a practitioner is taken by students who seek to gain enlightenment in others' problems in order to better understand their own emotional difficulties.

A clinical psychologist and personality theorist, J. F. Rychlak, has developed a typology of motives similar to that suggested by Sharpe. Based upon his impressionistic investigation he has reported three broad, somewhat overlapping but, nevertheless, differing motives for doing psychotherapy. For Rychlak they have to do with defining psychotherapy as *insight, cure,* or *self-growth.* The three corresponding motives for practicing psychotherapy are the scholarly, the ethical, and the creative (Rychlak, 1965).

THE SCHOLARLY MOTIVE

These are people who practice psychotherapy to learn more about people in the objective sense that Sharpe referred. Rychlak includes Sigmund Freud in this category, pointing to the well-documented statements by Freud that he was never greatly interested in being a physician. His interests were not primarily to cure so much as curiosity and the desire to draw general universal principles about human behavior in order to help resolve universal social problems. Thus, Freud's main emphasis in the technique of psychoanalysis was a tool for discovering truths about humanity, rather than a means for the amelioration of individual patients. This does not necessarily produce an ineffectual practitioner, but may, in fact, contribute to therapeutic effectiveness, as I will seek to demonstrate later in this chapter.

The relationship of Freud's Jewish cultural values to his scholarly pursuit still has significance to those who become practitioners today. Henry (1971) indicates that over 50 percent of the practitioners in his large study were Jewish or of Jewish extraction. Burton (1972) argues that:

> The archetypal values of being a Jew, reinforced by ever-present survival needs, are part and parcel of what every Jewish boy has dinned into him. Only a rare few can escape their fate. One of the values is the love of wisdom and the love of learning. In [the cities of] Lvov or Kiev, the Jewish father was not expected to work and support his family. His work was to study the Talmud and become wise in Jewish ritual and law. The rabbi was not only a religious and spiritual man but was the secular leader of the community. He served as judge and jury about most matters of daily living. He was the wise old man backed by millennial tradition, contact with God, and morality, and an ethic of health and happiness. (p. 13)

These archetypal values—whether they emerge in the backgrounds of a child from a Jewish family or from a non-Jewish family (with similar archetypal values)—shape the calling for practicing psychotherapy. These are people who rather typically have an accentuated need to understand themselves and others and to help others understand and come to terms with their way of seeing the world. Jewish tradition strongly emphasizes that the individual's life is a treasure to be lived fully. To do so, each person must be willing to examine his/her own motives and deepest fears. This exploration necessitates the individual asking him/herself in countless ways and situations the question, "Why are we [am I] in the world?"

Those who become psychotherapists seem to view and respond to this question in particular ways. Psychotherapists seem to share a view about human conflict. Conflict generally is regarded by them as a struggle between feeling and reason. But unlike the dictates of moral philosophy of the past, neither reason nor feeling is regarded as the authentic faculty. Conflict is regarded as inherent in the human condition predicated on the demands of a preexisting society on the emergence of each individual consciousness. Psychotherapists seem to believe that people are born into a culture that defines to the smallest degree the acceptable and rejected behavior of our existence. If we were a simple organism whose function was to maintain itself in a hedonistic yet energetically conservative fashion, these strictures would not invite our regard, if indeed, they would exist at all. However, as the chapter on the personal journey should suggest, we are not creatures whose enduring pleasure can be simply met. We are complex beings who, at times, risk the simple pleasures and security we have gained in quest of more substantial joys and personal enrichment. We, then, are not creatures whose destiny is to fulfill our culturally prefabricated dictates, but beings whose quest is perpetual self-exploration and whose nature is never final and resolute unless we recant from the ordeal and give in to the cultural strictures. Human nature, if unfettered, is seen as continuously emerging and being redefined in terms of new experiences—new perceptions, ideas, feelings, and relationships.

Nevertheless, in the culture in which we dwell our intrapsychic and interpersonal explorations are transacted. We can never escape grappling with the terms of this human condition. As fully functioning individuals, consequently, we can no more disregard the demands of society than we can deny the prompting of our emergent being. To avoid the dilemma of embracing one set of demands at the unrealistic exploitation of the other, the individual must avoid the dilemma of regarding the human condition as a question that demands an answer. If the human condition is a problem, then it is a problem without an answer (Watts, 1961).

Our emerging nature is never finally perfected, nor are cultural demands ever absolutely set. Our own nature and the demands of others are in perpetual struggle. We may opt out and surrender our autonomy. In so doing, we become objects for others to manipulate, like, for example, a hospitalized patient who is pushed back and forth in a stereotype role as a categorical object rather than as a human being. In this way, we allow others to project their own torments and demands upon us and we will not protest or assert who we are and what we strive to be (Goldberg, 1970).

Psychotherapeutic examination stands neither for the demands of the culture nor for the separation of the individual from his/her social context—rather, it is a struggle which is authentic and must be viewed optimistically, although we realize that it is never resolved.

THE ETHICAL MOTIVE

Rychlak refers to Carl Rogers as the prototype of the practitioner whose practice is derived from an ethical motive. Rogers's theoretical and technical contributions have focused upon those aspects of the therapeutic situation that promotes what Rychlak refers to as "the ethics of self-determination through competent interpersonal relation."

Practicing from an ethical stance, whether as a theologian or as a psychotherapist, as I have already tried to demonstrate, derives from a sense of calling. It may seem pretentious to claim that the person who is drawn into the practice of psychotherapy does so as a spiritual calling. Nevertheless, it seems accurate to affirm that the choice of practice is not a simple, intentional vocational selection but has to do with early urgings to help others. The ways in which this motive is expressed in adulthood may take on a certain legitimacy of proficiency which stands in stark contrast to the helpless frustration many of the autobiographical accounts of psychotherapists revealed that they experienced in a nurturer role in childhood. Henry's research readily demonstrates that people who go into the mental health field frequently see themselves as more enlightened either socially, politically, spiritually, or intellectually than most other people. Of course, other types of people hold this belief, as well. It is the family nurturing role, however, that impels them with this sense of enlightenment to assist others in their own journeys for enlightenment.

The contrasting juxtaposition of childhood inadequacy and the adult expression of superiority suggests to me that one of the basic reasons people are drawn to a service profession has to do with an attempt to quiet their own concerns and apprehensions about human existence. The concern that a healing profession is founded on involves the question of what leads to human suffering—such questions as what induces internal suffering, why do people allow others to treat them as they do, and is suffering a destiny.

Not altogether consciously, psychotherapists are drawn to their subject matter in a magical hope that if they could study people long enough and intimately enough, they may come upon the eternal secret—the key to the mysteries of human existence. Lopez-Ibor, a Spanish analyst, tells us that he decided to study medicine so that he could draw closer to the mysteries of human existence (Burton, 1972). Such practitioners wish to learn to avoid the plights that have made other people fearful and incompetent to deal with universal uncertainties. We're all concerned about the fact that other people don't always understand us. We are distressed that they don't always care about us in the ways we would like. We wish we were stronger, smarter, and more able to accomplish what we want. We're also, at least in the periphery of our consciousness, aware of our finiteness. We know we are growing older. We fear that we are losing our vitality, our attractiveness, and our interest to other people. We try to find ways to assuage these fears and their painful awareness. But for us as practitioners "legitimately" to fashion solutions to these uncertainties in terms of the people we are, we need to feel that these solutions are part of an ethic of self-growth available to all—especially, to our own clients. Winnicott (1963) speaks of the capacity for concern as an outgrowth of the guilt experienced for ambivalent feelings toward those who cared for us in our own childhoods. We resolve our anxiety for harboring destructive feelings by being highly sensitive to the feelings of those who nurtured us. We continue to seek approval and to suppress our guilty feelings by generalizing these sensitive and responsive concerns to others in the world.

One practitioner told of a childhood and adolescence in which she felt considerable guilt because both her working-class parents held extra jobs and utilized all their savings to send her to boarding school and provide her with an excellent education. She felt a debt to them for giving her more than she felt she deserved. She could not return caring feelings towards them, however, because of suppressed rage. Her parents continually reminded her of what they were doing for her. Not being able to be intimate with her own family, she became an expert family therapist. In this way she nurtured others and satisfied her parents' philanthropic values at the same time.

Succinctly stated, to the extent that we feel guilty for our selfish and disdaining attitudes toward others, we develop ways of being helpful, caring, and concerned about others. Consequently, as practitioners, to pursue self-interest, given our character formation, we need to perceive these pursuits as having a corresponding altruistic possibility. So if, for instance, we go to a lecture or a workshop, we believe that we are attending not only because of our own interest, but also because it may abet our work with our clients.

THE CREATIVE MOTIVE

Quite obviously, people come to psychotherapy to be cured of their symptoms, their illnesses, and their unhappiness. However, those who practice psychotherapy seem to believe that if happiness is the ultimate goal of living fully, and if reparations are to be made for symptoms and illness, these objectives can only be derived from examining one's life and one's inability to find happiness in oneself and fashioning a new and creative way of being. Jewish mothers tell their children that it is a *mizvat*—that is to say, a blessing—to help people. It is deeply grounded in the archetypal values of being a Jew. It is also inherent in other moral traditions concerning human responsibility. Many of us feel guilty if we allow people to remain in pain. However, the specific kind of helping that we attempt is determined by experiential factors backed, of course, by the particular endowment we bring to the situation.

One practitioner's mother instilled in him a guilt for not helping those who were suffering but, at the same time, he came to believe that everything she told him was invalid for him. Thus, he unconsciously avoided situations that required his direct assistance with pain and suffering. He did help friends and people who were told of his intellectual faculty, but in terms of reasoning and creative solutions rather than by the expression of direct caring. Consequently, he was rather amazed during his formal training as a psychiatric resident to have patients express, with rather obvious sincerity, the appreciation of having been helped by their working together. He was responding to his mother's script for him but denying it at the same time, because her demand and his lack of trust in her beliefs were rationally inconsistent.

Autobiographies of famous therapists indicate that they had not completely resolved their own family romance. They are unusually sensitized by that proclivity to the emotional pain and suffering of the human condition. Identifying with those who suffer is a universal human attribute; and we are more puzzled by the lack of demonstration of kindness, caring, and humanity—even in our present cynical world—than in its expression. Nevertheless, psychotherapists seem to be, in their autobiographical accounts in Burton's book, even more sensitized to the deprived, the helpless, and the maimed than are most other people. In an earlier work, Burton (1970) indicated that the identification with suffering contains a basic rage "which motivates humanitarian efforts. This is the rage of aloneness and the requisite compensatory efforts to dispel it."

I agree with Burton, but I also believe that the rage against human suffering has to do with the sense of unfairness which some of us feel rather acutely. This rage may be rather influential in choosing one type of service profession rather than another.

What I mean by this is that not only are our societal institutions based upon regulated systems of expected and sanctioned, proper (that is, fair) exchange among social units, but a person's choice of life-style may, as well, reflect personal struggles with the meaning of equity. This was certainly true of my choice of a professional career. I was encouraged as a college undergraduate to pursue a medical career, but that was emotionally unacceptable to me. I have always felt uncomfortable with persons who are severely physically disabled, particularly if they were born that way or if they could do little to improve their condition. I felt uncomfortable because I could not discern in what way these persons were responsible for their afflictions. If they were not responsible, then their condition seemed to be grossly unfair. I am more comfortable with persons who suffer from emotional disturbance. Their condition has greater clarity and meaning for me, because I can generally discern how they are "responsible" for how others treat them. Because emotional distress has greater meaning for me than physical illness, I feel that I can be helpful to persons suffering from the former to a far greater extent than to those suffering from the latter.

Considering that there are several different motives for practicing psychotherapy, one might wonder if there is a preferred route for those who might be the most able practitioners. Sharpe's classical paper (1947) suggests that it would be a mistake to open only one door for therapeutic apprenticeship. She argues that psychotherapeutic practice and research requires people who have entered the field from both the objective and subjective paths. But she wisely indicates that to practice effectively the analyst needs to combine both attitudes. In her words,

> the scientific observer accustomed already to collecting and scrutinizing data from external objects, must, if he would understand human nature include himself as an object of inquiry. He may intellectually accept the concepts of psycho-analysis but there can be no inner conviction concerning their physical truth until through the subjective experience . . . he arrives finally at the same place from which the student starts who comes first to psycho-analysis in order to understand his own inner disharmony. The latter student is called upon to proceed through the discipline of facing his inner conflicts to the objectivity which characterizes the scientific spirit.

In purviewing the autobiographies of famous therapists (Burton, 1972), Sharpe's contention seems to be borne out. It seems to me that each of these men became renowned not only because of his reputation as a practitioner but also because of interest and proficiency in other areas of the profession. In short, each seemed highly directed toward at least two of the three motives postulated by Rychlak. I am not saying, of course, that celebrated practitioners are necessarily the most skillful and astute. Indeed, I am leery of those practitioners who spend considerable time on television talk shows or promotional tours for their books or for their radical new psychotherapy institutes. At best, these practitioners have little available time for careful work with clients. Moreover, many of them as self-promoters may be more concerned with selling their clients a technique and a life-style than in helping them come to terms with where their clients are "at." Just as the best teachers go unsung, perhaps, also, do the "best" psychotherapists. They don't write books, give lectures, or even teach. They are known only to their clients.

What I am saying is that the influence of the famous psychotherapist in Burton's book seems to have been derived from their combining several motives. And there is every reason to contend that this admixture of interests contributes to their therapeutic skill, as well. A practitioner, at best, is not only a skillful listener and interpreter, but is also a scientist who knows how to pose hunches and verify them in the material clients bring in. The practitioner is also an effective teacher in abetting clients' curiosity, interest (and, perhaps, even excitement) in learning about themselves and the world in which they live. Warkentin has said it well: "A good therapist includes being a good teacher, a sincere friend, a student of people, a lively person, and especially a good lover" (Burton, 1972; p. 261).

THE QUALITIES OF THE PRACTITIONER

I will, in this section, discuss the specific qualifications of the psychotherapist, at the same time admitting that there is no single best type of personality for practice. Of course, the personality of the therapist is of immense importance. Due to the interpersonal nature of practice the personality characteristics of the therapist are often regarded as the most important factor in determining the outcome of psychotherapy. This has led many to regard psychotherapeutic practice as an art (Bandura, 1956).

The practitioner's personality and character must be such that he/she can be personally and intimately committed as an involved person. In general, the practitioner must be able to be open with others and capable of engendering mutual trust. This is borne out in a study by Henry Grunebaum of Harvard Medical School (1983). He asked a group of psychotherapists—including practitioners from the four mental health disciplines—the important personal qualities in the practitioners they have chosen for themselves. Most respondents mentioned "warmth, liking, caring, and support" as crucial characteristics.

They chose a person who would provide them with a "feeling of being approved, appreciated, and respected." In contrast, they rejected practitioners whom they regarded as "cold fish, too distant, and ungiving."

In addition to the qualities mentioned in Grunebaum's study, an effective practitioner must have such skills as conceptual and intellectual ability. The therapist has to be able to move confidently from the concrete to the general and then to the abstract in order to understand what the client is referring to which cannot be meaningfully understood simply in terms of the discrete events and happenstance being described. Similarly, the practitioner must also be able to understand these discrete events in terms of pressing human concerns. In this endeavor, the practitioner should be able to help the client abstract and generalize the particular situation the client is dealing with to the central issues of the client's life.

To be able to perform these intellectual and dialogical tasks, the practitioner must have the ability to communicate effectively. Rudyard Kipling commented that words are our most powerful drug. Among the verbal skills he/she possesses, the practitioner should be able to mirror and echo what the client seems to be saying, but cannot effectively articulate in words, against what resonates within the practitioner's own psyche. To do this the practitioner should be able to communicate at different levels, to use his/her voice with varying modulations, and with a wide variety of expressiveness. The practitioner should be capable of employing vivid examples and analogies to converse with clients who possess intellectual skills, conceptual abilities, levels of education, and life experiences different from his/her own.

Paramount in the practitioner's skill is the ability to concentrate deeply and listen attentively. The recent work of practitioners such as Lacan, Schafer, Langs, Bion, and others have opened up new perspectives on listening which may serve to enhance our empathic comprehension of clients.

With deep listening as a stimulus, the therapist must be able to think metaphorically, and so doing, find illustrations, poetic phrases, philosophical associations, and literary references, as well as everyday phrases and expressions that contain the essence of what the client seems to be trying to express. In short, the practitioner must be able to combine practical experience with artistic awareness, as well as to combine technical knowledge of the tools of human interaction with the wisdom of deeply lived experience.

There are important attitudinal considerations, as well. Primarily, the therapist must be a person of good will. The practitioner should be hopeful and courageous. Therapeutic practice rests upon the assumption that although life is difficult, and the path through personal journey is not always clear, that by dealing steadfastly with one's own concerns, human life will be enhanced.

Still other attitudinal qualities are of special importance for becoming a competent practitioner. The therapist must have a capacity for both intimate and appropriate distance. This involves the practitioner being actively interested and curious about people, including the details of their lives. At the same time, the practitioner must be reflective about what the client is dealing with in terms of the client's intentionality and how these issues reflect the therapist's own experiences, particularly issues to which the practitioner has not given sufficient attention.

The practitioner should be a person who doesn't use curiosity about people in hostile ways. Kohut (1977) has cautioned us that empathy can be used in very destructive ways. Failures in therapeutic empathy underlie many of the difficulties and impasses encountered in treatment. The practitioner, therefore, must possess humility and a sense of decency. Even some of the best trained practitioners lack some of these vital traits. I once worked with a psychoanalyst who was regarded as an excellent supervisor and teacher. In a supervisory conference he strongly recommended that practitioners do as he does—charge group therapy patients for every missed session. This in itself is not remarkable, but in the event that only one or two appear for the group, he requests that they have an individual session instead of meeting with both in a group, and charges them *additionally* for the individual session (although he is getting paid already by all the group patients for the group time). His attitude seems to evidence boredom with practice and the need to get paid extra for his work, as the former reasons and benefits of practice were no longer sufficient. Such practitioners, I have found, have rescinded their capacity for self-criticism and the willingness to examine their own motives. On the other hand, the practitioner mentioned above had "solutions," "answers," and "uncontestable" interpretations for any clinical issue raised by colleagues and students in supervision.

The practitioner must also possess a capacity for nonintrusive caring (which will be extensively examined in Chapter 10). Unfortunately, there is often an inter-relationship between being intellectually sharp and sharp interpersonally. This is why many practitioners with fine minds are good theoreticians, diagnosticians, and researchers but are not effective psychotherapists. They lack sufficient sensitivity, empathy, and humility. They don't realize or seem to care that clients need to find their own solutions and cannot do so in a climate in which their therapist feels superior to them. Possessing psychological knowledge does not capacitate a person to become a competent practitioner. Wisdom is also required. Wisdom has an emotional component which knowledge generally does not. Wisdom consists of compassion and common sense. Unless the practitioner combines his/her knowledge and skills with compassion, common sense, and a sense of decency, the practice of psychotherapy is little more than an exercise in logic and aesthetics.

As an applied art rather than a science, in addition to knowledge, intellect, and good will, other factors are required for effective work. The availability of the practitioner's affective life, especially the capacity for concern, involvement, and interest are essential. In this respect, I believe I was a better therapist when I began my practice with an eagerness to learn about myself through other people than I was as a far more knowledgeable and seasoned practitioner who felt, frequently, that "I've seen it all already," during my disillusionment as a practitioner, of which I spoke in Chapter 2. Only now that I have rejoined my personal journey am I able to reach clients whom I may not have been able to reach if I had worked with them several years ago.

Finally, the practitioner who has a healthy sense of humor is well-served. Naturally, if the practitioner is not comfortable with wit, it is better if it is not forced. Creativity, flexibility, and optimism in finding ways of orchestrating tensions in order to go deeper into meaningful dialogue with clients serve, at least, as well.

In short, the practitioner must have at least the following qualities: The ability to use his/her own being; interest in other people; the potential for emotional intelligence and self-awareness; humility; courage; capacity for intimacy; curiosity; creativity; flexibility; optimisim; humor; and problem-solving skills. Different kinds of personalities have such qualities and may be equally suited as therapists (Foulkes & Anthony, 1957). Furthermore, whereas the very gifted and the poorly qualified may be easily recognized, often it is difficult to differentiate adequate therapists from simply mediocre ones. Perhaps the approach to defining a good or adequate therapist may be misleading and fatuous. Therapists have come to realize that no one kind of ameliorative approach is effective with all clients or even consistently successful with the same individual. Correspondingly, every therapist is not equally comfortable and successful with each of the therapeutic tasks at his/her disposal. The therapist's work must be a creative endeavor in which his/her style and the technique employed are congruent with his/her own personality, temperament, and the demands of the therapeutic situation (Foulkes & Anthony, 1957). The question, "What is the best therapeutic approach?" becomes "What is the best therapeutic approach for whom and by whom?" My opinion is that the personality theories upon which particular psychotherapeutic methodologies are based are not equally applicable for all age groups nor for all types of people. For example, certain psychotherapeutic systems seem more accurately descriptive of particular periods of life: Freudian psychoanalysis best captures childhood; Adlerian individual psychology, young adulthood, Jungian analytic psychology, the middle years, etc.

Obviously, a trained therapist is a better therapist than one without training. In addition to the necessary personal qualifications, a competent therapist should have adequate background in three areas: education, supervision, and experiential training.

EDUCATION

It is first necessary to distinguish between education as a person—wide liberal arts background—and education as a professional psychotherapist. The education of the psychotherapist-to-be should not have been overly weighted in favor of science and technical methodology. Phillip Rieff (1968) points to certain negative consequences of medical requirements for practicing analysis, considerations which hold true for all kinds of psychotherapy:

> More often than not, the contemporary candidate for training in one of the institutes is straight out of medical school with precisely the wrong kind of education, for which a reading of Freud's case histories and various other courses in the development and structure of psychotherapy cannot compensate. [In contrast] the early psychoanalysts were *educated* men

First, it might be best to start psychotherapists-to-be in another field than psychology or medicine, such as literature, history or theology This is based upon the belief that before you can examine human problems, it is useful to become aware of what it means to be human. (Le Shan, 1984). Without the leveling influences of humanism, science tends to become mechanical and aimless. A serious and continuing interest in history, philosophy, and the arts is indispensible for a practitioner who is required to relate conversantly with people in all walks of life and who are troubled by many of the same concerns that have plagued people from the dawn of time. In training and supervising psychotherapists I find that many practitioners are frequently ignorant of philosophy and the metaphysical premises behind psychological ideas and practices. This ignorance confounds our theories and our clinical work. (I will examine these premises in Chapter 13.)

Another positive effect of humanism on clinical practice is that it is to be hoped that it would lessen the tendency of some practitioners to approach psychotherapy as a business rather than a service. Rieff (1968) tells us that some psychotherapy institutes have become trade schools preparing the candidate "for accreditation and the good life in some suburb."

In a word, the practitioner should have a broad, liberal education. He/she should be well-read in literature, philosophy, sociology—perhaps, ideally, in all possible areas, because the issues his clients bring to him may involve any of these areas. Not that he/she can become an expert, or as knowledgeable as clients in any of these areas, but he/she should be conversant with a broad spectrum of human thought and concern. For example, he/she may be working with an adolescent boy who reads comic books. To have some appreciation of the experience of this boy, it would be useful if the practitioner knew the kind of thought and conceptualization that goes on in this medium. Moreover, he/she should have academic training and preparation in all aspects: biological, philosophical, the physical

sciences, the social sciences, etc. His/her clinical training, furthermore, should not be too restricted in terms of any school of
thought, or any particular technique. He/she should be conversant with the whole spectrum of psychotherapy practice. Most
importantly, in terms of his/her academic and clinical training,
he/she should be appreciative of the discipline of dialectic dialogue. Dialectic discipline is an indispensable conceptual, and interactional tool for the psychotherapist. Studying dialectics enables the practitioner to understand how people interact and
develop ideas, formulating reactions in terms of the synthesis
and the point-counterpoint progression that is implicit in the
process of dialogue. Training in the dialectic process is a very
important area of experience for the practitioner. The dialectic
tradition in depth psychology can be traced back to the Socratic
method.

Socrates was a turning point in the history of Western philosophy. Unlike the pre-Socratic philosophers, who were mainly
concerned with the nature of the physical universe, Socrates was
obsessed with the human condition. His philosophical inquiry
concentrated entirely upon the problems of human life; that is
to say, to understand what it means to be a human being and
for what purpose one was in the world. Socrates equated knowledge with virtue, allowing for no compromise in its pursuit. For
him, knowledge was a real, personal conviction—a direct and
compelling inner vision of virtue, which comes only from one's
own efforts to understand (Chessick, 1982). Because of the importance of this subject and because I have found specifics of dialectic dialogue extremely helpful in the development of intimacy and the personal journey, I have devoted Chapter 11 to
this topic.

A practitioner must, of course, have a sound background in
the social sciences and scientific methodology. The practitioner
requires a comprehensive knowledge of theories of personality,
theories and techniques of psychotherapy, and theories of psychopathology. The therapist should also be thoroughly conversant with studies of group dynamics and small groups (the latter would provide him/her with an understanding of the vital
interrelation between personality development and milieu). In
short:

Education in psychotherapy should be designed to provide
sound grounding in present knowledge and skills, yet enhance

the student's awareness of how current approaches are but a point in historical development. The aim should be to convey knowledge and principles without dogmatism and rigid adherence to techniques qua techniques. Acknowledging the inevitability and desirability of change in the field should make it clear to the student that without his future creative and innovative contributions, the art and science of psychotherapy will become stagnant. (Bookbinder, Fox, & Rosenthal, 1969)

It is hard to conceive of an individual acquiring the forementioned knowledge, which can be regarded as only minimal preparation for being a practicing psychotherapist, without at least a graduate degree.

Psychotherapy educators argue as to whether training as a practitioner should be eclectic or devoted extensively to one theoretical position. Those who contend for a single position claim that those who study a little Freud, some behaviorisms, some cognitive theory and so forth know only a little about anything. These people are widely read, but shallow and skeptical of everything. I believe, however, that those who are only trained in a single theory are even worse off. They have to latch on to often inappropriate theory to explain and deal with anything they encounter in their work. They have difficulty knowing whether or not it is inappropriate because they have no other reference with which to compare it.

THE APPRENTICESHIP OF THE PRACTITIONER

Ernest Kris spoke of the practitioner's "formulative decade." He, like many master analysts in the past, believed that it was not possible to become a competent practitioner in less than ten years. In times past, practitioners spent many years, perhaps most of their professional careers, in apprenticeship with eminent and expert practitioners. They worked in psychiatric hospitals, clinics, family service agencies, and other institutions, acquiring their clinical skills with a wide range of patients and clinical concerns. After many years of training and clinical experience some began to see a few clients independent of their institutional work. Only a few psychoanalysts, some psychiatrists and even fewer clinical psychologists went into full-time private practice. This has greatly changed in recent years. There is a steady flow of practitioners into independent practice. Graduate students generally cannot wait to enter independent practice. Many prepare their professional cards while still in school, and some even practice privately before they graduate. These factors strongly suggest the growing depreciation for the need for apprenticeship in psychotherapy.[1] In my view, since psychotherapy is a creative art there is more of a need for apprenticeship than if psychotherapy were a science, such that a formula for practice and a proven methodology could be utilized in all clinical situations by any knowledgeable practitioner. As a creative art, the practitioner must develop therapeutic abilities over time under the guidance of experienced, expert practitioners. *Mentoring* is important to apprenticeship because while you cannot teach essential attitudinal qualities for practice such as common sense, humility, and decency, the mentor can model them in his/her dealings with students and others.[2]

Very few of the famous psychotherapists found in Burton's book had considerate things to say about their own personal or training analysis. In fact, several expressed extremely negative feelings about their personal experience. But what does come through in contrast is that most of these practitioners had a great deal of affection and appreciation for the person with whom they were in analysis. Although they felt that the process was defective, they also felt that their analyst had "tried hard and was quite human about it" (Burton, 1972, pp.313–314).

SUPERVISION

In many ways, supervision is the pivotal experience for the trainee in psychotherapy. It is the meeting ground between the practical, the theoretical, and the personal. To maximize the effectiveness of their relationship, the supervisor and supervisee need to relate to one another, similar to the therapist and client, in terms of their reaction to one another in the immediate situation rather than in regard to formal principles of therapeutic practice or on the basis of their previous experience with similar relationships. This highly immediate and personal aspect makes supervision a particularly relevant training device for the inexperienced therapist whose concerns go beyond the question of "proper" technique and "correct" understanding of the patient's behavior.

Generally, the most pressing concern of the inexperienced therapist is "what he/she is all about" as a person in a therapeutic encounter with another. Attention to the immediate personal aspects of psychotherapeutic training discourages an artificial distinction between didactic and practical education. The supervisor should be a good example in terms of clinical excellence rather than on the basis of academic achievement. The supervisor:"must be that which he attempts to teach others to be. It is not sufficient for the teacher to be highly competent in psychotherapy research or the teaching of psychotherapy theory" (Bookbinder et al., 1969, p. 4).

EXPERIENTIAL TRAINING

It is my belief that the traditional methods for training practitioners to work with others through passive and intellectual reception of theory and methodology need to be recast. Emphasis should be on learning through dynamic interaction, learning by participation, both as a leader and as a follower. One cannot properly attend to another's needs if he/she cannot experientially attune him/herself to the thoughts and feelings of others. Therefore, the therapist should obtain the direct experience of being "on the couch" as well as sitting "behind the couch." Personal dyadic therapy is highly important to the practitioner, but no less important is his/her exposure to a wide array of psychotherapy experiences. While in training the practitioner should be a participant in various types of psychological demonstrations and experience.

PERSONAL PSYCHOTHERAPY
FOR PRACTITIONERS

Research data seem in agreement that therapy is apt to be most successful when a warm, giving, optimistic therapist feels comfortable and experiences an empathetic bond between himself and his/her client (Mahrer, 1970). Therapists are not capable of relating equally well with each client who enters their consulting room. Therapists empathize best (and probably are most effective) with clients who have similar personalities and conflict areas. On the other hand, the therapists who have been unable to resolve their own personal difficulties in certain areas will have distorted interpersonal perception in these areas. As a result, their effectiveness will be reduced in areas that they share with their clients and with which they have not themselves successfully dealt (Dymond, 1950; Jourard, 1959; Strunk, 1957).

Each client is helped by particular procedures and therapeutic conditions, depending upon the state of the practitioner's psychological maturity and the nature of previous psychosocial experiences. Correspondingly, a therapist feels most comfortable and works most effectively with a technique which is congruent with the compromises and resolutions to the crisis in his/her own development. The skills of the psychotherapy practitioner are most closely related to his own intrapsychic and interpersonal development than are the skills of other professional disciplines. The therapist must acquire a fund of existential knowledge and skill that differs from the "factual" orientation of the behavioral scientist. His/her work with relationships between people requires a sense of his/her personal place in the world. In short, conducting therapy is more than simply a cognitive endeavor. A therapist who is not in touch with his/her own feelings and is unable to recognize his/her own inappropriate responses cannot avoid subtly encouraging clients' resistence patterns, their unwillingness to face up to their own perturbance. A practitioner who has not confronted his/her own problems in personal therapy[3] can be expected to be uncomfortable with clients who confront the practitioner. A therapist who has had personal therapy is more apt to recognize countertransferential reactions. The practitioner without therapy is less apt to deal with his/her own irrational notions when called to task by clients. Such practitioners turn these threats to their leadership back on clients by suggesting that it is their problem, not that of the practitioner.

After having said this, it is also necessary to distinguish between personal psychotherapy taken on the practitioner's own behalf and a training analysis or psychotherapy. The unanswered question one encounters in examining the literature on required personal psychotherapy during training is whether this experience is generally helpful, only sometimes helpful, or, indeed, even antagonistic to the maturation of the practitioner's ability to reach clients. We cannot tacitly assume that a training analysis or therapy should be a mandatory component of sound clinical training. It seems quite reasonable to maintain,

as I have above, that practitioners who have had personal psychotherapy are more likely to be available for their clients and,
at the same time, to argue that required personal therapy during the period of training may be deleterious to the objective of
freeing up the trainee. The paucity of empirical research available on the subject, as Greenberg and Staller (1981) indicate,
linking personal therapy with outcome as a practitioner is incon-
clusive. In their recent paper, Greenberg and Staller report to
have found only eight studies in the literature that examine this
issue. According to the authors, "Two studies hint at a positive
effect, four find no major differences, and two indicate a negative
effect."

The negative effect makes sense when we realize that mandatory personal therapy for professional reasons rather than due
to a strongly felt need may cause considerable resentment and
resistance on the part of the trainee. This negative effect is further explained by a study by Shapiro (1976) of 121 graduates of
a psychoanalytic training institute. Whereas the vast majority
of practitioners who answered the author's survey regarded their
training analysis as promoting favorable gains,

> over a fourth of these graduated reported serious problems in
> analysis during training that could not be resolved during the
> time of their candidacy. A very large percentage of this subgroup
> acknowledged significant personal pathology which contributed
> in many cases to the difficulties they may have experienced
> within their analytic relationships or with the complexities of the
> training situation.

We might infer from these findings that the requirement of
personal therapy, while being basically sound, is, as a forced
component of training within a limited time period, likely to disregard the unique issues the trainee brings into the period of
training, and is, therefore, ultimately self-defeating. This is because, while psychotherapy may eventually work through the
trainee's conflictual issues, training therapy is hampered by the
time-constraint placed upon it from the trainee's desire to complete treatment in order to fulfill training requirements. Consequently, any trainee with a modicum of common sense will realize that entrenched psychological issues that require more time
to work out than the period of time the candidate wishes to devote to his or her apprenticeship, need to be suppressed and not

revealed to the training analyst or psychotherapist. This suppression may lead to feelings of shame and inadequacy, which contribute deleteriously to his or her clinical work. My own analytic supervisor during my institute days told of how his own training analyst neatly separated training from treatment, enabling my supervisor to use the sessions therapeutically and profitably. For the first year of his training analysis, my supervisor carefully avoided conflictual material, bringing up only issues that suggested that he was a healthy, well-integrated person. One afternoon his analyst broke convention and announced heartily, "I just wrote the report to the institute passing you. Now let's get down to work!"

Finally, we also need to look at an insidious side to using personal therapy as a training component. I will touch upon it only briefly. Many people who have come from other fields of endeavor have used their experience in psychotherapy as a patient as being the criterion and the justification for being a practitioner. They conduct themselves as practitioners with little or no training. I believe that this begs the question of what a practitioner is. I think there are experiences necessary to being a practitioner that cannot be derived simply from the experience of being a patient. I question, and strongly doubt, the contention that the major training dimension of being a practitioner is one of personal psychotherapy. I believe it is only one, albeit necessary, component of psychotherapeutic training and experience.

In short, a well-trained therapist has a balance of experience and training in all of the areas described in this chapter. It would be injudicious to consider only one or two of these areas as sufficient for competence in psychotherapy or to assume that an abundance of training in some areas can compensate for a deficiency of training in others. Each of these areas of training blend together with the necessary intellectual and emotional equipment into a dynamic and mature gestalt.

NOTES

1. All of Burton's therapists felt that their true growth had come from direct clinical work. Much of this was self-taught.

2. Freud pointed to the importance gained from a lasting personal relationship, which often results between the apprentice practitioner and the mentor.

3. According to both Henry's respondents and the famous practitioners studied by Burton, personal analysis or psychotherapy was regarded as the most valuable component of the practitioner's education and training. Ironically, in only one of the four mental health disciplines, psychoanalysis, is there a requirement of personal analysis as a training component. Direct, clinical experience was regarded as the second most important component, particularly, but not necessarily, if the experience was supervised by a seasoned and able practitioner. Several of the therapists studied by Burton revealed that a varied and demanding range of clinical experience was highly instrumental even with minimal or no supervision. Several were fortunate to observe able mentors. But several others discussed considerable disappointment in watching the ineptness of eminent mentors. O. S. English writes:

> I cannot recall that I learned anything whatever from psychoanalytic supervisors. . . not one of them ever said anything or commented on the work reported in a way that has remained with me. . . I have often wondered why such great names in the field seem to mean so little in my training when I can still recall the helpful impact of many an unpretentious clinic patient. (Burton, 1972, p. 93)

PART II:

The Practice of Being a Healer

Chapter 8
Starting a Private Practice

To see a world in a grain of sand,
And a Heaven in a wild flower,
Hold Infinity in the palm of your hand,
And Eternity in an hour.
— William Blake

The young professional who has recently finished graduate school with an interest in practicing psychotherapy might well ask where to begin. Statistically, he or she is among a service force in the United States today that includes approximately 31,000 psychiatric social workers, 29,000 psychiatrists, 26,000 clinical psychologists, 10,000 psychiatric nurses, and 10,000 people who call themselves counselors. They treat approximately 34 million people annually on a budget estimated to be about $13 billion (Sobel, 1980).

The neophyte needs to look at the mental health scene realistically. Proportionate to the increase in population in the United States, positions in the mental health field have greatly diminished from the 1960s when I finished graduate school. In the 1960s there seemed to be unlimited amounts of funding for public programs and of third-party insurance monies available for private practice psychotherapy. We live in more conservative times today, with dire concerns about balancing the national budget and bringing down interest rates. Under tight monetary regimes, fees for psychological services are phased out far sooner than those for missiles and aircraft.

Accordingly, highly qualified mental health practitioners are expensive, considering the shrunken budgets of public institutions. In order to keep costs down, administrators are willing to hire beginning and less qualified professionals, who merely meet the minimal qualifications for the legal and professional standards imposed on these institutions. Because medicine and nursing are the two most closely related professions in terms of medical and legal requirements for public institutions, there are currently more positions available for psychiatry and psychiatric nursing than for social work and psychology. However, because master's level social workers and master's level psychologists can generally be hired at a lower salary than can Ph.D. psychologists, master's level professionals find more job listings than do the more qualified psychologists.

The following are the major settings in which mental health positions are available:

1. General hospital in-patient units.

2. General hospital mental hygiene clinics.

3. General hospital special programs; e.g., drug and alcohol abuse programs.

4. Community (public) mental health clinics.

5. Private profit and nonprofit mental health clinics.

6. State psychiatric hospitals.

7. Private psychiatric hospitals and residential programs.

8. College counseling centers.

9. Federal Veterans Administration hospitals and clinics.

10. Federal and state hospitals in forensic settings.

Quite obviously, the kinds of clients and the encouragement and time available for intensive psychotherapeutic work will differ among the above-mentioned settings. Moreover, because of the expansion of psychiatric services to medical units, the time devoted to any one service function, including psychotherapy, is more limited today as compared with the long-term-treatment psychiatric hospitals of the past. Many of the mental health workers, who in the past would have worked exclusively with psychiatric patients in intensive psychotherapy in these institutions, today find themselves assigned to medical services where they do psychiatric consultation, treatment and discharge planning and abundant administrative paperwork, with time available for only brief psychotherapy.

The young professional should keep these factors in mind in choosing the setting in which his/her skills for psychotherapy can best be honed. Inexperienced practitioners should also expose themselves to areas of clinical experience in which they have had relatively little experience. I have found among those I have supervised that practitioners who have not had early clinical exposure to clients with severe pathology that their understanding and ability to work with resistive mechanisms in less severely disturbed clients is appreciably hampered. Having a clear sense of normal and creative human development is indispensable to the skills of the practitioner; but so is experience with severe psychopathology. Moreover, an exposure to a wide assortment of clients and service modalities enables practitioners to more judiciously select an area of interest in which they would like to specialize. In considering a position in an institution, practitioners should also decide what other role(s) they wish to fill, in addition to being a psychotherapist. As I have suggested, due to limited funding, the practitioner is expected to carry out other duties in addition to direct work with clients. These functions include: (1) administration; (2) research; (3) public or in-service education; (4) supervision of staff and/or trainees; and (5) diagnosis and evaluation.

The practitioner should also consider which modalities he or she would prefer to work with: (1) individual psychotherapy; (2) group therapy; (3) family therapy; (4) psychoanalysis; (5) psychodrama; (6) art or music therapy; etc. I would recommend a sufficient exposure to all these modalities.

REASONS FOR A CAREER
IN INSTITUTIONAL SETTINGS

Many professionals prefer to stay on indefinitely in institutional or clinic settings. For some there is a lack of interest in independent practice because of its business and managerial requirements. Among these practitioners there is a disdain for the competitive struggles for clients among mental health practitioners in private practice. Many social workers and psychiatric nurses, for example, feel that public opinion favors psychiatrists and psychologists in independent practice. Social workers and psychiatric nurses who have remained in institutional and clinic settings, while their psychiatrist and psychologist colleagues have gone into private practice, often assume leadership positions in these settings. These positions give them the prestige and personal satisfaction for their contributions to the institutions, which compensate for the benefits unique to independent practice.

In addition, there are mental health professionals, notably psychologists and some psychiatrists, with research interest in institutional settings. Administrations eager for additional funding, which can be brought in by research grants, often provide the opportunity and encouragement of heuristic pursuits in areas in which funding is available.

PRIVATE PRACTICE

Despite limitations on funding (as compared with the past), the independent practice of psychotherapy has become increasingly more attractive to practitioners in recent years. Having determined that being a psychotherapist is his/her calling, the practitioner will, undoubtedly, at some point consider the possibility of entering private practice. In considering independent practice the practitioner should realize that competence as a psychotherapist is not alone sufficient for the demands of private practice. Whereas the independent practice of psychotherapy is a service-oriented endeavor, it is, at the same time, a business, involved with practical and managerial concerns. Few practitioners have had sufficient training and knowledge in business management. There is little or no attention to these issues in clinical training. Rarely have I heard of graduate school courses which deal with the problems of building a private practice. I know of no graduate school course which squarely addresses such significant concerns of the independent practitioner as where to get referrals, how to become sufficiently well-known in the community as a practitioner and how to select those clients which best maximize the practitioner's current skills, conversant knowledge, and the kinds of practice and goals toward which he/she aspires. Yet, these are considerations necessary for building a successful practice. Consequently, the practitioner needs to learn how to competently deal with business concerns after leaving graduate school.

WAYS PRIVATE PRACTICE DIFFERS FROM INSTITUTIONAL PRACTICE

The practitioner who works within an institutional setting is influenced by the mores, values, and philosophy the key institutional personnel have toward psychotherapy. His/her clients are also deeply affected by the attitudes institutional personnel have toward psychological treatment. Much of the practitioner's time as a clinician or psychotherapist, whether he/she realizes it or not, deals with the chafe and the unsettled feelings in clients that come from negative or resistive views about psychotherapy in these institutions. The clinician is both a representative of the institution and an advocate of the examined life. If these two positions are in conflict, his/her relationship with clients can be severely impeded. Often the practitioner may have to decide whether it makes better sense to take either a therapeutic or an administrative role with any particular client. Moreover, the caseload of each practitioner is often so large as to mitigate against treatments of choice for particular patients. These are, in short, often severe limitations in practicing psychotherapy in an institutional setting, which are absent in independent practice. On the other hand, working for an organization offers a number of clear benefits in comparison with private practice. There are health insurance and retirement benefits. In private practice, if we are ill or take off for vacations and other personal needs, we are not allotted paid leave time as we are in working in institutions and agencies. We are not allocated time to attend professional meetings, deliver papers, and give presentations. There are other disadvantages to private practice. Because we are less likely to work collaboratively with colleagues in private practice, independent practice may be rather isolated and lonely. We have also to be able to take cases without close supervision available and nearby. Moreover, there are often in institutions interesting clinical cases that we may rarely see in private practice. In addition, because of the protection a custodial setting offers, we may treat cases in a custodial institution that would be too risky to treat in independent practice.

Finally, I wish to point out another important difference and expense for the practitioner who works in independent practice rather than in an agency. The independent practitioner must obtain both professional liability insurance for the conduct of psychotherapy—to cover possible legal costs incurred because of the supposed deleterious effects of the therapist's actions (or lack of appropriate action) in regard to clients; as well as office insurance for injuries or accident occurring on his/her property. (The latter is generally included in the former.) The fees for liability insurance vary according to which discipline the practitioner belongs to. The fee for physicians greatly exceeds that for psychologists and social workers. Generally, the association of one's discipline, being quite large, offers the least expensive rates. However, these associations cannot hold back the tide of large settlements directed at professional malpractice. In the period between 1984 and 1985 the cost of professional liability insurance for psychologists increased by 600 percent.

Of course, there are, conversely, a number of advantages to having one's own independent practice. The potential remuneration is considerably higher. The practitioner is relatively free of the politics and endless paperwork of institutions and agencies. There is no one but oneself and one's clients to whom the practitioner is responsible. In short, private practice, with its independence, fees, and recognition for the practitioner as a skilled independent may be a very attractive enterprise.

EVALUATING THE RISKS AND REWARDS OF PRIVATE PRACTICE

Among the rewards of private practice are status, recognition, and financial compensation. It also gives the practitioner, who wishes to be more flexible in his/her own life, the independent means of creating his/her own schedule and life-style—to work in a way that makes sense and is meaningful for the practitioner. Working in institutions with other groups of practitioners can be confining. The practitioner's time needs to mesh with the schedules and the needs of colleagues.

There are financial risks, on the other hand, for practitioners in private practice. Independent practitioners have to rely on themselves. They have to generate their own financial security. They cannot depend on a salary or other kinds of institutional means of securing their financial support. There are also other kinds of risks for independent practitioners. There are crises, legal concerns, and problematic clinical situations which they must handle alone. Contrastingly, while working with other practitioners in an institutional setting, individual practitioners have built-in-institutional mechanisms and other people there to protect them and to deal with many of the other kinds of concerns. In short, in deciding whether to start a private practice, practitioners should examine their apprenticeship. They must answer for themselves whether they can now work independently with the clients they anticipate treating. If they believe that they will be overwhelmed by some of the issues they will be dealing with, they need to obtain appropriate supervision and consultation.

PART-TIME OR FULL-TIME PRACTICE

Therapists must decide whether they can afford to go into full-time practice or whether they need to limit private practice to part-time work. Most practitioners start to work for an agency, an institution, or a group practice and over time begin to develop their own independent practice. At the point practitioners feel there are a sufficient number of clients being seen privately, and adequate referral sources, they must ask themselves whether this is the propitious moment to go into full-time practice. This is a nebulous and risky moment because clients may drop out of treatment, referral scources may not come through adequately, and practitioners give up a dependable income from institutional practice. The question of when to go into private practice full-time is one many therapists struggle with for a long time.

There is really no way of safely knowing when it is the right moment to enter independent practice. Of course, it is wisest to make the decision when the practitioner has enough referrals to have sufficient clinical hours in order to maintain an adequate livelihood. However, even after carefully examining what practitioners have going for them in terms of present clients and promised referrals, and realizing that they are taking a risk, practitioners might also realize that it is a risk they need to take.

If working in an institutional setting is severely stultifying to one's development as a psychotherapist, the risk of independent practice should be seriously considered.

BUSINESS ASPECTS OF PRACTICE

The person who goes into private practice must be aware of the financial and business questions and issues involved in practice. Anyone who goes into private practice has to be well aware that he/she is a business person, as well as a professional service provider. Many neophyte practitioners are rather idealistic, with considerable antipathy for business practices. To earn a livelihood in full-time private practice, the practitioner needs to overcome this antipathy. If he/she is uncomfortable about this, getting business and psychological consultation is necessary.

When psychotherapists choose to enter private practice, they are, in fact, choosing to go into business for themselves. Practitioners are responsible for conducting their practice in such a way as to gain a livelihood. The practitioner is responsible for finding an office, selecting furniture, buying stationery and office supplies, sending out announcements of the opening of the practice, and finding means of referral. The practitioner may also have to borrow money for dealing with expenses that will not be covered by the fees from the initial practice. Practitioners must also manage their own time, deciding how many days, evenings, or hours to rent office space from another practitioner or whether to invest in a full-time rental. Even if the practitioner works at a home office, to manage his/her time best the practitioner must decide on which days to be available for client scheduling and on which days or parts of days to continue to pursue other employment to ensure some income until the private practice is able to support the practitioner sufficiently. To reiterate, the majority of private practitioners are in part-time practice, as they do not reach a level of receiving referrals that they feel confident will support them.

The above are issues with which practitioners who work full-time for an institution or agency rarely need to concern themselves; or if they do, it doesn't have the same gravity as for those in business for themselves. Beginning practitioners or even journeyman therapists who are considering entering independent practice need to question seriously their attitudes about business. The early years may be difficult and stressful. Do they have the aptitude and conation to go into business for themselves? Many a superb practitioner is a horrible businessperson. Those who recognize the unwillingness to promote themselves and to do whatever is necessary to secure a steady practice are in a position to get business management assistance. Sometimes this means simply hiring an efficient office manager or secretary or engaging a public relations service, or using money managers for financial planning. Those practitioners who are appalled at having to promote themselves and cannot acquire sufficient referrals simply by their name and reputation are wise to confine their independent practice to a small, part-time one or eschew the idea completely. They may be happier and more competent practicing, teaching, and training others in institutional settings. There they can devote their full energies to what they do best and allow the administrative personnel to handle the business aspects of psychotherapy.

Many a beginner is lured by the status and relatively good remuneration offered by independent practice. It is generally true that a practitioner can make considerably more income than those who work in public institutions. Nevertheless, a principle inherent to all business enterprises—psychotherapy not being exempted—is that you must spend in order to make money. True, the expenditure for the psychotherapy practitioner may be less in terms of money allocations than in most other businesses, but the expenditures of time the practitioner must make may be considerable in terms of giving lectures, talks, workshops, and consultation to agencies and self-help groups for little or no fee. The practitioner may also need to be willing to accept "difficult" and "undesirable" clients from colleagues and resign him/herself to charging initially somewhat lower fees than well-known colleagues in order to secure clients who cannot afford the others' fees. The practitioner must also free his/her schedule for a certain amount of hours, and at least initially, take the risk of not filling them. In a word, initial practice has the risk of a considerable portion of the practitioner's time not being remunerated.

The propensity for business is not the same as the skill of being a psychotherapist. There are many fine psychotherapists whose personalities are not those which immediately inspire confidence and trust among potential clients. As distasteful as the idea may be, most practitioners are not able to secure an adequate practice without promoting themselves. Some personalities are more receptive toward and skillful at promoting themselves than are others.

In short, the practitioner whose name and reputation will not guarantee him/her a thriving practice is wise to begin independent practice gradually, trying to work out flexible hours with the present employer or even leaving a full-time position and finding part-time teaching or agency work as the practitioner gradually builds a private practice.

PROMOTING ONE'S PRACTICE

There are many ways of promoting one's practice—basically, it is to become visible in the community—to practitioners as well as to other kinds of allied professionals, and to the general public. The practitioner may do this by giving talks; writing books and articles; being on radio and TV shows; and making him/herself known to ministers, rabbis, priests, church and synagogue groups, and community agencies. Often, the practitioner does this by representing him/herself to the general public or to other practitioners as having specialized skills, special knowledge and expertise in some area of concern.

PUBLIC APPEARANCES

Obviously, if the therapist wants visibility, public appearances are very important. How the practitioner represents him/herself and appears to others should be closely considered. Some practitioners claim that the most effective way to succeed in independent practice is to have a flamboyant personality and offer techniques that bolster clients' defenses rather than probing the underlying causes of their suffering. The practitioner's attitude toward him/herself is reflected in choice of clothes, manner of speech, and style of interacting with others. The practitioner should consider whether a more flamboyant or more conservative presentation of self is consistent with the types of clients the practitioner is interested in attracting. This is to say, whether the practitioner wishes to be seen as a lively *bon vivant* or a conscientious, careful practitioner.

GETTING REFERRALS

Therapists who enter full-time independent practice, as I have already mentioned, usually do so by gradual stages. Initially, they may be their own best referral. They may be able to bring clients they have seen in clinics and institutions into their own part-time practice. Getting referrals can also begin with the place one was trained. Generally, there is some type of implicit (sometimes explicit) agreement between trainees and training directors. The agreement says, in effect, that if the practitioner is regarded as an ethical and competent practitioner that he/she can expect to get referrals from the training center—whether the setting be a graduate school, or a psychotherapy or psychoanalytic institution. It is advisable, therefore, that, when leaving a training center, one encourages the staff who refer clients to psychological services to include the practitioner on the referral list. The same holds true for practitioners leaving their jobs in institutional and clinic settings. Many of these agencies only provide services for clients who cannot afford the private practitioner's fees. It is wise to let key personnel in these agencies know that the practitioner is available and the types of clients he/she is most willing and able to work with.

Practitioners should also inform students whom they have taught and supervised that they have opened an independent practice. They should also notify former fellow students who have busy practices, former teachers and supervisors who thought highly of them, and even former personal therapists, of their availability. For it is these colleagues who know their work best. It is from these people, together with referrals from former clients, that the practitioner gets the most appropriate referrals for the kind of clinical work that he/she does best.

In this regard, it is prudent for the practitioner starting a private practice to inform referral sources of specific types of clinical problems and clients that he/she works with best; otherwise, the practitioner may be regarded as simply one of the many private practitioners to whom to refer. As I have already mentioned, there are specific kinds of difficult clients with whom the *busy* practitioner is not interested in working. If the beginning practitioner is willing to treat these clients and other clients who cannot afford the busy practitioner's standard fees, he/she is more likely to get referrals than if the practitioner is only willing to treat the YAVIS (young, attractive, verbal, intelligent, successful) and more affluent client. Moreover, the practitioner beginning a practice should consider doing consultations for agencies in order to increase visibility, recognition of skills, and, as a result, referrals.

Renting office space from a nonpsychiatric physician, an attorney, or a dentist may also be useful. These professionals frequently wish to refer away to others patients and clients who take up their time with complaints stemming from psychological issues. A psychiatrist may be reluctant to refer to another psychotherapist, particularly a nonmedical practitioner, because of competitive strivings. The nonpsychotherapist professional, on the other hand, is less likely to experience competitiveness in referring to a practitioner from another profession. Moreover, sharing office space enables the professionals from these different professions to get acquainted with each other's work. It improves the chance of referrals, of course, if a mutual liking develops.

Each city and each area of the country seems to have its own preferred types of treatment to address the social and clinical problems peculiar to that area. The beginning practitioner is prudent to survey the specific needs of the community in which he/she works. It may be helpful to survey statistical records of the kinds of problems most prevalent in his/her county and the availability of resources to handle those clinical problems. Obviously, the practitioner is more apt to get referrals for services undeveloped in his/her community than those in which there are sufficient resources.

Giving talks and workshops for the community—both for laypeople and professionals—increases one's visibility. This holds for consulting to family service and religious organizations as well. There is still another potential source of referrals today: the singles world has become a highly visible and well-organized population. Many singles experience considerable distress in adapting to and dealing with their situation. They usually have time, interest, and motivation for programs conducted by professionals on handling the concerns of single people.

THE IMPACT OF GEOGRAPHY ON TECHNIQUE AND APPROACH

In differing parts of the country—say, in rural as opposed to certain urban centers—people practice differently. In small towns, one is very visible. There, one can't always have the confidentiality one might in an urban area, where the practitioner is less likely to run across clients in their daily lives. Also, the way one gets referrals will certainly vary with the geographical area. If one has the unfortunate experience of a client becoming inordinately upset, or a client who feels the therapy has been a disaster, it can have a devastating effect in any setting, but in a small community word gets around more quickly.

FEES

The practitioner who is beginning practice has to decide a number of things: (1) the going rate in the community; (2) the going rate for someone of his or her experience; (3) the going rate for someone of his or her discipline; (4) the competition for clients in this particular community. Also: If the practitioner is less well-known than other practitioners, will he/she be losing out if he/she charges the regular going rate? But if the practitioner charges too little, can he/she afford to practice?

Fees, therefore, depend upon many determinants. It is somewhat influenced by the discipline the practitioner has been trained in. Despite the similarity of the psychotherapeutic work among fifth-profession (psychotherapy) practitioners, the public still makes a distinction and expects a differential fee schedule among the four disciplines of mental health. Fees are also affected by the amount of clinical experience, type of experience, and type of training and prestige of the training institutions in which the practitioner has been trained. Fees are further determined by the type of service provided. Psychotherapists generally charge either a fixed or sliding-scale (in terms of ability to pay) fee for the 45-minute individual session, the hour couple or family session, the 90-minute group session, the half-a-day group marathon, etc. A psychologist may charge a set fee for a diagnostic battery of tests, based not solely on the amount of time spent administering the tests to the client, but on the approximate amount of time required to score and interpret the findings as well. Moreover, if, e.g., the person who is being tested is a child, the fee is based not only on the amount of time taken to administer the test, but also on the time required to discuss the results with the child's parents and/or the school personnel. Similarly, a forensic (psychiatrist or psychologist) expert may set a fee based upon the actual number of hours he/she spent waiting and testifying on behalf of a client in court, or, more likely, will set a fee based on the time necessary for waiting and appearing in court, which requires leaving open a block of professional hours.

There is, as mentioned earlier, a range of prevailing fees determined by the geographical location in which one practices. Generally, fees among the fifth profession as a whole are higher in large urban centers than in rural areas. Insurance companies keep up-to-date actuarial figures on fees based upon the abovementioned considerations. Generally, they are willing to furnish this information to practitioners.

Many practitioners refuse to discuss fees over the phone. They prefer to deal with fees in the larger context of the client's financial situation. These are reasonable practices, especially if the practitioner utilizes a sliding scale to set fees. Nonetheless, it is unreasonable for a prospective client to attend more than a session or two without finding out whether or not he/she can afford to continue seeing the therapist. If the practitioner's custom is to set fees after a face-to-face discussion, then the initial agreement about the fee for the first session should be reached before scheduling it. A practitioner's unwillingness to divulge his/her range of fees (and other administrative practices as well) before the prospective client makes a commitment to work with the practitioner might cast some doubts in the client's mind about the practitioner's openness on other issues vital to the client. Some other practitioners, who believe that accepting a fee implicitly assumes a willingness to work with a client, do not charge for the first interview.

Practitioners vary in the promptness they require for payment of fees. For a client with health insurance coverage, it is necessary to ascertain whether or not the practitioner is covered for his/her services on the client's policy and whether the practitioner requires to be paid directly by the client or is willing to wait for the third-party reimbursement. These considerations are of considerable importance if the client has little available cash. For some practitioners, fees have definite status value, but as with many expensive restaurants, there is probably no direct correlation between cost and quality. In most instances, fees reflect the going rate in a particular geographical area among the various mental health disciplines, with a practitioner who regards him/herself as a psychoanalyst generally charging the highest fee, a nonpsychoanalytic psychiatrist charging somewhat less, a psychologist still less, and a social worker or a psychiatric nurse the least (with obvious overlaps and notable exceptions). This fee situation is, of course, not always dependent upon the original discipline in which the practitioner was trained. Those practitioners who feel that public opinion favors psychiatrists and psychologists receiving the highest fees may modify the situation by getting a doctorate in social work or nursing, going back to graduate school in psychology or medicine, or becoming particularly proficient and well-known in some special area of clinical work, e.g., in psychotherapy for children, family, groups, or addicts. Other practitioners who feel discriminated against because of their discipline have entered psychotherapy and psychoanalytic institutes. They leave these institutes no longer referring to their academic degree, but rather to a title indicating their new area of expertise—"psychoanalyst," "Gestalt practitioner," "Ericksonian therapist," "neurolinguistic practitioner," etc.

A final addendum on fees (until we get to collaborative work) is that we live in a nation in which money is status. It may be prudent for the practitioner to view this in terms of the cognitive dissonant studies a decade or two ago, which demonstrated the more effort one expends in a task, the more one values it. To reshape the old business adage, "money attracts money." This is to say, practitioners who charge too low a fee are often suspected as not only uncertain of their worth, but perhaps, not even worth consulting. In New York, Park Avenue practitioners pay highly for their office space. Correspondingly, their fees may attract clients who assume that if they are on Park Avenue and charging a high fee, they are probably worth a high fee. I am not recommending charging exorbitant fees. I am, however, suggesting that it is often both deleterious to therapist and the client to charge too low a fee. In a number of cases, I and several of my colleagues have noted that charging too low a fee, less than the client could easily afford, impeded the work of therapy. It suggests that the therapist has certain countertransferential difficulties in terms of his/her worth as a practitioner. It speaks to the thesis of this book.

Many practitioners feel the need to help others, often at their own expense. Still others exhibit another type of dysfunctional attitude toward fees. Like Weinberg (1984) I am puzzled by therapists who, despite largely empty schedules, turn down referrals because the client can't pay enough. Weinberg (1984) wisely indicates, "Help people and they'll refer others to you" (p. 35). Ultimately, the question of fees can be reduced to the question,

"What are our time, experience, and effort worth and how do we demonstrate their value to others in such a way as to provide ourselves with a comfortable livelihood?"

INTERDISCIPLINARY WORK

Practitioners in the course of their work come into interaction and occasionally conflict with colleagues from different disciplines. Even in private practice their interactions cannot be avoided because certain clinical situations involve several practitioners, such as working with families whose members see more than one therapist or are being seen for social or other kinds of services by public agencies.

These conflicts have many possible causes, although it is reasonable to assume that the problems approximate the motives that draw a person into becoming a practitioner and result in jealousies with regard to the status, competitiveness, and power of other disciplines. Over the past several decades, the relationships among the various disciplines have changed fundamentally. This is especially true for the roles of the psychologist and those of the medical practitioner. There are often wide discrepancies in terms of how practitioners from these two disciplines see each other's role. Psychologists achieve clinical independence earlier in their careers than do physicians. This, in part, had led to misunderstandings and political struggles over clinical responsibility. Psychologists tend to regard physicians as overly authoritarian, whereas physicians generally view psychologists as lacking an appropriate appreciation for the complexity of illness. Further exacerbation of difficult relations among the professions occurs to the exent that practitioners employ different models of illness and psychopathology. To circumvent potential conflicts, Hetherington (1983) strongly recommends that the division of labor should be fully decided before collaborative projects are attempted.

I don't wish to seem as if I were trying to discourage interdisciplinary efforts. There is an increasing need for interdisciplinary contacts, not only among our mental health disciplines, but also with physicians in general, and with other social scientists. Efforts should be rendered to avoid the chauvinistic insulation of the viewpoint of one's own profession, which comes from viewing problems from a single perspective.

There are clinical reasons for interdisciplinary cooperation in addition to the intellectual and refurbishing effects. Each of the different disciplines focuses and specializes on overlapping—but nevertheless specific—areas of human behavior. Consequently, each offers the other an expertise that the other might not have. Each discipline has a certain perspective on any behavioral phenomenon. The essence of science is that there is no single valid level of discipline, or true perspective. Ultimately, knowledge is singular, but human beings, for their convenience, subdivide it into different areas. Every scientific discipline conceptualizes the same behavioral phenomenon at a different level of abstraction. At the same time, none of these levels is (nor the discipline) the most real or the most meaningful. Thus, each discipline offers one aspect of the whole phenomenon. By bringing together these various perspectives, one has a more holistic and integrated view of the phenomenon. Furthermore, one can validate by cross-checking the essence of the event from his/her discipline by correlating it with the perspective of the other disciplines. Moreover, each discipline not only views behavioral phenomenon from a different perspective, but deals with it from a different vantage as well. Psychiatry is clinically and practically oriented; social work focuses on organizational and psychosocial factors; psychology on research and scientific experimentation and testing.

PROFESSIONAL IDENTITY

For many practitioners, there is some need to separate their identity from their profession in doing psychotherapy. For example, a psychologist who is a psychotherapist is a member of a profession that consists of many who don't do psychotherapy. Instead, they are involved with research, teaching, or work in industrial or other kinds of non-clinical settings. Psychologists/psychotherapists feel more akin to, and have more in common with, clinicians and practitioners from other disciplines than with their own academic profession. These are issues that need to be looked at in terms of the associations and the professional societies to which the practitioner gives allegiance.

GROUP PRACTICE

Working in independent practice will differ from group practice in that in independent practice, the practitioner is not beholden to the interests, concerns and sensitivities of colleagues; the practitioner does not have to collaborate. For some practitioners this is a preferable way of working; for others, it is isolating, lonely and threatening. It is threatening because of the absence of a cooperative effort for sharing difficult situations and feelings, which can be supportively addressed in collaborative work or group practice.

However, choosing to join a group practice raises numerous issues related to other types of collaborative work. The research of Henry et al. (1971) has amply demonstrated that mental health practitioners are prototypically trained as individual psychotherapy practitioners. As practitioners who work alone with clients, we find our work substantially sequestered from the observations of our colleagues. However, when a practitioner selects to work collaboratively, the practitioner, in fact, exposes his/her reputation, skill, experience and limitations to colleagues. They no longer need to make assumptions or take his/her word about what kind of practitioner he/she is. They can not only actually observe what goes on between the practitioner and clients, but no less significantly can experience the impact of the clinician on themselves as recipients of collaborative efforts. The practitioner's reputation and vulnerability are always on the line in collaborative endeavors.

On the other hand, the practitioner who works collaboratively is no longer sentenced to a solitary existence in practice. The practitioner no longer has to handle all the crises and difficult processes alone. There are others with whom the practitioner can deliberate with and share resources. Moreover, to the extent that the practitioner can trust colleagues, the practitioner can also profit from their reactions to his/her work. Also, the practitioner has the opportunity to observe colleagues directly and learn from the effect the practitioner observes their particular ways of working have on clients and on self.

INDIVIDUAL VS. GROUP/FAMILY PSYCHOTHERAPY

Obviously, some practitioners, aside from their skills in any of the particular modalities, have personalities that are more appropriate for certain kinds of therapies than for others. They may be able to stay more hidden in dyadic, certainly in psychoanalytic, treatment as compared to family, group, and other therapies, where they are part of a social group and their social facilities or lack of them are more evident than in private therapy. The wise practitioner learns to find ways of working tailored to meet his/her specific character and temperament.

COLLABORATIVE THERAPY

Obviously, many issues have to be dealt with and examined when working with one's own spouse or with colleagues who also are friends. For some, this kind of collaborative work is quite gratifying and enriches their social and emotional relationships outside of work. For others, it has a very deleterious effect. The merits and drawbacks of collaborative work should be carefully examined, and there should be ongoing review and discussion, and perhaps consultation with another colleague when attempting this kind of treatment. Chapter 14 provides a model for co-therapy endeavors. Of further use to practitioners who work together collaboratively is a method of dialogue I have labeled "Basic Emotional Communication." This is a method that has two essential interpersonal functions: First, it is a means for persons involved in intimate and significant relations to explore their relationship; second, it is a model for resolving conflict and moving beyond impasse in the therapist-client relationship. This model is discussed in detail in Chapter 11.

Collaborative work, such as conducting a weekly therapy or family group with a colleague is not as profitable as when it is conducted by a sole therapist unless the fee charged each client is rather exorbitant. Nevertheless, there are occasions in independent practice when it does make sense to work collaboratively, such as when two practitioners wish to start a therapy group and neither has enough clients to hold a group. Moreover, they may believe that their clients will profit from co-therapy. Similarly, a less experienced practitioner may wish to run a group with a more experienced practitioner, with the understanding that one will leave the group at the point that the less experienced practitioner is able to conduct a group independently. The question remains in this situation of how to split fees. Should this be done on an equal-time, equal-pay basis, or disproportionately, due to the greater experience and skill of one? Again, the question raised in considerations for fee-setting is how much the practitioner's time is worth.

TIME MANAGEMENT

The practitioner must manage his/her time in such a way that will be financially as well as professionally rewarding. On the other hand, the practitioner needs to concern him/herself with personal social needs and not to overbook, squeeze in, work too many hours, in such a way that the practitioner becomes emotionally exhausted and existentially drained.

A therapist's schedule of appointments should be such that, within reasonable limits, the therapist is available to the client when needed. He/she should have times available that are convenient for the client. Some practitioners work best in the morning, and others in the afternoon or evening. The same is true for clients. Although I don't ever remember being asked by my clients when I work best, it does seem to be a reasonable and significant consideration in scheduling sessions. The conventional therapy session is 45 or 50 minutes, and practitioners with busy schedules generally prefer regular, conventionally scheduled sessions. If a client feels he/she can work better with an infrequent but longer session than with a typical weekly or semiweekly session, he/she may do better with a practitioner with a more flexible schedule.

FLEXIBILITY OF SCHEDULING

There is nothing absolute about scheduling clients for 45 or 50 minutes on a regular basis, i.e., once or twice a week. Frequently, a flexible schedule, based upon the specific problem and the means of working on these issues makes more sense. With especially difficult clients it is often less stressful when the time is flexible to extend or shorten sessions as clinically indicated. For example, early in my career I was a staff psychologist in a large federal hospital. I specialized in working with rather bright, quite disturbed paranoid-schizophrenic inpatients. In that I developed my own schedule I could see patients as frequently as I felt was necessary. I chose to see these patients more frequently but for shorter periods than is customary. I worked with individuals three to four times a week for 30 minutes and groups three to four times a week for 45 minutes.

This can, of course, be done in private practice, as well. A number of years ago I treated a client referred to me because of his incapacity to function without anxiety due to a number of specific fears. I first used psychological implosion and desensitization during biweekly sessions. When these techniques were unsuccessful because the client did not become anxious simply by imagining the situations in which he was fearful, I employed symptom scheduling in terms of *in vivo* situations. This required the client to do a considerable amount of the therapeutic work on his own between sessions. In the vernacular, he was given "homework" assignments. Consequently, the sessions were scheduled in such a way as to review the progress of the homework and to plan additional follow-up sessions. The duration of the session was not decided beforehand. Instead, they reflected the time required to review the homework, maintain a working alliance and discuss the next assignment. For some sessions this required only ten or 15 minutes. At other times, it took over an hour. The client was charged on the basis of a fixed amount per session. Since the client was self-employed, he came to sessions whenever it was necessary, as often as required. I scheduled these sessions in the afternoon when I had sufficient flexibility that I did not need to halt a session before that session's work was finished.

THE OFFICE

Weinberg (1984) states the office issue well:

Nothing is more overrated in importance, takes up more time and unnecessary effort than concern over the psychotherapist's office. Therapists, especially those starting out in private practice, are likely to displace many of their concerns onto their office. Not that it's irrelevent: it's the most immediate visible part of their work, and patients respond to it. But patients respond to much more, and after a while, they come to judge the office by the therapist. (p. 22)

Because the beginning practitioner generally cannot afford an expensive office and furnishings, his/her concern should be to secure an office that is clean, comfortable (having sufficient waiting space), and not noisy or having distracting sounds from the street or adjoining offices. Understanding the effect of noise is of particular importance to our understanding of stress in our work. Several studies have indicated the growing threat of noise, demonstrating its effect not only on our hearing, but on our behavior as well. These studies indicate that fatigue, irritation, increased accident proneness, and difficulty learning and performing are a consequence of long periods of encountering noise. The practitioner whose office is located in a noisy place must encounter this hazard regularly. A sound doesn't necessarily have to be high-pitched to be distracting or noxious. Noxious sounds have "attention-getting characteristics. Sounds that are repetitive rather than steady-state are the most annoying, although a very stable and loud sound can be very annoying...."[1]

In terms of location the office should be conveniently located and easy to find. In areas where clients do not usually drive, there should be reliable public transportation close by. The practitioner should also not situate his/her office in such a public place as to call attention to and embarrass those who enter the office.

In order to convey to clients that the practitioner's office is a place in which they can feel comfortable as in a sanctuary, a professor of psychiatry who teaches career-planning seminars for psychiatric residents noted the following trends in psychotherapists' offices:

> More sun, plants, fish and space—an acknowledgement of Eros's triumph over Thanatos. An absence of ashtrays and hidden club chairs—a statement of therapists' greater respect for their own health and less need to hide from their patients. Fewer secret exits and more waiting-room area—a recognition that psychotherapy in the'80s is often an elective growth phenomenon. A persistence of clocks—a reminder that therapy is spent in precious periods."[2]

PRACTICING: HOME VS OFFICE

There are obviously many issues that come up in practicing in one's own home. The most important issue is that of transparency. For some therapists there is discomfort in revealing more of his/her personal life than is necessary. For others, a more natural, homelike setting is congruent with their personalities and therapeutic styles. Similarly, some clients may do better in the therapist's home, in that it is less austere and less undisclosed than an office, as opposed to other clients, who don't feel safe and need the anonymous structure of a professional office to reveal their dark secrets.

ANSWERING THE PHONE

The young practitioner beginning a practice might wonder whether to answer the phone directly while in session, hire an answering service, or purchase a phone answering machine. Expense is, of course, one consideration, but so, too is the question of how the practitioner wishes to interface himself and clients and also with prospective clients. Some practitioners have found that some of their clients (especially more schizoid personalities) relate adversely to the practitioner's voice on a mechanical device. They maintain that a courteous, efficient, and professionally conducted phone answering service is more acceptable to their more fragile clients. Moreover, such a service can be quickly in touch with the practitioner in regard to emergencies and an efficient depository for messages the practitioner might leave for various callers he/she anticipates hearing from. A personal secretary with mental health training would be even better for these purposes but also more expensive. However, the practitioner may be "penny wise and dollar foolish" in these matters. Practitioners who have tried to save expenses by hiring the most inexpensive answering service they could find have frequently regretted it. To their chagrin and their callers' resentment, these services are often operated by unreliable and inefficient phone answerers who lose messages, are discourteous, and even fail to notify the practitioner of urgent messages. In working with clients experiencing a serious crisis, the very lives of these clients may depend on a reliable system of communication between them and the practitioner.

It is my impression that most practitioners these days utilize some kind of answering machine. There are all kinds of machines on the market with a wide range of prices depending on which special features are included. The beginning practitioner is wise to buy a machine which he/she will not quickly outgrow as the practice prospers and expands. He/she should purchase a machine which has features that will be efficacious for the expanding needs of the practice. For example, a machine with a remote control, to be able to listen to messages from outside the office, is extremely helpful. Consulting with colleagues who have found reliable machines is useful. Even more useful is researching these machines in the latest editions of *Consumer Reports* and similar publications.

Answering the phone directly indicates availability of the practitioner to callers. However, if the practitioner answers the phone during sessions, it may be distracting and insensitive to a client who is paying for the session. Exceptions to this are, of course, when the practitioner anticipates an emergency call.

Some practitioners do quite a "number" on callers by answering the phone during a therapeutic session and in an irritating tone indicate that they are in session. They make it quite evident that the caller is interfering with their work. The moral should be obvious! If a practitioner doesn't wish to be disturbed by calls, he/she should unplug the phone, have calls directed to an answering service, or recorded on a phone machine.

CLINICAL IMPACT OF THE WORK SETTING

Whatever goes on in therapy may have an impact on the client. This includes the practitioner's decisions in which setting to have an office, the way the office is decorated and how the business aspects of practice are conducted. The competent practitioner is aware of how these decisions present themselves in the client's material. For example, I worked with a therapist who was struggling with financial issues after a separation from his wife. He moved his office to his home. Not having the time or energy to care for them, the house and grounds were in disarray. Plants formerly cared for by his wife were neglected. One of his clients dreamed of plants begging for water and attention; others presented associations in their sessions replete with "displaced" stories of lost little children and an unfulfilled need for mothering.

In whichever way the practitioner is most clinically conversant, he/she is prudent to look for displaced effects of whatever business decisions and actions are taken in the practice. Depending upon the client to directly inform the practitioner of these effects will not suffice. In short, although considerations of the business aspects of the therapeutic work may be repugnant and tiresome to the practitioner, they are real and worthy of careful consideration. Whether or not the practitioner chooses explicitly to explore them as they impact on his/her work, they will, nevertheless, affect the therapeutic material that clients present.

CLIENTS WHO DON'T PAY BILLS

Weinberg (1984) indicates two typical causes that collusively contribute to clients not paying bills. The first is *overidentification* with the client. The practitioner who overidentifies with the role of helper in being a psychotherapist finds it difficult to make firm demands on people who are suffering or undergoing personal difficulties. The practitioner experiences him/herself as an ally, someone with unlimited empathy, patience, and understanding. This kind of practitioner finds it hard to admit that he/she is doing psychotherapy for a living.

The second cause is an even more unconscious and disabling attitude toward practice. The independent practitioner harbors a pervasive sense of inadequacy and a lack of credence in the psychotherapeutic method. Weinberg points out that in conveying that "money isn't important," the therapist is actually indicating that he/she doesn't deserve to be paid.

It is essential, Weinberg indicates, that the practitioner ac knowledge to him/herself as well as clients that "I do this *for a living.*" This can serve as an antidote to clients who don't like to part with their money or who wish for a "pure" relationship with the therapist.

CLIENTS TERMINATING TREATMENT

As Farber and Heifetz (1982) have found in their study of the sources of stress in practitioners, difficulty in receiving adequate regard for work well done is highly germane to therapist dissatisfaction with their work. Moreover, practitioners appear more affected by their failures than by their successes (Marston, 1984). Clients who terminate treatment, proportional to the extent that the practitioner feels that termination is premature because certain issues have not been adequately worked out and to the degree that resentments are borne between practitioner and client, a sense of failure is experienced by the therapist.

Several options seem advisable in the face of this problem. One, because clients who succeed are rarely heard from again, the practitioner might devote some worthwhile time to following up. Marston indicates that some practitioners learn to increase the amount of the rare positive feedback they receive by initiating a follow-up on all their clients after a period of time. This practice fosters more satisfaction and provides a method of systematically improving clinical services. Marston adds that this practice is a survival skill, which should be taught to all new practitioners.

In following up all clients who have recently terminated treatment, the practitioner looks for particular patterns—e.g., terminations because of nonpsychotherapy circumstances or because of unknown circumstances or because of deleterious factors in the practitioner's behavior and interaction with each of the clients who terminated. In exploring with former clients (as well as with clients in the process of leaving) the practitioner should be careful, of course, not to put clients in a defensive position because of termination. The practitioner serves self and client best by being nonjudgmental about client dissatisfactions. Having a contractual way of working and a straightforward means for terminating in a reasonable way with clients is invaluable in this endeavor. (This issue will be examined in the next chapter.)

Another means of review of the practitioner's work is to try to catch problematic issues before they result in termination. In this regard, a tape recorder is often the practitioner's best friend. The practitioner who encounters a rash of drop-outs may learn to pick up some of the reasons by taping sessions with the clients he/she is continuing to treat. When I was in analytic training at the Washington School of Psychiatry, my supervisor indicated that a tape recorder could be a practitioner's best supervisor. He was right! Listening to one's own clinical work closely renders feedback and should help one recognize missing, neglected, and misalliancing issues. If the practitioner is not able to find these problematic patterns by listening to a tape, supervision and consultation is a must. Not all clients are comfortable with a tape recorder. Some need to be prepared and reasons for taping carefully explained. With fragile, highly suspicious clients, taping should be avoided.

MANAGEMENT OF CRISIS

First, let us look at what is objectively meant by "crisis." In its most general sense, crisis refers to a decisive moment in which some *immediate change* is highly probable of causing the demise of the subject. Medically it may refer specifically to a disease or injury to a person; interpersonally, to the continuation of a marriage; physically, to a pending natural disaster; intellectually, to the development of a theory.

In terms of human development, there are basically three kinds of crises. First, there are *developmental* crises caused by the requirement of imprinting. These are critical periods in human growth when developing maturation skills are most optimal. Generally, development not achieved during these maturational periods results in retarded growth. Second, there are *identity* crises, such as Erik Erikson has so cogently described, in which age-appropriate emotional and social maturation is required. If mismanaged, they cause fixations and retardation in the emotional and intellectual development of the individual. Third, there are crises that are referred to as *emergencies-in-living*. It is usually the third type of crisis that causes us the most stress in practice. These are situations in which we are rarely given a second chance to appropriately respond, unlike the first two types of crises which have a period of currency. When working with suicidal, self-destructive and violent clients, we must be available at all times to handle emergencies. We cannot often safely stay within a conventional therapeutic role and realistically expect to handle the crisis. We may have to be active, directive, controlling, and even authoritarian. In these roles, we take the chance of severely contaminating our therapeutic neutrality. Obviously, it is better to have a live client who is no longer willing to work with us because we took a decisive action in saving his/her life or that of someone the client threatened to harm, than to hold to our neutrality in the face of a jeopardy to life.

Each of the three types of crisis has to be recognized and differentiated from the others, as each requires a different kind of intervention. Generally, the first two crises can be handled alone by one practitioner. The last frequently requires collegial support. This makes crisis more difficult for the private practitioner than for those in institutional work. The independent practitioner doesn't have the built-in resources and support for immediately handling crises that are generally avoidable in an institutional setting. When the practitioner cannot rely solely on his/her own individual resources, the practitioner must call in others for help. It is prudent that the practitioner rehearse possible emergency situations and go through a mental drill; if you have ever been to sea, think of the lifeboat drills. This is preparing for emergencies before they actually occur. Making a list of names and telephone numbers of key colleagues and emergency services, and working out a plan of action for each kind of emergency is well-worth the effort to offset possible later grief.

In conclusion, for the practitioner with minimal business knowledge, there are seminars and workshops on the business aspects of independent practice given by experts who visit various cities on their seminar junkets. I assume most practitioners receive flyers about these seminars in the mail. There are also several periodicals and newsletters on various aspects of private practice. The two best-known of these is a quarterly journal published by Haworth Press (28 East 22nd Street, New York, NY 10010) called *Psychotherapy in Private Practice*; and a newsletter, *Psychotherapy Finances*, 500 Barnett Place, Ho-Ho-Kus, NJ 07423.

In summary, we have in this chapter touched upon a number of the issues the practitioner must examine in working in independent practice. We will, in the remainder of the book, look at the personal and professional effect this work has on the practitioner.

NOTES

1. A story in *The New York Times*, quoted Dr. Thomas H. Fay, an audiologist at Columbia Presbyterian Medical Center, on the subject of disturbing noise.

2. These statements were made by Dr. Roger B. Granet, assistant professor of psychiatry at Cornell Medical College, in an article by Georgia Dullea entitled, "Therapist's Decor: Do the Patients Count?" in *The New York Times*, July 4, 1983.

Chapter 9
Structuring the Personal Journey in Psychotherapy

> A mind conscious of integrity says no more than
> it means to perform.
> —Robert Burns

In keeping with our theme of personal journey as a conjoint endeavor of both client and therapist, I will propose in this chapter that the notion of personal journey is integrally linked with contractual psychotherapy. Therapists who equate freedom and autonomy with independence tend to ignore interpersonal partnership as central to the therapeutic encounter, for if human beings are autonomous agents, then they must free their solitary will to assert themselves in seeking happiness, meaning, and security. In my contrasting view, the journey into self requires the presence of another. We come to know ourselves through the other. As a frame of reference for this venture, I have, in this chapter, made recommendations for establishing a therapeutic partnership by developing guidelines for negotiating and contracting for roles, tasks, and responsibilities in the therapeutic encounter. I have also proposed ways of rationally terminating psychotherapy. Where problems develop in a therapeutic relationship, I have recommended guidelines for utilizing consultation in dealing with them.

When a therapist and a client meet for the first time, each comes to the encounter with an implicit set of fantasies, expectations, and demands about what will happen as a result of their meeting together. When these expectations remain hidden or inappropriately addressed, there results an unproductive impasse, if not an outright vitiating consequence for either or both the client and the therapist. This state of affairs may seem to be a strange and unjustifiable occurence in psychotherapy—the reputed sanctuary from deceit, pretense, and inhibition; the supposed setting par excellence for the baring of the naked truth. The practice of psychotherapy, however, is a complex and difficult endeavor for its practitioners, no less than for their clients. Like their clients, practitioners are, at times, arbitrary as they are reasonable, foolish as they are perceptive, timorous as they are courageous, and irrational as they are rational—all the while, merely human. To be sufficiently cognizant of the existential dilemmas and ethical implications of the practitioner's behavior in psychotherapy, to say nothing of being willing to face up to the implications in order to avert counter-productive conduct, is an onerous task for even the best of practitioners. I am not speaking of deviation from ethical practices, which can only occur in situations in which clear ethical guidelines are available. Far more frequently, in my experience, the ethical implications of psychotherapeutic practice are equivocal and open to dispute (Goldberg, 1977). Nevertheless, if practitioners do not establish effective and meaningful guidelines for their conduct for themselves, it is evident that outside interest groups (e.g., governmental agencies) will impose rules and regulations on them. There has been considerable public clamor and pressure from the professional sector to police the practice of psychotherapy. In recent years several serious inroads into the once exclusive therapist-client relationship have been imposed.

MODIFICATION OF THE ONCE EXCLUSIVE THERAPEUTIC RELATIONSHIP

As psychotherapy in the past has been integrally tied to private health insurance, it is evident that the future of psychotherapeutic practice is closely related to the development of national health insurance. Advocates of national health insurance, who are concerned with the growing amounts of payments for psy-

chotherapy, are insisting upon peer review of clinical cases covered by third-party payment. Peer review has begun with medical practice. Its influence is now being felt by practitioners of other disciplines, as well. We, as practitioners, decry the long arm of governmental bureaucracy interfering with the private practice of psychotherapy. Nonetheless, until practitioners convincingly justify to federal legislators the conduct of psychotherapy as a private arrangement between a practitioner and a client with whom the practitioner chooses to work, psychotherapy as an exclusive conclave of client and therapist may soon be largely an anachronism. Already third-party payment has had a marked effect on the type of treatment offered, created problems of confidentiality and diagnosis, influenced the nature of the transference relationship, and raised complex issues for client resistance (Meltzer, 1975; Chodoff, 1972; Halpert, 1972).

Private health insurance carriers claim in their own defense that mental health services are being "overused" and "abused" by subscribers, making it essential for the insurers to have easy access to medical records to review mental health practices. Insurance companies have, as a result of such practices, created strong pressure toward the formation of peer review committees to oversee the practice of psychotherapy. These committees of colleagues have been utilized by the insurance carriers and by professional (e.g., state and county) associations to review the treatment plan and treatment rationale of the practitioner in his/her work with clients where third-party payment is involved. Malcom Meltzer (1975) mentions an acquaintance who confided to him that his psychiatrist's bill for the past month was $2,900. He indicated that he visits the therapist four times a week, his wife twice, each of his children individually, the children as a group, the family as a whole, and the parents as a couple. He, of course, would not be able to afford to be so involved in psychotherapy unless insurance coverage was at the 80 percent level. Meltzer, a clinical psychologist, indicates that the family he is describing is intact and middle class, and the members are capable and functioning. To justify expensive treatment, some therapists have distorted diagnosis and altered clinical data.

Mental health experts on social legislation believe that peer review committees to monitor the private practice of psychotherapy will also be an integral component of national health insurance. The American Psychological Association has initiated peer review committees to the rancor of its clinical membership, even prior to the enactment of national health insurance. It may well be in the near future that these reviews will be required even in instances in which the client is paying the entire cost of treatment out of his/her own pocket. The responsibility of the practitioner in cases under review will be to specify intended therapeutic outcome, and the practitioner also will be held responsible for arriving at these objectives within a specified period of time. Such a state of affairs will clash with the notions of clinical responsibility implicit in psychotherapeutic practice—even when the practitioner is a nonphysician.

Elliot Friedson (1976), a New York University sociologist, argues in his book *Profession of Medicine* that two assumptions have been regarded as fundamental to the healing professions in the United States: (1) once a patient has placed him/herself in the doctor's care, the practitioner has sole and complete responsibility for the treatment, and (2) clinical experience is the foundation of medical responsibility. Healing is regarded as an art rather than a perfected science. Cures cannot be effected by choosing the right procedures by objective appraisal of the patient's medical history. Parenthetically, this rationale denies that peer review committees are in a position to ascertain proper clinical procedures. Each doctor, Friedson writes:

> builds up his own world of clinical experience and assumes personal, that is, virtually individual responsibility for the way he manages his case . . . [In this way, the work of healing] gives rise to a special frame of mind oriented toward action for its own sake. (p. 172). . . Such action relies on first-hand experience and is supported by both a will to believe in the value of one's actions and a belief in the inadequacy of general knowledge for dealing with individual cases. (p. 178). . . [The healer believes] that his work is unique and concrete, not really assessable by some set of stable rules or by anyone who does not share with him the same first-hand experience. (p. 180)

In requiring justification for the goals of treatment, peer review committees operate from a different set of assumptions. Their rationale assumes that in claiming a genuine ability to influence clients, the psychotherapist must reasonably assume at least some of the responsibility for the nature of that influence, as well as being accountable for the manner in which that influence is conducted.

POLITICAL AND SOCIETAL IMPLICATIONS OF PSYCHOTHERAPY

Despite sufficient evidence to the contrary, the psychotherapy establishment has permitted societal institutions to assume and affirm that psychotherapists have the capacity to protect society from the "dark secrets of the mind." As a consequence, in such decisions as *Landau v. Werner*, the courts have ruled that a psychiatrist may be held culpable for malpractice for the destructive behaviors of his/her patients. The fact that multitudes have filled our large state hospitals and would still today if these patients weren't being discharged for budgetary rather than clinical indications attests that, in actuality, practitioners have little control over the dark secrets of the mind. Only when drastic controls are placed on a patient's environment or when severe alteration of the patient's neurology or body chemistry is rendered, is the practitioner able to modify appreciably the resistant patient's behavior.

These practices, of course, raise serious ethical concerns. Today, there is considerable concern among the populace about the utilization of psychosurgery, electrical shock treatment, behavioral modification, and involuntary hospitalization. Concerns have also been raised about the use of insanity in criminal defense; megavitamin therapy for schizophrenia; the vast expenditures, intrusiveness, and inefficiencies of community mental health; the dangers of new therapies; and the implicit fraud in the conventional therapies. The conventional therapies have been called antifeminist, proestablishment, anti-working class, prointellectual, and so forth. At the same time, a considerable number of therapists are anxiously scurrying around looking for newer, more exciting, more "relevant" techniques without seriously grappling with issues and values being called into question. Shepard, in *Marathon 16* (1971), for example, makes the claim that he is willing to try with his clients any behavior that he regards as not physiologically harmful to himself. In subsequent books he seems to be eagerly pursuing this challenge and promise in his psychotherapy practice.

The responsibility for the failure to seriously grapple with the issues and values upon which psychotherapy is predicated cannot be attributed to any single factor. Yet it is evident that although psychology is today the most popular college subject, as well as the leading source of scientific literature and college texts (London, 1974), and although countless books, movies, television dramas, and popular conversation broadly "portray" what happens in psychotherapy sessions, psychotherapy lies behind a mystique. It is not that practitioners don't know a great deal about influencing or changing human behavior, but that they often behave like romantic poets who believe that the power and efficacy of their practices resides in its mystique. Many psychotherapists, for example, have been annoyed by the publication of such books as Eric Berne's *Games People Play* (1964) and Wiliam Glasser's *Reality Therapy* (1965). The overt reason for this is the undue oversimplification of psychological conflict and its amelioration as presented in these books. Covertly, in my opinion, many psychotherapists object to the demystification of the psychotherapeutic process presented by such books.

There are even more serious implications of psychiatric mystique. The *Washington Post* reported in December 1975 that a research psychiatrist at Saint Elizabeths Hospital, a large psychiatric hospital run by the federal government in the nation's capital, acknowledged that patients involved in psychological research at the hospital frequently do not understand what they are being asked to do. The concept of requiring informed consent from human subjects, according to Schwitzgebel (1975), appears to have emerged primarily from the German war trials: "The investigation of German medical experiments by A. O. Ivy served as a basis for the 1946 decision of the Judicial Council of the American Medical Association to require for the first time the 'voluntary consent' of research subjects." When a profession, on the other hand, permits the practice and conduct of its practitioners to remain implicit and mysterious, while at the same time requesting the trust, financial resources, and difficult personal modifications of persons in distress and confusion, this profession, in my mind, raises many serious ethical concerns.

Unfortunately, there are no clear guidelines for the review of psychotherapeutic practice. Psychotherapy is not always a circumscribed ameliorative endeavor intended to heal the individual's emotional wounds. Psychotherapy has subtle social and political implications. Some psychotherapists openly affirm psychotherapy as a political activity (Halleck, 1971). The practitioner's prerogative, in their view, is either to encourage the client to rebel against an oppresive environment or to accept and adjust to his/her present condition (Blatte, 1973). Various programs of behavior modification and psychosurgery are the hall-mark of adjustive treatment philosophies. In their more insidious forms these programs are conducted in the absence of the informed consent of those who are being subjected to their influence.

A FRAME OF REFERENCE FOR PSYCHOTHERAPY[1]

The study of interpersonal influence and interaction is essential to the establishment of guidelines for exploring concerns in psychotherapy. Considerations for psychotherapy must rest upon the conditions that insure an effective working relationship between therapist and client.

Psychotherapy, like all other interpersonal relationships, consists of a host of complex and interacting dimensions and parameters, certain of which stand out in importance. In order to develop more fully the therapeutic encounter as a meaningful human endeavor, practitioners need to know how these factors interact and to appreciate more clearly the particular shape these parameters take in a wide range of different psychotherapy and clinical situations. This is to say, psychotherapy is, often, necessarily indirect. However, this does not excuse therapists from knowing what they are doing and being able to state it plainly when the occasion calls for it.

The thesis I will develop in this chapter is that if practitioners are concerned about the plight of the individuals in distress with whom they work, they must first uncover the issues that predicate the individual's place in the social order. Emotional disturbance, as I will argue, is a result of the deterioration and disequilibrium of equity and balance that an individual experiences in relation to significant others in the person's normative system. If equity and balance are essential interpersonal dimensions for maximizing one's place in society, the client must be taught to negotiate directly for restoration of these relations in his/her interpersonal and societal transactions. To seek out the reasons why the client has feared to ask for equity in his/her object relations is not sufficient. For the client to become a more responsible and effective person, the client needs to be given more responsibility for collaborating in his/her own emotional growth. This endeavor requires a partnership between therapist and client. The practitioner serves as a role model. The client

will be no more willing to struggle for meaning in his/her journey into self than the client senses the practitioner is in his/her
own personal and interpersonal journeys. As such, psychotherapeutic practice requires a rationale and a methodology that will
enable the practitioner to get in touch with the practitioner's
own, as well as the client's, loneliness and despair, to address
the conditions that present themselves in a therapeutic encounter in which therapist and client take each other seriously. To
the extent that a practitioner does not consciously experience
the struggles with his/her own humanity in the encounter with
a client, the practitioner tends to regard the therapeutic relationship as a function. The therapeutic relationship under these conditions becomes an abstraction, appropriate for description and
convenient for observation, but at the same time unavailable as
a meaningful human encounter in which client and practitioner
share concerns in regard to their being-in-the-world. The traditional therapeutic model:

> holds that the therapist, having already had his training, has lit-
> tle need to grow experientially in the therapeutic situation. He
> must, in fact, specifically guard against experiential rather than
> cognitive, rational involvements, for failure to do so is generally
> regarded as overinvolvement or "countertransference." Thus,
> although disclosure of self is an inherent part of all traditional
> models of therapy, it is almost all one way, from patient to ther-
> apist. (Dublin, 1971).

Strict adherence to the specific theoretical principles and
their implications for technique and treatment methodology is
necessary for scientific validation of theory. On the other hand,
although a practitioner may be inclined to wish for scientific
validation of the clinical work, he/she is first and foremost an
agent of the client and therefore clinically responsible to the client. The practitioner is responsible for abetting the client, even
if this requires deviating from the cardinal tenets of the theoretical position with which the practitioner identifies. It is inhuman
and improper to withold an intervention that will help the client because it does not accord with a theoretical position. There
are two "sick" jokes which speak to this issue. One is from surgery and the other from analysis. The first tells of a surgeon who
has a drink with his colleagues after a long and arduous surgery.
He tells his friends that the operation was successful because,
despite the patient's condition, he stuck to proper surgical

procedure—even though the patient didn't survive. The second joke is about three analysts who meet at a convention. The youngest of the three describes his very creative work with a sociopathic young man who did not meet the general requirements for analytic work. The senior of the three men smiles slyly at the other analyst and wonders out loud to the reporting therapist whether what he conducted in treatment was really psychoanalysis.

But, jokes aside, the ability to use common sense and compassion in deviating from theory can be a serious matter. I still vividly remember, while a candidate in a psychotherapy institute some 15 years ago, sitting and watching a seasoned practitioner conduct psychotherapy with a very fragile, suicidal young woman, while I and my classmates watched from behind a one-way mirror. The patient became inordinately upset during one of the sessions. She was in tears, screaming that the therapist was like everyone else who claimed to want to help her, but was actually indifferent to her. She jumped up, promising never to return to therapy because life wasn't worth holding onto. My classmates and I, concerned about the upset woman, called for the therapist to go after her. I don't know if he heard us. I don't know if it would have mattered. He sat there and didn't move. In our postsession discussion with him, he justified his actions on the basis of his theoretical position. His theory said that if he went after the woman, he would be manipulated time and again. The patient never returned. I believe that the therapist's actions violated their therapeutic contract, although no *explicit* contract had ever been made with this woman.

I will argue later in this chapter that all transactions between people are contractual. The therapeutic relationship I propose differs from that of other interpersonal situations in that the contractual obligations of the agents involved in a therapeutic encounter are or should be based upon a voluntary, intentional, informed, and goal-directed agreement as to how each will conduct him/herself with the other. By focusing upon the transactual and contractual dimensions within the therapeutic relationship, the therapist has the opportunity to become aware of the effect his/her own values and sentiments have upon shaping the client's behavior in ways the client may or may not wish. To foster a relationship in which the client can learn to contract for his/her wants in an effective and responsible manner, the therapeutic partnership needs to be viewed as an autonomous system. Neither therapist nor client can be beholden to any third party in their dealings with one another. Where the practitioner is a double agent—representing the state or a school of psychotherapy and its dogma or being reimbursed by a third party—there is serious intrusion upon the partnership relationship. In this therapeutic model, the client is not relegated to the role of victim of his/her inscrutable nature and circumstance and in need of being taken care of by the therapist. The therapist's function is not to change the client but to help the client discover his/her intentionality—this is to say, the direction the client has given his/her life—so that the client may have more conscious choices about how he/she lives his/her existence.

The traditional approach to illness, cogently formulated in Talcott Parson's (1964) concept of the "sick" role, places the patient in a passive and compliant role vis-à-vis the physician. The person seeking psychological guidance, regardless of his/her education and psychological sophistication, generally carries this role into psychotherapeutic work. The client initially interacts with the psychotherapist similar to how he/she approaches an internist—citing complaints and symptoms, giving time and place of their eruption and waiting for the practitioner to give a prescription, e.g., medication, advice, encouragement, or dismissal. The inherent imbalance in power and status make a shared personal journey impossible in this role relationship. Contractual psychotherapy is a means some practitioners have found highly efficacious in dissuading the client from assuming a "sick" role and eschewing the responsibility for being an equal partner in the therapeutic alliance.

Naturally, the very difficulties and resistances which disabled the client from continuing his or her personal journey prior to visiting the practitioner, will continue into the consulting room. Therefore, whereas psychotherapy as a contractual partnership offers the client a fair, reasonable and efficacious treatment modality, it may not always be a welcome prospect for the client.

Unlike the traditional medical model, in which the client places a blind trust in the practitioner's knowledge and healing powers, contractual psychotherapy replaces magic with hard work. The client may initially feel it is unfair to assume collaborative responsibilities when he/she is feeling confused, exhausted, and distressed. Because the client experiences him/herself as inadequate, the client willingly pays a therapist to resolve his/her difficulties. Only from the practitioner's willingness to share his/her own humanity with the client does the client come to the realization that the client cannot escape human responsibilities if the client is to find meaning in existence.

The next four chapters in this volume explore ways of structuring the personal journey in psychotherapy.

CONTRACTUAL PSYCHOTHERAPY

Every therapeutic encounter represents a series of contractual obligations that client and therapist have agreed to enact vis-à-vis each other. This statement may sound absurd to those who regard a contract as a highly articulated legal document, but contracts may be viewed within a broader context in which all social relations may be regarded as contractual transactions (Pratt & Tooley, 1964). People, finding themselves not self-sufficient, have found it necessary to make promises and agreements with others to exchange material and emotional resources for mutual advantage. We are able to establish agreements with others because of our capacity to create and utilize signs in establishing rules, language, and interpersonal games (Havighurst, 1961). By means of language games, we pledge ourselves to employ mutually accepted signs and sign obligations in fulfilling promises and agreements.[2] As a consequence, interpersonal influence is possible whether or not the agents involved have ever encountered, or even have prior knowledge of, each other.

Demands and expectations of another person are generally predicated upon rules, roles, and sanctions experienced with others in previous situations approximating the emotional requirements of the present situation. Communication difficulties arise when people differ in their willingness and ability consensually to validate and comprehend the interpersonal agreements and promises they have imposed on themselves. Each of these contractual modes may be characterized by varying degrees of explicitness and informed consent. Contractual arrangements among people are, as a rule, more frequently implicit than explicit, unconscious than conscious, coercive than voluntary, unilateral than mutually endorsed. Accordingly, contractual arrangements may harmonize relations among some people, while antagonizing and creating tensions among others.

Contractual behavior, although a fundamental human capacity, has only in recent history achieved social significance in everyday life.[3] A contract is, by and large, an arrangement between equals that, when explicitly formulated, rejects coercion and fosters personal freedom (Havighurst, 1961). As such, contractual relationships stand in sharp contrast to status relationships. Every type of discrimination that categorizes another person, such as those that regard a person as "sick" or "well," makes use of status relations. Every discriminating act toward another person deprives the person—by transforming him/her into the occupant of a predetermined status category (e.g., "patient" or "victim")—of the right to contract as to how the person will conduct his/her relations with others.

Psychiatry before Freud may be characterized generally as the administration of a curative methodology to a disease entity—a status type of relationship. One of Freud's most significant contributions to the practice of modern psychotherapy was his penetrating exploration of the therapeutic encounter as an interpersonal process. He clearly recognized the need for joint participation in the therapeutic encounter, an endeavor that has come to be referred to as "the therapeutic alliance." As early as 1925, Freud established contracts with patients or with their families (Pfeiffer, 1972).

Of further importance to the development of the therapeutic alliance, Freud and his followers have been rather encyclopedic in recording their insightful observations of the ways in which clients, through transference mechanisms, and therapists, through countertransference mechanisms, unwittingly resist the development of effective therapeutic alliances. Nonetheless, description of resistance does not by itself enable clients to assume therapeutically efficacious roles. Strategies for effecting interpersonal partnership are required. Until recently, these therapeutic strategies have remained at a primitive stage. Eric Berne (1964), George Bach (1968), and several other practitioners concerned with regulated interpersonal relations have, in recent years, catalogued a variety of strategies and games played in psychotherapy and other interpersonal situations. They have also suggested a number of therapeutic ploys to gain the client's cooperation. Berne regarded "a game" as a transaction in which the agents involved could, by knowing the rules, become skilled in strategizing to handle the moves of the other agent in such a way as to obtain a fair shake and a predictable outcome. When the practitioner appreciates the client's need for an equitable and predictable exchange in psychotherapy, the requirement for an explicitly contractual relationship becomes an ethical necessity. It will be my task in this chapter to come to terms with the contractual issue involved in a therapeutic partnership.

RELATIONSHIP AS CONTRACT
IN PSYCHOTHERAPY

Ideally, what differentiates the therapeutic encounter from other interpersonal situations is that the contractual obligations of the agents involved are based upon a voluntary, intentional, informed, and goal-directed agreement as to how each will conduct himself with the other. Szasz and Hollender (1956), in their now classic discussion of the basic models of psychotherapy, argue that the main intellectual and educative value of psychotherapy lies in the kind of model the analyst fosters to induce mutual and informed participation within the therapeutic relationship. Informed consent, the eminent psychiatrist Fritz Redlich indicates,

> is the basis of all psychiatric intervention and...without it no psychiatric intervention can be morally justified...the medical profession's exclusive hold on its system of ethics no longer exists. The fiduciary system, in which a patient puts his trust in the physician's ability and willingness to make crucial decisions, is being replaced by a contractual system." (Redlich & Mollica, 1976)

Redlich's statement is particularly important in consideration of the recent court decision in California, which upheld the dying patient's right to request termination of life-support apparatus. This decision has, of course, serious implications for all aspects of a person's existence.

A therapeutic contract, then, is a promise or a set of promises, the fulfillment of which each agent involved has agreed to assume as his/her duty. Existentially, a therapeutic contract is an attempt to enable each agent in a therapeutic encounter to inform the other agent involved of his/her responsibility in addressing the former's existential concerns. In this endeavor, client and therapist need to explore together the questions: Why are we here? How did we get here? Do we need to be here? Where do we go from here? To the extent that either agent fails to address these concerns, the client's quest for meaning is appreciably thwarted.

As my discussion should suggest, a therapeutic contractual arrangement is an attempt to combine the best aspects of a clearly defined set of work goals with a method for continual reassessment and review of the work in progress (Adams & Orgel, 1975). By "contract," then, I am not referring to a cut-and-dried, written document that either client or practitioner might insist upon at the commencement of the relationship and that is referred to again only at such time as one of the agents experiences the other as violating their agreement. I mean, instead, that goal setting and negotiation are essential parts of viable therapeutic work and go on throughout the course of treatment. Insofar as a contractual relationship divests psychotherapy of its mystique by defining its specific purposes and procedures, it increases the accountability of both agents for what transpires in their work together. A therapeutic contract, then, is a tool that clarifies the client's goals by enabling the client to take an active role in deciding on goals and meaningfully pursuing them. A client will derive as much out of psychological treatment as he/she personally invests.

Some modalities are more insulated from the immediacy of the client's concerns than are others. The goals of the various psychotherapeutic treatment approaches correspond to the existential views these approaches hold in regard to the nature of the self and its possibilities for emergence. For example, in the traditional Freudian position, the self (actually, the ego) lacks a purposive propensity. Ego is primarily regarded as having an executive and integrative function in rechanneling misdirected affective expression, resulting from energy systems in conflict with one another. The goal of analysis is to unite the unconscious with the conscious in order to convert neurotic suffering into the common suffering of humankind. In the Horney position, an inherent, teleological attribute is posited in the self. The goal of treatment, consequently, is the development of the Real Self, which is capable of continuous self-realization in forming cooperative rather than antagonistic interpersonal relations. In the Kohutian position, the self is, metaphorically, regarded as reflected images from parental mirrors. The goal of therapy is to provide appropriately permissive and encouraging mirror experiences which will enable the self to integrate its fragmented parts and form more optimistic and vitalized interpersonal relations.

To the extent that each person is not an unitary private self, but rather a composite of situational selves, responding to the various social and interpersonal contexts in which the person is being encountered, dyadic psychoanalytic treatment may, for particular patients, at certain junctures in their treatment, incur therapeutic impasse with regard to the developmental needs of the emerging self. These impasses have generally been regarded as due to therapist error and unexamined therapist countertransference. Clinically, we are aware that if these impasses are not appropriately handled, they quickly become negative therapeutic reactions on the part of the client.

In Chapter 12, I will examine the negative therapeutic reaction from a historical point of view, as well as how the term is currently employed. I will then explore clinical means for addressing the negative therapeutic reaction. I will argue that very frequently the manifestation of this reaction in dyadic psychoanalytic psychotherapy is not due as much to therapist error as it is to a definitive indicator that dyadic psychotherapy for that patient at that moment in the patient's development has inherent limitations. Obviously, in dyadic treatment the negative therapeutic reaction that emerges manifests itself in the context of a relationship of two people who are interacting in a relatively circumstantial setting. In contrast, the combined modalities of dyadic and group, marital, family therapy, and so forth, examines the phenomenological self of the client as the self emerges in interaction with a series of significant others in ways that are often not adequately addressed in dyadic treatment.

Family and marital psychotherapy has the distinct advantage of enabling the client to work directly with significant persons in his/her life with whom relationships are in conflict. Group psychotherapy enables the client to negotiate with other people who evoke conflictual feelings similar to those the client experiences with significant others outside of therapy. In dyadic sessions, the client generally has greater control of the process than in other therapeutic modalities. Working out conflictual feelings may be more easily avoided in dyadic than in group or family sessions, unless the practitioner firmly focuses upon the immediacy of the transactional relationship of therapist and client. By definition, a contractual arrangement focuses squarely on the transactional relationship. In this endeavor, there is a need to interface what the client is working on outside of therapy with what the therapeutic agents are working on together in their therapeutic encounters.

In addition to its pragmatic purpose, contractual psychotherapy has, of course, an *ethical* intent. The only certain way of effectively dealing with ethical concerns in psychotherapy is to focus upon the transactional and contractual dimensions of the therapeutic relationship. How can the practitioner be aware that his/her own values and sentiments may be shaping the client's behavior in ways contrary to the client becoming the person he/she intends to be, unless open discussion, assessment, and negotiation about what the client is working toward and about the roles and responsibilities required of both agents become integral components of the therapeutic encounter? In short, for the client to become a more responsible person, the client needs to be given responsibility for collaborating in his/her own living experience. In contractually oriented psychotherapy, the therapeutic relationship is

> determined neither by the patient's "therapeutic needs" nor by the analyst's "therapeutic ambition," but rather by an explicit and mutually agreed set of promises and expectations which is called the "contract." (Szasz, 1969, p. 7)

OTHER ALTERNATIVES TO PROBING PSYCHOTHERAPY

Psychotherapy is an expensive way to deal with problems, and it may indeed be a rather inefficient way to resolve some kinds of problems. Consequently, we need to explore whether there are less expensive and more efficient ways to come to terms with the problems for which the client is asking help. Ethically, a therapist must be open to this kind of exploration. Steinzor (1967) has stated the issue succinctly. In his discussions with his clients, he asks, "Why are we discussing this complaint and why are you not describing your feelings to your friend, your lover, your supervisor?" Steinzor explains that if the therapist does not raise this question, the implication conveyed to the patient is that only through the therapist will true revelation appear, like a miracle vision in the desert. The patient must be confronted with his choice in bringing any thought or feeling before the doctor rather than elsewhere (p. 9).

Clark's (1975) distinction between *therapeutic experience* and *therapeutic relationship* has bearing here; the quest for meaning and for a greater sense of being-in-the-world may lead people into therapeutic experiences as well as into psychotherapy. Therapeutic experiences may be renewing family ties; developing new, or reestablishing former, friendships; or joining in social, political, and educational pursuits. The quest for meaning and sense of being-in-the-world may be explored in time-limited, goal-limited therapeutic experiences, such as carefully chosen encounter and growth-oriented workshops and weekends. Moreover, for certain types of psychological problems, hardcore drug addiction or serious alcoholism, for example, self-help groups and residential treatment programs are frequently more effective than private psychotherapists doing psychodynamic psychotherapy. In instances in which the client will only accept removal of "the problem" (see Goldberg, 1977, Chapter 6), circumscribed therapy techniques such as behavioral modification, sex therapy, or psychosocial training may be more effective than psychodynamic psychotherapy.

THE CONTRACTUAL PHASE IN PSYCHOTHERAPY

Many practitioners appear to view contract negotiation as an endeavor that takes place when the agents first convene but is put aside once the client's objectives have been established. Those who hold to this attitude regard the work of psychotherapy as two distinct steps: first, trying to establish goals; second, striving to reach those goals. In fact, a viable therapeutic contract is a developmental process that is continually being negotiated and periodically being reviewed throughout the entire course of treatment. In most instances, the goals of psychotherapy are better understood and can, therefore, be more specifically stated as the therapeutic encounter unfolds. In discussing the role of contract negotiations in social work, Seabury (1976) states that the following stages usually characterize a therapeutic contract:

1. *Exploration and negotiation phase.* In this preliminary phase, both agents are sizing up and testing out each other. They are attempting to understand what the purpose of their encounter is and what each one's obligations are in this endeavor. In this phase, each agent explores what he/she needs to know about the other in order to develop a working alliance.

2. *Preliminary contract phase.* There is in this working

phase a tentative agreement as to why each of the agents is in the encounter with the other and how each expects to be treated. This agreement is generally characterized by considerable reservation and ambivalence.

3. *Primary working agreement phase.* The terms and conditions of the therapeutic relationship are clarified as to what the specific task and time limitations are and how each has agreed to treat the other in this relationship. This phase gives rise to a variety of secondary, as well as behaviorally specific, contracts. Moreover, there is some agreement in this phase as to how the outcomes can be evaluated and reviewed and how provision can be made for grievances.

4. *Termination phase.* After specific actions have been taken, both agents evaluate the outcome of their attempts to achieve their agreed-upon goals. Mutual agreement is given for terminating the working relationship or continuing with new goals.

According to those who have surveyed the practice, few practitioners actually employ written therapeutic contracts, unless urged to do so by their clients (Adams & Orgel, 1975). The following are the components that The Mental Health Study Group (Adams & Orgel) suggests should be contained in a written contract:

ELEMENTS OF A CONTRACT

1. Name of each agent.
2. Date of beginning and end of agreement.
3,4. Length of each session.
5. Goals of sessions stated as specifically as possible.
6. Cost per session and when payable.
7. Definition of services provided by psychotherapist (stated as clearly as possible).
8. Provisions for cancellation:
    a. no penalty for termination.
9. Renegotiation at end of stipulated period.
10. Allowance for changing goals within stipulated period.
11. Definition of nature of services; no guaranteed results; guarantee of intention and good faith.
12. Establishment of access by client and therapist to documents that become part of client's records; guarantee of con-

fidentiality and control by client over medical record and its contents and use of any information therein.

In my view, a viable, contractually conducted therapeutic relationship does not require a written contract. There is, after all, a major distinction between a therapeutic and a legally defined relationship. Proof and evidence are the strengths of a written contract. Evidence or proof of stated intent will not alone, however, enable therapist and client to act responsibly in a relationship. What seems to me to be more important to a viable therapeutic relationship is an evolving awareness of what each agent is asking for, an awareness that proceeds from implicit (silent) hopes, fears, and expectations into explicitly (directly) articulated and openly negotiated roles and responsibilities. This kind of process is difficult to capture in a written document. When documentation is desired, audiotape and videotape are expensive, but preferable. My own concern is that a contractual negotiation process take place in psychotherapy, not that it can be documented once having occured.

Contractually, the client's roles and responsibilities in psychotherapy are similar, with one important exception, to a person's roles and responsibilities in buying a house, contracting for its construction, and securing proper services in its maintenance. A buyer is entitled to the commodities and services he/she purchased, not because he/she is lonely, nor because he/she is upset or has emotional problems, but because he/she has requested them, the seller has agreed to deliver them, and a fee has been exacted to validate their agreement. A person would be imprudent to buy a house without investigating the market for the best available houses and without obtaining information about what he/she would attend to in a well-constructed and functional edifice. The one exception to the fitness of the analogy between buying a house and contracting for psychotherapy is that a customer would be foolish to purchase a house without obtaining a written contract guaranteeing the specifics of the negotiated agreement of what the purchaser has bought, since the goodwill of the seller cannot be sensibly presumed. On the other hand, the client can enter into a therapeutic arrangement with a therapist without benefit of written contract because the goodwill of the therapist is generally not suspect,[4] even if the practitioner's competence doesn't measure up to his/her best intentions. Frankly, my lack of faith in a written contract has to do with the tenuous nature of the therapeutic situation. Few practitioners are foolhardy enough to guarantee results. The therapeutic contract does best as a means of focusing on how client and therapist may best cooperate in devoting their best efforts to addressing the client's best interests.

OUTLINE FOR ESTABLISHING
A THERAPEUTIC CONTRACT

1. Clark (1975) recommends that the initial task in a therapeutic situation should be an exploration of the relationship issues and concerns. This proposal makes infinite sense to me. Clark states:

> Ordinarily clients use the first session to discuss the problems they feel are causing their difficulties. Partly because they want relief as quickly as possible, partly because they think the therapist expects them to explain why they have come to psychotherapy as fully as possible, most clients submerge the questions they have about psychotherapy. This is a mistake. The best way to use the first session is to outline, with the therapist, the basis for the psychotherapy relationship. (p. 75)

2. For the client to get as much as possible from the therapeutic relationship, the client must assume that the therapist is there to hold up a mirror, but the therapist must rely on information from the client since he/she is not able to read the client's mind (Viscott, 1973). The client should be ready to present him/herself actively rather than wait to be drawn out by the practitioner's inquiry.

3. It is essential in formulating a therapeutic contract to avoid the use of technical terms and complex concepts. Operational terms, such as how the client might look, feel, and act at the conclusion of the therapeutic relationship, may be employed and should be made as specific as necessary for each of the agents to be cognizant of what is being asked for and what each has agreed to fulfill.

4. A contract must define the nature of therapeutic work by addressing such concerns as: Why are we here? What are our expectations of one another? What do we have to offer one another? What would we like to gain from our experience together?

What is the meaning of asking help from the other? In this dialogue, the therapist seeks to ascertain the client's notion of psychotherapeutic work and replies in terms of his/her own beliefs and also according to the best evidence he/she has available about psychotherapeutic endeavor.

5. I am aware that in their initial discussions many practitioners are unwilling to inform the client fully of how the therapeutic experience may be of help and, particularly, of its possible limitations. This may be due to the therapist's awareness of unconscious material he/she believes the client either cannot tolerate without serious psychological repercussions or is not psychologically receptive enough to acknowledge early in a treatment relationship. In my view, this is not a therapeutically useful attitude. It is the therapist's responsibility to provide an assessment of what he/she foresees as the conditions of the work ahead for each of them. (This is referred to as a "prognosis" in medical terminology.) The practitioner's assessment is based upon what realistically can be accomplished in regard to:

>   *a.* the client's hopes, wishes, demands, and expectations of the therapist and psychotherapy, in terms of the client's problem-solving capacity and his/her personality attributes;
>
>   *b.* the client's strengths and limitations, with specific regard to the transference object (s) the therapist may likely evoke for the client and to the client's complementary role relationship with the therapist (based upon the client's family system);
>
>   *c.* the therapist's skill, expertise, and personal attributes; and
>
>   *d.* their combined ability to influence environmental conditions that would lead to the most favorable outcome.

6. The conditions of the contract must be equitable and realistic. The requirements must be within the capability of each agent. Both agents are responsible for the relationship. Since the *client* is the ultimate judge of his/her own needs (as the therapist is of his/her own), the client cannot allow the therapist to withold "threatening" material from his/her awareness. In this endeavor, the client must hold the therapist responsible for answering such questions as:

>   *a.* How does the therapist see the situation that the client is bringing into treatment?
>
>   *b.* What does he/she hear the client asking to accomplish in therapy? That is, what does he/she perceive to be the hopes,

wishes, demands, and expectations the client has of the therapist and of therapy?

c. Which of these appear to be conscious but unarticulated and which are presently beyond the awareness of the client?

d. What does the client seem willing to do, so that the therapist will meet his/her expectations?

In developing a contract, it should be noted that the therapist may assume that he/she has both a responsibility to the client at the present (C1)—i.e., the client suffering from a lack of integration and purpose—and to the client at some time in the future (C2), the integrated and more finished journeyer. Consequently, the therapist's perception of the client's needs may differ from that of the client, or he/she may conceive of the client's goals in ways the client might not recognize. Many therapists feel that it is legitimate to sell a suit to a client who is only asking for a hat. For example, the client "might want to erase his stutter, rash, or anxiety, while a psychoanalytically trained therapist might see these as symptomatic and manifestations of repressed hostility, and might formulate his own goal as freeing up the patient's impounded aggression. In effect, he sees C1 as different from C2 and works the contract with a C2 who does not yet exist, trusting that when C2 arrives, C2 will be happy with the results" (Michaels, 1973).

7. The practitioner has a responsibility to the client to explain:

a. if diagnostic tests are to be performed, the nature of these tests, the reason for their being employed, and any significant risks involved;

b. if medication is recommended (by the practitioner or by another practitioner to whom the client will be referred for medical supervision), the expected results and possible adverse effects;

c. which techniques (in terms the client can understand) he/she intends to employ and the expected results, risks, and complications, as well as other techniques appropriate to the client's concerns and the reasons he/she has decided not to employ them;

d. the alternatives and options to psychotherapy should the client refuse treatment or decide at some point to discontinue therapy; and

e. the expected outcome of therapy (in terms the client can relate to in his/her everyday existence), if the client stays with it for the period of time therapist and client have agreed on.

8. A therapeutic contract must specify the negotiable and nonnegotiable aspects of the therapeutic relationship. The psychotherapist cannot let the client decide for the practitioner how the practitioner is to meet the needs the client wishes to have addressed. These considerations require an intensive exploration and negotiation in which the concerns of both agents can be explored. Let me illustrate this from a common phenomenon in psychotherapy that might aptly be referred to as the "purchase of love." There are probably few practitioners who have not encountered clients who demand love. The client pleads from need and desperation that he or she deserves unquestioning love, not labor. The therapist may well ponder whether he/she has agreed to give love or sincere endeavor. If the practitioner has contracted to give love, what kind of love has the practitioner agreed to? Has the practitioner agreed to make the client more important than others in his/her life, or is the practitioner promising only partial love, such as sexual involvement or paternal support? Meaningful love, of course, cannot be rendered on demand, however deserving the client may be.

I have sometimes responded to the attractiveness of some of these offers and the reasonableness of still others in the following way:

Where did you get the idea that I agreed to give you my love? I agreed to give you my unselfish attention and the product of my understanding of your situation and its effect upon me. Are you not asking me for my love as a substitute for what you have not found in your life? In any case, I will not be a substitute for it. To do so would mitigate your attempts at genuine love outside of this special situation. If I experienced love as freeing you, I would give it as best I could, but love will not free you as long as you are a prisoner of your fears and silent dreams. Indeed, only when you experience your own internal "permission" to care as much for me as you need or want to *without my having to* care as much for you, will you free others to care for you as you need or want them to. I may have some of your fears. I refuse, however, to fall into your illusion. I have committed myself to struggle with these fears—in you, and in myself. You may choose to join and work with me or you may choose not to work with me. This is your prerogative! Mine is not to mask my fears and yours with an illusion!

Aware of the dangers of seductive patients in an emotionally charged relationship, Freud (1915) wrote that a love affair would be a great triumph for the patient, but would be a complete interference with the cure. It is genuine love, not love on demand, that the client seeks. As such, the client deserves more than an illusory relationship. Whatever the therapist is promising must be made clear early in their relationship.

9.   A viable therapeutic contract must have provisions for its fulfillment and a modus for addressing grievances and dissatisfactions. For example, a second opinion or consultation should be encouraged by the therapist before rendering heavy medication, electric shock therapy, hospitalization or, indeed, any therapeutic intervention about which the client is deeply concerned. The terms of the contract must be flexible enough to be renegotiated whenever client or therapist believes that the terms are nonproductive.

10.   There must be a clearly understood means for terminating the contract and psychotherapy. The practitioner should be sincerely willing to deal with termination as a real issue at any time this concern is raised by the client. What hangs up many therapists is the notion of a complete analysis. With the exception of Ferenczi, even the psychoanalytic masters did not believe that a complete analysis was possible. Freud was certainly pessimistic about a complete analysis. Nonetheless, the practitioner's omniscient wishes may transcend this reality.

Emotional disorders, because they are expressions of disorientations to reality, are also disturbances of time. The psychotherapist has a dual function: Not only is the practitioner expected to enable the client to call forth repressed and dissociated impulses; the therapist must also serve as a "representative of reality who tries to reeducate the patient to an optimal reintegration of reality" (Weigert, 1952). In this endeavor, each agent must be clearly cognizant of how he/she uses or misuses therapeutic time. Objective time is a dimension of reality that both agents share. It is also the quintessence of reality upon which all other dimensions of reality depend. Time, in this sense, predicates the possibility of human meaning and purpose. Toward this aim, client and therapist must struggle with contract termination and its implications for the fear of nonbeing when not intimately involved with another person.

What implications does the contractual orientation have for time structure in psychotherapy? The role the therapist assumes differs from the roles and relationships the client has taken with others in that, from its beginning, psychotherapy is a process of preparing the client to take over for him/herself, vis-à-vis significant others in the client's life, those functions the therapist is assuming at that time and place. The more uncertain and vague the period of treatment and the goals to be worked on, the greater the influence of irrational and magical notions and attitudes the client may have toward therapeutic work. The more specific the period of treatment and the goals to be worked on in treatment, the more appropriate and rapid the confrontation with these refractory attitudes in the work to be accomplished in therapy (Goldberg, 1976).

11. Therapist and client need to reach some initial agreement about how upsets and acting out by the client will be handled by the therapist. The practitioner should inform the client the controls the practitioner is willing to assume. In a word, will the practitioner become personally involved when a client becomes inordinately upset, or will the practitioner handle it by medication, hospitalization, or termination of the relationship?

12. A therapeutic contract must begin with an outcome; only then can it be decided which procedures are needed and how to evaluate what happens. The goals of the therapeutic relationship must be evaluated mutually, even though evaluation is a term that makes many practitioners anxious. Standards for assessing therapeutic progress must be decided upon before the evaluation of results.

13. Proper evaluation concerns itself with both internal and external criteria. The therapeutic contract is just part of the client's life contract. The therapist must continually draw the client back to the interrelated concerns of: What have I learned in therapy that can help or is already helping me with concerns in my daily existence? And conversely, what am I learning from my relationships with others that can help me with my work in therapy?

14. There should be an understanding and agreement about the relationship (which could run the gamut from phone calls to personal involvement) or nonrelationship of the agents outside their ascribed therapeutic sessions. A similar understanding must be reached among members of therapeutic groups about their relationships with one another, as well as with the therapist.

15. In summary, a therapeutic contract must establish a

mutually agreed-upon and explicitly articulated working plan (in medical-model parlance, a "treatment plan"). The working plan consists of the following six elements:

   a. the goals client and therapist have agreed upon working toward;

   b. established means for working on these goals;

   c. a prospectus on the ways the therapist plans to intervene in or stay out of the client's issues, based upon how the client tries to draw the therapist into the struggle;

   d. a prospectus on ways the client has agreed to work on his/her issues;

   e. means for reviewing and evaluating the therapeutic work; and

   f. means for addressing dissatisfactions in the working alliance.

CONTRACT NEGOTIATION BETWEEN THERAPIST AND CLIENT

My use of contract negotiation is derived from a theoretical model delineated in terms of the effects of the participants' expectations and obligations upon their cooperative or conflictual transactions with others. This model emphasizes both those articulated benefits the individual expects to derive from a treatment encounter and those benefits he/she is unable or unwilling to identify consciously. Sager, Kaplan, et al. (1972) indicate that there are three levels to contracts between persons involved in an intimate relationship:

   1. *Conscious and verbalized expectations:* the hopes and demands that each agent expresses to the other in clear and understandable language.

   2. *Conscious and nonverbalized expectations:* the expectations, plans, beliefs, and fantasies that each agent withholds from the other because he/she is fearful or ashamed to express them to the other.

   3. *Unconscious expectations (wishes beyond awareness):* needs and desires that frequently are contradictory and unrealistic, initially not accessible to the client's awareness.

Obviously, to the extent that the client's expectations remain implicit rather than clearly articulated, it is unrealistic for the client to expect them to be fulfilled by others.

EQUITY AND BALANCE

My model attempts to delineate how the clients I work with seek to achieve, maintain, or avert a position of equity with significant others. An important focus in my work is to indicate how the people I work with use the equity issue in the forms of justification, rationalization, illness, and weakness to assume positions of inferiority, passivity, and irresponsibility or, on the other hand, domination, oversolicitude, and overresponsibility (Goldberg, 1973).

Closely related to the concept of equity is the concept of *balance*. The principle of balance in interpersonal relationships is basic to human functioning. Structuring of experience is a universal tendency. We tend to see definite forms and patterns and make of them definite images. Over time, our memory of these entities and events may be modified and transformed, structuring our experience still further. Heider (1957) has described this psychological tendency toward structuring of experience as *cognitive balance*. A state of harmony exists if entities that, in our experience, belong together are all positive or else all negative. If closely related entities are perceived to be of different valences, then a state of tension or disharmony is experienced by the perceiver. Jordan (1953) experimentally demonstrated that when a person finds him/herself in an unbalanced situation, psychological forces within act upon the person to achieve balance. The traditional power-behind-the-throne, manipulative roles played by women with their husbands and sons may be regarded as attempts to balance their societally deficient power roles. Unable to realize their ambitions by their own endeavors in the past, women often sought to seek satisfaction of their objectives through pressure brought to bear on the men in their lives (Gelb, 1972). It does not follow, of course, that people seek or desire relationships that are perfectly balanced. Fiske and Maddi (1961), on the basis of a large number of diverse psychological studies, argue that the human organism inherently seeks novelty and excitation. Perfectly balanced relationships would result in states of stagnation and boredom.

In brief, in negotiating for a contract, the first step is to make explicit what is implicit in the expectations and wants of those involved in the ameliorative endeavor. The second step is the establishment of balance: A successful contract cannot be rendered unless each agent feels he/she has something of value to give as well as something he/she wishes to receive. This necessitates a period of work in which the therapist and client discuss what they want from and can offer each other. Basic agreements are set down for the giving and receiving of assistance, and the consequences and handling of broken agreements and dissatisfaction are discussed. This gives the client confidence that his/her feelings and behavior are being responded to in a nonarbitrary way. There are, as a result, clear dictates about the consequences of the practitioner's behavior and of the persons with whom the practitioner is working with clinically. I believe that this collaborative structure, conducive to establishing feelings of equity and balance in the working relationship, is an essential component of an effective therapeutic contract. The final step is that of negotiating the exchanges among those involved in the ameliorative endeavor.

In sum, the contract negotiation approach I have delineated is intended to enable the practioner to help the client clarify from the onset what the client is seeking help for, what roles and responsibilities the client and the practitioner are willing to assume, and how they, together, can implement the client's goals. Once having reached these goals, client and practitioner then decide together the next step in the client's quest for psychological maturity.

Having explored the contracts people make with themselves and with others, I have employed in my own practice many different types of contract negotiation approaches, ranging from nondirective to directive verbal techniques, and to various action modalities. These are explored in depth in my book *Therapeutic Partnership* (1977).

THEIR IMPLICATIONS
FOR INTERPERSONAL RELATIONS

The roles of equity and balance in object relations suggest to me a number of important principles that have serious implications for interpersonal relations, including, of course, therapist-client relationships. The result is three psychological premises that order my conceptual frame of preference.

First, both socially aberrant and emotionally disordered behavior are generated by disturbances of regulated and common systems of expected and proper (equitable) behavior between significant persons. If an individual cannot derive desired material and emotional exchanges in accordance with what the person has come to expect and feel entitled to from the referent system of equity under which he/she operates, aberrant or emotionally disordered behavior results. George Homans (1950), in canvassing numerous sociological and anthropological studies, arrives at a somewhat similar concept underlying social behavior:

> [I] envisage human behavior as a function of its payoff—social behavior [is] an exchange of activity, tangible or intangible and more or less rewarding or costly, between at least two persons—the more to a man's disadvantage the rule of distributive justice fails of realization, the more likely he is to display the emotional behavior we call anger. (p. 75)

A second psychological premise that orders my conceptual frame of reference is that the reestablishment of a mutually acceptable and equitable system of conduct between persons involved in conflict and emotional upheaval tends to lessen conflict and harmonize interpersonal exchanges. Moreover, for those individuals who have had early developmental experience pervaded by psychological exploitation and inequity in interpersonal relations, training in skillfull negotiation with others is an effective ameliorative endeavor. The concept of equity in object relations is a natural bridge to a psychotherapy that emphasizes the establishment of a working contract and the development of skills in negotiating and strategizing for need satisfaction. When the individual lacks effective negotiating skills, interpersonal accommodation, that is, the matching of his/her personal needs with the resources to satisfy them, clearly becomes difficult to attain.

Third, and most important, equity can best be achieved in interpersonal relationships when the relationship is balanced. In a relationship in which one person gives more of him/herself than does the other, the recipient becomes less valued both by the provider and by the recipient him/herself. Quite recently, social psychologists have attempted precisely to define equitable and balanced relationships by means of a "mathematical" formula. The formula says, in effect, "Two people are in an equitable relationship when the ratio of one person's outcomes to inputs is equal to the other person's outcome/input" (Walster & Walster, 1975). For my purpose, however, a phenomenological statement is preferable: a balanced relationship is one in which both agents perceive that they have something of value to give to the other and something of value to receive in return. According to Homans's analysis:

> [The] more frequently persons interact with one another, the stronger their sentiments of friendship for one another are apt to be. (1950, p. 133)

> [The] more frequently persons interact with one another, when no one of them originates interaction with much greater frequency than the other, the greater is their liking for one another and their feelings of ease in one another's presence. (1950, p. 243)

In summary, the concepts of equity and balance offer an understanding of the maintenance and deterioration of interpersonal relationship. Persons in significant relationships who are regarded by their partners according to arbitrary rather than explicitly negotiated standards of conduct experience their relationships as frustrating and unfair. In order to restore balance in the relationship, they react with retaliatory mechanisms. These observations suggest to me that attention to the normative system structuring the client's relationships must be combined with psychodynamic formulation in working with clients involved in conflictual interpersonal relationships. Similarly, attention to the normative system is essential to an understanding of the therapeutic relationship.

A CONTRACTUAL APPROACH FOR DIFFICULT CLIENTS

Obviously, techniques do not resolve characterological client resistance to therapeutic work. Psychotherapists are not infrequently faced with deciding whether to treat, and how to treat, the unwilling client. Generally, clients come into encounter with a psychotherapist because they are "overwhelmed by anxiety" or, contrastingly, they are concerned because they "feel nothing." In either case, they are generally dissatisfied with the direction their existence has taken. In other instances, people feel "forced" to enter therapy by the persuasion or coercion of others, and these clients resist treatment. I have found that the contractual approach need not be abandoned in these instances.

The contractual partnership model is the ideal psychotherapy prototype for which I aim in my practice. I realize, nonetheless, that clients are, in varying degrees, characterologically unwilling or unable to assume a responsible relationship with me. If they could, many of them probably wouldn't be seeking psychological amelioration in the first place. To varying degrees, clients generally prefer to assume positions of confusion, helplessness and inadequacy, or indifference—in order either to be saved by the omniscient magic of the therapist or to have fulfilled their belief that their personal situation is without remedy so that they can "legitimately" continue to harbor resentment and hurt and react with retaliatory mechanisms toward themselves and/or others. This is exemplified in my work with a couple, both of whom have had some professional experience in the helping arts. Alice tries to undo Barry's negotiating attempts to gain her approval and dissolve her rage at him by indicating that if she accepted the idea that personal differences could be resolved in a reasonable manner, she then would have to give up her lifelong survival mechanisms. She has only been able to survive, she tells us, by being "tolerant" of the manipulations of her psychotic mother and seductive father rather than through confidence and trust in another person's intentions.

I try, therefore, to work from whatever attitude the client comes with to engage the person in a relationship in which I provide him/her with the opportunity to negotiate for becoming the kind of person he/she wishes to be. *Therapeutic Partnership* (Goldberg, 1977) examines a considerable number of these cases in depth. It occurred to me when writing this book that power relations are implicit in our struggles with our clients.

THE UNSPOKEN DIMENSION OF POWER IN PSYCHOTHERAPY

If there is a single characteristic common to all who seek psychotherapy, it is the sense of loss or absence of personal power, with the concomitant sense of lost adequacy. Psychotherapists appear to agree that despite the diversity of symptoms and complaints clients present upon entering treatment, the common feeling is one of self-denigration. The psychotherapeutic experience is designed to supplement the client's natural group associations where they have failed to meet his/her needs adequately. Psychotherapy is devised precisely to resist rules and directives that have frustrated the client's previous attempts at a consistent and gratifying conceptualization of self. This section is intended to give the reader a greater appreciation of the significance that therapist-client power struggles have in the course of psychotherapy.

It is the nature of human interaction that people try to influence one another. Many of these endeavors are conducted in such a way that people can choose whether or not they will be influenced. In many other situations, however, people have little or no choice about the nature and the impact of how others will try to influence them. In which category is psychotherapy? As an influence process, is psychotherapy a democratic or egalitarian endeavor, as many of its practitioners claim? Are therapist-client struggles for control, therefore, essentially attributable to transference and countertransference distortions? Or are these struggles more frequently the *sine qua non* of interpersonal relations, without which psychotherapy would represent a pale imitation of social reality?

Power dynamics should be a basic concern in the conduct of psychotherapy. Power in psychotherapy refers to the awesome capability the therapist is given by the client (reinforced by societal sanctions) to affect the client's life and the lives of others who, though not clients of the therapist, live within the societal system of the client who is being treated (Gelb, 1972). In my view, neither theorists nor practitioners of psychotherapy have given sufficient attention to the issue of power in psychotherapy; for the most part, it remains as unacknowledged dimension.

Three analysts (Gadpaille, 1972; Gelb, 1972; Enelow, 1972) who have concerned themselves with the denial of power in the conduct of psychotherapy argue that an important reason for failures in psychoanalytic therapy has to do with the analyst ignoring the client's distorted and often exploitative interpersonal relationships with people in the client's social system. Because of the focus on the client's internal psychological processes, the manifestation of the client's conflictual interpersonal relations may be less appreciated in an analytic situation than it can be in psychotherapy in which interactions are encouraged. In this chapter, I will limit my discussion of power relations to the denial of power struggles within the therapist-client relationship. I believe that this denial supports a basic dishonesty that contradicts the ideals of autonomy, informed choice, and psychological freedom that psychotherapy as an enterprise manifestly purports to engender.

In New York City, a number of years ago, I was a participant in a workshop for experienced group psychotherapists. The workshop dealt with the rationale and technique of group supervision. The workshop leader was a renowned and rather strong-willed female analyst. Several other participants and I were disconcerted by the direction the workshop had taken. The workshop leader had told us that the workshop was ours (the participants'). It was all right with her, she said, to discuss whatever topic we wished and to explore these topics in any way we wanted. Nonetheless, it appeared rather difficult if not impossible to launch into issues that some of the participants wanted to explore. In answer to questions of procedural direction raised by the participants, the workshop leader offered psychodynamic explanations categorically supporting or denying the usefulness of our comments for the consideration of what was transpiring in the workshop.

The most salient issue that was shaping the covert tensions and the direction the workshop had taken, it seemed to me, was the workshop leader's use of power. When I pointed this out to her, she became rather annoyed. She indicated that "power has no importance in psychotherapy. Psychotherapy is an almost democratic process. We must always deal fairly with our patients—otherwise it is a countertransference problem. It needs to be worked out in the therapist's own analysis. But I don't want to talk any more about power. It is not important. Let us talk about other things!" The concept of power seemed repugnant to her. This led me to believe that in her view the struggle for power was essentially the client's problem, not that of the therapist.

Was the workshop leader correct in describing psychotherapy as an almost democratic enterprise? I was struck by the modifier "almost." To me, the term "almost democratic" conceded a threat, a fear, and a cover-up by the analyst and the therapeutic orientation that she represented. This orientation suggested to me that the therapist and clients are equal, but like some of the creatures in George Orwell's *Animal Farm,* the therapist is just a little more equal and just a little more knowledgeable about the direction the therapeutic relationship should take than are his/her clients. It is this inherent imbalance that gives the therapist the right to be less than equitable with his/her clients. If my inference is valid, then it seems to me that a psychotherapist, operating from this orientation, is espousing a hypocritical status denial. The psychotherapist says implicitly to his/her clients, "We are all in this situation together—to learn and grow. Just because you people pay a fee and I collect it, doesn't necessarily mean that I am different or better than you. You must realize that I, like you, need to eat and provide for myself. (But here is the catch!) You experience yourself as not being able to deal with your condition because you essentially feel powerless. But, then, I don't feel that way about myself. I don't feel powerless as long as you believe and act upon the notion that I am worthy of being paid and continue to look to me for help. I guess, then, we're not alike, after all!"

POWER AND SUICIDE THREAT

Therapeutic and clinical data provide abundant evidence that therapists and their clients are frequently, if not inevitably, involved in point-counterpoint power maneuvers with one another. In this process, the psychotherapist may become threatened by the client's manipulations. In turn, as Haley (1969) has forcefully described, the therapist may revert to reactive manipulation of the client and his/her situation in order to regain control over the therapeutic enterprise and thus diminish the threat to his/her reputation and sense of adequacy as a therapist. Occasionally, a therapist becomes so frightened, angry, and vindictive that the practitioner is unwilling or unable to examine critically the irrational, reactive posture the practitioner assumed toward his/her client's power ploys.

One of the most potent and frightening power tactics employed by clients is the threat of suicide. Psychotherapists often experience their reputations, self-esteem, and sense of adequacy as integrally linked to their effectiveness in checkmating the client's suicide threat. At least one well-known psychotherapist prefers to regard his manipulative therapeutic strategies as intentional, clinically indicated techniques rather than as emotional reactions to his clients' power ploys. This therapist, who undoubtedly represents countless other therapists who have the need to deny their own emotional reaction to client power, says,

Humanitarian fervor aside, it's the therapist's job to take power over the patient, push ahead with solving the problem, then convince the patient he or she is better, even if it means being devious. He can develop ploys beyond the wildest dream of a car salesman. One is to make patients work or suffer to get into therapy and so increase their belief in its value. (Gillis, 1974)

The following are just three provocative examples of the checkmates that therapists with a manipulative orientation employ to invalidate a client's suicidal power ploy: A client calls the therapist late one night and says that he/she is seriously contemplating suicide. The therapist tells the client to come to the office the next morning and not to take any action until then. As the client enters the office, the therapist greets him/her with, "You are going right into the hospital and you are not coming out until I have some assurance that you have stopped acting like a child!" Or the therapist may say, "Threaten me with suicide, you bastard, and I'll make you a promise that if you succeed and kill yourself, I'll go over to your grave and piss on it. Just keep that in mind." Or the therapist may say, "Look, friend, my practice is confined to clients who want to work on their problems. I won't stand for your wasting my time nor with threatening me with suicide. If you are to continue to work with me, I will insist that you secure a life insurance policy that names me as beneficiary." These ploys have been used by several experienced psychotherapists of my acquaintance. The first of them is so ubiquitously employed by therapists that the strategy has long since attained the stature of a clinically indicated technique, which, nonetheless, doesn't alter the fact that it is a very powerful and often devasting checkmate.

There are those practitioners who not only refuse to give in to their clients' power ploys, but actually seem to enjoy the challenge of a client's suicide threat. One such practitioner refers to himself as a humanistic guru. One of his clients called me. The client was a psychotherapist himself and had worked with me as a colleague a number of years before. He told me in a rather agitated conversation that he had been seeing this guru psychologist for a couple of years. In the past year or so the client had become increasingly more depressed and suicidal. He had even bought a second-hand pistol. He told his therapist that he felt so worthless and confused that he had been seriously considering going out into the woods and putting a pistol to his head and blowing his brains out. His guru reacted with a barrage of abusive and denigrative statements, telling him that he was clearly a coward, and probably a fag as well. Indeed, the therapist emphasized, this opportunity might be the client's moment of truth—a test to see if he had any guts. The client faced his moment of truth. He fulfilled his fantasy and put the gun to his head and pulled the trigger. Apparently the gun was in poor condition; fortunately, it didn't fire. Was this moment of truth a productive growth experience for the client? He didn't think so. He hadn't resolved the issues for which he had gone into therapy, and now he had to struggle with additional rage, confusion, and fright about the power he had given to the therapist over his life. Those who deny that power is a significant unspoken issue in psychotherapy would undoubtedly write off the above illustration as the flare-up in the guru of serious and unresolved feelings of countertransference. Whether or not the issue is simply one of countertransference, innumerable cases I can cite suggest that the use and potential abuse of power is central to the therapeutic relationship and frequently lies at the heart of many of the covert tensions.

Many therapists are anxious to avoid employing checkmating power strategies that divest the client of his/her power and sense of adequacy. They realize that a therapist cannot be a useful agent for the client if the practitioner cares too much whether or not the client succeeds. If the therapist cares too much—indeed cares more than the client cares for him/herself—the client can manipulate the therapist's caring in order to retain neurotic and psychopathic patterns. This creates a situation in which the therapist is the center of the therapeutic process and the one who determines therapeutic success. The psychotherapy is based upon the therapist's choices and their consequences rather than upon those of the client.

Adding to the problem of power is the fact that, whereas a practitioner may be anxious to avoid abusing his/her power in a therapeutic relationship, the clients frequently wish to divest themselves of power and adequacy in dealing with their life situation, leaving themselves incapable of taking care of themselves. The following case accords with Thibaut and Kelley's concept (1959) of *dyadic connection,* indicating that in a stressful interpersonal situation in which a client experiences him/herself as having no direct control over his/her own outcomes, the client can use the ability to act in a dysfunctional manner to control the other's outcome so as to influence his/her own payoffs, i.e., have the other take care of the client. In psychodynamic terms, this is referred to as *secondary gain*. The psychotherapist is placed in the bind of having to choose whether to take care of the client—in many instances, as in the following case, with personal loss to him/herself—or to withold from the client the psychological attention the client acutely requires.

A hippyish-sounding 25 year-old woman telephoned a therapist, whose name she had received from a hotline referral service. The woman stated that she had been in treatment for over two years with a rather passive female social worker who simply interpreted her behavior and at the same time let her avoid issues with which the client felt she needed to deal actively. The client claimed that she needed a confrontative therapist. However, she was not currently working and could not afford the therapist's full fee, though she expected to get a job and health insurance shortly. The therapist agreed to see her at a reduced fee set during the initial interview. There were three sessions. They agreed that the client would pay at the time of each session because the client had difficulty budgeting her money. At the third session, the client reported that she had forgotten to bring a check. The therapist indicated that according to their agreement he would need to receive a check before he would schedule another session. She agreed to mail him a check that day. A week later no check had arrived. The client called and said that she had been raped that week and needed to see the therapist. The therapist agreed to see her but sheepishly pointed out that she had not complied with her agreement. The client angrily indicated that she had lost her job and wouldn't be able to pay for that session, either, and she reproached the therapist for his materialistic attitude. The client did not show up for the scheduled appointment. She called later that day, saying that she had been detained at the police station concerning the rape. She asked not to be charged for the session since she couldn't afford the money and she especially needed help then.

It is my impression that what traditionally has been regarded as unethical therapist behavior frequently occurs at this kind of juncture in the therapist-client relationship in which the client fails to keep the payment clauses of the contract. The therapist, feeling exploited and used, may ask implicitly to be repaid in love for his caring and taking care of the client. Sexual exploitation may also arise from the therapist feeling disdain for the client because of the practitioner's sense of superiority. Sexual exploitation may also result from the therapist believing that he/she has something of extraordinary value—something others have not been able to give the client, e.g., an inorgasmic woman, a climax; a schizophrenic, understanding. This exploitation generally results from the therapist's frustrating inability to help the client by indirect, psychological means. I am speaking here of *love treatment,* whether it involves sexual intimacy or not. Love treatment refers to potentially very potent abuses of the therapist's power. There are some people who can in perhaps no other way gain the power, influence, and love they can as therapists drawn into the field of psychotherapy. To avoid slipping into the exchange of love for caring, there is a need for clarity about the specific goals therapist and client have for being in a therapeutic encounter.

The exchange of a fee for a service, as materialistic as it may appear, serves to reinforce the essential notion that psychotherapy is an exchange that benefits both agents. Without a clear reciprocal consequence for the practitioner's involvement, there is often confusion about why the agents are involved in an encounter, and a firm understanding about fees can help to avoid this.

For the therapist whose sense of personal adequacy is well integrated, the transference phenomena reflected in the case I have cited serves as a useful therapeutic dimension. For the therapist who doubts his own adequacy and avoids critically assessing his illusory powers, however, the potential for abuse is serious and manifold. He/she is apt to feel, "Maybe I am lovable and desirable after all. Maybe it is not the patient's distortion, but that *he/she knows something others cannot or will not see. I must hold on to him/her because he/she makes me feel powerful and adequate!*"

Perhaps the most crucial question that these cases raise is also reflected in the statement of a well-known psychiatric educator, Hans Huessy, about ethical concerns in the conduct of psychotherapy:

> I suspect that instead of finding too many kinds of gross abuses, the more difficult problem that [needs to be addressed] is how is the decision made as to what kinds of therapy are used for what kinds of patients. The caricature of American psychiatry and psychology is that the treatment is not determined by the patient's ailment but by the therapist's predilection. (personal communication)

THERAPIST'S RELATIONSHIP WITH A CLIENT

A contractual model in psychotherapy requires that each agent negotiate with the other without resorting to abuse of power, tactics of coercion, or manipulation. Therapists are more likely to resort to power strategies at those junctures in the therapeutic process in which they regard the client as "resisting" treatment. Too often, in their client's experiences outside of therapy, the client has become overwhelmed with an inability to express disagreements with others, and as a result, the client has chosen to cherish personal differences with others as too sacred to question. In previous interpersonal encounters, therefore, the client has refused to examine images of him/herself and others in an open and negotiable manner. The client brings the same resistance into the therapeutic relationship. The occurence of resistence in psychotherapy indicates that the client and the therapist have reached a crucial point in their interpersonal encounter. The therapist must help the client to experience difficulties with external intrusion and learn to handle them in a constructive manner. Concurrently, the client must alert the therapist that he/she is experiencing a personal difference with the therapist and wishes assistance in dealing with his/her feelings. The therapist who is able to help the client tolerate the experience of opposition to others does so by personally demonstrating that the occurrence will not cast the client adrift from human company.

I agree with Schafer (1974) that *speaking personally* rather than "objectively" and "clinically" with a client is the preferred mode of dialogue in a therapeutic encounter. The power of the psychotherapist to help the client stems from the relationship; human power has very little meaning outside the context of a relationship. The practitioner's progressive and spontaneous personal declaration of understanding where he/she is in relation to the person with whom he/she is in encounter confirms that there is meaning and purpose in the client's being-in-the-world, and that the difficulties the client experiences in pursuing his/her humanity may be dealt with by means within the client's own power and capabilities. When a client experiences his/her behavior being responded to in terms of explicitly negotiated roles and responsibilities, the client experiences the relationship as incomparably fairer than a relationship based upon implicitly set rules he/she had no part in establishing. In the former type of relationship, the client experiences him/herself as having permission to utilize his/her own personal power in meeting his/her needs. By freely negotiating the terms of their relationship, the therapist supports the client's prerogative to seek whatever he/she wishes to be because, although therapist and client may be interrelated in a caring relationship, they are ultimately and ideally separate and autonomous persons.

Even the best intentions and practice, however, will not prevent the therapist's values from shaping his/her stance toward the client. At some point, ignorance, insensitivity, or a momentary slip will cause one of the agents to interact with the other in disregard of the established way of interacting. The inevitable clash of values has, of course, serious consequences for the therapeutic relationship. The therapist, by dealing immediately and directly with his/her own reactions to behavior about which he/she has strong feelings and convictions, conveys to the client that the client's concerns are not his/hers alone to solve. Problems, tensions, strains in the therapeutic relationship are issues that can be openly and mutually dealt with. Strains within the therapeutic relationship involve both client and therapist, deeply and personally. Such conflicts in therapy are not procedural issues that require merely technical manipulation. Having encountered a resistance, the therapist and client together explore ways of discovering the source, be it in the therapist or in the client or, more likely, in the condition of their interrelationship (Goldberg, 1977).

The therapist enables the patient to become what the client intends to be by respecting the client's potential for autonomy and self-development. The practitioner does so by not trying to protect the other from making mistakes nor does the practitioner impose his/her value system on the other. This sentiment is rooted in both existential and psychoanalytic theory: We can't force the patient to grow, we can only coax him. Only he can prefer it; no one can prefer it for him (May, 1961). "The patient should be educated to liberate and fulfill his own nature, not to resemble ourselves [the therapist]" (Freud, 1919).

The therapist presents his/her point of view as the therapist's own. The therapist enters into the therapeutic relationship with the intention neither to persuade the other, nor to accept the other's behavior uncritically. The practitioner treats the other as he/she expects to be treated—openly and congruently. The practitioner presents him/herself as an autonomous person and exudes the potence of being autonomous. The practitioner proposes by his/her own behavior that interpersonal exchanges be made on the basis of negotiation rather than by use of threat, manipulation, or authority. The practitioner acts responsibly, accepting his/her behavior as being of his/her own choosing. The practitioner deals openly with the consequences of his/her choices. The practitioner also protects his/her own integrity and that of the therapeutic relationship. If the client fails to act responsibly, that is, if the client is unwilling to comply with the contract they have both agreed upon and will not negotiate for another, the therapist severs the relationship without anger or condemnation. The practitioner explains precisely the reasons for his/her decisions. The practitioner points out his/her responsibility to him/herself and his/her work not to be exploited by the other. Szasz (1969) stated this attitude clearly and succinctly: "The analyst tries to help his client, he does not 'take care of him.' The patient takes care of himself" (p. 24).

To this we may add H. F. Thomas's (1967) advice: "An important aspect of therapy is the therapist's refusal to allow the client to use emotional disturbance as an excuse for not facing responsibility."

Sally did not feel she was able to pay her monthly therapy bill. Her insurance company had not sent her the previous two months' payment. She also failed to contact her insurance company. The therapist, rather than treating her as sick and disabled, regarded her as separable from the therapist and his choices and therefore as responsible for her own decisions. The therapist calmly inquired if she were asking his permission to call her insurance company. He asked, on second thought, if Sally were asking to be excused from her scheduled payment because she had been irresponsible in following up her obligations. The therapist informed Sally that if he accepted a late payment in this situation, he would be condoning her irresponsibility. A person's striving for autonomy, completion, and mastery over his/her own growth and development are fulfilled when the person takes responsibility for his/her own actions. Taking responsibility for oneself is a prerequisite for accepting one's personal worth and finding the meaning of one's existence (Goldberg, 1973).

The purpose of this chapter has been to explore specific ways in which practitioners and their clients can effect a meaningful therapeutic partnership by being cognizant of and responsive to the manifestations of equity and balance in their relationship. The following factors are, in my experience, integral to a meaningful therapeutic encounter:

1. Attention to the manifestation of equity and balance in the therapeutic relationship.

2. Exploration of the manifestations and utilization of power in the relationship and its effects upon the feelings of adequacy of each of the agents.

3. Clarity of contractual roles and responsibilities.

4. Clarity of therapeutic goals.

5. Exploration of how permission and informed consent are manifested in the relationship.

6. Exploration of how each of the agents communicates and meets needs in the relationship.

7. Clarity about the administrative contract.

8. Exploration of how the above-mentioned issues are negotiated for in the relationship.

9. Provision for review, evaluation, and modification of the working relationship.

In the next four chapters we will explore how the issues raised in this chapter are articulated in psychotherapeutic work.

NOTES

1. The ideas and concepts found in this chapter are developed in more detail in the author's *Therapeutic Partnership* (1977).

2. It is hardly surprising that we regard the schizophrenic who violates language roles and signs as infrahuman.

3. The sacredness of contract is integral to the American character. It is zealously guarded by American courts, beginning with the landmark decision *Dartmouth College v. New Hampshire* in 1819.

4. "Unlike the businessman, who aims to sell products, compete and make a profit, the professional's first goal is to perform a service. Therefore, society gives the professional certain privileges based on the expectation that professional ethics will prevent exploitation" (Shore, 1973).

Chapter 10
The Role of Intimacy in Psychotherapy

In every consulting room, there ought to be two rather frightened people: the patient and the therapist. If they are not frightened, one wonders why they are bothering to find out what everyone knows.
—W. R. Bion

To examine meaningfully the role of intimacy in psychotherapy, we need some perspective about the relationship of intimacy and human suffering. If this contention is not readily apparent at the onset of this chapter, then it should be by its conclusion.

HUMAN SUFFERING

Both philosophy and psychology have been concerned with the nature of the self and how it comes into being. Neither of these disciplines, however, appears to have very definitive ideas about how the self is developed and constituted, which results in some people responding to the suffering in their human condition with courage and fortitude, while others are host to alienation and despair. Suffering is not a subject to which philosophers have paid sufficient attention. George Simmel, the highly respected German philosopher and social theorist, is reported to have remarked that suffering is not what philosophy is all about, as if there is something tainted or unclean about the subject matter (Natanson, 1981). Moreover, physically, the presence of suffering in others can easily be ignored. Unlike related subjects like evil, which requires an audience, suffering can be borne silently and alone.

Correspondingly, psychologists cannot rightfully chagrin other disciplines for not forthrightly dealing with suffering. Those of us who are clinicians are expected to be concerned with human suffering as part and parcel of our daily professional endeavors. But we have done little more than treat the symptoms of suffering. Admittedly, some philosophers, such as Albert Camus, have claimed that a person's first responsibility is to struggle with the suffering caused by other humans. Nevertheless, few philosophers or psychologists have attempted penetrating examination into the etiology and meaning of human suffering. In this chapter, I will seek to demonstrate the strong interrelationship between the mirror image and the experience of suffering, and how this interrelationship pertains to the role of intimacy in psychotherapy.

I will begin by addressing one of the most common manifestations of suffering—loneliness. Daily and in large numbers, people consult psychotherapists with a slew of complaints, such as depression, addiction, marital conflict, etc. Few realize that it is loneliness for which they are actually seeking help.

In the last few years, a number of writers have helped loneliness[1] to escape from the closet. In former times, to admit about oneself, or even to describe someone else as lonely, would have been tantamount to an indictment of immorality. It were as if the statement of loneliness was a demonstration of loss of faith in the divine powers, no less than a lack of benevolence toward other human beings. This attitude was reflected in the statements of those who insisted that loneliness was a companion of selfishness. No one, they claimed, would need ever to be lonely if they were concerned with others. According to this point of view, it is egocentric interests which lead to loneliness. Personally intimate with loneliness, the Danish philosopher and theologian. Søren Kierkegaard (1954) wrote that the person who is seen frequently alone in the street is pitied and shunned, whereas the person who is rarely seen alone is envied. I believe that this attitude of pity and disdain for the lonely still forcefully pervades modern humanity's sentiments and attitudes. I also believe that it evokes considerable discomfort and disdain to be confronted by another's loneliness. Other people's grief mirrors our own. We wish to avoid the mirror of our own inner being. A recent feature article in the *New York Times* by Susan Jacoby (1983) rhetorically asked, since grief is a universal human experience, why do "so many people find themselves unable to offer the right sort of consolation even when they desperately wish to do so?" To offer true consolation, Jacoby answered, is to "share something of the taste of grief."

An incident in which I was involved about a year ago showed me that even those who are supposedly the best informed on the subject and involved in treating the maladies emanating from loneliness, may show considerable discomfort in the presence of the lonely and forlorn. Late one afternoon, while attending a medical conference, a psychiatrist friend and I observed a crowd gathering in the lobby of the hotel in which the conference was being held. There were 15 or 20 poorly attired, sad-looking men and women linking arms and silently sitting on the floor of the lobby. Some even looked frightened. A few held poster cards protesting against electric shock treatment and excessive psychopharmacological treatment. Among the bystanders we recognized a number of physicians from the conference. We were told that the protesters had been sitting there for a few hours. During the time we stood there these people expressed neither hostility nor provocative action toward anyone. In fact, they neither spoke nor moved from where they sat. After we were there about an hour, six police officers appeared on the scene and began to disrupt the calm. First, a police sergeant and a plain-clothes officer spoke with each of the protesters. After a while, police reinforcements arrived. They began pulling each of the people from the circle. Since they had joined arms in an attempt to maintain their position within the circle, they had to be separated forcefully. The resistance, however, was quite passive. Two officers were assigned to each protester; one by one each protester was dragged through the long and crowded lobby of the hotel and taken who knows where.

By this time, we developed strong feelings that these people, who were causing no apparent harm to anyone, were being abused. My colleague and I went to investigate the cause for their removal. We were told by one of the officers that there had been "orders" and that we, by our inquiry, were obstructing these "orders." We were told that if we continued, we were liable to be arrested. We, nevertheless, stated that we had an objection to what was being done to these people. We were referred to the hotel management who, we were told, had requested the presence of the police. The assistant manager turned out to be a very pleasant young woman. She explained to us that the hotel management had no grievance with the protestors, that the request for their removal was in response to a number of doctors from our conference who had sternly reproached the hotel management for not having the protestors removed from private property. Clearly, the hotel management did not want to antagonize its clients. What was most disconcerting to us was the response of the physicians who requested or demanded the removal of silent objectors. That some members of the healing professions could not tolerate the manifestations of a silent controversy from people who appeared to be suffering does not say much for the courage or caring of our colleagues. Their actions did much more to confirm the validity of the protestors' accusations than all the placards in the world.[2]

In her thoughtful article in *The New York Times,* Susan Jacoby indicated that in our contemporary society there are social forces that encourage us to ignore the suffering of others. Americans, she points out, "tend to become impatient with those who do not make haste to 'get on' with their lives." Therefore, "we tend to ignore grief that is somewhat removed from the predictable social order." Perhaps the physicians who protested the presence of the protesters could assume concern and involvement with their suffering patients in the clearly defined role of "doctor," in a setting in which the sufferer is clearly defined as a "patient." On the other hand, removed from the confines of these allocated roles of doctor and patient, they could or would do no more than express their inhumanity.

SUFFERING AS LEARNED

Organisms experience pain, but pain does not become suffering until it is translated in a category of meaning. This category of meaning is derived from assumptions and expectations conveyed to us by others. We do not know what we are experiencing, in many instances, without trying to see ourselves as others do. Suffering, therefore, is an interpersonal and learned process. It is a socioemotional statement that our state of being is intolerable because it is contradictory to how we have been led to believe our existence should be experienced (Goldberg, 1984b). The Polish philosopher Josef Kozrelecki indicates in reaction to the overinclusive existential notion that humans are constantly suffering, that, in fact, what is more accurate is that they suffer only when their highest values are threatened. "The loss of other desirable things and experiences can only give rise to feelings of unpleasantness. Most people suffer when they lost their health, when love comes to an end, when they have no daily bread and no roof over their heads [or] when they 'lose face' " (Kozrelecki, 1978).

The self, as sociologists such as Charles H. Cooley (1900) and George H. Mead (1934) conceptualized it, is a "looking-glass self," consisting of the reflected appraisals of others. A person and a mirror, similarly to a person in dialogue with another, create a self. In assuming the attitude of the other in dialogue with our mirror, we see ourselves through the eyes of others. In short, the mirror teaches us to see ourselves as we imagine others see us. The bold sight of one's own vulnerabilities through the inferred eyes of others evokes the threat of suffering. In order to reverse the threat of suffering, the self may attempt to undo its image and remake itself, concealing parts of itself in the process. The mirror graphically conceptualizes the self's relation to the world, and as such, provides the opportunity to rehearse its relationship with the world. It has been said of Shakespeare's Richard III that throughout the play he seems to be watching himself in an unseen mirror, measuring his emotions to meet the vexing challenges of his world (Gussow, 1982).

Those people like Roger, who was discussed in Chapter 2, who have not been able to find beauty and contentment within themselves, seek external mirrors to validate their existence. The price one may have to pay for being mirrored by another person is that, at times, the "mirror" may reflect an untoward and threatening representation of the self. These adverse reflections may evoke terror and dread in the person being given his similitude. Those who will not, or cannot, share these terrors with others are forced to suffer their terrors alone.

Several years ago, on a Friday evening about supper time, I stopped off in a rather unpretentious coffee shop in the midst of the quite fashionable upper East side of Manhattan. I had a few hours on my hands before I was to meet a friend for dinner. As I sat and drank coffee, I canvassed the faces along the counter and those in the booths along the opposite wall. Of these, one person captivated my attention. She did not stand out because she was particularly attractive or because of her attire. Rather, she seemed intent on being unobtrusive. She appeared to be in her late thirties, with an intelligent face and drab-looking clothes. She conveyed a sense of loneliness and the lack of attachment to any caring other person. Although she did not appear indigent, she only ordered a bowl of soup. She drank it thirstily, with what appeared to be more greed than gusto. It was as if this bowl of hot soup was all to which she felt entitled.

As I sat observing her, a short story of Franz Kafka came to mind. The fable concerns a young man who attempted to treat his sense of inner emptiness with methodical desperation. Kafka informs us that the young man was a petty bureaucrat in some insignificant governmental office in Prague. One day he awoke and realized that his life was scheduled by his attention to a series of meaningless activities. He decided to free some of his time so that he could attend to more worthwhile pursuits. First, he stopped shaving in the morning. Next, he totally stopped grooming himself. After a few days, due to his self-consciousness about his unkempt appearance, he remained in his apartment. After a while, he would not leave his couch. He just lay there until he died.

When I first read this story in college, I interpreted Kafka to imply that the young man died of prolonged boredom. More recently, after many years as a psychotherapy practitioner, I have come to regard the story differently. Many people, it seems to me, go through life with little awareness or interest in what is happening *inside* themselves unless they are experiencing physical or psychic pain. With all the trivial activities of his life removed, Kafka's young man had no means of distracting himself from what was happening inside of himself. He was forced to listen to the sounds of terror within his psyche. He must have died quite quickly of sheer fright. Kafka leaves us with the same alarming message in all of his short stories and novels: that which is most basic to human existence is the terror and fright of being alone in the world. And yet, in some intuitive sense, each of us knows that loneliness is not intrinsic to our being in the world. It is the unavailability of others, or our inability to reach for others, to share these terrors which lead to loneliness. For some people, protective subterfuge is required in order to remain in contact with other people.

Gina, a lovely and lonely social worker of 35, lived with her mother. Her mother had deserted her at about age five. Gina had searched for her for many years. It was only at age 30 that Gina found her. Yet, finding her mother unfortunately did not put to rest her fears. She attempted to protect herself from her terrors of being taken by surprise by others, by always having her phone answering machine on, even when she was home. She did not, under this arrangement, have to talk on the phone to anyone without knowing beforehand who the caller was. Gina's voice on the phone machine had become her double, a second self, which was for many callers the only image of Gina available to them. In some ways, the voice on the machine was more real than Gina, herself, because the machine message was presented to the world of others, while Gina was hidden and undisclosed. In this sense, the phone machine served as a mirror object (a subject we discussed in Chapter 2) to hide Gina's fears and vulnerabilities. Gina's phone message to others remained constant and unaffected by her own feeling states. The cost of this deception, of course, was Gina's increasing loss of contact with others and the resultant loneliness and alienation.

The foregoing has depicted the mirror, or mirroring object, as a dangerous object. Clearly, however, the mirror has a potentially constructive function, as well. The self, as reflected in our image, is the medium for the person's relation to the world of other people. I would not need a sense of self other than in relation to another person. Moreover, the affectivity which I experience in regard to how I perceive how I present myself to the world reflected in my mirror image enables me to become aware of my relation to other people. For most of us, mirrors and mirroring relationships are a continual and inseparable part of the endeavor to make sense of who we are.

To face the mirror squarely and probingly, courage is required. Unfortunately, social scientists have not given the concept of courage much attention. This has had deleterious effects on the practice of psychotherapy because, as I will try to demonstrate in this chapter, the psychotherapy practitioner needs to devote as much attention to fostering passionate attributes in those he/she works with as in encouraging an understanding of behavior.

THE NEGLECT OF COURAGE
IN THE BEHAVIORAL SCIENCES

Courage, as I have been using the term, is both an acceptance and a willingness to transcend, by active modification, a world that is experienced as not intrinsically or essentially based on justice, equity, accountability, or compassion. In both acceptance and transcendence, the self requires passion and commitment toward itself in order to suspend, modify, overcome, or endure the self's fears in being and acting in a required or desired way (Goldberg & Simon, 1982). Interestingly, Freud's definition of psychotherapy implicitly assumed a similar definition of courage. Freud defined the goal of psychotherapy as "the willingness to change that which can be changed and accept that which cannot."[3] Courage, therefore, should make possible a fuller appreciation of one's own personal truths.

If this is valid, then, the psychotherapy situation—as a reputed sanctuary from deceit, pretense, and inhibition, the setting *par excellence* for the baring of naked truth—should be an ideal arena for examining the nature of courage. However, the exploration of the role of courage and risk in psychiatry, as psychoanalyst Leon Salzman (1974) has indicated, has long been neglected. This is unfortunate. Narcissism and other so-called modern psychiatric "illnesses" have to do with the fear and unwillingness to make meaningful and deeply experienced commitments. Acts of courage may serve, then, as antidotes to narcissistic dilemmas. As such, psychotherapy clinicians need to understand how courage develops and matures. Unfortunately, courage is a concept that has been assiduously avoided by behavioral scientists and modern philosophers in explaining human behavior. To the behavioral scientist, no doubt, courage is a term best left with athletes, soldiers, and true believers. Courage is an attribute of passion, which cannot be readily accounted for in scientific and deterministic terms. To the behavioral scientist, no doubt, it smacks of ascribing enviable characteristics to behaviors that would have inevitably occurred without the imposition of the hypothesized emotion we call "courage." A mechanistic view of human behavior would suggest that the imputation of courage is not actually necessary for accounting for human action. But, without the attribution of courage, human dignity and passion become quickly dismantled (Goldberg & Simon, 1982).

I believe that psychotherapists are particularly uncomfortable about appearing to promote concepts having to do with passion in psychotherapy because they fear that it might reveal certain of their own narcissistic inclinations. As I am sure the reader is aware, in today's society to refer to anyone as "narcissistic" is an act of derision.

It may be of some value to review some of the confusions and controversy about narcissism in the psychotherapy field for the reader to appreciate the tumultuous identity problem in which the psychotherapy establishment is now involved.

THE CONTEMPORARY VIEW OF NARCISSISM

In our day, narcissism has become a ubiquitously recognized and misused concept. Due to the contradictory and manifold formulations of the concept in the psychoanalytic literature over the years, narcissism has fostered considerable controversy and confusion even in its narrow technical meanings. The seeds of ambiguity about the meaning of narcissism closely follow the vicissitudes in the growth of psychoanalytic conceptualization. Roberta Satow (1982) has indicated that Freud in his writings employed the concept of narcissism in at least four different ways:

1. As a defense against painful disappointments, within context of libido theory, narcissism was referred to as energy directed towards the ego as opposed to objects.

2. In terms of object relations, as the ego attempts to control other objects in order to maintain a blissful or perfect existence, narcissism was characterized as a type of object choice and a means of relating to these objects.

3. From a genetic perspective, narcissism was viewed as a normal developmental stage in which libidinal energy is neutralized.

4. From a structural point of view, narcissism was discussed in terms of difficulties in denying the self's limitations and imperfections in the regulation of self-esteem.

The legion of writers on the subject of narcissism have produced divergent emphases and contradictions because they have predicated their theoretical and clinical formulations in terms of different meanings of the concept. Currently, the concept has become a rallying point for almost every and any dispute and contradiction among the various proponents of psychoanalytic theory and practice. Moreover, as the leading figures of psychoanalytic cults, such as Otto Kernberg and Heinz Kohut, have achieved almost the status of folk heroes, many of their ideas about narcissism have descended to society-at-large in some rather unfortunately reductionistic and pejorative ways (Goldberg, 1984[b]).

Those who support this reductionism generally argue that narcissistic personality features such as self-aggrandizement, the quest for unlimited self-expression and accentuated individualism refer less to specific intrapsychic dynamics and psychopathology as it does to cultural attitudes and values shared in common in society-at-large. Other social scientists, such as Clement (1982), have argued, in vehement opposition to this view, that the eager willingness to label social experience and ourselves in terms of a particularly unattractive psychiatric diagnosis is no less a manifestation of a "masochistic" American tradition as it is narcissistic. Again, we must be aware that the use of diagnostic terms such as "masochism" misappropriates a specific intrapsychic description in order to interpret cultural phenomenon at another level of analysis. I do not have space in this chapter to examine this interesting controversy in detail. The interested reader is referred to Clement's excellent article.

A CHANGING ROLE:
PSYCHOTHERAPIST AS AFFECTIVE AGENT

The psychoanalytic tradition has until recent times cautioned the practitioner against his/her full participation in the therapeutic process. With a misunderstanding of Freud's legendary dictum of "Where id is ego shall be" (Freud, 1960 [1921]), therapists have sought to specialize in rendering their cognitive contributions to the therapeutic alliance. Although there has been growing recognition of the need for the therapist to be affectively receptive to the client, nevertheless, the therapist is trained to transform his/her affective reception of the client's material into cognitive premises in terms of his/her responses to the client. In other words, the therapist is trained to use affect to understand and then employ understanding cognitively to help the patient express his/her own affective intent. Therapeutic expression that is affectively expressed rather than transformed into cognitive expression has been regarded as clinically inappropriate, a countertransferential reaction of the therapist and inimical to effective analytic work. This is because affective expression is seen as self-relevatory of the therapist. Generally, analytic theory posits that self-revelatory expression by the therapist leads to repressive tendencies in the patient.

In sharp contrast, in my work with rather disturbed clients suffering from preoedipal conditions, I have found that the therapist's use of his or her own affective expression is vital to the therapeutic process. Because the expression of emotion is vital to any intimate experience, it cannot be denied in psychotherapy if the endeavor is to be a meaningful one. The delineation of these issues will be described in Chapter 12.

In the following pages I will discuss a particular paradigm of psychotherapy which takes into account the issues, phenomenon, and concerns already discussed in this book. This paradigm is not beholden to or in allegiance with any particular school of psychotherapy. I believe, rather, that it is central to all sound psychotherapy.

THE ROLE OF INTIMACY IN PSYCHOTHERAPY

How does therapeutic intimacy differ from intimacy experienced in everyday life? Therapeutic intimacy has a *time,* a *place,* and an imposition of *explicit comment* upon its ongoing process. These three components are necessary because the bond between therapist and patient is not that of love—rather to say, love is not required—but of shared intimacy. The striving for intimacy emanates from an accentuated sense of aloneness and a wish to bridge the separation between the self and the other. The hallmark of intimate strivings, in contrast to love, is an *immediate* encounter and exchange with its desired object. The act of love may intend toward, but not necessarily require the presence of, the other. Because the immediacy of the other is required in the intimate moment, the magical fusion of self and other is encouraged. Without the imposition of realistic limits upon the therapeutic relationship, that is to say, with unlimited time and space, there is no distinction between therapeutic situations and any other intimate relationship. The client can then expect, indeed, demand, that all his/her intimate needs be met by the therapeutic relationship. Without limits imposed on their relationship, the practitioner's ego boundaries as "therapist," as opposed to the timeless requirements of "lover," become blurred and diffused. It is this role diffusion that may contribute to confusion about intimacy between patient and practitioner and contribute to subsequent abuse of the intimate relationship, which will be discussed later in this chapter.

In D. W. Winnicott's terms, the psychotherapeutic situation has the structure of a holding environment (1958), or what W. R. Bion (1962) called a "container." It is this container, or holding environment, which serves to frustrate the full experience of relationship so that the client will gradually direct his/her intimate needs to others in which full expression of intimacy is more appropriately met. Within this structure, however, both client and practitioner are permitted to explore the full range of emotion. According to Winnicott, the emotional enactment within the container is a process of *play.* In a therapeutic play the expression of the fantasies of each participant invites a response from the other. In the enactment of this free play the various aspects of the self are given permission to be revealed. The container and the free-play process represent the parental roles. When they are combined in a meaningful manner, they serve as a normalizing or corrective emotional experience. But, of course, the process within the therapeutic container would remain solely emotive and, perhaps, at best, cathartic, without the imposition of *comment.* Comment on the process transforms the intimate moment, which we defined earlier, as experienced "as if time stopped," to a context which has the attributes of time and space. This is to say, explicit comment on the emotive experience between client and therapist reveals the meaning of the experience to the ongoing lives of its constituents. As the guardian of space and time, the practitioner is expected to relate the meaning of the ongoing process to the client's place in the continuum of his/her life. Whether the therapist has a historical, contemporary, or teleological orientation, the therapist is concerned with the implications of the therapeutic relationship in terms of what the client intends to be.

Therapeutic comment, in what I would regard as effective psychotherapy, generally moves from mirroring to transmutation to personal statement. In the *mirroring* phase, the practitioner emphatically reflects to the client those aspects of the self which have been frustrated and denied in the mothering relationship effecting the presence of a double. The therapist mirrors the disavowed aspects of the client's self by empathic rapport. In doing so, the practitioner reacquaints the client with missing aspects of self. The therapist, by expanding upon and redirecting the client's metaphors and disguised messages, seeks to help the client become aware of how his/her *phenomenological* self—self as experienced in time and space—and the sense of double (shadowy memories of bodily sensation once deeply felt but since disavowed) continue to interact in the way the client experiences the world. Therapeutic skill is evidenced in the practitioner's ability to manipulate a series of mirrors at different angles and perspectives to capture the client's premature integration of self, the illusion that is derived from unpalpable external feeding. On the other hand, the gradual acknowledgment and bodily reexperience of once deeply felt and yearned-for sensation and emotional touch helps bridge and integrate the self and its disavowed attributes. It helps the phenomenological self feed itself, digest and retain experiential nurturance.

In transmuting the deficits of self-esteem experienced by the client in the bonding relationship to more integrated functioning, the therapist acts from the realization that his/her clients require from their intimate relations with the practitioner more often courage than ideas. Clients generally have ideas about what they want to do with their lives, but lack conviction. As the early Greek philosophers demonstrated, there is no answer to the question of life except courage (areté) and optimism in the face of what is. We are keenly aware of the need for an accentuated sense of surging courage and fortitude in the face of extraordinary and trying exigencies of life. But it is actually the day-to-day sense of courage that should concern us most. Courage in everday life is, of course, related to the meaning of life for a particular person. Understandably, this sense of purpose may be experienced as fleeting, unclear, or lacking permanence for any particular person. The meaning of courage in everyday life must, under these circumstances, be sought in the exploration of what impedes, what prevents, what eludes the individual's finding purpose in living at any given moment. Quite frequently, these impediments are due to a premature closure in leaving open the question of one's purpose in living. This results in responding to the existential prerequisites of one's life in superficial and negative ways. These manifestations are evident in depressive and suicidal orientations, no less than in life styles held together by addictions.

In fact, courage is little more than one's acceptance of one's intentionality—the allowing of one's own actions to be statements of one's purpose and identity. Courage is a willingness to allow one's life to flow and a commitment to staying with the flow by directing one's existence *in vivo,* rather than by calculated decisions. The notion of a personal journey is related to this process. A personal journey is an attempt to discover by invention the meaning of one's life. The paradoxic and ironic nature of the personal journey is that the task involved is to invent a self that one is already. One does this by experiencing the authority of being one's self as one intends to be. What I am saying is that there are two separate but related processes within the self. One is intentional and *active* and the other is a process of *becoming without effort.* What a person intends to be and what he or she allows to develop must be courageously struggled with and reconciled. Neither can be fruitfully subsumed by the other. In this sense, courage as an everyday endeavor is the willingness to open one's life, to share one's commitment and passions with others. It is sharing and involvement with others in contrast to being demanded upon or of "giving" of oneself. It is a trend away from secrets, from "embarrassment of being," and from explanation rather than revelation and presence. This dialectic intentionality will be described in detail in the next chapter.

The point I wish to impress most on the reader about courage is that it is not a character attribute, an essential entity that one possesses and that necessarily precedes courageous action. Courage is not a mysterious quality, bestowed at birth or as a result of being, metaphorically, struck by lightening. In fact, courage is an empty and illusory concept except as a term used to describe a series of specific behaviors and activities, behaviors that can be observed and commented upon. It is, indeed, as I have said earlier, an illusory belief that courage is a trait or attribute that some people have and others don't, which disables people who don't regard themselves as courageous from carrying out acts and behaviors which they are capable of if they didn't impute the requirements of courage for their behavior. This consideration was necessary in my work with Roger discussed earlier in this book. After he experienced considerable agitation over a life experience that he had never faced before and that he manifestly handled rather well, I indicated that he acts as if he is reborn every day. He seemed to forget his past accomplishments and his getting through them. I felt that he could manage his difficulties again. I hoped that he wouldn't run away as he had in other fearful times in his life before psychotherapy and sell himself short. Because he was uncourageous previously, he did not necessarily have to be now. He had to take each situation and event, one at a time. In my own experience, to free myself up to be "courageous," I have needed to realize that I have in the past acted at various times in ways I and others regarded as "cowardly." At each moment, however, I have the freedom to act as I intend, regardless of what I have done before. I need no special motivation, cause, or support. These considerations may make my act of intention easier, less lonely, or less uncertain, but they are *not necessary* for me to act as I intend.

An additional concept, *caring,* is essential to our discussion of the development of intimacy. Caring is essential to intimacy. It is related to the mentor's willingness to allow the apprentice to find his/her own direction and symbols, as discussed in Chapter 1. Intimate caring is a demonstration of respect for the other's growth and mystery. It is a willingness to be there with the other rather than to do for the other. It is exemplified in a willingness to listen responsively to the other and to make personal statements rather than to give advice or problem-solve for the other. When the other is in distress, the self's concern is that the other's struggle to examine the assumptions he/she makes about his/her being-in-the-world will be worthy to enable him/her to be as he/she intends rather than how someone else wants him/her to be. Roger's mother tragically failed him by not respecting his need to mature by struggling with the realities of life. In their relationship all that was required of Roger was that he act desperately and contritely. She bailed him out of situations which he preferred not to face, rather than responsibly listen to his fears and share her own concerns with him. In a word, Roger's mother failed to share her humanity with him. In this sense meaningful intimacy may be defined as a moment in which the participants share their humanity with each other. In every-day intimacy, it may happen with a look or a touch or in some other, nonverbal way. In psychotherapy it requires a personal statement. I will give a poignant example of this from my own experience.

Several years ago I was on the clinical teaching faculty of the Department of Psychiatry of a medical school. During the first year of my appointment to the faculty, I was asked by several psychiatric residents to be the faculty discussant at a clinical case conference in which they would be presenting a difficult patient who was under observation in the psychiatric unit. I was flattered because they indicated that they had heard from other residents whom I had supervised how effectively I worked from an existential and humanistic orientation. Their other supervisors were more psychoanalytic and the residents were eager to see how I viewed this difficult case. At the conference, which was held in a room crowded with psychiatric residents, medical students, and some other faculty, one of the residents presented the patient's history. The patient was a middle-aged, upper-middle class woman, highly intelligent and well-educated, who owned an art gallery. A friend of her and her husband was a psychiatrist. He had hospitalized the woman because she had become increasingly secretive, guarded, and hostile. During the conference, I was asked to interview her. In our conversation, she said, in effect, that she did not belong in the hospital, did not want to be in the hospital, and if she needed any help I was not qualified to be able to understand or help her. As the interview proceeded, I became extremely self-conscious of how poorly I was doing. Although I felt that my questions and my manner were clinically sensitive, it was to no avail. She made it clear that she did not want to be there, nor me to be interviewing her. I became increasingly concerned with the effect this interview would have upon my teaching career in the medical school. I regarded my poor performance as due to the woman's lack of cooperation in being interviewed, which, of course, I regarded as her psychopathology. My discomfort resulted from my need to act as if I were in control and to deny the obvious fact that she was directing the interview and I was not effective in getting her cooperation. When this dawned on me, I decided whether or not I succeeded in doing a better job of interviewing, it made no sense for me to stay anxious. I realized that to handle my anxiety I needed to reveal, rather than to try to hide, that I was anxious. I commented to the patient that I had been asked to interview her because supposedly I had some expertise in cases like hers. I added that I had no idea from where this foolish notion had come. She must be aware, as was everyone else in the room, how poorly I was doing. I said that I appreciated her tolerating my ineptness. In the process of liberating myself to express myself more freely, I became aware and disconcerted that I was more concerned with my persona to the professionals and students present at the conference than in how shameful and difficult this interview might be for the patient. I felt humiliated at being concerned with my own professional behavior at her expense. Curiously, however, as I spoke of my embarrassment with the patient, she became more and more responsive and willing to have a dialogue with me. She told me that I was not doing such a bad job, but that she did not want to be the only person in the room who would admit to having feelings. In only a few minutes after I started to talk about my anxiety, the woman and I were involved in a rather intimate dialogue which, unfortunately, had to be interrupted as the conference had drawn to a close.

When I have related this story, in teaching psychotherapists, it is often pointed out that, as an experienced psychotherapist and one who has taught and written extensively about paradigmatic approaches in psychotherapy,[4] I must have been aware of the effect disclosing my feelings would have had on the patient. Actually, my anxiety at the time as a young practitioner, trying to impress my colleagues, blocked any awareness of what effect my behavior might have had. I only was aware that my anxiety was interfering with my interaction with the patient and that my own anxiety had to be dealt with before I could effectively deal with the situation. In the process, I discovered that I would only be able to have a meaningful dialogue with the woman if I could experience and express myself freely.

To offer a *personal statement* about how the therapist experiences client and self in a relationship, the practitioner must allow him/herself to experience freely. When experiencing freely, the practitioner tends to experience the encounter more emotionally than when feeling comfortable. He/she may experience choking up, giddiness, irritation, anxiety, sensuality and the other emotional reactions that are apperceptively filtered out by more clinical and "professional" formulations and notions of certainty about what the practitioner should be attending to in a therapeutic encounter. It is only from an immediate and continuing commitment to the real possibility of a relationship with the person with whom the practitioner is involved in a therapeutic encounter—a commitment that is not bracketed off by oaths of conduct, statements of clinical interest and responsibility for the other, rather than responsibility for the therapist's own intentionality—that the practitioner and client become aware of their separation. The more they get in touch with their ultimate estrangement, the more they can appreciate what they are currently sharing together and the preciousness of the present moment.

THE STRUGGLE IN PSYCHOTHERAPY

There is always a struggle in psychotherapy about how each shall make himself known to the other. The underlying conflict existent in every therapeutic encounter is how therapist and client will address their personal concerns with each other. Awareness of this prevents the therapist from managing the lives of clients and moving them to therapeutically logical conclusions that may be in contradiction with the existential needs of his/her clients' existence. The practitioner's therapeutic system represents value-orientations as to how the practitioner requires clients to address their human condition. Unless the practitioner is comfortable in exercising considerable power on a client's behalf, and unless this influence is openly explored with the clients, their work together will be replete with implicit, if not manifest, struggles of will and moral persuasion. The psychotherapist's power resides not in the validity of his/her explanations but in the audacity in being willing—with the client's conviction or, at least desperate need—to reduce all matters of importance to psychological terms, which the therapist "knows" better than does the client. Under these conditions the client is not obliged to validate the therapist's explanation in terms of his/her own experience. Therapists who do not examine their own power ploys in their work operate from theoretical models which try to induce the client to play the game by the rules of their psychological system rather than accepting and working at where the client is. In this enterprise, the only power left to the client as long as he/she remains in the therapeutic system—conceptual or real—is the utilization of subversive power. Each of us, as practitioners, has experienced our clients' subversive power—the various indirect strategies clients employ to negate our misdirected efforts to help them and/or protect ourselves. Our clients deserve the opportunity to acquire more direct power than this! The therapist, to be effective, then, must begin where the client is, not where the therapist wishes the client to be. He/she must find ways of bridging the difficulties between the client and the practitioner by use of such means as will be suggested in Chapter 12 together with the practitioner's willingness to learn from the client and to use the client as a consultant rather than someone whom the practitioner needs to suppress and to persuade to see things as he/she does. To do the latter would be to simply exacerbate the very issues which the client has brought into treatment and from which he/she seeks redress.

REALIZING THAT HUMAN RELATIONSHIPS ARE DESTINED TO FAIL

Therapists, above all others, must recognize that no relationship can meet magical aspirations. Consequently, the practitioner must allow the client to know that while the practitioner is available to understand and to help the client know him/herself, the practitioner is not there to take care of the client. No person can provide a relationship that will assuage all the hurt the client has experienced and that will repair all the psychic damage that has occurred or make good all the bad relationships the client has had. And, ultimately, it is necessary to realize that although they do not fully understand each other, and do not always agree on how to make life work for the client, that this is the best they can do and that the effort has been worth making. The reader might ask, isn't there a way of working with clients that will circumvent therapeutic conflict? In short, can the traps and dilemmas encountered in therapeutic situations be avoided? No, not if the endeavor is to be a meaningful human dialogue. Avoidance should not be the goal of therapy. Rather, it is ideally a journey of deeply felt experience, understanding, and transcending intentionality. Whatever the difficulties that have arisen, the therapeutic question generally remains an attempt to understand how their own ways of being and how their coming together have gotten in the way of an effective partnership. Consultation and supervision can often be effective in this process, as I will discuss in the following chapters, but so will examining the beliefs we, as practitioners, hold.

THE THERAPEUTIC SEARCH FOR TRUTH

Psychotherapy represents an authentic search for the meaning of one's existence. Some systems of therapy, certainly psychoanalytic therapies, purport to seek the real motives of behavior, as if there was a solitary reality and a single truth. When therapy is unsuccessful, the practitioner may feel that in some way he/she has been involved in a fallacious endeavor. The practitioner may question his/her own limitations and truthfulness. It is important for the practitioner to see that although psychotherapy searches for truth that these truths are actually "functional truths." In another book (Goldberg, 1980) I have explored the unquestioned assumptions of behavioral scientists that they are experts in regard to the realities of other selves. In doing so, I have returned to the work of Arthur Schopenhauer, the nineteenth-century German philosopher. Schopenhauer, in his simple and profound opening statement in *The World as Will and Idea* (1966 [1818]), says, "The world is my representation (idea)." Schopenhauer is implying that the world simply "is." How I experience the world consists of my assumptions about the world, having little or nothing to do with how the world really is. Schopenhauer's statement leads to the realization that no person can actually be an expert in regard to objective reality, much less the idiosyncratic realities of other selves. This is as true for the therapist as for the client. Nonetheless, personal responsibility is predicated upon the individual's commitment to withstand varying degrees of discomfort and emotional risk in questioning the validity of his/her assumptions about what it is to exist as a person and move around the world, as the individual constitutes his/her world.

Functional meaning, therefore, has to do with the practical considerations of how people come together and deal with their human existence. It has to do with the specific kinds of meaning that they give to their existence. Psychotherapy is a very important place for examining functional truth. However, if the search in psychotherapy is for objective truth, the work is illusionary and, ultimately, disappointing. Nietzsche, in his caution, said it well. He indicated that all truth needed to be confronted with the question, "Can it be lived?" In a word, can the beliefs that we, as practitioners, hold be meaningfully lived by both our clients and ourselves?

ULTIMATE GOAL IN PSYCHOTHERAPY

The theme of a popular and rather thought-provoking Broadway play of some 15 or so years ago concerned "the impossible dream." In the play *Man of La Mancha*, Don Quixote reaches for "impossible" goals. One of the most important dimensions of psychotherapy as I have indicated earlier is that it enables the client to dare to reach for whatever psychological aspirations the client desires. The client may reach for things he/she has only silently hoped for or, perhaps, even denied to him/herself. Each of us needs to have an "impossible dream." When we reach our goals, particularly, if done with relative ease, there is nothing else for which to live. It is vital to creative growth that we aspire beyond our ready horizon. Of course, we must also reach for "realistic" goals. But beyond, there always should be some star that we reach for, some ideal which shapes our existence for which we continually quest. In a word, we should encourage our clients to live fully in the present, but also dare to dream and aspire beyond the horizon.

To model this process, the therapeutic journey must involve risk. In enduring a risky ordeal experienced together, people come to truly know one another and develop, as a result, a genuine liking and respect for one another. At the moment in which they lose the sense of certainty and security provided by theoretical and clinical procedures, so that they can no longer predict the outcome of their being together, the possibility of a meaningful encounter lies before them. It is to the degree that the client senses, as the relationship manifests itself, that the practitioner is willing and able to negotiate how the client is to be regarded and treated that both agents within an encounter can cast aside reactive fears and the need for safety, and can accommodate to each other. In so doing, each, in exploring their intimate relationship, comes to experience him/herself and the other with increased meaningfulness.

THE PERSONAL JOURNEY IN PSYCHOTHERAPY

I view psychotherapy as the personal journey of two in order that each finds him/herself. A personal journey means a search to find something in oneself. It is a journey of two because one cannot find him/herself without the other in this endeavor. Nor can this quality, sentiment, or realization be found passively or simply in contemplative aloneness. It requires a trek together to find something externally that mirrors something inside. Plato's dialogues, especially the *Symposium* and the *Prado,* are early models of the personal journey through dialogue. In more recent times, novelists Somerset Maugham in *The Razor's Edge* and James Michener in *Rites of Spring* depict the personal journey.

I will discuss the case of Abe, whose situation cogently touches upon the issues already raised in this chapter. When I worked with him many years ago, Abe was a scientist in his late forties with a brilliant mind and the needs of a child because his needs were not met at the proper time in his development. He still had a child's curiosity. He had a need to know purely and simply, without any commitment to ever use the knowledge on his own or others' behalf. He had been extremely drawn to a young woman in his therapy group. Laura was a schoolteacher, WASP, sophisticated, and coolly attractive. Abe was Jewish, unsure of himself with women, and had been married from early adulthood to a woman in whom he had lost sexual interest many years previously. He had gone from mother to wife-mother without a loss of stride. He never had with either of these women nor with any other, for that matter, an intimate relationship. Laura was everything he had romantically dreamed of in a woman. He was unable to express his feelings directly about her in the therapy group. His fears of actual intimacy confined him to fantasy and to asking himself hundreds of "what if" questions designed to embellish his fantasy world with her. Fearing the disapproval of the therapist and the members of the therapy group by speaking of his feelings for her in the group, he surreptitiously called Laura on the telephone and asked her out for dinner. She refused and insisted that he deal with these feelings in the group. He panicked and stayed away from the group for several sessions. Laura reported Abe's telephone call to the group.

After the second session that Abe missed, the therapist phoned him. Abe confessed what had happened. He reported feeling humiliated and unable to face the group. The therapist recognized that this extremely guilt-ridden man who had nearly more therapy years than the therapist had years of living did not need more insight. Abe was a person who had never had the opportunity to rebel openly. He was a man who claimed that he could remember every bad thought that he had ever had about himself. The therapist, therefore, did not try to interpret the difficulties Abe was experiencing. Abe had enough psychological expertise to do that for himself. Instead, the therapist wished him courage in protesting the misery that for so many years he had accepted and had passively tried to understand in regard to how he was responsible for that misery. The therapist confirmed Abe's right to rebel against therapy. The therapist hoped that he could do this and still attend sessions. However, if the only way he could rebel was by not attending sessions, then the therapist told him to come back only when he felt he had made a sufficient protest. After another missed session Abe called the therapist. He wished to discuss whether his protest was sufficient. The therapist indicated that Abe would be ready to come back when he no longer would continue to ask only to *understand* himself. He must also learn to *do* something about his understanding. Abe would be ready to come back to therapy when he was ready to accept himself as being strong as well as intelligent. He had survived a bizarre childhood, but he must use his strength now to go forward rather than guard against encroachment of past ghosts. The reader may be aware that what Abe was being told is a reversal of what we usually would expect to be the reasons for clients attending psychotherapy. Abe was told to come to therapy when (because) he was strong. Typically, we believe people should be in therapy when they are disabled (weak) and leave when they are able and strong. In a way, the therapist was asking Abe to forget all he had learned in his many years in therapy and simply come back to the difficulty he might face in the group as an act of courage. In the phone conversation, Abe said confidently and unhesitatingly that he was ready.

What is the point of the story? I have tried to demonstrate that courage is an indispensable attribute to the therapeutic attitude for both therapist and client. The therapist who suggests and supports the notion that psychotherapy is *only* a preparation for life—that the psychotherapist's office is the place where the client learns about psychological skills he/she someday *may* use to become the kind of person he/she would like to be—does his/her client a serious disservice. Psychotherapy is life. To encourage precaution in living in the immediate world, rather than active courage in facing up to one's responsibilities is to reinforce and entrench the difficulties the client has brought into therapy. In recent years, many practitioners have come to appreciate that those therapeutic orientations that emphasize the examination of the client's repressed motives, while having general merit, suffer from being too slow and far too speculative and indirect for a majority of clients with whom we work. Of course, some clients act too impulsively for their well-being. But almost all our clients suffer from the lack of courage of their convictions and a reluctance to stand up for what they believe and deserve. A therapeutic approach which restrains the activity of these clients stifles what little spontaneity they have permitted themselves.

It is the ownership and passionate scrutiny of one's convictions—along with the awareness of the fear and uncertainty accrued—that comprise courage. There is always courage involved in acknowledging the dissonance between one's ideology and aspirations—and the conditions in which one finds oneself-in-the-world.

In the context of what we have said about the role of courage and intimacy in the therapeutic situation, what can the practitioner best offer the client? Clearly the practitioner shares with the client the existential requirement to give some direction to the client's own life. The therapist can enable the client to derive meaning from the client's struggles by offering the courage the therapist has found and the values she has derived in experiencing her own personal journey. Simultaneously, by freeing herself to discover the caring in her own despair, the therapist may find herself and enable her client to find value and meaning from the client's own suffering.

ABUSES OF THERAPEUTIC INTIMACY

The client needs to experience the therapist's caring. However, whereas this is a necessary phase in the therapeutic relationship, it is not sufficient for meaningful therapeutic endeavor. Where the therapist's caring is the client's payoff for therapeutic work, it can only lead to deleterious impasse, if not therapeutic seduction. Therapeutic caring is a demonstration of respect for the growth and mastery of the client. Therapeutic seduction—whether it involves physical intimacy or not—is deleterious to the client because it leads the client away from the integration of his/her own phenomenological self and double. A psychological mirror holds a threat to the bearer as well as to the gazer. The therapist uses him/herself as a mirror to help the client integrate. However, the mirror is reversible. The therapist, too, must witness unbearable parts of him/herself in the client. In therapeutic seduction, the patient's phenomenological self serves as a mirror for the therapist's own double. A more constructive option is where the client experiences the openness of the therapist's phenomenological self to his/her double. It is not difficult to see that courage is necessary in caring in order to permit the other to experience the self as the self "is." Courage is involved in the self's "letting go" to permit to emerge that which the self is experiencing at the present moment—in terms of values, desires, and vulnerabilities—as the phenomenological self constitutes itself-in-the-world. The process of "letting go" requires a caring for oneself without the defensive-protective stance of constraining other selves in relating to the self. "Letting go" is the preferred stance of the self in seeking intimacy. Letting go permits an openness for the phenomenological self to experience its avoidances rather than seek reassurances and certainty about its assumptions about how the self must be in-the-world and how others must treat the self. The self receives meaningful caring from another by sharing its preferences and concerns with the other, freeing the other to relate to the self as the other experiences the self, rather than in regard to how the self believes it needs to be regarded.

As Paul Tillich (1952) has so cogently delineated, courage mediates anxiety in our experiencing our being and the being of the other. Courage, in this sense, is the openness and curiosity about how the self uses and avoids itself in its human condition.

Fear and anxiety are, in their existential sense, the implicit assumption that if the self "let's go" of itself—its conceptions of its boundaries and properties—that is to say, metaphorically, if it "forgets" itself—the self will go out of existence. This existential fear prevents union and intimacy with another. Only by "letting go" of itself can the self transcend itself—its present boundaries—and come together with another and emerge in a new way, with new possibilities and a joining of self and double. Consequently, difficulty with intimate relations are acts of dissipated courage—the failure of courage to let go of self and reemerge in a new union.[5] But within the intimate therapeutic container a creative process can occur. Creativity, in the sense we are using it, is the willingness to let go of stereotypic, conventional ways of seeing, believing, and acting, and the permission to let emerge what is—the *waiting upon* of which Martin Heidegger (1966) spoke. From the unconscious playing with constraints of conventional reality, there emerge possibilities from the unconscious—to perceive new unities in the nature of things within oneself and within the world in which the self is in context, and to seek a more meaningful integration.

A purview of the literature on intimacy in psychotherapy suggests to me that abuses of the therapeutic relationship emanate from the practitioner's feeling about self—that he/she is incapable or fearfully uncertain of meaningful intimate relations. We should be able to see, then, that the therapist's "seduction" of the client leads each away from his/her own integration. The client is entitled to more than this. When we get down to it, courage has to do with taking seriously the belief, "So why not the best!" This means: "I am entitled to work with a practitioner who willingly struggles to be fully there with me.

THE DOUBLE AS SOULMATE

Psychoanalytic theory has persuasively argued that the ontogenetic quest for union with another person, such as in sexual relations, is to unite with the mother. I suggest another basis. At its core, sexual endeavor contains a wish to merge with one's other—one's double—the denied, unaccepted, unattainable parts of oneself. In the sexual act one may wish to truly discover and realize oneself through the stranger. This requires courage for profound sexual exploration may evoke considerable anxiety and trepidation. Courage and intimacy are closely related. Acts of intimacy demonstrate a willingness to suspend certainty and allow the self to plunge into its own and the other's unknown. To do this, however, the self needs a sense of confidence that what it has inside itself is basically positive so that in combination or synthesis with the qualities of the other self, the resultant will be essentially beneficial. Those who feel empty inside experience themselves at the mercy of the unknown powers of the stranger. Those who feel malignant inside fear the destruction of both self and other (Goldberg & Simon, 1982).

Roger, who was discussed in Chapter 2, felt empty inside because he could not hold on to experiences. This was especially true of positive experiences. He felt worthless in spite of his considerable gains in psychotherapy and in his life in general. To reiterate, it was as if he were reborn each day. When his needs were not met as he expected or demanded, he would feel desperate and had no internal resources to depend on. Several of his suicidal attempts were at times of desperation, because a lover or friend would not spend the night with him. He could not bear to be alone. He was not even able to fall asleep without alcohol and/or sleeping pills. Moreover, because he could not trust his own internal processes, he experimented, tried out, and quickly discarded everything in which he was involved. He ate his food and downed his drinks rapidly and took drugs bombastically. Similarly, he quickly parried and prematurely judged statements directed to and about him. He had never learned to take in substance, hold on to it, cogitate about it, and then decide to digest or disrepute it.

Roger could not find intimacy in his relations with lovers because he insisted that they prove their love by various clever and sadistic ploys—not even falling short of suicide gestures and attempts. His lovers soon tired of these tactics. Roger could not trust himself or others in intimate experiences. He would rather be humiliated and denigrated by those with whom he was sexually involved than share with them his sense of inadequacy, emptiness, and the continual terror evoked by the lurking shadow of his own self-hatred.

Personal comments and biographical data about Oscar Wilde (1982) and other authors of double-self tales attest that painful secrets were as true for these authors' personal lives as for their fictional characters. The numerous legends of the double self suggest that each of us seek his/her second self, in terms of the aspects of self that are experienced as lacking and necessary for self-integration. Human suffering results from the tenuous and conflictual phenomenology required of the self in attempting to validate the invention of its various selves (its doubles) as reflected in the mirror with the world of others. In a word, suffering comes from lack of self-integration. It is derived from the feeling that part of oneself, which is contained in another, is necessary for completion. This notion pervades our world. Readily, we are drawn into all sorts of emotional and physical interrelations with others. Milton's version of creation in *Paradise Lost* tells us that God made Eve because Adam in himself alone was incomplete. Eve's qualities of grace and beauty were necessary to temper Adam's attributes of strength and wisdom. With her joined to him, Adam was superior to what he was alone.

Joyce Colony (1982) has indicated that we are drawn together by a force as inescapable as magnetism. At least once in each of our lives we encounter another person who seems to mirror our innermost thoughts and hidden ambitions. There seems to be some unspoken understanding that if we let go of our tenaciously held securities, that the other would become intensely joined to us. And yet, we may be uncomfortable with this interdependency because generally we are taught to be self-sufficient. Our yearning for companionship often runs counter to the ethos of an American culture which emphasizes autonomy, independence, and personal freedom. To be lacking in ourselves is experienced as a shameful and morally inferior condition. Indeed, one of the major beliefs about evil is that it is an "incomplete good." This parallels the notion of the double self. Many of us, out of fear and disappointment about not living up to our human capabilities, create the illusion of integration, of being self-sufficient. Some people attack others because they feel that they have been robbed of completion by deprivation of love, status, security, recognition, etc. According to the ethos of the double-self legend, suffering is derived from desiring one's other half—in Martin Buber's poetic terms, an "I" yearning for a "thou"—in order to complete and fulfill the self (Buber, 1970).

Despite the role of the double in suffering, the seeking of one's other self is not necessarily pathological. A psychoanalyst, Harold Searles, who has done exciting, innovative work with rather disturbed patients, supports this contention. Searles, who at one time regarded a multiple identity as purely pathological, existing in the persons suffering from a borderline psychotic condition, now sees that the psychologically healthy person's sense of identity is far from being monolithic in nature. It may involve, rather, myriad internal objects functioning in lively and harmonious interrelatedness and all contributing to a relatively coherent, consistent sense of identity, which springs from and comprises all of them, but does not involve their being congealed into any unitary mass. The more healthy the individual is, Searles maintains, the more consciously does he/she live in the awareness that there are myriad "persons"—each bearing some sense of identity value within him/her (Searles, 1977).

I have sought to demonstrate in this chapter that the person the self tries to invent or create does not spring from nowhere. It ushers out of the desire to unite and become integrated with its soulmate, its magical self.

The eminent abstract painter Ad Reinhardt has written: "We

have lost our ability to look. We can not look without verbalizing what we see. If you want to see you must be prepared to look."[6] To truly look is to plunge into the unknown to experience in union with something outside of ourselves that which the self cannot experience by itself. It prototypically leads to birth, hope, and possibility. The path to self-integration requires a perilous journey in search of self. We must recognize our double as a soulmate and companion in our journey rather than as the enemy.

NOTES

1. A number of years ago, Carl Rogers indicated that the sense of loneliness and alienation consists of two major determinants. The first is "*an estrangement of the person from himself* and his own experiences." In this fundamental rift, Rogers points out,

> the experiencing organism senses one meaning in experience, but the conscious mind and self rigidly cling to another...meanings sensed by physiological organism being denied and ignored, until they break through unbidden. Thus, we find man lonely because of an inability to communicate freely within himself. (Rogers, 1961)

The second factor is *the lack of significant others* with whom we are willing and able *to communicate* our deeply experienced *sentiments.* To the extent that we are unable to communicate,

> both aspects of our divided self—both our conscious facade and our deeper level of experiencing—then we feel the loneliness of not being in real touch with any other human being. (Rogers, 1961)

Rogers regards this kind of loneliness of recent vintage. He indicates that,

> In earlier times the individual also distrusted or ignored his experiencing, in order to keep the regard of significant others. But the facade which he adopted, the meaning he now felt that he had found in his experience, was a unified and strongly supporting set of beliefs and meanings. His whole social group tended

to perceive life and experience in the same way, so that while he had unwittingly given up his deepest self, at least he had taken on a consistent, respected, approved self by which he could live. (Rogers, 1961)

2. We had been told by the assistant manager of the hotel that some officials of the medical organization had been notified and had told the hotel management to call the police. Recently, after we had written a letter to the official journal of the organization, we received a call from the chief security officer of the organization. We met with him. He told us that in fact the organization not only did not order the arrests, but tried to delay the arrests, but were not successful in this effort. Although the assistant manager and the security officer's information seem somewhat inconsistent, we regard both as truthful. What seems evident, however, is that a number of physicians were personally distressed by the poorly dressed protestors in their midst at a time they weren't professionally required to interact with them.

3. Alcoholics Anonymous has added to this code of courage (which seems implicit in the ethical systems of every religious order of which I am aware), "God grant me the serenity to accept the things I cannot change, courage to change the things I can, and the wisdom to know the difference."

4. See C. Goldberg (1980[b]); also see Chapters 7 and 8 in Goldberg (1980[a]).

5. This is what I believe the reknowned theologian Paul Tillich (1952) had in mind in discussing the evolution of the self in his classic book, *The Courage to Be.* New Haven: Yale University Press, 1952.

6. Found in an explanation of his paintings at an exhibit of Reinhardt's work at the Whitney Museum, New York City, in 1983.

Chapter 11
Developing Intimacy

Communion is that union which makes differen-
tiation possible. Man becomes an individual
through participation.
—T. Hora

To recapitulate what I have said in Chapter 9, if practitioners are concerned about the plight of individuals in distress with whom they work, they must first uncover the issues that predicate the individual's place in the social order. Emotional disturbance is a result of deterioration and disequilibrium of equity and balance that an individual experiences in relationship to significant others in his/her normative system (Goldberg, 1977). It is the absence of equity and balance in an interpersonal relationship that make it extremely difficult for an individual who is experiencing an estrangement from him/herself to communicate deeply experienced sentiments to another person. Consequently, if equity and balance are essential interpersonal dimensions for maximizing one's place in society, the client must be taught how to negotiate directly for restoration of these relations.

People today have a greater appreciation of their psychological impact upon one another than they had in the past. Contemporary psychotherapy therefore must develop a methodology to take the most advantage of its transactional arena. This methodology must teach those we work with definitive interactional skills for obtaining equity and balance in their relationships; this will enable them to minister to their own (and significant others') loneliness and despair, and to address the problems of alienation and existential exhaustion, of which contemporary man has become so acutely aware. This problem concerns the journey in search of self.

The journey into self is most productive in a climate in which each partner is present and involved in the seeking of an increased awareness of his/her own identity. Each needs to explore, experience, and hopefully come to terms with the contradictory attitudes, assumptions, and paradoxical ways of being that each has defined for him/herself and that each has allowed others to impose upon him/her in avoiding becoming that which the person seeks to be. The cogent "paradox" this journey attempts to address is how each participant may retain and fulfill his/her own individuality while at the same time being a functioning partner in an interrelating, interpersonal unit (Goldberg, 1977). Rather than focusing on simply changing unsatisfying modes of behaving—trying to become something or someone else—the journey into self requires each to encourage the other to explore the fulfillment of avoided behaviors so that each may *become that which they are.* These notions address the interface of self and other and the roles of intimacy, courage, and caring in the development of creative meaning in human development.

BASIC EMOTIONAL COMMUNICATION: 25 PRINCIPLES

In the following pages I will discuss a special kind of dialogue which I have labeled "Basic Emotional Communication." In previous books (Goldberg, 1977; 1980a) I have proposed Basic Emotional Communication as a model for resolving conflict and moving beyond impasse in the therapist-client relationship and for improving the communication of couples in marital therapy and in family therapy. I am concerned with Basic Emotional Communication as a means for persons involved in intimate and significant relationships, such as a personal journey together, to explore their relationship courageously and creatively.

Basic Emotional Communication (BEC) consists of a dialogue occurring between two or more individuals involved in a significant relationship, in which the needs of each are both heard and responded to—emotionally as well as cognitively. A useful analogy to the process of Basic Emotional Communication would be to keep a Ping-Pong ball in motion on a table through the continual strokes of each of the two players. This type of exchange requires that neither player try to move the ball out of the reach of the other in order to win a point; otherwise the ball would hit the floor and cease to be in motion.

BEC is built upon the guidelines of a dialectical process[1] and, as such, has a temporal structure. The partners

> alternate in their presentations, and each successive statement has to reflect at least the one immediately preceding. Incorporating only the preceding statements represent, of course, a minimum requirement for a dialogue. A maximum is attained if each utterance reflects all of the earlier statements. Strictly speaking, one never enters the same dialogue twice. Each utterance must be consistent with the [other's] own views and must represent equally consistent or systematically modified reactions to all statements made by the [other]. (Riegel, 1976)

Moreover, each alternating statement must reflect the same basic theme the speaker has presupposed and, until that moment, not consciously realized. If a reflective coordination is not built into the dialectic process,

> the dialogue would degenerate into alternating monologues in which each [partner] would merely follow up on his or her earlier statements without reacting to the [other's] elaborations. The [other's] statements would appear as distractive interruptions and the only remaining feature would consist of the alternations between the [partners]. (Riegel, 1976)

At the present time, BEC consists of the following 25 principles based upon the issues and concerns presented in this book.

1. *Speak directly and personally to the other.*

Assume that the other self has no previous information about you, that the other will know you entirely on the basis of what you are willing to reveal in this specific encounter.

2. *Make "I" statements, rather than "you" statements.*

Take ownership of your statements. This will move both partners away from blaming, dependent, object-fused stances and toward positive, direct statements of want and desire.

3. *Make statements out of your questions.*

This keeps the momentum going in a dialogue by moving the exchange away from excessive reflection, intellectualization, and hence, hesitation. Many people try to get to know other people factually. They ask endless questions in order to collect information as would an interviewer. They then attempt to use these facts to compare the other with others they or their friends have met or those they have read or heard about. They use these comparisons, based upon what happened in other situations, to make judgments about a personal involvement in the present situation. That is, they judge the present person and situation on external criteria rather than by their own immediate sense. Many people don't trust their own feelings and judgments. They prefer that the other or external events make the decisions for them. Making statements out of your questions emphasizes the willingness to be personal with the other rather than factual and objective.

4. *Make statements of your present feelings rather than of your thoughts or previous feelings.*

Interpersonal conflict, particularly in significant relationships, centers around the issue of arguing "facts" rather than stating preferences. Making statements of present feelings, therefore, moves the exchange onto an emotional and experiential place, in which the wants and desires of both partners are open to sharing, exploring, and negotiating, rather than one in which demands are presented as concluded (fixed) and closed (non-negotiable). Emotions are facts not limited to any single means of expression. Using a constructively selfish approach,[2] you ask directly for what you want and do not attempt to "protect" the other from your "selfishness" (i.e., your wants). To do this, you need to regard the other as capable of responsible and rational agreement or disagreement with your requests.

5. *Make statements of your desired expectations rather than of what you hope to avoid.*

This enables each of the partners to become aware of what is gratifying to the other person rather than only of what the other wants to avoid. Psychologically, it is easier to initiate new behaviors than it is to terminate old ones. To do this, each of the partners must avoid apologizing for feelings and needs.

6. *Specify exactly what is wanted.*

It is important to be exact about what you are asking for in an exchange (e.g., time and place) rather than simply to speak of wanting behaviors initiated or terminated. This is because, psychologically, an individual can best adjust behaviors in a situation in which he/she knows specifically when these behaviors are most crucial to the other as opposed to a situation in which he/she experiences him/herself as being expected completely to adapt or drop existing behaviors.

7. *Keep your statements brief.*

Clear and terse statements make it more convenient for the other to respond immediately. Elaborate tangential statements are apt to cause the partner to lose the essence of the communicative intent.

8. *Give feedback for clarity.*

Periodically summarize (play back) what you have heard as objectively as you can. This provides a mirror for you to reflect upon what you are about to present to your partner.

9. *When examining conflict in the relationship, avoid interpretations and value judgments.*

Employing interpretations and value judgments effects an imbalance in the relationship by informing the partner that his/her behavior needs to be morally restructured according to your system of equity rather than according to explicitly negotiated norms established by both partners.

10. *Keep the momentum going in the exchange.*

A relationship feeds on the balance of energies contributed by the external system (i.e., the two partners). You cannot, therefore, allow yourself to let the exchange abort by becoming upset or angry and tuning out.

11. *Use active terms in the exchange.*

We experience ourselves and others in the world in terms of the conceptualizations revealed in the language we employ. The use of active and dynamic terms and descriptions also helps to keep the momentum going in an exchange. The excessive use of passive terms reveals the passive use of Self and of its perception of itself as tentative-in-the-world. Passive conceptualization leads to the loss of momentum in the exchange.

12. *Use subjunctive clauses of speech which perpetrate active intent toward the other rather than those which cause cessation of action.*

Beware of, in yourself, the tendency to use "negative qualifying" conjunctive terms and clauses in your dialogue when feeling fearful. "But" is a ubiquitous manifestation of this tendency. For example, I want to get close to you, *but* I am afraid ("*but* I don't know how," or "*but* I don't know if it is safe," etc.) A rather different sentiment is expressed by changing "buts" to "ands," for example, "I want to get close to you *and* I am afraid." A rather open and courageous sentiment is evinced by admitting the fear, including it in the struggle to become more intimate rather than implying the cessation of the struggle because of the fear. This speaks cogently to the issue of loneliness discussed previously in this book. The important thing to be aware of in feelings of loneliness is that it is rare that the "lonely" person feels lost, empty, or desperate at the moment of the awareness of being alone. Rather, these emotions are contingent upon a *conjunctive clause* by which the person judges and evaluates his or her state of being and comes to the conclusion that this state will be continued. In other words, loneliness and desperation come from the statement to oneself, "I am not with anyone at this moment, which is all right, *but* I fear that this state will continue to be—that is, I will always be alone; there is no escape." In short, change your "buts" to "ands."

13. *Move from a statement of needs to a statement of preference.*

Necessity and preference are often confused conceptually, as well as emotionally. Most people can meet their basic needs in order to survive, but they do not experience the "permission" (i.e., power adequacy[3]) to want more than to meet these basic needs. Consequently, many people force themselves into positions of isolation, desperation, depression, and despair in order simply to secure some human contact. You don't have to need a response from your partner to want it and to ask for it.

14. *Be aware that your interpersonal involvement in a dialogue is dependent on your interpersonal risks.*

The cautious, introspective person becomes isolated and detached in an exchange because he/she feels a need to express only statements of which he/she feels certain. This cautious stance erodes the dialogue until it loses momentum. A basic emotional exchange is intended to be an opportunity for you to explore uncertain, uncomfortable, and threatening aspects of yourself with another person.

15. *Periodically attempt new modes of behavior with your partner.*

It is particularly relevant to "do something different" when you feel threatened by your partner's not fulfilling your expectations of how you would like to be treated. To the extent that the Self maintains typical modes of behavior, it is threatened by loss of its essence—its "real" Self. To the extent that the self periodically attempts new behaviors, it experiences energy and expansion of Self rather than a need to conserve its integrity against attack.

16. *Say "no" but never say "never."*

View the dialogue as an experiential laboratory for searching for greater awareness of yourself and your partner rather than as a situation in which personal limitations are to be judged. Let your partner know where you are at the moment, but leave the possibility of modification open for the future.

17. *View strong feelings in an exchange as mediators of intentionality.*

If, in an exchange, you feel bored, misunderstood, or unloved, you are required to act. Interpret states of feeling not as calls to remain passive and deprived but as enabling you to enact the state of being you feel is lacking.

18. *A person's presence in a dialogue comes from the "waiting for" of denied and underpresented aspects of self.*

A person's energetic presence in a dialogue with another seems to come from the harmony and balance of natural rhythm—of passivity and activity, thought and emotion, etc. When too much emphasis is given to one side or the other, imbalance, tension, and conflict are effected in the self and the result is disequilibrium in the dialogue between the partners. Each partner can enable the other to be more fully present by enabling the other to experience what aspect of the partner is missing, denied, or underpresented in their dialogue. Clinical evidence demonstrates the importance of denied aspects of our lives. This is to say, what makes our lives happy or unhappy, conflictual, or content, is often not what we are currently involved in but what we deny the importance of and suppress in our lives. Thus, the "successful workaholic" generally is unhappy not because he is successful at his work (although clinically we know there are such people), but because the joys of meaningful leisure are absent from his life. His whole existence is caught up with being productive, even in his leisure. Contentment seems to come from a harmony and balance of natural rhythm. When too much emphasis is given to one side or the other, imbalance, tension, conflict, and disintegration occur in the personality of a person.

19. *Act with the other as if the other partner is the person with whom you would like to be involved and as if you are the person you intend to be.*

I view personality, as I have reiterated in this volume, as a process rather than a fixed entity. A person becomes that which he/she seeks to be through action and intent rather than through passively inducing intrapsychic arousal and stimulation. A person is constructively shaped toward being the kind of person another seeks him/her to be when the person is treated as if he/she were that person. A person's intent, therefore, serves to role-model desired attributes he/she seeks in another.

20. *When you experience unfulfilled gratification from your partner, initiate behavior which is gratifying to your partner.*

From my clinical experience it has become increasingly more evident that people treat the other in terms of how the other feels (and how the other conveys in one way or another) that he or she *deserves to be treated.* This is why so many people get the same kinds of responses, regardless of with whom they are involved. Consequently, if you feel unloved, it is likely that you are treating yourself as unlovable. Acting as if you are lovable, you convey that you deserve being loved. In an exchange, partners often become hung up on justification of their behavior by expecting and demanding reciprocal behaviors from their partner. It is important to consider the possibility that one acts lovable toward another, not only to evoke desired responses from the other, but to evoke desired responses in oneself.

21. *Realize that you and your partner are not responsible in a dialogue to any outside agent.*

In conflictual relationships, each of the agents attempts to manipulate the other into assuming his/her idiosyncratic system of equity in exchanges based on the justification of how other people behave. Functional and gratifying dialogues result from realizing that neither partner is responsible to any outside agent or system of conduct in his/her interactions with the other.

22. *Explicitly review norms, standards of conduct, and other values brought in from society-at-large in preparation for negotiating them within the relationship.*

Because you probably view your partner's contributions to the dialogue in the context of implicitly assumed societal values and sentiments, you need to decide together how they should function within the particular relationship with your partner. Because the dialogue between you and your partner represents a contractual agreement between just the two of you, it should be open to renegotiation in order to improve functioning.

23. *Avoid giving or asking for declarations of essence.*

Many of the depressed and passive-resistant clients I have seen in psychotherapy who have had unsuccessful romantic relationships are caught up in the tragic trap of saying, "I don't really care how he (or she) treats me, as long as he (or she) says, 'I love you!'" and "I don't care whether the relationship ends or not as long as I feel that he (or she) loved me!" Love, or any other emotional condition, is not a single entity; it is a series of specific ways of relating to another person. The individual who refuses to ask directly for equitable and meaningful, specific responses from his/her partner is left with an empty declaration.

24. *Appreciate the nonverbal language you communicate with your partner.*

Each of us is conveying signals—direct and indirect, verbal and nonverbal—about what we expect from others, how we wish and wish not to be treated. Because these cues are for the most part nonverbal and indirect, we often are consciously unaware of the effect we have upon others and they upon us. We set up moods in others and others in us which cause us to react in ways we do not acknowledge. By monitoring our physical sensations we can often detect discrepancies between what we are verbally and nonverbally communicating. For example, one may be sitting across the table from a very attractive and interesting person, but one's body may be leaning back and away from this person. If one is aware of one's own bodily posture and sensations, one can realize, let's say, in this situation, that he/she feels constricted and not allowed by this person to express him/herself freely. With another, perhaps less objectively attractive and interesting person, one is leaning over the table toward the other, feeling free to be whoever one is and intends to be. In a word, our visual and intellectual assessment of the other may report an impression that is contradicted by the veracity of our proprioceptive reactions.

25. *Ask for compensation to restore equity and balance in a relationship.*

We live in an age in which people are not wont to act toward us in ways we regard as just or fair. It is our responsibility to ourselves (perhaps, even to the other) to educate the other toward their relationship to us. I believe that all self-help education and, indeed, the ethos of all liberation movements can be reduced to a single core value—a need to educate others toward their responsibilities toward us. This is clearly exemplified in assertive training and the various rights movements. In this sense, courage, as a moral act, is a willingness to confront and educate those who deny us our integrity. This task has become increasingly more urgent in the age in which we live. It takes daily courage to live in a world in which few things seem to work properly. The use of indignation is sometimes required. Indignation is a passionate statement about an age in which people take little pride in their craft or the quality of their existence. It says, "I care about what happens to myself and to the world in which I live." It, too, is a statement of courage and a call for others forthrightly to address their grievances. A typical example of this, which occurs so frequently that we may lose sight of its significance, is the societally sanctioned manner for cancelling out acts of inequity, insensitivity, and mistreatment by saying, "I am sorry." This too-often-perfunctory statement, however, does not usually assuage aversive feelings. I have found out that when a person asks for compensation for inequitable treatment, and does so with a legitimate sense of entitlement, balance is restored to the relationship which helps dissipate aversive feelings toward the partner.

In summary, in terms of the partners' personal journey, basic emotional communication is designed to enable each of the partners to answer (at least) the following questions:

1. What am I actually experiencing?

2. What does the experience mean in terms of the person I intend to become; this is to say, what is the relation of my experience to my own core values?

3. What fears and conditions are interfering with my experiencing my existence?

4. How can I reexperience my experience, bringing my experience into fuller awareness; that is, what experiments, exercises, and ways of being will help me complete my experience?

5. Having reexperienced and completed my experience, I should have a more lucid conception of who I am. How do I put these values into action?

The model for Basic Emotional Communication comes from a theory of personality development I have proposed in a previous book (Goldberg, 1980a). This theory specifically focuses on the pursuit of individual enlightenment as an emergent and intentional endeavor. In developing a theory of self-development, I have delineated the process of personality growth by indicating the specific developmental tasks the self has to address in a five-phase developmental theory in which the self first becomes aware of possibility (sensory-self phase), turns toward possibility (courageous-self phase), creates meaning by intuiting how it constitutes itself in the world (intuitive-self phase), establishes relationships with others (intimate-self phase), and creates a direction for expression of its sense of meaning (creative-self phase).

NOTES

1. "Dialogue" and "dialectic" are being used here in the Hegelian sense of creative synthesis of thesis and antithesis, rather than in the Socratic sense of interrogative.

2. There are two classes of selfishness. *Destructive selfishness* rewards weakness and failure. People who are overweight and claim they wish to diet may, for example, reward (console) themselves for the emptiness of their lives by consuming rich foods. They, in short, eat to celebrate the inability to feel good about themselves. *Constructive selfishness* rewards (celebrates) work and success. People with an alcohol problem, for example, no longer have a drinking problem when they only celebrate accomplishments that make them feel good about themselves. In short, they celebrate their *ability* to feel good about themselves.

3. *Power adequacy* I have defined elsewhere as the inner experience of being aware of one's personal needs; knowing that the resources to satisfy them are available; and realizing that to utilize one's power, one needs the ability and permission to obtain these resources. (See Goldberg, *Therapeutic Partnership*, pp. 95–97, for relationship of power adequacy to psychotherapy.)

Chapter 12
Dealing with Difficult Clients

—that which we are, we are—
One equal temper of heroic hearts,
Made weak by time and fate, but strong in will
To strive, to seek, to find, and not to yield.
—Alfred, Lord Tennyson

I will describe in this chapter a means of dealing with difficult clients. First, let us be clear about who these clients are. By "difficult client" I am referring to those clients the practitioner regards as "difficult to work with," "impossible to help," "resistant to therapeutic endeavor," "recalcitrant to a relationship," and so forth. The term, "difficult client" is generally applied to those clients who invoke anxiety in practitioners because of their aggressive or seductive manners, or because their psychological distancing mechanisms don't allow them to respond to the practitioner's endeavors at relationship and alliance, at least not in the ways the practitioner is comfortable working (Goldberg, 1983ª).

What are the psychodynamics of difficult clients? I will start this discussion by describing the converse to the difficult client. Clients do best in psychotherapy who possess, in sufficient degree, the following personal attributes; insight and analytic reasoning skills; accountability for their own behavior; and the ego strength sufficient to form relationships with others in which the clients in question must tolerate critical scrutiny of themselves and be willing to disclose their own painful, threatening, and also tender and compassionate concerns to others. Therefore, these are persons who take responsibility for their own thoughts, feelings, and actions. They come to therapy, not to persuade the therapist to accept their attitudes and beliefs about themselves, but for a candid exchange with another. They are also persons who experience anxiety consciously and are, as a result, aware of their distress. But they also must be able to tolerate tensions engendered by their own hostile expression and that of others toward them. When they experience a situation warranting it, they need to be able to express anger without fear of loss of control (Goldberg, 1973, pp.85–88). Difficult clients lack in important ways some or all of these personal attributes.

Behavioral scientists have culled at this point sufficient empirical evidence to realize that the specific method of treatment—psychoanalytically oriented, humanistic, behavioral, cognitive, or some eclectic type—is less salient in the therapeutic outcome than are the experience, skill, and personal concern of the therapist.[1] But what is even more important is the qualities of the client. Hans Strupp and numerous other clinical researchers have amply demonstrated that the qualities of the client decisively determine the outcome of psychotherapy.

The difficult client poses for the practitioner the problem of how to deal with a person who does not respond to the usual strategies and maneuvers of the therapist situation (Pines, 1975). Indeed, the art of psychotherapy is characterized by the endeavor not to be averted by the recalcitrance of the practitioner's clients. In this endeavor, practitioners have continually sought newer and more impactful therapeutic approaches (Goldberg, 1983a). In this pursuit, it is generally assumed by the general public that as behavioral scientists, practitioners of psychotherapy rely upon scientifically verified means of dealing with clinical dilemmas.

To the contrary, practitioners have not been particularly interested in research. Each practitioner tends to believe his/her own point of view about what is best for clients. Practitioners see it in such a personal way that they believe that their effectiveness cannot be properly measured, since each therapist and clinical situation is idiosyncratic.[2] Therefore, like most other areas of psychotherapy research, investigation toward effective means of developing a therapeutic alliance with recalcitrant clients has not been very fruitful. Research findings report no more than the obvious.[3]

The major findings suggest that motivation factors strongly influence therapeutic outcome. Clients who have suffered in their lives tend to have stronger incentives for pursuing treatment than those who have suffered less, providing that their symptoms are not overly severe and they don't distort reality excessively. Consequently, clients who make a strong positive contribution to the therapeutic alliance have good treatment outcomes. Those who establish and maintain a positive attitude toward the therapist and the work of therapy achieve the greatest benefits. On the other hand, clients who contribute negatively to the therapeutic alliance have poor treatment outcomes (Marziali, Marmar, & Kiupnick, 1981). Strupp, Fox, and Lessler (1969) have indicated that these negative reactions become evident at the outset of therapy and persist throughout. Consequently, the important research and clinical question, as Marziali et al. (1981) have indicated, "would be the study of specified therapist actions aimed at establishing a therapeutic alliance with patients who develop a negative reaction to the therapist or the treatment situation." This question will be pursued in this chapter. I will begin with an historical perspective.

NEGATIVE THERAPEUTIC REACTION

Freud (1923) coined the phrase "negative therapeutic reaction" to elucidate the psychodynamics of those patients who responded in an aversive manner during psychoanalysis. In situations in which the analyst conveyed optimism about the progress of the analysis these analysands indicated personal discontent directly or, instead, evinced deterioration in their psychological functioning outside of psychotherapy. Sandler, Holder, and Dave (1970), in reviewing the psychoanalytic literature on the negative therapeutic reaction, indicate that Freud linked this clinical manifestation

> with the operation of what he saw as an unconscious sense of guilt, due to the operation of the patient's conscience...[The patient's] symptoms may represent a need for punishment or suffering, an attempt to appease an unduly harsh and critical conscience...which could lead to the negative therapeutic reaction, might in some cases be reinforced by a concealed unconscious masochistic tendency...[therefore] a neurosis which has

defied every therapeutic effort may vanish if the subject becomes involved in the misery of an unhappy marriage, or loses all his money, or has been replaced by another. . . .(Freud, 1924)

With increased clinical understanding of therapeutic resistance some analysts expressed hope of successfully treating the negative therapeutic reaction in analysis. Joan Rivere, a British analyst, indicated, according to Sandler et al. (1970), that

the negative therapeutic reactions as described by Freud did not mean that the patient was always unanalyzable. . .Much of Rivere's discussion relates to what we have described as resistances due to the threat of the analytic work to the patient's self-esteem and resistances due to 'fixed' character traits. Other aspects related to the absence of an adequate *treatment alliance* in certain types of patients.

A major advance in analytic understanding of the negative therapeutic reaction came from the interpersonal oriented psychoanalytic work of Karen Horney. Horney (1936) recommended that the analyst not indiscriminately formulate every deterioration in the client's functioning as an indication of the emergence of a negative therapeutic reaction. Horney suggested

that only those instances ought to be included in which one might reasonably have expected the patient to feel relief. . .The negative therapeutic reaction is embedded in persons with a particular type of "masochistic" personality structure. In such persons the effect of a 'good' interpretation by the analyst [is experienced by the patient]: (1). . .as a stimulus to compete with the analyst. The patient is resentful of what he feels to be the analyst's superiority. . .fused with [the patient's] ambition is an inordinate amount of hostility. . .(2) [The interpretation is] regarded as a blow to the patient's self-esteem when it reveals to him that he is not perfect and has 'ordinary' anxieties. . .(3) [The interpretation evokes] a feeling of relief, however fleeting, and the patient reacts as if the solution means a move upwards [toward] recovery and success. . .While on the one hand the patient feels that if he attains success he will incur the same sort of envy and rage that he feels towards the success of others, on the other he fears that if he makes a move toward ambitious aims and fails, others will crush him as he would like to crush them. Such patients recoil from all aims involving competition and impose a constant inhibiting or checking process on themselves. (4) The interpretation is felt as an unjust accusation, and the patient constantly feels as if the analysis is a trial...(5) [The interpretation is experienced] to be a rebuff, and takes the uncovering of his own difficulties as an expression of dislike or disdain on the part of the analyst. [The patient has] a strong need for affection and an equally strong sensitivity to rebuff. (Sandler et al., 1970)

These above described perspectives on the psychodynamics of the difficult client are, obviously, one-sided—viewing the client as responsible for therapeutic failure. The crucial connection of the analyst's involvement in the patient's resistance was generally poorly understood until the work of Heinrich Racker. Racker, a South American psychoanalyst, systematized and elaborated upon several "loose threads" in the psychoanalytic literature, which had moved away from Freud's monolithic view of countertransference as the singularly disruptive force in psychoanalytic work. Racker (1957) suggested that the analyst's unconscious resistances are emotional clues which may potentiate an understanding of hidden meaning in the client's material. I will turn to this consideration presently.

THE PSYCHOANALYTIC TRADITION

Psychoanalytic tradition has, until recently, cautioned the therapist against full participation in the therapeutic process. As Roy Schafer (1974) and other writers have indicated, practitioners with a misunderstanding of Freud's legendary dictum of "where id is ego shall be" have sought to specialize in rendering their cognitive understanding of the client in their therapeutic work. From the work of intuitively oriented practitioners such as Theodore Reik (1948) a growing recognition has emerged over the last few decades of the need for the analyst to be *affectively* receptive to the client's unconscious by the resonance of the material in the analyst's own unconscious. It was, however, Heinrich Racker's writings that provided a systematic approach to an understanding of the analyst's involvement in the patient's resistance.

Racker (1957) differentiated three meanings of countertransference. (1) Similar to Freud's view of transference, countertransference may be for the analyst an interference in understanding the client. (2) At the same time, it can be an important vehicle for assisting the analyst in better understanding and interpreting the client's unconscious. (3) Most important, to Racker, the analyst's countertransferential reactions affect his or her functioning:

> It interferes with his action as object of the patient's re-experience in that new fragment of life that is the analytic situation, in which the patient should meet with greater understanding and objectivity than he found in the reality or fantasy of his childhood.

It is the tenuous and double-edged capacity of countertransference to affect not only the analyst's understanding, but the practitioner's behavior as well that, in Racker's view, renders the use of countertransference, potentially, the most effective tool in the analysis of the client's transference. According to Racker,

> Understanding of transference will depend on the analyst's capacity to identify himself both with the analysand's impulses and defenses, and with his internal objects and to be conscious of these identifications. This ability in the analyst will in turn depend upon the degree to which he accepts his countertransference, for his countertransference is likewise based upon identification with the patient's id and ego and his internal objects... Transference is the expression of the patient's relations with fantasied and real countertransference of the analyst. For just as countertransference is the psychological response to the analysand's real and imaginary transference, so also is transference the response to the analyst's imaginary and real countertransferences. Analysis of the patient's fantasies about countertransference, which in the widest sense constitute the causes and consequences of the transference, is an essential part of the analysis of the transferences. Perception of the patient's fantasies regarding countertransference will depend in turn upon the degree to which the analyst himself perceives his countertransference processes...on the continuity and depth of his conscious contact with himself.

In practice, this affective understanding of the client has generally been translated in the analyst's conscious mind to cognitive terms, which are interpretively expressed to the client. In other words, the analytic tradition has dictated that the therapist utilize this affective response to the client to enable the analyst to *understand* and *empathize* with the client. With the empathetic bond as a guide, the analyst enables the client to gain insight into unconscious (or, perhaps, technically more proper, preconscious) processes and to express his or her own (i.e., the client's) intentions with affect. The analyst in this endeavor is encouraged to "separate" his or her own ego, which is both a perceptive and emotive faculty, into observing and experiencing selves. As an emotive self, the analyst "participates" and affectively registers the tensions being evoked in his/herself and, by extension, in the therapeutic field. As a "trained" cognitive self, the analyst interprets and makes sense of what he or she is experiencing, in cognitive statements to the client (Goldberg, 1973).

In contrast, therapist responses which are *expressed affectively* rather than transformed into cognitive concepts have generally been regarded as clinically inappropriate—a countertransferential reaction which mitigates effective analytic work. As I indicated in Chapter 9, the rationale for this contends that the affect of the analyst's expression unveils the person of the analyst. Self-revelation by the analyst, analytic theory posits, leads to regressive tendencies in the client—a return to the id impulse rather than to mature ego functioning. What are the implications of this material for psychotherapy? I believe that the practitioner's affect must be utilized in somewhat different ways than traditional psychoanalytic theory has posited. I will examine this in the following sections.

FOSTERING A THERAPEUTIC ALLIANCE

In my ongoing research with difficult clients, I have identified twelve essential issues that need to be addressed in fostering a therapeutic alliance and creating a responsive climate for effectively utilizing the therapist's induced reactions during conflict. These 12 issues may be classified under one of the three major areas of clinical consideration: values; transference-countertransference interface; and technique.

Values

The imperative that values impose for the therapeutic endeavor is the question of who each of the participants is in terms of his/her existential struggle-in-the-world and how free each is in exploring these concerns with the other. This is the area in psychotherapy, as I have discussed elsewhere (Goldberg, 1977), that has received the least attention from practitioners. Indeed, even to this day, practitioners are cautioned to regard questions of values as matters beyond the province of psychotherapy. Nevertheless, difficult clients quite evidently crystalize for us the underlying conflict existent in every therapeutic encounter as to how therapist and client shall address his or her concerns to the other (Goldberg, 1980ª). The following are value issues in the therapeutic work that need to be addressed in working with difficult clients and therapeutic conflict. These issues will be illustrated by clinical examples.

1. *A recognition that the client's "aberrance" is an attempt to make meaning of his/her existence.*

Much of the problem in training psychotherapists is that they are oriented to look for (and to only believe in) what is *wrong* with the client. This is to say, what is hidden, denied, or pathological. A therapist needs to balance the search for the pathological with what is *right*, what is healthy and hopeful in the lives of those with whom he/she works. This continual searching for the pathological is also very stressful for the practitioner. Consequently, the practitioner must free him/herself from concentrating on the "patient" aspects of the client, otherwise the healthier aspects of the client's personality are "frozen." The practitioner must respond to the client's emotional needs, not simply render these needs intelligible by interpretation. If psychotherapy is a process within a relationship, the relationship must be nurtured so that the enabling processes can be activated. A brief example of this point may be evinced by transactions in a professional training group in which one of the group members was being "scapegoated" for her dissatisfactions with the group. To help the group examine their unwitting projections, the group leader suggested that one could only go so far in finding fault with other group members and indicated that the group members had not yet explored what they wanted from one another (Goldberg, 1970, pp. 291–322). The mediating gestures and supportive concerns of the therapist fosters the openness and trust that must precede psychotherapeutic growth (Goldberg, 1973). Healing is not a single decisive act, but a series of discrete steps and developmentally challenging recognitions.

2. *The recognition that therapeutic struggles are inimical to meaningful therapeutic progress.*

Therapeutic struggles, of course, should not be encouraged, but neither should they be discouraged or avoided. They need to be viewed as both inevitable and important consequences of significant human interaction. Most theories of psychotherapy tend to disregard therapeutic conflict (Friedman, 1975). These positions tend to attribute the struggle either to the client's distortions or that of the therapist (or, in a few theories, to the nature of their coming together). But generally, therapeutic conflict has been regarded as that which gets in the way of allowing the practitioner to get on with the business of proper psychotherapeutic procedure (Goldberg, 1977).

The problem of the practitioner "getting on with the business of proper psychotherapeutic procedure" is that *trying to help* frequently antagonizes difficult clients. Their experience with "helping" and "nurturing" has been anxious and adverse. The client experiences his/her aloneness as unbearable. What the client wants the therapist to do is just to be there and do nothing. The therapist frequently gets caught up in therapeutic conflict because the practitioner doesn't really want to be there because it is boring and painful, but since he/she must be there, the practitioner insists on trying to help.

I view psychological problems as symptoms developed by the client to avoid the insoluble existential concerns. The difficult realization that our human condition impresses upon us is that we can do nothing to avert these concerns. The important question is not what we try to do to solve them, but rather how we allow ourselves to experience our human condition. In working with difficult clients the practitioner is wise not to concern him/herself so much with what to do for the client as with being *responsive* to and *curious* about the client. In this sense, the therapist represents being, not doing, a topic discussed in Chapter 2.

3. *Central to the issue of values in psychotherapy is the view taken of the client's refractory attempts to relinquish habitual and self-defeating behavioral patterns.*

Resistance to therapeutic work is evoked from the client's need to ward off the practitioner's intrusion into his/her value system. The resistance phenomenon posits a value clash between therapist and client. Such a clash is an inevitable dynamic of human encounter. It is also the *sine qua non* of ameliorative endeavor without which therapy is a pale imitation of reality. One of the few practitioners and theorists who refuses to deny the claim that psychotherapeutic work is heavily value-laden is Erik Erikson. He has indicated that the therapist *must* always recognize "that he is taking a planful place in an ongoing life—we all know this but we do not always act on what we know, and we are not always aware—that our interpretive habits are *social* actions" (Evans, 1967, p. 97). The occurrence of resistance in therapy indicates that client and therapist have reached a crucial juncture in their interpersonal encounter. The therapist must help the client experience his/her difficulty with external intrusion and learn to handle it in a constructive manner. Concurrently, the client must alert the therapist that he/she is experiencing a personal difference with the practitioner and wishes assistance in dealing with these feelings. Too often in the past, the client has become overwhelmed with an inability to express disagreements with others. As a result, the client has chosen to cherish differences with others as too sacred to question. The client, therefore, in past interpersonal encounters, has refused to examine his/her images of self and others in an open and negotiable manner. We can expect the same reluctance in therapeutic encounter. The practitioner who is able to help the client tolerate the experience of opposition to others does so by personally demonstrating that the expression of opposition will not cast the client adrift from human company (Goldberg, 1973).

To aid in this endeavor, the therapist may obtain consultation from the client. The practitioner may do so by such straightforward means as expressing his/her own uncertainty about what is going on and asking for assistance from the client. This brings us to the second category of essential issues which need to be addressed in working with difficult clients.

Transference-Countertransference Interface

Countertransferential factors were reported by a study of the scientific committee of the American Psychoanalytic Association to be the most important determinant of discontinuation for most of the analysands who prematurely terminated analysis (Aaron, 1974). Nevertheless, our progressive understanding of effective work in psychotherapy teaches that we can no more deny and eliminate countertransference reactions by the therapist than we can eliminate transference reactions by the client.

Instead, therapists must use their countertransferential reactions in creative and constructive ways.

The issues to be addressed in terms of the transference-countertransference interface in working with difficult clients are:

4. *The recognition that the practitioner frequently encounters him- or herself in a therapeutic impasse with a client.*
The anthropologist Weston La Barre (1980) indicates in his examination of charisma that it is the close similarity of the psychic structures of the shaman and his followers which make charisma possible. Moreover, it is the disavowal of the common hopes and fears of the followers contained within the shaman's expression of prophecy which gives the shaman's charisma such potence. I was once a consultant to an in-patient drug rehabilitation unit of a federal psychiatric hospital. The program was based on a therapeutic community approach in which the patients shared responsibility with staff for setting and enforcing rules for living in the unit. This responsibility was essential to the rehabilitation of people whose style of life was floridly sociopathic. In this hospital was an eminent research psychiatrist, the author of several monograms and textbooks on sociopathy in forensic patients. He was studying several of the patients on the ward in depth. One of the patients whom I will call "Jim," refused to follow the rules of the community. He would telephone the doctor whenever he wished to avoid duties in the program. The doctor promptly came over to the unit and walked out with the patient. Jim returned, usually several hours later. No other patient on the unit had Jim's privileges. When I confronted the doctor about his undermining the program, he indicated that he was conducting important research. (He had been able to get away with his misuse of power because the program lacked a physician and the nursing staff were not willing to risk their jobs by antagonizing the doctor. I was in a more fortunate position.) I told him in rather strong terms that his behavior was unacceptable and would no longer be tolerated. If he wished to interview patients from that unit, this was to be done in concert with the unit staff. He promptly went into a hysterical fit. He screamed about his poor health and his wife being in a hospital. He left the unit yelling that I was interfering with his important work. His behavior throughout was clearly sociopathic. His behavior was indistinguishable from the patients. Conclusion: When either or both client and therapist deny their commonal-

ity with one another, magical rather than realistic expectations and demands result.

Curiosity is related to the issue of therapist-client identifications. Natural curiosity is what keeps us alive and well. A common characteristic of persons in psychotherapy is the paralysis of their natural curiosity. Clients take on self-curative attitudes and get in touch with their own natural rhythms by regaining curiosity about themselves and their place in the world. Therapists cannot directly teach or enable clients to become curious. Rather, it is therapists' curiosity about themselves that will free clients to be curious about themselves. The child is naturally curious about his/her place in the world. Children have seemingly endless interest in toying with and involving themselves with things that we, as adults, have long past become bored with. We, as adults, too frequently act as if curiosity were no longer needed because we sufficiently comprehend everything. To reiterate, it seems to me that one of the common denominators of all those who come into psychotherapy regardless of their symptoms and despite different backgrounds and education is a loss of curiosity. They have lost interest in who they are, where they are going, and how others actually respond to them. This lack of curiosity is, of course, closely related to depression. Depression is a symptom that is common to all emotional problems. I believe that one of the most important or useful ways of viewing depression is as a defense against curiosity.

How does the adult lose this apparently innate need to become interested and involved in the world? Probably, he/she was discouraged from reaching out. By this, I mean both physically reaching out for objects and intellectually and emotionally reaching out to try to understand another person. Reaching out was threatening to significant people around the child. The child was told, "No! Don't do that!" or "Why do you ask that? What's wrong with you?" The child was told that there was something wrong in trying to know and learn by reaching out. And if what the child felt within him/herself was bad, painful, or hurtful, the child was not safe *within* either. The child who cannot escape by going into self or by reaching for the comfort of other people is in an intolerable dilemma. We know from experimental evidence with laboratory animals that when a subject is punished (in this case, also self-punishing) for whatever option the subject takes, what is called "experimental neurosis" or "experimental psychosis" ensues. In a more subtle way, some parents do the same with children. Consequently, in trying to understand psychological problems, we need to examine what happened to the person's curiosity interests. Every person goes through life with some apprehensions. For some it is an overwhelming sense of foreboding and doom. We look for reassurance in order not to be so afraid. Psychological symptoms are ways we find to try to defend ourselves against these continual dilemmas of the human condition. These defenses have, however, the unfortunate side effects of thwarting our curiosity strivings, by traumatizing the search within ourselves to express our pressing concerns. We, instead, reject the vehicle of dialogue and allow our symptoms to speak for us and, in return, direct our destiny.

Let me give you an example of this. The young child who fears school because of a threatening teacher, taunting and ridiculing classmates, or unpreparedness for exams, may not know how to tell his/her parents about these aversive feelings directly. The child may feel that they won't understand because the child does not have the words to express these feelings or because of guilt for having fears. The child finds by chance or by observation that by having a stomach ache the child's parents become concerned. They say, without anxious effort on the child's part, to express such thoughts and feelings, "You seem ill, so you'd better not go to school today." The child has now found a defense against the fears. This defense suffices for the moment because anxiety is blocked. Over time, however, the child who is not encouraged to struggle courageously with inner promptings and express them to others will develop more and more entrenched physical and psychological illnesses which serve the low self-esteem person with not having to deal with immediate fears. Moreover, these illnesses have interpersonal secondary gain. For those who have been unable to receive caring by asking directly for it but feel entitled, a compromise has been found for receiving caring through being cared for during illness. The sufferer has derived a means of getting people to respond because the other feels compelled through guilt and concern. These are family members and friends, who, as frequent responders to family manipulation in assuming the roles of caretaker, are being shaped for healing careers. Of course, some practitioners are more prone to responding with insufficient detachment to the sufferer's manipulation cues than are other practitioners.

As a child, Evelyn was continually in competition with her

accomplished older sister. Because approval for external accomplishments were blocked for her, she learned to gain appreciation from her family by being sensitized to their unmet psychic needs, particularly how her parents' very different cultural backgrounds and personalities effected a mistrust between them. They continually drew her into their disputes to disarm the potent hostility ever present. As a therapist, Evelyn is still quickly induced to feeling depressed and to expressing her clients' resentful feelings just as she was with her parents. She often is unable to separate her feelings from those of her clients. Not suprisingly, she finds psychotherapeutic work exhausting.

Another practitioner working with a violent patient in a forensic hospital became resentful toward the staff of the patient's unit because they restricted the patient to the unit after he assaulted another patient. The patient could not attend his three weekly therapy appointments because of this restriction. The therapist felt that psychotherapeutic work was the prime consideration in the patient's rehabilitation and, therefore, nothing should stand in the way of therapy. In supervision he realized that he was being manipulated by the patient. The young practitioner seemed more concerned and responsible about the patient's treatment than the patient was himself. The practitioner was overidentified with the patient. The reader will recognize that a special kind of identification—projective identification—is involved in these cases.

The psychological mechanism of "projective identification" is a term coined by Melanie Klein, which has come into increasing popularity in the clinical conceptualizations of psychologists and other mental health practitioners. It refers to the observation that a person who finds a certain aspect of his personality quite unacceptable, let's say, unreasonable anger, detachment, or narrow-mindedness, tends to find this attribute consistently in (an)other person(s). Understandably, the attributor also tends to relate to the other person(s) as if he (they) actually possessed this attribute in considerable degree. To the extent that the other responds in a manner consistent with the undesirable attribute the attributor finds confidence in his ability to detect flaws in other people. Whereas projective identification is a mechanism utilized rather ubiquitously during periods of emotional agitation, it is, in fact, used to some extent by everyone.

The therapist has to be aware of what the patient is projecting onto him and to be able to separate that from his own personal distortions, asking himself whether this is something he was experiencing before he came into the session, is this the way he generally sees the patient, or is there something that has happened in the session that he has not been aware of that is inducing him to respond in a particularly unhelpful way to the patient. Once he has made this countertransferential separation he can handle it more properly.

This will happen to the extent that in working with difficult clients we, as practitioners, are curious about ourselves. Otherwise, the practitioner experiences his/her difficult client as being boring and frustrating. He/she resents having to be there. He/she wants to get the clients out quickly and back into the world because it is very tiring, if not painful, to be with that person. So he/she tries to help the client get through therapy and terminate with the practitioner. Unfortunately, the difficult client is often a person whose experience with other people trying to help him/her has been very disappointing and painful. The people who claimed they cared or attempted to help him/her were harmful. Consequently he/she doesn't trust helping.

Of course, you can't teach someone to be curious about him/herself. It's not something you learn in graduate school. It's a natural response, and I think that the way the therapist deals with his/her own boredom and pain in working with a difficult person is also the key to helping the client deal with his/her own issues. The practitioner might ask him/herself, "How am I like this person?" "In what self-threatening ways am I like this person such that I wish to deny our similarities?" And, "what can I learn about myself at such a time as I am willing to identify with the client?" When therapists become curious about their own identifications and how they deny them (which I have called "identification denial"), they become aware of what they can gain from being there with a client whom they experience as difficult. It makes therapeutic work a meaningful experience for the therapist and, at the same time, it models for the client being curious about self, and the world in which he/she lives. When this happens, there often ensues the beginnings of a meaningful relationship and a basic honesty about who each of the participants of the therapeutic journey are.

In short, when practitioners become bored or resistive in engaging clients, they should explore the identifications and identification denials they experience toward their clients. In this endeavor they need to ask themselves what *personal* concerns can be addressed by working with these clients.

5. *A recognition that the therapist's unconscious disavowal of identification with a client gets in the way of relationship and healing.*

As the foregoing should suggest, when the practitioner is not sufficiently aware of identification with clients, unconscious reaction to his/her own unacceptable attributes encountered in the client make therapeutic alliance unattainable. As I pointed out in Chapter 6, in such situations the practitioner may work arduously at a manifest level to develop a relationship with the client. Covertly, however, the practitioner resists this relationship. Naturally, these incompatible objectives generate conflict in the therapeutic work.

6. *A recognition and separation of the practitioner's induced feelings from subjective and historical countertransferential reactions.*

(This is often a difficult introspective task, which will be discussed later in this chapter.) Having done this, the therapist can reflect these induced statements back to the client in such a manner that the client is compelled to address and examine his/her own feelings about the therapeutic work the client has been resisting.

A clinical example of the practitioner's affective expression of therapeutic resistance and conflict will help examine this issue. A newly formed group consisted of nine clients, including four practicing psychotherapists. The group recently experienced its first drop-out—an isolated older man, who somatized his anxiety and expressed the sentiment upon leaving that he could get nothing from the group experience because even the group members who were therapists in their professional lives couldn't help themselves. The group members he was referring to had interacted in the group mainly in their professional roles, reluctant to expose their more vulnerable attributes. In the ninth session of the group, the group therapist was sitting on the periphery of the circle, as was Ann, a nontherapist member of the group. Ann was chronically late and relatively uninvolved and silent in sessions, as she was similarly uncommitted to conscious goals and directions in her life outside the group. The therapist, upon being invited to move to an empty seat inside of the circle of chairs said, "It is a very emotional place to be"—indicating that to move to an empty chair in the middle of the group would be emotionally uncomfortable. The group members expressed strong reactions to the therapist's unwillingness to sit in the middle of the group. They wondered aloud whether he was being serious or sarcastic. They explored what was so threatening about them and why a therapist would be reluctant to be in an emotional spot in the group. The discussion raised the emotionality of the group. There was considerably more affect present in the participants' interactions during this and subsequent sessions.

In working with difficult clients, it is often necessary to speak at once to several levels, as the client will resist interventions aimed at a single level. Consequently, the therapist's statement was intended on several levels. He was reflecting his identification with Ann, who was sitting outside the group, but was unable or unwilling to articulate her isolation. On a group level, the therapist was setting a tone, early in the development of the group, for an open affective expression of immediate experience. As a role model for the others in the group, he was indicating that therapists are also capable of experiencing threat. Implicitly, he was suggesting that useful behavior was often impaired by analytic examination of other group members' behavior, if, in the process, one's personal feelings were denied. Parenthetically, clients generally assume that their task in a therapeutic group is to be helpful to others in the group. It is necessary for the therapist to indicate that they are not there primarily to help one another (although this is frequently an incidental and fortunate consequence of group encounter). The major reason for clients to join in a therapeutic group is to explore their *own feelings* about themselves and others in the group in such a way as to ascertain how these sentiments influence them. To the extent that each group member openly explores his or her own personal concerns in the group, that member encourages and enables others to take responsibility for themselves in the group (Goldberg, 1977).

This brings us to the final category of essential issues in working with difficult clients.

Technique

Technique is a question of educational considerations; having studied, read about, or experienced various kinds of therapeutic interventions in one's own treatment or clinical demonstrations, the practitioner must decide which of these seem clinically indicated at a particular juncture in the process of an ongoing therapy. The issues that relate to technique and need to be addressed in working with difficult clients are:

7. *A recognition of the importance of a metaphorical under-standing of the client's world view, and the therapist's effec-tive use of the client's metaphorical model in creatively deal-ing with therapeutic conflict.*

Therapeutic impasse is frequently a consequence of the prac-titioner using his/her own metaphorical system of reality, rather than the client's in conveying possibility to the client. In ther-apeutic conflict, therapist and client are trying to induce each other to operate in terms of their own world view (Goldberg, 1980b). The practitioner, therefore, needs to utilize the client's metaphors contained in the client's statements and the psy-chosocial development implied in communications with the cli-ent to influence the client. The kinds of metaphors contained in the client's expressions and behaviors is indicative of the level and type of experience the client is receptive to at his/her stage of development.

A metaphor is a figure of speech in which one quality comes to be known in terms of *another* quality. Similarities are noted in objects or ideas that at first glance may seem unrelated. Metaphors are used because the direct use of language is restric-tive. Our language emphasizes those objects and experiences that are necessary to the survival and the well-being of our so-ciety. The Eskimo language, for example, supposedly has 80 terms to denote snow, whereas the English language has, essen-tially, one. Being restricted to only expressing literal language would limit an individual's thoughts, feelings, and actions, which are, of course, dependent upon available concepts for processing experiences and realizing possibilities. Fortunately, poets and artists expand our experiences by the metaphors and images they produce in creative endeavor. So do our clients, but more often, unfortunately, in painful endeavor. The therapist's function during conflict is to ally with the client's painful feel-ings. The therapist may utilize the client's metaphors to create this bridge.

In the clinical example described, the therapist realized that he had the option of unintrusively moving into the chair in the middle of the circle. This was what the group members, in their polite social attitude, expected him to do. The therapist could, of course, have simply interpreted their invitation as, for exam-ple, an attempt to include him as a group member in order to deny the power and the mystique he held for them. However, he sensed that interpretations would not enable them, at that mo-ment in the development of the group, to contact the fears that fostered their resistive pattern in the group. The therapist, there-fore, expressed affectively what was consciously unexpected by the group members. He viewed the empty chair not only as an empty chair, but as an inner emptiness and an interpersonal separation that members of the group experienced and projected (then disavowed having done) onto the empty chair. The ther-apist's response was intended to indicate that he recognized and experienced this separation and would not attempt to bridge it until the group members indicated that they wished him to join them in meaningful endeavor.

8. *A need on the part of both the client and the therapist for courage in recognizing client-therapist identifications and in dealing with therapeutic struggles.*

The therapist must be able to dream and dare to express, as well as to enact emotionally, what the client dare not even im-agine (Goldberg, 1980a). What does it mean for therapists to use themselves creatively and to enact what clients dare not even imagine? All forms of treatment—other than *immediate* face-to-face encounter with clients—such as medication, hospitalization, advice-giving, referral, reflect the therapist's unwillingness to go beyond some point, whether in terms of structure—time and place—or process, to avoid the ascendence of the therapist's de-spair, repressed rage, hunger, insanity, or whatever. To main-tain an alliance with difficult clients, I try to influence them to take responsibility, even if it is responsibility for their "irrespon-sibility" (their being "difficult"). For this to happen, we need a *working model* for each client, from which we can direct our in-terventions. In working with difficult clients—perhaps in work-ing with anyone—this model should not derive from abstraction (someone else's theory) but from *our own immediate* experience of our clients as we *directly* and *personally* relate with them. By using our own fantasies and associations (assumed to be in-duced), we can create a model of how the clients present them-selves to us and we can know how and when to intervene. This model is interactive as well as induced. It emanates from the progressive verbal and nonverbal interaction between par-ticipants.

To understand the dynamics of the therapeutic situation in which I am a participant-observer, I allow my unconscious full rein as my apperceptive faculties engage the client's choice of words, facial expression, bodily posture, etc. A therapist's im-pressions may take the form of images and fantasies, but they are not helpful to the client if they are entirely in the therapist's head. Only from actions are people really known and understood. Therapists must allow the deeper recesses of themselves to contact and respond to the other. They cannot predetermine what effect their behavior will have upon themselves or on the persons to whom they are responding. Only by responding emotively as involved participants and reflecting upon the effect of their behavior can therapists properly assess their influence upon others and adjust their behavior accordingly. This is illustrated in the following case example of a client seen in group psychotherapy.

Jane is an appealing, slight girl with large brown eyes often filled with panic. More than others in this group she lacked meaningful relationships in her life. She claimed to have a number of fears but was unable to specify any. She was also quick to sense danger in the group when others seemed comfortable with the mood. She became very agitated if "wounds" inflicted during one session remained unassuaged until the next. As Jane had been unable to name and challenge her fears, she could do little more than flee from them. I fantasized about her in the group. I imagined a large bulky figure pursuing her, waving a crooked finger at her. I felt my heart pumping rapidly. I looked at Jane and, speaking from my fantasy, said, "Have you had enough punishment, Jane?" She didn't answer with any sounds, but her eyes pleaded, "Yes, but how do I stop the pain?" I said, now more consciously aware of my words, "You have a right to tell that part of you punishing you to 'cut it out' " Out of the welled recess of her repressed feelings poured memories she claimed to recognize only from dreams. She described when she was an adolescent slapping her mother and cursing God's name after finding out that she was adopted. She had felt unloved since that day, but until that moment had not remembered why. Until that group session she had not been able to discuss these feelings. She had been in therapy for several years and a member of a previous group for two years. Others had discussed painful feelings of self-denigration. Nevertheless, not until the therapist's direct affective involvement with her fear had she felt that she could really be understood because others had natural parents they remembered (Goldberg, 1973) and she didn't.

Some readers may feel that therapeutic action in this case was overreactive and intruded itself too much on the therapeutic relationship. I must point out that the client had remained "frozen" for almost three years in the group because the others in the group, through their projective identification with her, were "protecting" her by withholding strong reactions, which they believed she could not tolerate. Only the therapist "dared" to have an impact. Otherwise, Jane would simply reexperience the group as she did her mother.

As the above illustration suggests, the vital task for therapists in rendering affective responses is appropriately utilizing countertransference. This task is not simply a clinical technique, but emanates from the emotional involvement of therapist and client in therapeutic encounter. Consequently, the most difficult issue for practitioners not accustomed to working with difficult clients is to move from trying to understand these clients theoretically in terms of their psychodynamics to realizing how to influence a working alliance with them.

To understand someone psychodynamically means we are able to explain their motives and behavior as it defies common sense. This is to say, psychodynamic explanation delineates why people act in ways that seem pernicious to their best interests. To develop a therapeutic alliance, we need to return to common sense. We need to adapt our behavior and encourage the client to respond to us in a way that makes sense to both of us. Learning to recognize the various manifestations of countertransference is requisite in this endeavor. Ormont (1980), elaborating on the theoretical contribution of Racker, writes that there are two main classes of countertransference:

> The first is purely *subjective, historical*...The first form of [countertransference] is the *repetitive*...The therapists repeat the meaningful story of their lives without changing it or learning from it...Sometimes therapists not only replay their own past but also attempt to repair damage done. We call this *reparative* countertransference...When therapists see their groups' suffering, it unconsciously revives their own suffering. They feel impelled to alleviate it with some act. They want to make life better for their patients than it was for them...Resolving the reparative countertransference frees therapists to do the job which is uniquely theirs—understanding the group...The objective countertransference also subdivides well into two types: the matched (or Racker, 1957, calls it, "concordant") and the complementary. With the *matched* countertransference the therapist feels sad. No empathy is involved. The therapist is just matching the patient's emotional state...The matched counter-

transference can give us particular trouble if we take these reactions to be solely our own. In other words, we are unaware that we are merely mirroring the patient's reactions and accept them as our invention...Finally, we come to the *complementary* countertransference. This is the response of therapists to the roles in which their group members cast them. As before, the therapists identify with the group members. But with complementary countertransference, the identification is with important incorporated objects of their childhood...Some of their fellow [group] members may accept the parts they assign them, but others [of the group members] contend, expose and confront these maneuvers and role-casting. We, as therapists, take a different course. While the patients experience the feelings they had toward their original significant figures, we know we are replicating through our countertransference reactions the feelings they attribute to these figures. From these feelings we can reconstruct their early histories and understand them.

Ormont's comments about the various forms of countertransference suggest a rationale for utilizing induced feelings in working with difficult clients and therapeutic conflict. I recommend the following steps in utilizing induced reactions for therapeutic interventions:

a. *Don't attempt to interpret the meaning of behavior until you understand it affectively,* as well as intellectually. For example, the therapist's proprioceptive reaction to Jane was influential in experiencing Jane's fear. In training psychotherapists to work with difficult clients, I have been struck by the therapists' strong efforts and resulting frustration in trying to rid clients of their resistance without first understanding the meaning of resistance. Attempts to dissolve resistance without the therapist and client first understanding affectively what the resistance is about to both are ineffective and frequently deleterious to therapeutic work.

b. *Side with the resistance,* in order to reflect the difficulty the client is experiencing. In the incident above, the therapist's siding was not expressed directly. It was reflected by his identifying with Jane by experiencing the bulky figure pursuing her. In other instances, the therapist may verbalize joining behavior, such as when the therapist expressed his unwillingness to sit inside the group. The joining relaxes client defensiveness and makes alliance more acceptable;

c. The most crucial aspect of the effective use of induced

feelings is the *availability of the therapist's complementary countertransference.* By experiencing the internal resonance of the client's projection of painful introjects, in reaction to the client, the therapist has a clearer understanding of the basis for and strength of the client's resistance. I will use a somewhat extreme example. From experiencing intolerable, "murderous" rage toward a client, which is not the therapist's usual feeling toward a client, the therapist may reasonably conjecture that these are reactions that significant figures had toward the client in his or her early development. The client's intractable aloofness and indifference, let's say, were mechanisms to prevent counter-rage and psychological annihilation. Indeed, the client's current resistances were successful survival mechanisms, which have now outlived their usefulness. Thus, the therapist asked Jane if she had had enough punishment ("the punishment" was inferred to be a compromise reaction for fear of much greater punishment for not experiencing guilt); and

d. Having understood the meaning of the behavior's defensive function, the therapist *interprets or redirects it* (for example, the prescriptive statement by the therapist to Jane), *once the client expresses curiosity and concern about his or her behavior.*

9. *The development of a therapeutic alliance is created by the practitioner's close attention to and facilitation of productive working norms.*

These norms should emphasize commitment to work; open examination of thoughts, feelings, and actions; and the trust that these efforts will be meaningful and worth the effort they require. These are endeavors to create alliance by means of mutual exploration and shared undertaking. It is essential that we utilize our clients as "consultants" in recognizing the issues and values being struggled with during therapeutic conflict.

In a therapeutic group of eight members which had been in existence for about a year, the Christmas-week session was seen as an occasion for relaxation of the usual group conduct. There was the typical chit-chatting before the session, but it continued even after the group convened. Frieda, one of the usually more psychologically mature group members, brought in a box of cookies, which she proceeded to distribute to the group members, after first acknowledging that she was breaking the rules. Instead of accepting a cookie, the therapist stated the obvious— that the group wished to avoid therapeutic work and were test-

ing to see how far they could go. The group members acknowledged their refusal to work, saying that they were tired of
"always analyzing everything." They claimed that they were entitled to a respite for this session from "heavy psychological
work." The therapist "joined" their resistance. But he didn't experience it as a choice. He felt angry, misunderstood, and stub-
bornly unwilling to give of himself. He remained totally silent
until the last five minutes of the session. He was aware that
there were several attempts to manipulate his guilt—trying to
make him feel that he had failed the group members by his
silence.

Much of the session was spent in listening to a client who recently joined the group discuss a problem with considerable expression of upset. The usually helpful group members did little
or nothing either to support her or to help her examine her issue. No one in the group directly questioned or confronted the
therapist until the last five minutes of the session. At that point
several members exploded with rageful words at him, while
others expressed surprise and disappointment. These expressions were encouraged by the therapist. They were followed up
in the next session in which group members spontaneously were
able to identify their own anger and resentment about how the
group had been working for a few weeks. They identified with
the therapist's silence and realized that what they expected from
the therapist they, themselves, were refusing to give. The therapist indicated that it would be folly for him to care more about
the group than the group members did, but that he was willing
to share the responsibility of creating a meaningful group climate with the others. Psychotherapeutic practice requires a rationale and methodology based on a realistic assessment of the
existential conditions in therapeutic encounter. This rationale
must enable the practitioner to get in touch with his own, as well
as his client's, loneliness and despair, to address the conditions
that present themselves in a therapeutic encounter in which
therapist and client take each other seriously.

Issues of existential concern are denied in a setting in which
the therapist suppresses his own intentionality (Goldberg,
1975a). I am in agreement with Hugh Mullan (1955) that therapists frequently impose ritualistic requirements—for example,
not speaking until the client has, answering a question with a
question, or leaving unclarified the statements the client makes
about the "nontherapy"-related aspects of the practitioner's

life—supposedly for the benefit of the client, to promote his "cure," but they are actually a means for the therapist to avoid his own anxiety about the common struggle he shares with his client in their mutual quest for their own humanity.

Jules Older, a New Zealand psychologist, has discussed the conditions that, when absent in psychotherapy, limit the success of the therapeutic endeavor. According to Older (1977), there are four current taboos that may contribute to failure in psychotherapy. These taboos are against touching, embarrassment, noisy emotions, and long individual sessions.

The issue of touch is a controversial one in the modern healing arts. Physical and emotional touch can exacerbate the hurt and trepidation from the client's previous painful physical contacts. Psychoanalysts are especially cautioned against touching their patients in order not to encourage infantile symbiotic needs on the patient's part and to discourage seductiveness on the analyst's part.

There is no simple means of ascertaining whether touching clients is appropriate or not. Obviously, the safest way is to eschew touch in any way. But there seems something pathetically fearful on the practitioner's part to operate from such a blanket rule, and to disregard the special clinical significance of touch with particular clients. Older argues that by forbidding direct physical contact with those with whom we work, we have cut ourselves off, as practitioners, from very basic ways of relating and providing comfort to our clients. In some instances, Older indicates, it is the only way of reaching a client. This can be easily seen from analogy. Would the therapist avoid physical contact if the client tripped and was on the verge of incurring an injurious fall? If the client were in an agitated state and ready to injure him/herself in the practitioner's presence, would not the therapist seek physically to restrain the client? Similarly, and more usually, there are times when this emotional hold or simple touch is appropriate—times of great misfortune and grief, etc. These are times when some emotional touch, whether it is physical or not, is a sign of *decency.* Any psychotherapeutic system that is able to cancel out acts of decency are not systems of healing that are on the side of their clients.

Older tells us, "Touching is not a technique, not-touching is a technique." Like any other therapeutic intervention it needs to be used wisely—on the basis of common sense and compassion for the client. It is not surprising, therefore, as Older points out, that there are practitioners who privately admit touching their clients in therapy, but would never speak of it publicly out of a fear or misunderstanding of their motives and possible professional sanctions.

When I was in graduate school out West there was another graduate student in psychology from the Northwest with whom I became close friends. He was a rather bright and sensitive fellow who had struggled with his sexual identity into his mid-twenties. He spoke to me of the most significant aspects of his own therapy. His therapist—a rather tall, strong, and athletic fellow—sat and held his hand for most of the sessions of the second year of his therapy. He told me that the experience of being with another man who was so clearly masculine and yet was comfortable enough with his masculinity to hold his hand was a turning point in his own integration and acceptance of uncomfortable aspects of himself.

Similarly, Older argues that quiet and rational discourse is frequently an avoidance of emotional concerns. Discussion of pain isn't necessarily the expression of hurt, but may be, instead, its avoidance. It may be inconvenient or difficult for a therapist to allow the expression of noisy emotions in his/her office, but getting in touch with deep hurt is indispensable to meaningful psychotherapy. When this hurt is experienced, it may emerge with considerable noisy release. Correspondingly, the avoidance of embarrassment in psychotherapy constitutes an implicit agreement between therapist and client to avoid troublesome and painful concerns. This pact may be firmly maintained for years. Older points out that the silent agreement not to discuss painful and embarrassing subjects reinforces the client's feelings of self-denigration and unacceptability that he/she brought with him/her into psychotherapy. "For if even the therapist, fully imbued with transference, omnipotence, and gratitude, can't talk about something, it must be awful, indeed" (Older, 1977). According to Older, prolonged sessions increase the likelihood of the intimacy experienced in therapeutic encounter, dissolving the taboos against noisy emotions, the discussing of embarrassing concerns, and physical touch. It is Older's practice to maintain individual sessions as long as necessary to work through an emotional crisis.

10. *Separating induced reactions from personal distortion.*

In considering the optimal affective climate for therapeutic work, an issue not yet addressed is how practitioners ascertain whether they are experiencing and expressing the projective identifications (induced feelings) of their clients or, instead, are evoking their own personal distortions.

To separate induced feelings from personal distortions, practitioners must monitor what they bring into the session. Ideally, they "prepare" for the session by considering the concerns they are currently working on in their own lives. They explore how well they are doing with these issues, to elucidate their current pressing needs and the impediments toward meeting these needs. This introspection informs them of what may interfere with their effectiveness as facilitators for others. Following this reflection, they can interpolate their own personal pressing concerns into what they are struggling with as practitioners. To avoid being overly didactic and detached in their work, they need to cast aside, for the time being, that which they have already figured out about neurosis and human nature. Preconceived formulations and firm convictions about their work will issue forth more quickly than is necessary when they become uncomfortable during a therapeutic encounter. To be most in touch with the struggles of the people with whom they are working, they need to be aware of their own dissatisfactions as practitioners (Goldberg, 1977). Having monitored what they are bringing with them into the therapeutic field, they can allow conscious awareness of themselves to descend. To effectively utilize induced feelings, practitioners must sense and participate in the client's experience *as real people.* They must let themselves go fully—well, almost, with the only reserve being a firm conviction that when they experience a *hesitation,* or a sense of limitation in their own or the client's participation in the encounter, they will respect their hesitation. At such moments, they will hold back from full participation with the client and will seek to understand the source and consequence of that hesitation (Goldberg, 1980a). The experience of hesitation may be a signal that the practitioner is involved in an inappropriate countertransferential reaction. Other clues to countertransference include recurrent thoughts about the client outside of sessions, dreams about the client, and the urge to talk to others about the client.

In addition to the approaches already discussed, there are, of course, more traditional means of monitoring countertransferential reactions. The most typical are by expert supervision, a peer supervision group, control analysis, or co-therapy.

Ellen, a young psychiatrist, was being supervised in a therapy group she was conducting for family members of seriously ill patients on a medical unit of a teaching hospital. Ellen indicated that everyone, including herself, was afraid of a very red-faced, angry-appearing man in the group who had a myocardial infarct affliction. Hospital staff were afraid that if he became angry in the group he would either have a cardiac arrest or become violent. The supervisor asked Ellen if anyone in the group (including herself) had said to him, "I am afraid of (for) you." The supervisor said that he, himself, could not be effective in therapy if he held back the verbal expression of affect, particularly fear, when this emotion was strongly experienced. He also said that he did not believe that pretending not to be experiencing strong emotion was useful for an angry patient or for others in the group. His experience with violent patients indicated that unexpressed fears sensed by the patients, but unspoken by those around him or her, would evoke the patient's terror and loss of control. By expressing her fear directly, the therapist would demonstrate that she was in control of herself and could provide safe limits for the patients to express their own fears. In this newly formed group, with little psychological sophistication and preparation for a group experience, the therapist needed to model affective expression. Seasoned supervisors realize that beginning therapists are threatened by their countertransference and it generally takes some time for them to become comfortable and effective in utilizing it. Acting out by clients is frequently suggestive of therapeutic countertransference by the therapist. It often emanates from a confusion about the therapist's core values. The therapist's affective contribution is a value-laden attempt to make the treatment situation a viable and meaningful endeavor. Ellen's bland cognitive statements in her group were barren of the affects of the disavowed, projective identifications of the group members. These affects needed to be returned to the group in order for them to do their therapeutic work. Because Ellen was apparently threatened by strong, affective identification, she tacitly assumed the helpless role the group put her in.

To avoid destructive client collusion, the therapist must let what the client is saying and doing resonate within his/her own internal experience and ascertain how it affects the practitioner at that moment in the session. Practitioners must continually evaluate their role in the therapeutic relationship. By doing this, they can, at any point, question the role the client has placed the therapist in and with which the practitioner has apparently gone along. In the "empty chair" incident, the therapist questioned his own unwitting joining with the group in "helping" others and had the feeling that some of his own feelings, and those of the group members, were not being met in this way. The therapist then questioned his own motives for colluding with the group and thereby permitting them to avoid looking at some important processes taking place in the group. Similarly, in the "silent" session the therapist realized that he would not behave this way in the group by choice. However, having acted this way, he took responsibility for his behavior. He became aware that his reaction was both subjective countertransference and the induced anger and feeling of being misunderstood by the group members. By staying with these strong feelings and examining them, he was able to separate them and utilize them constructively. An unwillingness to acknowledge strong affect can be therapeutically deleterious.

In a supervision group at an analytic institute, a candidate commented that the supervisor sounded rather vehement when he went around the group in a simulated demonstration of how to handle scapegoating in a group composed of clients regarded as unsuitable for dyadic analytic work. The supervisor agreed, saying that in group psychotherapeutic work, he would express as much emotion as necessary when group members denied their involvement in behaviors that led to a group member being physically or psychologically injured. In terms of the group being supervised, the supervisor perceived that there was a splitting mechanism taking place. The client group members, in their panic, were covertly asking the therapist to set firm limits on their inability to control their own sadism. Unless the therapist spoke firmly and directly, psychotic-like reactions would be quite likely to erupt. But the therapist's inability to stop the scapegoating in his group indicated his unwillingness to face up to angry feelings directed at him. The cognitive statements he used in trying to stop the angry outbursts were technically accurate, but they were not sufficiently impressive affectively to dissolve entrenched preoedipal patterns in the group.

11. *Therapeutic responsibility*

In working with difficult clients we do not have an ideal situation. Normally, there is little opportunity for careful deliberation in examining conflict and effectively engaging these issues.

If the client is not there, nothing therapeutic can happen; no matter how thoroughly a practitioner understands a client, after he or she leaves treatment it will be of little avail. Therapists need to *engage* difficult clients. To move from therapeutic impasse, practitioners need to act quickly to facilitate the examination and expression of conflictual material. To do so, they must apply what is missing in this task. In the clinical examples described in this chapter, the therapist utilized (or was encouraged to use) his countertransferential reactions to reflect what the clients were unable to articulate.

To take a less directive role and only to interpret or attempt to wait out the resistive patterns would be ineffectual. In working with therapeutic conflict, practitioners' responsibility is not simply to handle immediate exigencies, but to model the processes they believe will foster ongoing effective therapeutic functioning. However, like other kinds of significant learning experiences, this modeling requires that practitioners *inspire* the client to incorporate the sentiment that their efforts will be meaningful and worthwhile.

12. *The installation of hope.*

Frank (1961) and Yalom (1970), among others, have also indicated the importance of the installation of hope in the curative process. Thus, in the "empty chair" incident, the therapist "rewarded" the group members at the end of the session. He expressed appreciation for their hard work transforming a session in which group members had previously seemed unconnected to a session with a climate of involved relatedness.

CONCLUSION

A theoretical and clinical rationale for working with difficult clients in therapeutic conflict has been presented. The model delineates several essential issues that need to be addressed in working effectively with these clients. The essential contribution of the therapist to the affective and inspirational substratum of the treatment situation has been demonstrated. This model may appear in certain ways to be in opposition to certain analytic principles; however, I do not believe that this approach actually contradicts analytic principles. It should be realized that those analytic principles restricting therapeutic activity are essentially economical in that they generally simplify therapeutic practice.

This economical consideration should not be confused with therapeutic contraindications, especially in working with difficult clients, who require ingenuity, creativity, and courageous strategies in order to be engaged.

Finally, I would like to suggest several questions which the practitioner may find useful to consider when working with difficult clients:

1. Who are the therapists who generally work with the most difficult clients?

2. Why are we involved with another person in distress?

3. What do we learn about ourselves in working with difficult clients?

4. What do we, as practitioners (aside from the client), wish to acomplish in our encounters with another person in distress?

5. How far are we willing to go in helping our clients?

Having said that, we must, however, face certain realities. We are forced to realize that there are certain clients and certain clinical situations in which we should not get involved. In theory we have been trained to believe that we can work successfully with any client if we try hard enough to understand or if we have our countertransferential impediments removed. In practice we come painfully to recognize that if we don't like a client, we cannot work meaningfully with that person. Of course, it is to our edification and professional responsibility to try to understand our reaction. But it is to the detriment of the client not to refer him/her to someone else if after sufficient time we are not able to get past our dislike.

NOTES

1. Except for the short-term superiority of behavior therapy for phobias, compulsions, obesity, sexual problems, and cognitive therapy for nonpsychotic depression, no single therapy has been demonstrated to be significantly more efficacious than any other.

2. I have stated that there is very little research of direct value to the psychotherapist on this topic. The reader may be interested in a study that tried to sort out the most and least common mistakes by neophyte practitioners. These are found in table 12.1.

Table 12.1

Supervisor's Ratings (*N* = 20) of the ten Most Common and ten Least Common Mistakes in Psychotherapy Made by Residents*

Therapist Mistake	Mean Frequency of Occurrence[a]
Most common	
Wanting to be liked by the patient	3.37
Inability to "tune-in" to the unconscious of the patient	3.21
Premature interpretations	3.21
Overuse of intellectualization by the therapist	2.90
Inappropriate transference interpretations	2.89
Assuming a stereotyped "analytic psychotherapist" stance regardless of the actual treatment situation	2.89
Lack of awareness of countertransference feelings	2.84
Therapist's inability to tolerate aggression in the patient	2.84
Therapist's avoidance of fee setting	2.84
Least common	
Therapist lack of interest	1.44
Excessive voyeurism in the therapist	1.50
Consciously disliking the patient	1.68
Therapist's revealing personal information about himself or herself	1.68
Therapist dissembling	1.68
Therapeutic nihilism on the part of the therapist	1.68
Seductiveness by the therapist	1.84
Therapist's lack of empathy	1.88
Competitiveness with the patient	1.89
Absence of psychological-mindedness in the therapist	1.89

[a] 0 = not at all; 4 = very often. Group mean = 2.98; two-tailed t test between means of 10 highest rated and 10 lowest rated items revealed significant difference, p < .001.
*Buckley, P., T. B. Karasu, & E. Charles. Common mistakes in psychotherapy, *American Journal of Psychiatry, 12 (1979)* 1578–1580.

3. In fairness to the psychotherapist, I must point out again that mental health practice has not reached the maturity of a science. It is also clear that interest in investigating the outcome of psychotherapy has not kept pace with the growing utilization

of psychotherapy, particularly in private practice. In fact, interest in the research of psychotherapy, in general, has never been an abiding concern for more than a small minority of practitioners.

Chapter 13
A Prospectus for Dealing with the Concerns of Practice

We are wiser than we know.
—Ralph Waldo Emerson

In previous chapters I have sought to demonstrate the interrelationship between the satisfactions of psychotherapeutic practice and its hazards. This perspective was predicated upon the theme of the vulnerable healer in personal journey. In this chapter I seek to show how the practitioner, in being aware of this theme, can reduce some of the unnecessary stresses of practice while enhancing professional and personal goals. I will begin with some individual concerns of the practitioner and expand them to the larger philosophical issues of psychological work.

TAILORING PROFESSIONAL OBJECTIVES TO THE PRACTITIONER'S PERSONALITY

The psychotherapist's personality—his/her strengths and weaknesses— are the tools of practice. Unlike other professionals, the practitioner of psychotherapy has no external instruments with which to work. Consequently, the way the practitioner works should be congruent with his/her own personality and theoretical perspective. Generally, this perspective was found useful in his/her own personal therapy and apprenticeship, and honed in workshops and continuing education. As such, it should be congruent with the practitioner's view of the world. Every psychotherapeutic system has implicit a philosophy of what the world is like and, as such, imposes questions such as "What is human nature?," "How do people become what they are?," and "How can people change and get rid of impediments to constructive and creative growth?" The techniques of practice are designed to implement and the latter questions, predicated upon the point of view the therapeutic system takes toward the former two questions. Among psychotherapists, Erik Erikson is notable in recognizing the vital interrelationship of the practitioner's personality and therapeutic style. Erikson (Evans, 1967) writes,

> It is not enough for the psychotherapist to claim that he has learned his method only because he knew it would work better than any other (reasonably honest) method. The fact that he can really learn only a method which is compatible with his own identity is a minimum condition for his effectiveness with patients to whom his method has appeal. It is no coincidence that all over the world a large percentage of the first psychoanalysts and probably also of patients were Jewish. I think Freud believed himself, that in some ways the whole logic of psychoanalysis has much to do with highly verbal and self-conscious gifts, and we know to what extent book learning and verbal drive have been an important part of Jewish identity and adaptation over the centuries. So it isn't just a question of which method is the best for patients, but also of which method the therapist feels most at home with and creative in. Only then will he be a really good therapist for the patients whom he has learned he is good for. (p. 95)

THE PRACTITIONER'S LIFE PLAN AND GOALS

Just as many practitioners explicitly suggest to their clients that they develop life plans and goals, so, too, this existential project is valuable for the practitioner in assessing the course of his/her career. Practitioners should examine what they devote their time to in practice. In this examination, at least, the following three questions should be asked: "Is the practitioner specializing too exclusively in certain types of clients, which limits the practitioner's effectiveness with other kinds of clients?" "Have the limitations the practitioner imposed on him/herself resulted in feelings of staleness and boredom?" "How can the practitioner broaden (or, in some cases, narrow) the directions the practitioner wishes to take in his/her life?"

To provide a broad enough perspective for the practitioner's planning and examination, it may be helpful to formulate a five- or ten-year plan."

EXPANDING ONE'S CLINICAL PERSPECTIVE

First of all, it is important in the growth of every practitioner that no matter how conservative his/her practice is or even how successful, that the practitioner take on one or a few different types of clients (maybe, even difficult clients) than he/she usually works with on a regular basis. It may be useful to experiment, even to a limited exent, with some other therapeutic approaches than how the practitioner customarily works. Like the traveler who learns more about his own culture through the eyes of the foreigner, he may learn more about his own practice, in addition to the important benefit of becoming invigorated by these occasional journeys into previously unexplored areas of clinical work.

In short, there is a need in practice to have a variety of clients and activities. This prevents the practitioner from "assembly-lining" his/her professional life. The contrast between different kinds of clients creates a variety of perspectives on human existence. A perspective on human existence becomes artless and slanted whenever the practitioner assumes a position of having finally figured out human existence. Contrasts among the clients he/she sees should constructively challenge these beliefs. The practitioner who believes that he/she is capable of formulating his/her work into a universal schemata of human nature will have clients who suffer from unknown aspects of their complexity as human beings even after many years of treatment. Human existence requires a continual response from each of us. It re-

jects all final answers. In return, we will only reject human existence if we attempt to impose final answers upon our human
condition.

Second, just as the seasoned practitioner needs to accept new
types of issues for his/her own growth as a practitioner, so
should the practitioner reject those who do not promise growth,
and instead perpetuate stagnation. Maintaining the growing
edge in practice, Burton maintains, requires a careful selection
of those with whom we work.

> After more than 25 years in the practice of psychotherapy, I
> have come to the place where I accept only those clients for a
> therapeutic relationship where there is not only some promise
> that I can help them, but who offer something for me for my own
> growth. (Burton, 1969)

Third, it is important that neither the practitioner's financial
nor therapeutic satisfactions depend upon one or a few clients.
The practitioner should never keep a client for personal satisfactions, whether they be financial, intellectual, or emotional.

Fourth, because of the built-in frustrations and limitations of
dealing with very disturbed clients, it helps to balance the practitioner's energies by applying his/her talents to other areas of
psychological work. The seasoned practitioner who works with
only difficult borderline and schizophrenic clients may receive
little positive regard from clients. By sharing his/her experience,
knowledge, and concerns with students and supervisees, or simply in devoting his/her professional time to those areas of interest and skill the practitioner does not normally use in private
practice, the practitioner may receive satisfactions not obtaina-
ble in his/her daily clinical practice.

Fifth, the practitioner who works exclusively with individual
clients may profit from devoting some of his/her practice to
group and family work. Among other values to the practitioner,
it may serve as an invaluable tool for understanding his/her own
countertransferences. Let me illustrate!

THE PROBLEM OF COUNTERTRANSFERENCE

One way that group therapy is preferable to individual psychotherapy is that the group members serve as guards against

the therapist's countertransference. They enable the practitioner to act more appropriately and more spontaneously in the present group situation. They alert the practitioner against carrying over biases and expectations from the practitioner's relationship with persons who are not members of the present group (Goldberg, 1973). This is illustrated in the following group protocol:

Helen: (discusses her former therapist) Whenever he said things he put it in terms of himself, and I was so impressed with that because it made him so real to me. I guess I wish you could do that, too!

Therapist: You want to hear more about me?

(Other patients "protect" therapist, claiming the therapist has been responsive and supportive of them.)

Therapist: Well, what about Helen's statement? She would like to hear more about my experiences than I have revealed.

Helen: It was a question of the way you put it. Dr. Sprite, in the other group. . .every once in a while would mention that this was an experience he had. It was natural.

Therapist: Uh-huh. What does this do for you?

Abe: (a patient who also wanted the therapist to talk about his own experiences) Well, I think it makes it real. The problems we are all struggling with are the problems of people no matter when, where, and how . . .

Murray: You seem to be saying I wish you could do that, too. I think you are saying I wish you were Dr. Sprite, and I think that this is a difference in personality. *(Helen tries to break in)* Wait, let me say, I feel very comfortable with the way he [the therapist] handles the group, comfortable with you [the therapist] and if you choose to tell more about yourself, I guess I would feel comfortable about that, too. . . .

From this discussion the therapist realized that he had self-protective feelings caused by events outside the group. He came to a clearer understanding of his reactions in recent weeks to clients in his groups. Experienced group practitioners recognize that the therapist is not always the person who is most in touch with each of the client's needs. Haigh (1968) indicates that:

One outstanding value of group experience is that there is often at least one member of the group who is personally stirred by the expression of deep feelings and who closely identifies with the person expressing the feelings.

It is these group members who help monitor the practitioner's overreactions as well as underreactions to clients in the group. The therapy group utilizes the strengths and resources and also clearly crystallizes the weaknesses of clients and therapist.

PERSONAL EXPERIENCE, RESEARCH, OR AUTHORITY?

I have made the argument in previous chapters that one's work should be based on personal experience. Obviously, where research is available, the practitioner is beholden to ethical and scientific aegis to be aware of such findings and to consider their implications for his/her own work. However, I believe that there is very little sound clinical research available that can lend relevant guidelines for psychotherapeutic practice at the present time.

Moreover, there are instances where authority is required. There are times when practitioners should take a stand. Practitioners need to be clear both to themselves and their clients about what they are trained to do. They should clearly let the client know where their expertise lies and stick to that. Moreover, there are times when they need to indicate that they are being manipulated or required to act in ways that they feel are not accordant with their own values. In a word, among other functions, practitioners serve as experts on certain matters. To be authoritative is not necessarily to be authoritarian. They can offer information without imposing it and without manipulating client guilt because the client does not accept the therapist's point of view. Practitioners should not shy away from the fact that they are professionally trained and specifically knowledgeable about psychological and interpersonal functioning. Generally, however, they should work with their own personal experience. Their work should be predicated upon their life experience and their clinical experience as practitioners. This should be the basis of the encounters and interactions between them and their clients. Their knowledge of themselves is maximized by their relating to the issues that brought the client into treatment, with respect to how both involve themselves in their encounter together in the therapeutic session.

VOYEURISM VS. ACTIVE PARTICIPATION IN LIFE

Therapists often have a tendency to be reactors rather than initiators in life. Some of the stress they experience has to do with finding themselves "snowed in," because they have lost sight of what they want of life other than being there for their clients. Therapists, in many ways, can be viewed as "voyeurs," whose lives center on learning from and identifying with their clients in terms of their excitement and fantasies about the client's life, rather than active participation in their own lives. There is a danger of "starvation of reality" inherent in being a practitioner. Therapeutic practice needs to be balanced by active involvement in the real world of the therapist. As in the Broadway play *Equus*, the effectiveness of the therapist who lives without passion must be critically questioned. Refusing to participate in the passions he is obsessed about, the psychiatrist in the play, Dysart, was unable to articulate meaningfully the fundamental concerns with which he was struggling intellectually. As Dysart's statements suggest, he is only able to speak about his "struggle," but not capable of speaking *from* the experiences of that struggle. Thus, his existential questions are expressed with extreme vagueness:

> ...questions I've avoided all my professional life...I don't know. *And nor does anyone else.* Yet *if* I don't know—if I can never know that—then what am I doing here? I don't mean clinically doing or socially doing—I mean *fundamentally*! These questions, these whys are fundamental—yet, they have *no place* in a consulting room. So then, do I?" (Shaffer, 1975, p. 88)

A sense of well-being requires a balance of psychic energies—those directed toward both reflective and initiative behaviors. Practitioners tend to be inordinately reflective. Many have learned early in life that it is safer to observe than to be observed. Consequently, their major source of pleasure is through vicarious identification with their clients. There is a cost to this identification. The price is competition with and envy of those through whom we live vicariously. The practitioner may get him/herself caught up in a vicious bind of both needing his/her clients to succeed in order to satisfy his/her succor needs, while at the same time to fail in order not to thwart his/her competitive and envious sentiments. To the extent that the practitioner feels actively involved in his/her own social world, the force of this vicious cycle is lessened. The practitioner generally takes an active participant role in therapy from experiencing an active, refurbishing and gratifying life outside the consulting room.

WHEN PERSONAL AND SOCIAL NEEDS ARE NOT MET

The need for a safe haven at home, close friendships, interesting activities, and involvements outside his/her practice seem vital when we recognize that the times of greatest stress for the practitioner are generally those in which he/she must face the everyday onslaught of emotional issues without feeling that his/her own emotional needs are being met. For practitioners, whose marriage or caring relationships are depressing, attraction to clients, as well as the loosening of defenses against looking toward them for emotional sustenance, may follow. No one but a masochist would endure endless therapeutic practice without having his/her own needs met. Of course, a masochist is hardly the role model desired for the practitioner's persona!

PRIVATE PRACTICE AS A WAY OF LIFE

Winston Churchill once said that he thought it was fortunate that his avocation was also his profession. Robert Frost said something similar, "Let my avocation be my vocation as my two eyes make one in sight." There is, however, a real problem when one's personal and social life become less important than one's practice. From my discussion about the backgrounds of psychotherapists and their response to the "spiritual calling" of therapeutic practice, it is hardly surprising for us to recognize that for many practitioners one of the most serious hazards of practice is that it consumes the whole being of the practitioner. We have given numerous examples which well-illustrate that, for many practitioners, clients become home, family, mission, and destiny. It was said of Harry Stack Sullivan that his clients were his closest companions. Apparently, at various times, several of them boarded with him in his large townhouse. Henry et al.'s (1971) research certified that, for most mental health practitioners, their relationship with clients was more emotionally intense and satisfying than with their own spouses and children. In my view, therapists need to balance their practices with satisfactions, gratifications, and interests in other aspects of life and human existence. When this does not transpire, they become fused with clients. Because they cannot appropriately be there for clients, they begin to use clients to meet their own needs and satisfactions. Ralph Greenson (1966) has pointed to the importance of a safe haven for the practitioner. This is a place to be less than perfect—a place to be a husband or wife, a mother or father, and/or a friend, and not a special person with omniscient and omnipotent qualities.

LONELINESS AND BOREDOM IN PRACTICE

When the practitioner loses curiosity and enthusiasm for therapeutic work, such that the details of people's lives are no longer of excitement or interest, the practitioner becomes bored. This is particularly true of analysts and other practitioners who work only with individual clients, without much interaction transpiring between client and therapist. When practitioners see client after client, day after day, in such a way, their professional lives become rather lonely. In essence then, when the practitioner loses curiosity and enthusiasm for work, he/she feels hopeless and cynical. When he/she does not see the potential for realization about himself by learning from clients, boredom sets in. This often comes from a depression in which the whole of life has become restricted, painful, and ungratifying.

In short, the feeling of boredom in practice is generally symptomatic of a more pervasive *ennui* in one's life. In that people who are drawn toward practicing psychotherapy are generally people who are highly stimulated by and responsive to the inner life, a state of boredom in the practitioner stands in sharp contrast to the practitioner's usual stance. If the onset has been sudden, it may be due to acute hurt and disappointment in life and with his/her sense of self. However, if it is chronic, it may have to do with the practitioner having lost touch with the goals,

purposes, and directions with which he/she entered his/her career. But in almost all instances the feeling of boredom signals
the abandonment of the examined inner life. It represents the
externalization of satisfactions. It represents the requirement
that other people provide the practitioner with sources of contentment which formerly the practitioner hoped could be found
within him/herself.

IMPACT ON ONE'S FAMILY

The therapist who can't share professional concerns with family will feel increasingly insulated from his family. If he/she
cannot share concerns with family, his/her clients will become
more important than family. Inevitably, the concerns of practice
are experienced both by therapist and client. It is reasonable to
infer that the practitioner will feel closer to those clients with
whom he/she shares the most personal thoughts and feelings.
It may be to these clients the therapist unwittingly or even in-
tentionally turns during prolonged and painful periods of estrangement.

PERSONAL INVOLVEMENTS WITH CLIENTS

In an emotional setting with people who have become significant to him/her over time, the therapist may be drawn and attracted to clients—sexually, intellectually, or emotionally. If
he/she doesn't realize this or can't make clear to him/herself the
appropriate function and purpose of their being together, serious problems develop.

WHEN SEXUAL PROBLEMS ARISE

It is not hard to understand that sexual attractions develop
in therapy in that most psychotherapy clients are female and
most psychotherapy practitioners are male. It is certainly not
unusual, nor is it untoward for an attraction to arise toward
someone the practitioner works closely with, someone whom he
cares about and he feels cares about him. This may not be particularly difficult to examine therapeutically if the client's feel-

ings are "eroticizing" rather than erotic. For example, the client who says "I think I love you," or "I fantasize about being physically close to you" implicitly recognizes the transferential quality of her romantic feelings toward the practitioner. In sharp contrast, the client who says, "I love you, let's have an affair," probably doesn't, and poses a far more difficult situation for the practitioner.

The problem comes when the practitioner feels the need to act on the client's feelings, particularly when they are erotic rather than eroticized. The practitioner will feel the need to act on these feelings, largely to the extent that sexual and emotional satisfactions are not available in the practitioner's personal life. In both personal and professional life, there is a need for a balance of exchange of emotional gratification. When the practitioner experiences that his giving greatly exceeds what he receives, he may unconsciously expect gratification from clients, which is therapeutically unreasonable and deleterious to the therapeutic relationship, in the form of, e.g., love, admiration, and appreciation.

Furthermore, as Harold Searles has shown in many of his brilliant clinical papers, clients rather apperceptively pick up the therapist's loneliness, sexual frustration, etc., and attempt to provide what the therapist needs. Searles tells us that the client's unconscious motive is to help the therapist integrate and to become whole in order to be able to provide the emotional resources required by the client for the client's own integration. Analogously, it is as if a child tried to save the mother from danger because the child unconsciously realizes that he will starve to death if the mother perishes.

In a word, if the spouse or significant others in the practitioner's life are not available, so that the practitioner feels neglected, he/she may manipulate clients into taking the role of caretaker of the practitioner.

SEXUAL ATTRACTION IN PSYCHOTHERAPY

In dealing with this, the therapist first has to be aware of how he/she is responding to clients. If the therapist feels that he/she can't deal with the problem alone, then consultation is needed. Whether that means going back into treatment, having case supervision with a seasoned colleague, or bringing it up with colleagues in a peer group, the therapist needs help from others. Often, feelings of embarrassment and shame prevent the practitioner from getting help. The troubled practitioner should bear in mind that self-help groups, as well as personal therapy and consultation, are available from caring, nonjudgmental colleagues. The merits of the latter are obvious, so let me speak briefly about self-help groups for practitioners. There are such groups available for virtually every kind of personal problem the practitioner may experience. They bring colleagues together for mutual assistance and offer a reliable support network for the practitioner. I will, in the next chapter, discuss in detail peer groups for practitioners.

Of prime importance, the practitioner should utilize his/her own countertransferential reactions to best help clients, not to regard such reactions as something to avoid examining and confronting. Some therapists avoid these reactions by referring away any clients to whom they have a strong sexual attraction. What is essential to realize is that having more than one kind of relationship seriously affects the therapeutic process. A therapist who assumes more than one hat with a client seriously impedes his/her effectiveness as a psychotherapist. (On the other hand, the client who is looking for a love affair would be wise to look elsewhere. Why pay an expensive therapy bill for a lover when there is no reason to believe that therapists are more responsive lovers than persons in any other walk of life!)

BEING REAL AS A PSYCHOTHERAPIST

The beginning practitioner may wonder whether to be different inside the therapeutic hour in presenting oneself to clients than one is with family, friends, and others outside therapy. This concern can be answered from both a semantic point of view as well as by the practitioner's theoretical orientation. The semantic inquiry would be, "What does "being different" mean? Can the therapist ever be other than him/herself?" The retort to this inquiry is, "Well, no, he/she is always him/herself. But which aspects of self does he/she utilize in a session? Are there parts of the self that he/she holds back because he/she feels shameful and threatened by their expression? Or because there are clear and reasonable reasons for their being held back in the session?" As I said earlier, for the therapist to be effective and meaningful within the psychotherapy frame, ideally, the therapist needs to be aware at all times of his/her own human frailties and how the human condition impresses upon him/her. The therapist needs to be open to every human experience in order to be able to register all human emotions. But how he/she expresses it is seen differently by each school of psychotherapy. Each system of psychotherapy looks differently upon how open or how undisclosing the therapist is to be, in expressing his/her repertoire of human responses.

I strongly believe that the reduction of a person's life, interests, interactions, motives, and sentiments to a few psychological motives diverts the practitioner from the directness and immediacy of what both therapist and client experience together. It is unfortunate that the methods of psychological inquiry, which once sought to free the human being from the bonds of repressed motives, have come full circle, rendering practitioner and client alike prisoners of a never-ending obsessive search for truth. The practitioner is, too often, less concerned with what he/she is directly experiencing with others than with what he/she infers or seeks to find is the "real" reason or motive behind his/her own and others' behavior (Goldberg, 1980a). In my view, effective psychotherapeutic work examines magical and transferential elements in the therapeutic relationship *without dismissing* or relegating the *real relationship*, as Greenson (1966) has called it, to secondary importance. The question we need to address is whether the therapeutic alliance actually can ever become a truly egalitarian partnership.

THE EGALITARIAN PARTNERSHIP IN PSYCHOTHERAPY

This is an ideal toward which therapist and client must aim. Some schools of psychotherapy, certainly those that engage in humanist forms of healing, would agree that an egalitarian relationship actually takes place in their therapeutic work. I think, however, that all schools of psychotherapy claim that this is their ultimate objective. Each would also underscore the importance of the therapist examining how he/she gets in the way of an effective egalitarian relationship. On the other hand, those systems that regard the "infantile" needs of the client as the focus of the work, e.g., behavioral therapy, would claim that it may be inappropriate, that is to say, asking too much of the client, to assume an egalitarian relationship, at least initially. This theoretical assumption about the inherent inability of clients to assume egalitarian roles has had some untoward consequences. Stanley Greben (1984) points out that

> Sigmund Freud, attempting to make the new discipline scientific, had cautioned its practitioners to be objective, reflecting back what the patient said, as would a mirror, or operating in a 'clean and sterile' field, without excessive personal involvement, as would a surgeon. This sensible and well-meant advice had been perverted, over almost a century of practice by those who followed him, to something he could never have intended. [Practitioners] often became ridiculously unresponsive to their patients. When they should have been caring human beings who worked hard to understand and to help people in trouble, they became cerebral pseudoscientists who trained their patients to accept their neglect of them. (p. xvii)

The practitioners Greben speaks of are unable to express concern. Arnold Bernstein (1972) has spoken eloquently of the practitioner's fear of compassion, a fear that interferes with feeling and expressing concern.

THE FEAR OF COMPASSION

Many therapists have the notion that they can be most helpful to the client by not gratifying any of the client's needs other than that of self-understanding. This attitude fosters a rather barren atmosphere in which to relate. It is also a misunderstanding of Freud's dictum about the therapist getting too involved. There are times when it is clinically necessary for the client to feel the therapist's compassion. Expressing concern and compassion is not by itself sufficient for therapeutic gains, but as a mediating gesture, when properly used (see Chapter 12), it is necessary for maintaining a human relationship. The practitioner should not be afraid to show compassion and concern. Sidney Jourard (1964) indicates this ethic in his eloquent statement about the I-thou relationship in psychotherapy: "No patient can be expected to drop all his defenses and reveal himself except in the presence of someone whom he believes *is for him*, and not for a theory, dogma, or technique" (p. 65).

In curious contradiction, the preponderance of the training for mental health practitioners that I have found available over the past several years has been concerned with psychotherapeutic technique. This is particularly true of workshops held at professional psychotherapy conferences. These workshops emphasize the theoretical and methodological considerations in how to do therapy: considerations that are designed to help the practitioner work with certain types of difficult, borderline, and narcissistic client populations; techniques that Gestalt practitioners, for example, claim to have more impact than analytic techniques; techniques that psychodynamic practitioners believe to be better thought through than those of transactional analysis or psychodramatic methodologies (Goldberg, 1977).

I believe a curbing of the operational orientation to psychotherapeutic practice is seriously needed. I have written this section because some practitioners undergo considerable distress in struggling with whether or not to underscore their own values in their therapeutic encounters. Sigmund Freud made rather clear his belief that the practitioner's style and technique must be in keeping with the person he/she is, not based upon a ritualized technique for all. Freud indicated that:

> The technical rules which I bring forward here have been evolved out of my own experience in the course of many years, after I had renounced other methods which had cost me dearly...I must, however, expressly state that this technique has proven to be the only method suited to my individuality; I do not venture to deny that a physician quite differently constituted might feel impelled to adopt a different attitude to his patients and to the task before him. (Freud, 1919)

The above has implications for how therapists present themselves in their therapeutic encounters.

THE THERAPIST AS ROLE MODEL

The claim of the humanistically oriented therapist that he/she above all must be a "real" person to the client has reached the point of overstatement and cliché. Can the therapist ever be unreal in therapy—how can he/she be anyone other than who he/she is? Even in assuming a role, a person chooses to reveal certain aspects of him/herself. It is inconceivable to regard a therapist as a blank "projective screen." What a therapist chooses to be is predicated upon his/her own values. In this sense, the detached, withholding therapist is real. Unfortunately, he/she is too prevalent! In assuming an aloof, impersonal role the therapist has chosen to avoid responding to other aspects of him/herself that cause anxiety.

It is important to recognize that whatever way a therapist behaves in therapy, the behavior is intended to deal not only with the client, but also with his/her own anxiety. This kind of behavior is not necessarily counterindicated. All of us act in ways that are designed to avert our own anxiety. Some of us, for example, become therapists because we need to feel helpful; we may be desperately trying to counter and deny our own dependency needs or be suffering from an array of other anxieties. Thomas Szasz (1969) points out:

> . . . Freud abandoned the use of mild faradic currents for treating neurotics, not merely because it was not very effective, but because he could not stand the fraud implicit in it. Similarly, he disliked hypnosis, not only because it did not work well enough, but because he realized that his personality was unsuitable for it; the authoritarian intrusive role of the hypnotist was not for him. In developing the psychoanalytic method of treatment, Freud followed his own needs, not the needs of his patient. . . Harry Stack Sullivan's modification of analytic technique reflects his need for a more personal relationship with patients than is possible in analysis. Sullivan was a lonelier and more isolated person than Freud; he used his patients as companions and friends to a greater extent than did Freud or the early Freudians. (p. 42)

What is important is not that the therapist is trying to avert his/her own anxieties, but that the therapist realize that it is he/she who is uneasy and it is he/she who strives to become more comfortable. Only insofar as the therapist recognizes his/her own discomfort is the therapist able to negotiate with the client in an open manner to make the relationship comfortable for both parties. If the client is doing something that disturbs the therapist, the client has a right to know about it. Openness and congruence are essential in therapy, for without them the exercise of choice and responsibility is difficult, if not impossible, to induce. A cardinal goal of therapy is to develop the ability to make more conscious choices, even if, for example, the choice is to terminate therapy. (It is unfortunate that some therapists assume that the major goal of psychotherapy is to perpetuate treatment.) The therapist, through his/her disclosure and congruity, serves as a role model for the client. Openness, however, creates anxiety for both therapist and client because of the uncertainty of knowing how to respond to new aspects of one another. Openness transforms the therapeutic relationship by requiring each person to take a new stance toward the other (Goldberg, 1973).

THE THERAPIST'S EXISTENTIAL CHOICE

The more unstructured a situation is, the more it evokes a projective screen for activating disturbed and unresolved emotional proclivities in clients. The detached therapist fosters a lack of involvement in those he/she is treating. The involved therapist, rather than serving as a mirror or as a figure from some other time and place, uses his/her own experiences as an assessment of what is transpiring. He/she relies upon direct experience with the client rather than on textbooks.

An integrative (in contrast to transitory) experience does not transpire between client and therapist unless the client experiences it as "real." It is real to the extent that each person treats the other as he/she would other significant people in his/her life. If the client is to avert transference distortions, the practitioner correspondingly, as I discussed in Chapter 12, must curb his/her predilection for regarding the client in a stereotypic manner. He/she must free him/herself from concentrating on the patient aspects of the person.

Elaine, a client in a private group, had strong counterdependent defenses. She was sensitive and responsive to the needs of the others, but reluctant to share her burdens with them. I found it helpful to say to her in a session in which she wrestled with a decision to make a commitment to a man still responsible to a wife and family: "My feeling is that you and your friend can work out this situation by yourselves. I am more concerned with your reluctance to bring your burden to the group and share it with us." Elaine's unavailability for others who wished her to share her burden with them should come as no surprise when one learns that she was a psychiatric social worker who worked with profoundly psychotic long-term in-patients.

I believe that the rationale for making mediating intervention as illustrated in my example above, deserves more attention in the psychotherapy literature than it has received. High-powered theory for making interpretations already exists in abundance. Even James Strachey (1934), with his emphasis on the mutative transferential interpretation, realized that effective interpretation must ensue from a well-attended therapeutic alliance. Mediating responsiveness fosters an autonomous enabling process in the other. In an encounter where the other is treated as an impersonal object, he/she feels manipulated and exploited, and tension and strain inevitably occur.

When the client senses that the therapist is willing to negotiate how the client is to be regarded, the client is free to reveal him/herself as he/she seeks to be known. When both agents can cast aside reactive fears and the excessive need for safety, they can accommodate themselves to each other and explore their interpersonal domain, each coming to know him/herself and the other with increased meaning. This is expressed in Carl Rogers's (1961a) conception of the existential choice:

> In the actual relationship both the client and the therapist are frequently faced with the existential choice, "Do I dare match my experience with my communication? Do I dare to communicate myself as I am or must my communication be something less than or different from this?" The sharpness of this issue lies in the often vividly foreseen possibility of threat or rejection. To communicate one's full awareness of the relevant experience is a risk in interpersonal relationships. It seems to me that it is the taking of this risk which determines whether a given relationship becomes more and more mutually therapeutic or whether it leads in a disintegrative direction.
>
> To put it another way, I cannot choose whether my awareness will be congruent with my experience. This is answered by my need for defense, and of this I am not aware. But there is a continuing existential choice as to whether my communication will be congruent with the awareness I do have of what I am experiencing. In this moment-by-moment choice in a relationship may lie the answer as to whether the movement is in one direction or the other in terms of this hypothesized law. (pp. 345–346)

THE LIMITS TO INVOLVEMENT WITH CLIENTS

Therapeutic practice draws the practitioner into emotional involvement with those with whom he/she works. I have discussed the physical limitations of involvement. There are also limits to emotional connection. Reik (1948) has written that in the empathic congruence between client and therapist, without which therapy cannot occur, the therapist shares the experience of the client, not as if it were his own, but *as his own*. I experience the demands upon me for relationship immediate and genuine in therapeutic work. I, too, attempt to participate in the experience of the other. However, I also concur with Rogers (1949) that empathic understanding of the client must come from the therapist "sensing the client's internal reference without the therapist losing his own emotional existence."

Although I take up the experience of the other, I need to make clear to the other what I am and what I am not. I do not wish to stand for someone else—a father, a mother, a son, a daughter, a teacher, or a former therapist. As a person involved in a relationship with another, I wish to have impact on the other as a real person rather than as a fantasied figure. On my part, for this to occur, I must be willing to regard myself as a real person, capable of foibles and human errors, rather than as a judge or a detached observer. Arthur Burton (1964) has aptly said:

Transference and countertransference are insufficient as complete therapeutic formulations in themselves. I have always felt that they lacked sufficient breadth and scope as parameters for a most complex relationship phenomenon, and now firmly believe that not all of the psychotherapeutic relationship is a transference neurosis, and not all of the feelings of the therapist are countertransference.

There is a part of the psychotherapeutic interview which is not historical and which is not transference. That is, the reaction of the patient to the therapist, and vice versa, is *pour soi*— for itself—and may have no reference to past figures...Some of the most transcending of human relationships...have *immediacy* and *presence*, and their effects are not necessarily altered by an analytic attitude or by analytic applications.

In agreeing with Burton's point of view, I also admit to being no less wary of my own motives in therapy and those of my clients in relating with one another than my psychoanalytic training taught me to be. Motives do not spring forth new, virgin, unfettered by unresolved trappings of fantasied and former relationships. This, however, in no way denies the relevance of the spontaneous, immediate interpersonal encounter with those with whom I work. Inspection of the client's history is an appropriate endeavor insofar as it frees the being together of client and therapist, client and client's self in terms of the present interactive encounter. On the other hand, if the inspection of the client's past allows the therapist and client to avoid dealing with the present situation, it denotes a collusive resistance in both practitioner and client (Goldberg, 1973).

PSYCHOTHERAPY AS A SYSTEM OF KNOWLEDGE

Today, psychotherapy is more of an intuitive art than it is a science. It is not that we have not learned from empirical studies about various factors influencing the therapeutic process. But what we have also realized is that to the extent that we prematurely regard psychotherapy as a science, we miss the essential determinant of the therapeutic endeavor—the encounter between two people involved in a deeply emotional endeavor. This encounter cannot be meaningfully understood by reducing the difficulties this encounter evokes to a limited number of key elements. Nothing as complex and richly human as the meeting of client and practitioner can be reduced to a simple formula. We should become aware of this when we recognize that the practice of modern Western psychotherapy is a practice of healing predicated upon certain presuppositions.

To render this more meaningful for us as practitioners of Western healing practices, I will compare the rationale and methodology of shaman practices with that of modern Western psychotherapy. In doing so, I will contrast vastly differing ontological and cosmological concepts of existence.

Of course, there is always the temptation to make judgments about the superiority of one system over another. This will lead nowhere. Rather, my hope is that we can better appreciate what we, as healers, seek in our own journey and better assess the prejudices and hidden agendas in our own quest by contrasting our practices with those of the venerable practices of the shaman tradition.

Because of space constraint I will be discussing shaman and Western psychotherapy as if they were two distinct practices. For the most part, I will be making no sharp contrasts among the practices of Western psychotherapy and will be collapsing all non-Western healing methods—including the oriental practices of the Zen masters, the brujo tutelage of the western-hemisphere shaman, and the shaman in the nonliterate Siberian cultures—together.

Logically, of course, if the existential premises of Western healing in comparison to shaman practices were totally distinct, we could learn little by examining these practices comparatively. However, if we look deeply into such ways of life as Buddhism, Taoism, Vedanta, and Hinduism (Yoga), as well as the spiritual premises of societies in which shamans practice—we do not find either philosophy or religion as these are understood in the West. We find something nearly resembling psychotherapy (Watts, 1961)

In examining this contention, let us start with a given: All formal systems of healing involve a relationship between the healer and the person who is to be healed. The exact nature of this relationship is presently unclear (Burton, 1977). From his extensive examination of shaman practices, psychiatrist Jerome Frank (1961) insisted that the religio-magical methods of behavior change have great commonality with what we have come to accept as scientific psychotherapy. Central among the similarities is the power structure of the healer, the quasi-magical belief systems, faith in rationality and science, the need for personal fulfillment, hope, suggestion, charismatic influences, etc. These are the so-called "nonspecific" factors crucial in all healing relationships.

In brief, the main resemblance between shaman practices and Western psychotherapy is in the concern of both with bringing about *changes of consciousness*, changes in our ways of feeling about our own existence, and changes in our relation to human society and to the natural world. The Western psychotherapist has, for the most part, been interested in changing the consciousness of peculiarly disturbed individuals. Non-Western philosophies, particularly the disciplines of Buddhism and Taoism, are, however, concerned with what may be broadly called "liberation," which is not destroying the social construct that is "maya" or illusion, but seeing through it—seeing it for what it is (Watts, 1961). In an important sense, non-Western practices do not really cure the distressed individual of "something" as they cure him of "nothing." This concept concerns the notions of "maya" and "samsara," to which I will return presently.

Now I come to one of the central themes in the discussion of shamanism. I am concerned here with an attempt to understand Western and shaman practices through an appreciation of different notions of consciousness. This is to say, before we can turn to the comparative practices of shaman and Western healing, we must first look more formally at the systems of knowledge within which each operates.

EASTERN AND WESTERN THOUGHT CONTRASTED

Western philosophy, the discipline that endeavors to convey knowledge about the nature of the human being and the world to the constituents of Western society, is based on the venerable exercises of *logical* and *rational* constraints to thinking. These constraints are part of a language game played by rather definitive rules. The rules informing these exercises are composed of certain suppositions that cannot be put to the test. In short, logical thought is derived from reasoning that follows from its premises. Like all exercises and games, whether language-based or not, logical thought starts from given premises that cannot be questioned or doubted, for, to do so, an endless progression of questions would ensue that can never be finally substantiated.

Logic, then, tells us nothing about the real world. Logic only reports to us what would follow *if* a hypothetical situation, consisting of several basic assumptions, *were* true. It also is a practical language game, for the most part, enabling its participants to communicate thoughts, feelings, and intentions in a systematic and agreed-upon manner. The dissolution of any logical argument, therefore, is to state simply, "I don't accept your premises."

The second component of Western thought is rationality. Rationality is another language game, which maintains that cognitive reasoning enables the self to best understand the world in which he/she exists by putting to test certain hunches about how events occur in nature. Rationality is based on the premise that the self can predict the course of events by first observing prior events, seizing upon certain patterns and similarities contained in each of these events, in contrast to all other events, and, as a result, classifying these purveyed events into distinct categories. This is to say, by selecting events that more or less accord identical patterns to earlier observed events, an observer can predict the course of these events.

Western thought derives from the premise that mastery over human existence emanates from interpreting the laws of nature. Having mastered the laws of nature, human beings then can control and direct nature by anticipating (predicting) the lawful actions of animate and inanimate objects. In this endeavor the rationalist is asked to assume an indifferent (an unbiased) attitude toward the outcome of his/her observations. There is ample reason for this requirement. Evidence throughout the annals of science (Rosenthal, 1976) has demonstrated that if an observer has a bias or is ego-invested in the outcome of his/her observations, the investment can and does influence, often radically, the outcome of the observations.

In contrast, Eastern thought is based upon the premise that the human being *is* nature and therefore cannot stand apart from nature in such a way as objectively to observe nature. In Eastern philosophy, human beings are exhorted to act with, or perhaps better stated, act *from* nature. As such, the control and prediction of events are neither possible nor useful. The human being comes to know the world by the unfolding of the world within. Consequently, definitions of truth as "consensus reality" as determined by scientific methodology makes absolutely no sense to the Eastern mind. In Eastern thought truth is known from the experience of harmony. The universe is viewed as in a state of continuous flux between order and chaos. The Eastern mind experiences harmony by relating without bias to both sides of the vital interrelationship between order and disorder. This is very clearly the message that the eminent Indian philosopher J. Krishnamurti (1972) emphasizes. He eschews attempts to resolve conflicts by analytic or critical thinking. In his words:

> in analysis there is the problem of the "analyzer" and the "analyzed"—as long as there is a division between the "ob-

server" and the "observed" there is conflict—When the "observer" is the "observed" the conflict ceases. This happens quite normally, quite easily. In circumstances when there is great danger there is no "observer" separate from the "observed," there is immediate action. (pp. 4–6)

A psychotherapist trained in both Eastern and Western traditions indicates that each of the psychotherapeutic approaches found in Wesern society focuses on limited features of our entire being. At the same time, each system asserts the importance of that aspect of our being over the other parts of our functioning. Ajaya (1978) points out that:

one school emphasizes the uncovering of unconscious motivations, another directs itself toward changing behavior and a third stresses interpersonal relations—Each method seems to compete with others in asserting itself as the most efficient process of inducing psychological growth. Yet, there seems to be no objective evaluation which compares and assesses these divergent schools of thought. Furthermore, there is almost no discussion of where these approaches are complementary or antithetical to one another. In modern psychology we do not seem to have a comprehensive theory and methodology which considers all of the facets of human functioning and explains their proper place in the total person.

Said in another way, the considerable advances in knowledge of specific cellular structures and instrument technology in Western medicine has rendered the modern healer further and further removed from treating the whole person. This fragmented practitioner model has been adopted by the psychotherapist, as well. To rectify this limitation, Ken Wilber (1979), a psychologist conversant in both Eastern and Western philosophical traditions, has proposed a *psychologia perennis* for the spectrum of consciousness. Wilber indicates:

At the heart of this model lies the insight that human personality is a multileveled manifestation of expression of a single consciousness, just as in physics the electromagnetic spectrum is viewed as a multibanded expression of a single, characteristic electromagnetic wave. More specifically, the spectrum of consciousness is a pluridimensional approach to man's identity; that is to say, each level of the spectrum is marked by a different and easily recognized sense of individual identity, which

ranges from supreme identity of cosmic consciousness through
several gradations or bands to the drastically narrowed sense of
identity associated with egoic consciousness—The core insight
of the *p.p.* [*psychologia perennis*] is that man's 'innermost' consciousness is identical to the absolute and ultimate reality of the
universe, which, for the sake of convenience, I will simply call
'mind'—is what there is and all there is, spaceless—timeless and
therefore eternal, outside of which nothing exists.—This level is
not an abnormal state of consciousness, all others being essentially illusions.

If Wilber is correct, then we might ask why do Westerners
have such a different phenomenological sense of the world in
which we dwell, divided and fragmented as we often experience
it, than that described above. Wilber indicates that the Eastern
concept of "maya" best accounts for this discrepancy. Maya pertains to our experience of making distinctions in our experience
based upon a false dualism. The basic distinctions we make
have to do with the separation between subject and object, self
and nonself, good and evil, life and nonlife and real and not real.
G. Spencer Brown (1972) explains the reasons for our dualistic
illusion,

> We cannot escape the fact that the world we know is constructed
> in order (and thus in such a way as to be able) to see itself. This
> is indeed amazing. Not so much in view of what it sees—but in
> respect of the fact that it *can* see *at all*. But *in order* to do so,
> evidently it must cut itself up into at least one state which sees,
> and at least one other which is seen. In this severed and muti-
> lated condition, whatever it sees is *only partially* itself. We may
> take it that the world undoubtedly is itself—but, in any attempt
> to see itself as an object, it must, equally undoubtedly, act so as
> to make itself distinct from, and therefore, false to, itself. (p. 104)

This view accords with that of Alan Watts (1961), who has
maintained that our Western style of individuality stems from
the "skin-encapsulated ego," separating soul from its fleshy
receptacle and providing us with the sense of ourselves as isolated containers of consciousness distinct from the external environment and other beings.

Wilber indicates that the act of severance and ecapsulation
of our psyche from the objective world is only apparent; it does
not actually divide the world. As such, the world remains exter-

nally indistinct from itself. The original dualism or act of severance Campbell (1968) evinces from mythical legend separated
the world in heaven and earth, day and night, male and female.
Epistemologically, Wilber (1979) indicates:

> it is the separation of subject and object, knower and known, ob-
> server and observed; ontologically, it is the separation of self and
> other, organism and environment . . . Man's identity apparently
> (not actually) shifts from the nondual All to his organism.

This separation simultaneously creates *space*. As soon as the
human being identifies with its organism, the problem of "being" and "not being" is created. Having separated self from environment, the human being becomes conscious, in the words
of Hubert Benoit (1955),

> that his principle is not the principle of the universe, that there
> are things that exist independently of him; he becomes con-
> scious of it in suffering from contact with the world obstacle. At
> this moment appears conscious fear of death." (pp 33–34)

In terrorizing flight from the shadow of nonbeing, the human
being creates an idealized image of self. In erecting an idealized
image, the human tries to flee "his mutable body and identifies
with the seemingly undying idea of himself. Hence, his identity
shifts from his *total* psychophysical organism to his mental
representation of that organism" (Wilber, 1979). Finally, Wilber
indicates, in the ultimate act of severance, the human being denies the unity of the idealized concept of self and identifies with
only a portion of it. The human being disowns, denies, and casts
away unacceptable parts of self and regards them as belonging
to hostile beings in the surrounding world. (This account, the
reader may be aware, is consistent with the development of the
intimacy paradigm I raise in Chapter 2 and discuss clinically in
Chapter 10.)

In his extraordinarily interesting account, Wilber goes on to
delineate how each of the present-day psychotherapies are
responses only to particular dilemmas created by the sequential
stages of separation and dualism, which I have briefly described
above. As such, each Western psychology and psychotherapy is
only partial and incomplete. Wilber adds "that the therapies of
any one level tend to view experience at *any* level 'beneath'

theirs as being pathological, and are hence quick to explain away all lower levels with a diagnostic fury."

The whole question, then, of "right" therapeutic technique or "true" interpretation ignores the epistemological problems we, as psychotherapists, have not adequately addressed. Indeed, today there is considerable discussion in psychoanalytic circles as to whether psychoanalysis is a method for recreating factual events or whether the material presented by the analysand is more properly regarded *hermeneutically* as metaphorical explanations of the psychological recreation of earlier events in the person's life.

Chapter 14
The Practitioner's Continuing Personal and Professional Growth

Whoever strives, him we can save.
—Goethe

Realizing the considerable amount of stress attendant to practicing psychotherapy, the practitioner requires support. The cynical reader may say at this point that this chapter is simply beside the point. He/she may insist that personal psychotherapy is the only real answer both to the practitioner's professional and personal concerns. True, Freud recommended that the therapist return to treatment every five years. In Freud's view, therapy was not a terminal process but an ongoing endeavor in which the practitioner needs to review his/her life, as well as deal with new professional issues interfering with his/her effectiveness as a practitioner and his/her satisfactions as a person every few years. Nevertheless, there are professional issues that may be helped by personal psychotherapy but for which therapy alone is not sufficient. I also believe there are professional issues with which the practitioner struggles that are not best handled in treatment. Just as many of us tell our clients that there is real life outside the consulting room, such that some issues should not be relegated to issues for treatment, so, too, for us as practitioners, the answers to life's vicissitudes cannot be fully met by the therapeutic session.

Winnicott (1960) pointed out that the practitioner's personal analysis does not free him/her from neurosis—rather, it increases the stability of his/her character and the maturity of his/her personality. This is the basis of professional conduct and ability, in order to maintain a working relationship with clients. Winnicott also indicated that our professional codes of behavior are actually descriptions of an idealized version of ordinary men and women. As such, the practitioner is under continuous stress in maintaining a professional attitude—at all times, under all conditions and at different stages of his/her own development as a practitioner and as a person. According to Winnicott, even repeated doses of personal treatment do not remove this distress.

It is for these reasons that the practitioner needs advice, consultation, variation in his/her life-style, and emotional and social sustenance beyond whatever assistance personal therapy has to offer.

THE PERSONAL CONCERNS
OF THE PRACTITIONER

There are several important issues that concern practitioners throughout their careers. I have alluded to them previously. The practitioner should carefully examine throughout his/her career the reasons he/she has chosen to be a psychotherapist. Practitioners need to know what they are trying to achieve aside from the usual goals that one has in any kind of profession or business—making a good livelihood, earning status and recognition for successful work, and the sense of accomplishment of doing a job well. The practitioner should examine how his/her practice addresses personal incentives; this is, whether the way he/she practices furthers or antagonizes personal incentives. Let us look more specifically at the concerns of different levels of training and experience as a practitioner.

THE CONCERNS OF THE BEGINNER

The neophyte is attempting to understand the foundations of therapeutic practice. He/she searches for the ingredients of successful therapeutic work, such as developing a sound therapeutic model and the methods of making a good livelihood. The neophyte questions whether he/she has sufficient professional qualifications and the proper personal attributes for being a competent and successful practitioner; and whether he/she is able to practice independently or still requires supervision, consultation, and additional training. Deciding that further training is necessary, the beginner inquires where to get this training. Moreover, in seeking further training, the practitioner asks him/herself which doubts, mistakes, and other concerns should be shared with colleagues and with supervisors. For the practitioner who decides that his/her present skills are competent, questions about getting sufficient referrals and competing with more seasoned practitioners for referrals, recognition, and acceptance come to mind. There are also latent concerns about being sufficiently loved, admired, and appreciated by clients for his/her work that any self-inquiring beginning practitioner cannot easily put aside.

THE CONCERNS OF THE
JOURNEYMAN PRACTITIONER

This is the practitioner who has been in the field for a while. In examining her career the practitioner should ask him/herself whether he/she is going in the direction that she expected when beginning practice. If the practitioner has taken a different path, what has led to this new direction? The self-inquiring practitioner wonders what she now understands about him/herself and clinical work which were not recognized at the start. If the practitioner finds his/her work stultified and limited, to what factors can this be attributed—to boredom, loneliness, frustrations, and dissatisfactions in his/her personal life, or something else. In short, the practitioner questions the reasons which get in the way of self-realization as a person and as a practitioner.

ADDRESSING THE GROWING CONCERNS
OF THE SEASONED PRACTITIONER

The practitioner has been in the field for many years. He is experienced and knowledgeable. He has some of the same questions that the beginner and the journeyman ask. But he is also moving toward the end of his career. Is he satisfied with what he has accomplished? If not, what is still missing? What hasn't he still learned? What has he still not achieved for himself or with the people with whom he works or has worked? And, how can he now address these missing concerns?

Having asked these questions, what are some of the ways in which the practitioner may address them? Let us begin with some of the time-honored ways.

Private Supervision

Seeking out the most eminent practitioners and theorists for supervision is not always wise. Setting aside the fee, the most eminent practitioners may not be the most appropriate and best for a particular practitioner. They may have their own system of therapy to sell. Of course, on the other hand, their brand of treatment may have earned them eminence because of their success. Nevertheless, the really important question is the effect that the supervisor has on your work and growth as a practitioner. Trust your own senses.

Making the supervisee's choice even more complex is the fact that a good supervisory experience cannot be guaranteed even by referral to an outstanding practitioner. The temperament and personality of both agents must be congruent. The most important single consideration in selecting a supervisor is the quality of the interaction between trainee and supervisor. The supervisee must evaluate for him/herself whether the supervisor seems to understand that with which he/she is struggling. Many supervisors are capable of offering supervisees empathy, comfort, and reassurance, but these qualities alone are not sufficient for a meaningful supervisory encounter. The supervisor must be able and willing to enable the supervisee to articulate his/her concerns in such a way that the supervisee can understand, come to terms with, and gain mastery over his/her own struggles. Discomfort arises over time in any meaningful personal encounter. The crucial issue is whether both agents are able, in their being together, to deal openly with their discomfort.

Every psychological belief system from which supervisors operate is based on certain existential and philosophical assumptions and value orientations. The supervisee must ascertain whether the supervisor is willing to articulate his/her orientation in such a way that the supervisee is clear about what is expected of him/her in supervision, and most important for the supervisee, whether these values and assumptions are consistent with the kind of person the supervisee is seeking to become.

A meaningful supervisory relationship involves a partnership between supervisee and supervisor. Does the supervisee feel like a collaborator in formulating a working plan, or does the supervisor unilaterally inform him/her what he/she should be working on? Is there open and effective negotiation for roles and responsibilities necessary for attaining the supervisee's objectives in training?

With this general orientation for selecting a supervisor in mind, you, the supervisee, should also consider a number of specific concerns and suggestions of which to be aware in choosing and working with a supervisor:

a. Don't fly blind in seeking assistance. Give the consideration at least as much thought as you would in buying a house or a car. Before launching into supervision, give considerable thought to why you are seeking training. Having clarified this for yourself, or having at least become in touch with the questions and concerns about yourself you want to address, you can more efficaciously decide which kind of psychological training experience is best for your deeper needs, rather than your more transitory ones; this is to say, a superficial supervisor flatters the practitioner into believing he/she is as competent as necessary. A true mentor inspires the supervisee to develop still untapped potential.

b. In entering supervision, if you have doubts about the supervisor's ability to help you or about how motivated you actually are to undergo intensive work, ask for a short-term arrangement. Knowing that the commitment is for a specific period, you are in a better position to recognize your unwillingness to get deeply involved in the work if you experience an intense desire to terminate the supervision before the time you agreed to stop (Clark, 1975).

c. Anyone who considers entering training should immediately divest him/herself of the fiction that psychological work is a science and the practitioners are essentially objective and value-free. Be wary of practitioners who appear to have axes to grind. Steer clear of supervisors with a doctrine to sell. Avoid supervisors who try to coerce a reluctant trainee to be "honest" and "open" about his/her self-doubts rather than enable the trainee to develop sincere dialogue and a free give-and-take with them. After all, once training has ended, the trainee will be living his/her own life, not that of the supervisor. The supervisor's value system should be one that gives at least as much attention to what you consider your healthy attributes as to your disabled ones. In addition to the ability to work with your countertransferences, the practitioner needs to have a definitive model of human growth and development. It is a dubious assumption that once a trainee is unfettered of therapeutic conflicts, he/she will spontaneously and naturally become a competent practitioner.

d. Nonverbal communication and body language may be excellent sources of information about the supervisor. Be aware of your own bodily reactions to him/her. If you are uncomfortable, attempt to ascertain if there are discrepancies and contradictions between what the supervisor is communicating bodily and what he/she is stating in words.

e. An effective teacher should make sense to you, and should be someone who is able to lay out your issues in such a way that you two can work together. Be aware of the supervisor's unwillingness to accommodate his/her own behavior to the goals of training. For instance, does that person do things, such as answer the phone during the session, that are irritating and uncomfortable for you? How does the supervisor respond to your objections to these behaviors? Does the supervisor take a personal responsibility for his/her behavior and demonstrate a willingness to deal with it, or does the supervisor make it your problem by suggesting that his/her behavior shouldn't bother you? Does the supervisor make up appointments he/she is forced to break at a time of mutual convenience? In short, does the mentor you are working with take you seriously as a person or does this person treat you as a disabled patient? Supervisors conduct their work to suit themselves, but if their behavior is getting in the way of helping you, they must be willing to explore their own involvement in your discomfort. A particular supervisor may refuse to do so. The supervisor may indicate that you are concerned because this kind of upset is the problem that brought you in for consultation; the supervisor may suggest that, as an expert professional, he/she knows better than you what should and should not be explored in supervision. The supervisor may even tell you that the kind of supervision he/she practices precludes discussing his/her behavior with you. The supervisor may inform you that he/she fully explores his/her work with a personal consultant, but not with supervisees. In any of these cases, you would be wise to wish your present supervisor well and find a more responsive supervisor who makes sense to you.

f. After having been involved in supervision for a while, you should ask yourself the following questions to help you review the supervisory relationship:

1. Does he/she seem to listen responsively?

2. Does he/she regard your objections and negative feelings about the relationship as negotiable concerns or does he/she reduce them to manifestations of your problem?

3. Does your supervisor explore by initiating options, that is, is he/she willing to try more than one way of reaching you or does he/she only *react* to your initiations?

4. Are you regarded as a collaborator and a colleague or as a patient?

5. Does the supervisor share his/her feelings as well as his/her thoughts (including doubts) about the supervisory relationship?

6. Do you have more clarity about the concerns that brought you into training than you did when you began supervision?

7. Do you experience more viable options in your clinical work than when you began supervision?

8. Do you feel more optimistic and experience more constructive energy (emotionally, intellectually, and physically) in your own practice than when you began supervision?

9. Are you now able to connect and emotionally appreciate the interrelationship between your various concerns and conflicts about your work that, prior to entering training, seemed isolated, vague, or irreversibly fused?

10. Have the events of the past, present, and future strivings in your work taken on new meaning?

g. If you have not experienced yourself making progress in these dimensions after a reasonable amount of time, seek another consultation. Not all supervisors click with every trainee.

A competent practitioner generally senses this before the supervisee does and should him/herself suggest consultation. It makes no sense to remain in training to avoid an unpleasant confrontation with one's supervisor or to avoid hurting his/her feelings. Even when you sense that the serious underlying conflicts in your interactions with your supervisor are emanating from your personality, it may make sense to leave training, should you feel that your supervisor, after a reasonable amount of time has not been able to help you get at these issues effectively. It is important to recognize that a client's resistance, whether a psychotherapy client or a supervisee, is not entirely related to his/her intrapsychic makeup. In such a case, however, you should be prepared to follow up this unsuccessful training relationship with another supervisor who may be of greater help to you. The right to terminate a psychological situation you experience as noxious is your major source of protection (Clark, 1975) and should in no way be denied by a practitioner, regardless of how much he/she thinks you still need training and supervision.

h. Getting supervision free may be even more of a problem than receiving treatment without cost. It is important that the practitioner carefully examine his/her motives and those of the supervisor before entering such an arrangement. If someone receives something of value, something of value should be expected in return. If not a fee, then, what are you offering the supervisor?

There are many practitioners who live in rural areas or areas that do not provide easy access to expert supervision and training. They may do what others have done—take off a day or two a week (or, if they cannot afford this, a day each month) to fly to a city in which they can get intensive supervision and training on a regular basis. Most psychotherapy institutes provide this kind of scheduling for the convenience of out-of-town trainees.

Growth by Collaborative Endeavors[1]

Outside private practice, the preponderance of therapeutic situations involve more than one practitioner, albeit frequently indirectly through supervision and consultation. Moreover, cotherapy or multiple therapy (and various other appellations for psychotherapy conducted by two or more therapists with one or more clients) is hardly a rare occurrence in private practice, either. Nonetheless, there is a dearth of literature on models for working with one's co-therapist.

Unfortunately, the literature on multiple and co-therapy does not provide practitioners with ready models of interpersonal partnership. The various reports on co-therapy in the literature deal essentially with the special types of transference and countertransference that lend themselves to treatment in co-led groups.

Co-therapy originally came into being as a shortcut for the training of group therapists (Gans, 1962). The child guidance clinics that Alfred Adler and his co-workers established in Vienna in the 1920s provided not only group therapy but co-therapy as well (Dreikurs, 1950). The similarity of the multiple therapy situation to that of the family group soon became apparent, and this feature has remained central to the co-therapy modality for the past half-century. The principal value of co-therapy, according to this school of thought, is in its ready applicability to clients' oedipal and preoedipal problems (Mintz, 1963a) and to the resolution of special authority figures. Clients who secure a warm, protective relationship with one therapist are enabled to venture forth and explore feelings toward the more feared therapist (Mintz, 1963b; Loeffler & Weinstein, 1953–4). The therapists' stance recommended by this co-therapy model is that of neutral transference figures. This stance enables each of the therapists to provide objective and validated observations of the interplay of the different levels of transference present in the group (DeMarest & Teicher, 1954).

There are several factors that investigators of the co-therapy relationship have postulated as being significant in a co-therapy working alliance. Bailis and G. Adler (1974) have found that the success of co-therapy is heightened by (1) a felt compatibility of the co-therapists, (2) a felt approval from each other, and (3) the presence of a postgroup discussion. Hellwig and Memmott (1974) indicate, as the reader might expect, that differences in orientation can become a source of antagonism between co-therapists if each does not accept the value of the other's knowledge. In another investigation, Solomon, Loeffler, and Frank (1953) showed that the activity level of each of the therapists may significantly affect compatibility between them. An active therapist, they say, must always be paired with a more passive therapist because two active therapists will compete with each other and two passive therapists can't support one another. J. Adler and Berman (1960) have suggested from their work with delinquent youngsters that one co-therapist should be aggressive and "masculine" and the other protective and "feminine." In this way, one therapist will be reacted to with more or less fear and guilt, while the other will be perceived closer to the idealized image of the parent. This is in general agreement with Mintz's (1965) observation that one therapist should represent the reality principle for the client while the other therapist allows the client free play with fantasy.

What concerns me is not whether these recommendations are clinically valid, but that they are based on models that will lead to serious obstacles in the development of a growth-producing collaborative, personal psychotherapy experience for each of the therapists. Because my own model of co-therapy, which I will go on to explain, emphasizes the importance of the therapists as role-models of interpersonal partnership, I believe that each therapist must feel free and willing, as the situation warrants, to move from a position of care-giver to one of care-seeker. Therapists who must assume fixed roles in therapy, in keeping with a transferential model, cannot be expected to be successful in pursuing their own growth in co-therapy. Negotiation between the co-therapists requires that they move out of fixed roles.

Moreover, I would question whether what co-therapy investigators have regarded as complementary therapist styles may actually be therapeutically antagonistic orientations. The passive-nondirective therapist, for example, may find it difficult to maintain a positive relationship with a co-therapist who is active and directive, while the more active therapist might find the relationship unfulfilling, although the two therapists might be the best of friends outside of their professional roles (Paulson, Burroughs & Gelb, 1976). The lack of usefulness of fixed roles pertains to sex roles, as well. Several writers have argued for male-female pairs (for example Mintz, 1963a; 1963b). Rabin (1967), on the other hand, maintains that therapists of the same sex who are reasonably clear about their own sexual identities can successfully work together to enable clients to introject sexual self-acceptance.

Advantages and Limitations of Co-therapy

Since each co-therapist is a finite being with his/her own skills, sensitivity, and experience, co-leaders who are complementary offer the client a wider array of responses and opportunities for exploration than a solitary therapist does. Moreover, two therapists give the client the opportunity to observe how responsibility can be shared in a working relationship. Each co-leader can take his/her turn initiating interactions and interventions and the other serve as participant-observer who conveys personal reactions to what he/she experiences going on in the group. At various junctures, the observing co-leader may express puzzlement or disagreement with the more active co-therapist, with concomitant statements of data in support of the former's view (Goldberg & Goldberg, 1975).

Perhaps, most important, in working with rather disturbed families, the lone practitioner is bombarded with noxious induced feelings from the family members. To investigate a system in depth exposes a myriad of diverse and highly subtle nonverbal signals being transmitted by the participants. These signals, or cues, as they are frequently referred to, communicate powerful and urgent emotion. Shifts in the mood of the system are reflected in changes the participants make in posture, gesture, facial expression, and muscular tone, as well as in verbal expression. Because the family members are well-known to one another, they may deflect and defend themselves against urgent emotional impact in a way that a practitioner still familiarizing him/herself with the system cannot. The practitioner may experience him/herself as psychologically decompensating during family sessions. It is extremely helpful, often direly necessary, that the practitioner be able to sort out these messages and their meaning with a trusted colleague. Collegial work provides not only emotional support, but also another set of eyes and ears to sort out these subtle and often toxic cues.

An important function of a therapist in psychotherapy is to provide a client with the opportunity to experience the therapist as a role model. In brief, *role modeling* may be defined as a dimension enacted in psychotherapy in which the therapist presents him/herself in such a way as to convey effective and gratifying interpersonal strategies and problem-solving skills to the client. Indeed, whether or not the therapist intends to present him/herself as a model for emulation, the practitioner does so from his/her initial contact with the prospective client. In a co-led group, there are three interrelated, yet separate, interactive systems: the therapist-client system, the client-client system, and the therapist-therapist system. (These relational positions are more fully elaborated when there is an ongoing and intimate relationship between the therapists, such as spouses working as co-therapists.) In this situation, clients have the opportunity to observe and experience not only how each of the therapists relates to clients in the group, but also how each therapist relates to the other.

The therapist-as-partners, through their utilization of self-disclosure, congruence, and personal responsibility in pursuing their own growth, serve as expressive role models for the group members. Their goal-setting, negotiation, and effective work attitudes serve as an instrumentally oriented role model, which renders interpersonal relations a therapeutic and enabling experience beyond its inherent influential, educative and affective stimulating qualities (Polsky, Claster, & Goldberg, 1968; 1970).

Co-therapy thus offers each client in a therapeutic group or family group an opportunity to observe and, if he/she chooses, to adopt interpersonal strategies demonstrated in the therapist-therapist system that differ from those he/she presently employs. Co-therapy also offers him/her an opportunity to work with two practitioners who effectively solve problems as partners through their competence in relating in terms of meaningful, basic emotional dialogue. No less important, the client occasionally sees, in the therapist-therapist system, struggles with the inability to be understood and nontherapeutic expressions of anger, annoyance, and other emotion; but at the same time, he/she may see the practitioners' refusal to deny or rationalize these states of being. It is as important for practitioners to acknowledge and struggle with their imperfections as it is for them to demonstrate competence.

Despite the wide use and obvious advantages of co-therapy, some practitioners have reported deleterious experience with co-leadership work, and have formed cautious and restrictive attitudes toward the utilization of this form of therapy. These points of view should be taken into consideration in exploring the co-therapy model. A number of practitioners have indicated that in some respects the co-leadership model is more fraught with hazards than are groups that are individually conducted. In a co-led group the client is being confronted with a clinical situation more closely resembling the reality of his/her own conflicts than in a group with a single therapist. If the client senses a lack of respect, some disharmony, or infantile competitiveness between the therapists, similar to that which marked his/her own earlier years, then the restorative functioning of psychotherapy may be not only subverted but, indeed, reversed, effecting additional psychological damage (Lundin & Aronov, 1952).

Other disadvantages may be stated as follows:

1. There is already a shortage of qualified psychotherapists. Co-therapy further limits the number of persons who may be treated at one time (MacLennan, 1965).

2. Interest in co-therapy work is often a manifestation of the beginning group therapist's anxiety about clinical responsibility and a need for protection (MacLennan, 1965).

3. Co-therapists may act out their countertransferential distortions more than a single therapist will in a group (Solomon et al., 1953).

4. Co-therapists as a team may be as vulnerable and limited as a single therapist (MacLennan, 1965).

5. When hostility is generated between the co-therapists, there is often a tendency for one of the therapists to give up attempts to work with the client's concerns and to displace his/her aversive feelings onto the group (Solomon et al., 1953).

6. Co-therapy may intensify already existing countertransferential reactions toward a client in such a way that the therapist him/herself feels threatened. He/she may then ally him/herself more strongly with the client in order to avoid dealing with these conflictual feelings (Solomon et al., 1953).

7. More complex patterns of resistance may develop in a co-led group, given the more complex stimulus field, than a single-led therapy group (Pine, Todd, & Boenheim, 1963).

8. In order to avoid dealing with their fear of one of the therapists, clients may attach themselves to the more benign co-therapist and develop an indifferent attitude toward the threatening co-therapist (DeMarest & Teicher, 1954).

A Model for Co-therapy

The protection, care, and socialization of the young have traditionally been the principal functions of the consanguine family system. Basic to group therapy is the concept of the designed group as a new family in which earlier, distressing life experiences can be examined, modified, and more satisfactorily reexperienced (Goldberg, 1973). My model for group therapy led by co-therapists goes beyond the repair-adjustment model of therapy; it focuses upon growth and active development in the new family group by affording considerable attention to the co-therapists' relationship. This model stems from the concept of interpersonal partnership discussed in Goldberg (1977), in which the major feature is individuality as a partner in a functioning, interrelating unit. Hence, my partnership model gives special attention to such issues as how the co-therapists work through their courtship contract (which I will discuss presently) with one another; how they communicate with one another; how they deal with systematic processes in their relationship, such as equity and balance; and how they negotiate with one another for the personal and professional growth each intends for him/herself. The fact of two therapists working on their relationship with each other can constructively modify the other relational systems in a therapy group (Goldberg, 1976), but in this section I wish to concentrate primarily on aspects of the co-therapists' partnership.

To understand properly the transactions within a co-therapy relationship, knowledge about the co-therapists' personal history and psychodynamics is, by itself, insufficient. Also required is an awareness of the therapeutic situation as a normative system that is ordered by various structural and dynamic properties and shaped by principles of interpersonal functioning and by the assumptions of the agents involved in the system about the amelioration of psychological disturbance. As with any partnership, both practitioners who agree to work together bring to the situation an implicit set of fantasies, expectations, and demands about what will happen as a result of their joint endeavor. These expectations and demands must be openly and explicitly communicated if they are to collaborate effectively. Frequently, however, these expectations remain hidden and unexpressed, resulting in an unproductive therapeutic impasse, if not in deleterious consequences for each of them and their clients. In my view, it is of utmost importance in a co-therapy relationship to avoid these problems by establishing at the beginning a contract binding the practitioners together as partners. To be viable, a working partnership must adhere to the principles of equity and balance (Goldberg, 1976) by stating clearly and explicitly the expectations and demands of each of the partners involved in treatment—that is, what each has to offer and what each is to receive from the other in the therapeutic partnership (see Chapter 11).

The concept of a courtship period, described in a previous book (Goldberg, 1977) applies as well to the initial period of a working relationship. The courtship period in the life of a partnership is characterized by intense, intimate, and idealized feelings about the prospect of a new relationship. Just as in the marital relationship, each working partner brings unresolved issues from past relationships and intense hopes and expectations for resolutions in the new relationship. The partners form a courtship contract (see Goldberg, *Therapeutic Partnership*). To render a therapeutic relationship a viable working partnership, therapists must work together (and perhaps with a third colleague acting as a consultant) to transform their courtship contract into a *working contract*. To do this, each therapist's task is not to diagnose or collect data about the partner, but to engage him/her in a meaningful dialogue at relevant moments in their work together in order to relay appropriate information and sentiments to the partner and receive these data in kind in return. In my model, the aim of each partner is to increase his/her own choices in the conduct of his/her own life, beginning with how each wishes to involve him/herself with the partner in a therapeutic endeavor. This requires the specification of the roles and the responsibilities of each partner in the relationship. My model proposes that the partners begin their work by asking themselves and each other the questions: Why are we here? What are our expectations of one another? What would we like to gain from this experience? How can we, as collaborators, go about achieving these ends? (Goldberg, 1976)

If a working contract is not clearly specified in co-therapy, certain problems will almost surely emerge throughout the course of the work that follows. First, without a clear set of objectives as to what constitutes *work* and *task* behavior in the therapeutic situation, there is nothing but subjective value judgments against which to measure interpretations or interventions by the other therapist. This applies to interactions between the co-therapists as well as to their interactions with clients with whom the partners are working. Second, goals and expectations that remain implicit and unexpressed are not likely to be satisfied by the other partner. Insightful critical evaluations and attempts to deal with dissatisfactions in a therapeutic partnership are not viable without clarity about what is being sought and how each partner conceptualizes the means for achieving these ends. In the absence of negotiation, what frequently arises is a battle of wills in which therapist and clients end up working at odds with each other, none realizing why this is happening. This may be seen in terms of the striving for increased intimacy between the partners. The openness between the therapists frequently creates anxiety for both therapists and group members because they are unsure of how to respond to new aspects of one another. Openness transforms the therapeutic relationship by requiring each partner to take a new stance toward the other (Goldberg, 1973). It is this ongoing transformation that keeps the momentum going in a relationship. However, when uncertainty results in excessive amounts of anxiety, it can break down the partner's ability and willingness to stay in emotional contact with the other. At such times contractual considerations and basic emotional communication can be used to assuage the excessive anxiety and restore systematic balance and momentum for the free exploration of personal concerns in all three relational systems previously mentioned in the co-led therapeutic group.

It is my conviction that gratifying and enabling relationships develop when the partners grow together over time. For this to happen, a relationship must be enjoyed in its own right, regardless of its enduring quality. D. H. Lawrence says in one of his books, I believe it was in *Women in Love*, of the ideal marriage: Each partner is like a separate star, brilliant in his or her own respect, but more brilliant for their coming together. That is the ideal for which co-therapists might aim.

In many relationships this sense of autonomy is absent. To the extent that an individual does not permit him/herself the opportunity to enjoy the potency of his/her own autonomy, that individual becomes distressed. This disturbance emanates from a feeling deep within the self that that which the individual seeks to become is being denied (Goldberg, 1973). To experience the potency of his/her own being, a person must first disengage from the relationship in which his/her happiness and productivity are dependent upon the feelings and regard of another. Properly speaking, the co-therapists are not in the group to help or support each other; they are in the group to investigate openly their own condition in the group.

Basic emotional communication (described earlier) can be applied in this model for co-therapy to help participants arrive at maximal personal responsibility.

Co-therapy as Personal Psychotherapy

An important aspect of co-therapy is its parallel function of providing personal psychotherapy for the therapists. Freud (1919) recommended analysis for the physician who practiced psychoanalysis. He was aware, however, that analysis would remain incomplete following formal therapy. He further recommended a continuing self-analysis. A therapist in a group is a participant as well as a facilitator. Hence, I periodically ask myself what I would like (what I need) from the experience in which I am participating. Co-leadership raises the question of whether the growth needs of therapist and client are mutually exclusive. The advantages of co-therapy from the clients' point of view have already been discussed. Working with a co-therapist can provide an opportunity for continuing personal psychotherapy or, in many instances, it can impede professional growth.

I myself have found that in working with a co-therapist who is more comfortable with particular responses to clients than I am, I tend to rely on my partner to tender these responses. I also tend as a co-therapist to be more of a specialist in focusing and articulating certain processes and interactions, eschewing others, than I can afford to as a solitary therapist. Clients who have observed me with and without a co-therapist tell me that I am more responsive when I work alone. Yet, working alone I lose the reactions to my work of a respected colleague. The solution for me is to work with a colleague who both differs from me and won't permit me to specialize in the group. Such a partner restimulates my personal journey to further my own development.

My goal for myself while working with a co-therapist is to retain my individuality while fully functioning as a member of an effective interpersonal partnership. To reiterate what was stated in Chapter 12, I pursue my own growth as a therapist in a co-therapy partnership by concentrating on my own being-in-the-world. I consider the concerns and issues that I am currently working on in my own life. I explore how well I am doing with these issues in order to assess what my current pressing needs are and what the impediments are to making progress with these concerns. These subjective data inform me of what may interfere with my effectiveness as a facilitator for others during therapeutic encounters. Following this reflection, I interpolate my personal concerns into my current concerns as a practitioner. Then, to avoid being overly didactic and detached in the therapeutic encounter, I cast aside for the time being what I have already figured out about neurosis and human nature. I realize that my preconceived formulations and firm convictions about my work will issue forth more quickly than is necessary when I become uncomfortable during a therapeutic encounter. To be most in touch with the struggles of the people with whom I am working, I must stay as persistently as I can with my own dissatisfactions and unfinished work. All through this process, a trusted co-therapist who challenges my firm convictions and preconceived formulations enables me to continue my growth as a therapist and as a person.

My model for co-therapy, by enabling each of the therapists to retain his/her individuality while functioning as a partner in an interrelating unit, promotes continuing personal growth. This model is intended for practitioners who agree with Warkentin, Johnson, and Whitaker (1951) that psychotherapists enter their profession to find solutions to their own personal conflicts. However, the co-therapists' work together is not to be taken as a substitute for personal psychotherapy or for clinical supervision. My model is intended as a preferred modality for ongoing personal and professional growth, developed in a partnership with a colleague, in which both practitioners have already had their own personal psychotherapy and are well trained in the various therapeutic modalities. It is intended for therapists who are prepared, at a gut level, to achieve parity and share their deep fears and fantasies with their co-therapists during their work together.

Another potential vehicle for personal and professional growth is a rarely utilized type of consultation. I call it "conjoint consultation with clients."

Conjoint Consultation with Clients and Colleagues

Conferring with a senior or expert colleague is regarded as necessary for the practitioner who, though trained as a psychotherapist, is less experienced than his/her practice requires. The relationship that ensues between the practitioner and his/her senior colleague is referred to as *supervision*. Supervision is part of a defined didactic model in which the senior colleague is the teacher and the less experienced practitioner is the student. There is generally implied, if not stated, a function of the supervisor as permission-granter for the supervisee's behavior, conduct, and performance in his/her therapeutic encounters with clients.

The concept of *consultation* overlaps that of supervision, though the roles of consultant and consultee are generally more vaguely defined and the element of permission, which characterizes supervision, is generally absent. The consultant is brought in as an advisor. As an outsider without administrative responsibility for the practitioner's work, his/her advice and point of view may be rejected or not acted upon without any consequence to the consultee other than disapproval and possible termination of the relationship. In this agreement, the consultee theoretically has as much influence over the consultant's behavior as the consultant does over the consultee's.

Consultation to Assess Progress and Impasse

I labor to make a fine distinction between supervisory and consultative relationships because the model represented by the consultation relationship has direct bearing on the psychotherapeutic relationship: It approximates the therapeutic partnership I have endorsed in this book. In contrast, the supervisory-relationship model parallels the majority of current therapeutic relationships today. The use of consultation, unfortunately, generally is poorly understood, largely neglected, and frequently misused in the psychotherapy enterprise. Just as the consultee is free to decide how or whether to use a consultant's advice, the client should be entitled to dismiss the therapist's influence or hold it in abeyance while he/she obtains a second opinion if he/she has serious questions about the practitioner's influence on him/her.

The value of consultation is better understood, better accepted, and, in my view, more functionally utilized in medicine, legal counseling, and other professions than it is in psychotherapy. When a client confers with another therapist about problems that he/she is experiencing with "his/her own" therapist, and does so without his/her therapist's explicit permission, this consultation is generally treated as acting-out behavior. The client is frequently accused by the therapist of trying to avoid dealing with painful material he/she is experiencing with the therapist that is, according to the practitioner, in actuality, a transferential reexperience of unresolved conflict with others in his/her life. Yet the practitioner may consider consultation as appropriate for him/herself. At his/her own discretion, the practitioner may confer with a consultant or may even be in supervision or control analysis with a senior colleague. The client is rarely informed of this situation. This suggests that therapists frequently use their power to secure support, objectivity, and redirection through consultation, while at the same time not informing their clients of its potential usefulness to them and even actively preventing them from its use. This state of affairs is in obvious contradiction to an egalitarian partnership.

Separate consultation for client and therapist is a useful adjunct to viable psychotherapy. Consultation for both together is, I believe, an idea worthy of consideration, though to my knowledge it is seldom employed.[2] Conjoint consultation would tend to demystify the process of psychotherapy and reduce the omnipotence of the therapist. Some practitioners may object that it would also result in breach of confidentiality and loss of the valuable exclusive relationship of the patient and his/her doctor. These objections are invalid to the extent that consultation and supervision are acceptable practices, even though they, too, "violate" confidentiality and diffuse the therapeutic relationship.

I propose a consultation model that approximates conjoint marital therapy, which is a partnership model in contrast to concurrent treatment or treatment of one spouse but not the other. In a conjoint consultation the client feels part of a collaborative endeavor in which problems, tensions, and strains are not his/hers alone to deal with nor are they the therapist's prerogative to resolve; rather, they are part of a process in which both client and therapist-as-partner are intimately involved. By demystifying the therapeutic process and reducing the therapist's omniscience, each agent is permitted to recognize the limitations of his/her own knowledge and personal resources. This realization frees them to secure appropriate assistance. Through conjoint consultation, therapeutic progress can be objectively assessed, treatment can be productively redirected and, when indicated, rationally terminated or meaningfully referred elsewhere, all without the anger and misunderstanding attendant upon a consultation sought by the client on his/her own. Not infrequently, a result, or at least a subsequent condition, of unilateral consultation is that the client terminates treatment with the first therapist and enters therapy with the consultant or another practitioner recommended by the consultant. Conjoint consultation may make this result less of a threat to the therapist because he/she is present and involved in the consultation process. There are, of course, numerous practical issues involved in conjoint consultation that require careful consideration, such as who is to pay for the consultation—the client who is getting additional professional services, or the therapist who is getting consultation.

Peer Supervision Groups

Another potentially useful professional experience for the practitioner is peer supervision. Among other features, it has the value of longevity, which is not generally found in the consultations already mentioned.

As practitioners move from clinical practice in large institutions and agencies into private practice, they often feel increasing isolation and existential exhaustion. Frequently, these experiences develop into the feeling of being "burned out"—evoking disillusionment about one's work, its importance, and its impact. Many practitioners in the throes of this existential malaise seriously consider leaving the practice of psychotherapy. Some actually do. We live in an age in which the individual experiences an accentuated need for personal identity, significance and unification (Goldberg, 1980a). There is clearly a need for practitioners to find an opportunity for exchange with trusted colleagues, for the evocation of deeply encountered feelings about their work and the processes and directions toward which they aspire as purposive beings (Goldberg, 1981).

Practitioners share with their clients the existential requirement to give some direction to their own lives. Without the exchange of deeply experienced and meaningful sentiments with others, practitioners, no less than their clients, come to realize that their values are vacuous, their pursuits are bereft of happiness, and their endeavors lack direction and purpose (Goldberg, 1980a).

Peer supervision, if purpose and process are well-attended, offers a viable modality for growth and refurbishment for the practitioner of psychotherapy. There have been relatively few reports of this important supervisory modality in the literature (for an exception, see Ormont, 1980).

Based upon my own experience in various leaderless peer groups, discussions with colleagues who have participated in successful peer groups and reports in the literature, I will examine in this section the problems elicited by peer groups and will offer guidelines for dealing with these concerns.

Why Peer Groups Are Formed

The reasons that psychotherapists join peer supervision groups may be conveniently grouped within the following four categories:

1. *Clinical.* Many experienced psychotherapists find that, at their advanced level of experience, peer supervision is more appropriate to their professional needs than are the more traditional forms of supervision, training, and continuing education (Nobler, 1980; Woods, 1974).

2. *Professional.* For therapists in private practice, the peer group is viewed as an excellent place for securing and exchanging patient referrals. Because fellow group members are familiar with their work and the specific needs of their practice, they generally feel that they can be given more appropriate referrals than from other sources. The peer group also may be viewed as a propitious arena for demonstrating the professional competence and personal skills that may enhance the referral of clients from peer group colleagues. For many in private practice, their clients are the only persons available to attest to the practitioner's skills.

3. *Emotional.* Many practitioners regard the peer group as a potential source of support and encouragement. It also may be a vehicle for catharsis of the pent-up feelings that practitioners feel would be unsafe and imprudent to express to their clients or to the colleagues with whom they work directly (Kline, 1972; 1974).

4. *Social.* Due to the isolation of private practice and to the atmosphere of mistrust and apprehensiveness in the agencies in which many practitioners work, a peer group may provide a place for friendship and warm interchange. In this setting, colleagues experience a choice of association, which they may not find in the work setting in which they practice.

Hidden Agendas That Impede Productive Peer Supervision

Practitioners who are attracted to peer supervision may be seriously deficient in clinical education, training, and experience. They may have had insufficient supervision with senior and expert colleagues. As a result, these participants may impede the learning experience for others who have had considerably more training and experience. Practitioners may also join a leaderless peer supervision group in a dysfunctional attempt to get help for serious personal problems that are interfering with their professional and personal effectiveness. For these colleagues, joining a peer group is an attempt to deny their need for psychotherapy. This indirect petition for treatment is experienced as exploitative by the other group members. Rarely can these troubled colleagues continue in the group unless the others begin to assume therapeutic roles with them.

A certain amount of competitive fervor for referrals and professional esteem, in terms of what Woods (1974) has referred to as a "narcissistic anxiety inherent in disclosing one's clinical work with peers," is undoubtedly an appropriate attribute of professional life. Excessive competitiveness, criticalness and lack of concern toward colleagues will, of course, be disruptive to a productive peer-group experience.

Likewise, reaching out for social contacts and relationships among one's colleagues is certainly an understandable and necessary response to professional isolation. However, as a major impetus for joining a peer group, the social relationships of group members outside the group frequently mitigates against candid exchanges. The appeal of group members in terms of their providing regard, approval, and respect for the individual participant is, of course, at work in all groups. However, in groups in which participants have a greater investment in being liked than an openness for learning, the potential for defending against social exclusion by coupling and subgrouping is imminent. In groups in which this occurs, some colleagues will feel isolated and misunderstood, and will drop out. Others will split from the group together to form their own groups. These disturbances frequently have to do with unexamined sexual conflicts and innuendoes expressed in the group. Let us look now at some useful ways of establishing a peer group.

Guidelines for Forming and Maintaining a Peer Supervision Group

1. *Purpose.* As suggested above, the reasons for joining a peer supervision group vary greatly. Generally, I have found that those who join are in private practice—at least, in part-time private practice. In instances where the colleagues are employed

by institutions and agencies, they assert that appropriate clinical supervision is unavailable or so tied into administrative matters that they are unwilling to express themselves candidly in their work setting. Whatever the original motive for joining a peer group, these motives should be openly shared by the members of the group. Unrealistic aims should be examined early in the life of the group (or at the entrance of a new colleague to the group) to avoid later disappointment and resentment.

Just as our clients often have "hidden agendas" for entering therapy, so frequently do our colleagues for joining peer supervision. Several years ago, Doris, a middle-aged colleague who had recently received her doctorate and was a member of a professional association to which I belonged, asked me to join a leaderless peer supervision group she was interested in forming. Her clinical work was clearly not a financial necessity, as her husband was a successful and wealthy businessman, but she had a considerable need to mother and take care of others. Her relationships with her own family were rather strained and conflicted. She brought together four psychologists younger than herself. Sessions were held at her large home, where she offered elaborate, catered snacks and luncheons. I sensed that at some level she wanted the whole group to move into her house and expected the infusion of four surrogate children to render her unhappy abode a warm homestead. Within a few months, this group disbanded. It is prudent for those who join a peer group to have an accurate sense of the motivation of the others in the group.

It is also important that, for whatever reasons colleagues join a peer group, they give it a high priority on their personal agendas, and that they make sincere efforts to attend regularly. The firmness of colleagues' commitment may not be apparent initially, but it doesn't usually take long to discern whether they regard the group as a priority or in terms of convenience. I would question the profit to be gained from a group which is willing to allow participants to attend at their convenience. Several members were away for a protracted period of time from a peer supervision group that I found generally profitable. An issue vital to the continuance of the group arose during their absences, resulting in the group experiencing a great deal of difficulty reconstituting when the absent colleagues returned.

2. *Frequency, place, and duration of sessions*. Whether the peer group meets for luncheon in a restaurant, in a colleague's

private office during the day, or in a group member's home in the evening, with or without refreshments, reflects both the manifest and covert purposes for the existence of that particular peer group. Some thought should be given as to where the group meets and why they have chosen such a site. During the period of existential malaise I discussed in Chapter 2, I joined a leaderless peer supervision group with five psychiatrists who were purportedly interested in discussing their private therapeutic groups. This group met every two weeks for luncheon. Unfortunately, in many of these places the tables were so close or the restaurant so noisy and distracting that open and comfortable discussion, particularly when it concerned sensitive material, was difficult or impossible.

In my experience, practitioners generally devote considerably less thought to planning a peer supervision group than they do their therapeutic groups. Careful consideration of the format and process desired in sessions is necessary. The frequency and the amount of time that the group meets should concur with the realistic demands of the colleagues' professional schedules and personal lives and be in keeping with the amount of intensity and intimacy which the participants need or want. As these needs change over time, a periodic review of this issue is prudent. It would be easy to dismiss this statement as self-evident. It is my experience, however, that many peer groups do not handle the issue of how intensive they wish the group to be with careful consideration. In these instances, group members may use indirect or acting out strategies to dilute or to intensify the peer experience.

3. *New Members*. In the original formulation of a peer group, colleagues may petition interest by word of mouth, notices in professional newsletters and bulletin boards in agencies, and by other indirect means. Once a group has come together, however, indirect approaches are more atypical. Generally, group members report that a colleague of theirs is or might be interested in joining the group. The "introducer" is generally held accountable for the appropriateness of the colleague in terms of desirable professional and personal attributes for that particular group. Reflecting the quality of their own commitment, or, perhaps, a need to infuse new blood in a depleted or troubled group, the group members may agree to accept a new colleague without first meeting the colleague and with little or no discussion of the new colleague's background and motives for attending the group.

On the other hand, the group members may ask that the prospective group member attend one or more sessions, part of which are used to "interview" the candidate about his or her training, clinical experience, and most importantly, motives for wishing to join the peer group. One or more trial sessions enable both candidate and other group members to exchange feelings and reactions to one another and allows the candidate to view how the group attends to its purported tasks. A trial consideration also removes from the introducer, to some degree, the onus of having to verify singularly the appropriateness of the candidate. This accountability is never fully removed, however. During strains in group process, startling accusations of having let the group down by inviting an inappropriate colleague may be made. Consequently, adding new members should be examined in terms of possible mechanisms of denial and avoidance of uncomfortable agendas existent in the group.

In a peer supervision group comprised of three young male psychologists and three young female social workers, the male psychologists quickly developed an unspoken but obvious competition for being the most competent practitioner, among various other issues. The group had met only three or four times when two members proposed inviting a nationally known, middle-aged nurse to attend. All quickly agreed. The nurse attended one session. It was decided to hold the next session at her home. She called the other members the day before the scheduled meeting, saying that she had to be out of town and that she would get in touch with them about the next meeting. She never did, nor did the group ever convene again. This peer group avoided its considerable tensions by bringing in a new member, who tacitly was given the responsibility to dissolve the group. It is prudent, therefore, that an ongoing peer group explore whether adding new colleagues avoids issues the existing group must confront, so that the new members are less disruptive of the group's development.

4. *Drop-outs.* I have never been in a peer supervision group that succeeded in resolving its conflicts by allowing a "difficult" group member or two to drop out. As practitioners, we are aware not only that "difficult" group members bring their own personal concerns into the group, but that the very nature of their personal proclivities and concerns sensitizes them to the undercurrent of threatening and disavowed motives unconsciously being expressed by the other group members. Through displacement and projective identification, these "difficult" colleagues

represent the implicit conflicts experienced and denied by their colleagues (Goldberg, 1970).

In a peer group I attended, an obese and very dependent practitioner quietly dropped out of the group after having attended for about four months. No one bothered to call her to inquire why she left. Although she was not actually disliked, her constant need for attention and approval had been disruptive. In the next session, people smiled and agreed that now they could get down to work on a more meaningful and intimate level. Within a month, three other group members dropped out or were away on extended leaves. In short, "drop-outs" may make more impact by leaving than by their presence: In the group in question, the difficult member's departure signaled the covert conflict in the group.

Whenever possible, a group should request from colleagues the courtesy of *reporting* in a session their intention to leave the group rather than by giving indirect message. In fairness to all, the reason for such a procedure should not be to convince a colleague to stay (although, certainly, everyone should be free to share his/her feelings about this) or to criticize the impact the departing colleague has had on the group. As in a therapeutic group, feelings about participants who are leaving should be explored. The reciprocal sentiments from the departing colleague about remaining group members may provide useful feedback about unexpressed conflicts and agendas.

5. *Outside contracts.* The fact that the peer group is talked about by its members on the occasion of chance or planned encounters is testimony to its impact. However, as in a therapy group, the extent to which participants discuss those feelings and reactions about other group members and events that are not shared with the others—whether in sidewalk discussions following sessions or, most especially, in separate meetings—reflects strains within the group and a sense of mistrust about exploring the issues in the larger group. In a leaderless peer supervision group, as a result of a series of separate meetings by its various members, one participant, Doris, referred her own adolescent daughter to another group colleague, Betty, for psychotherapy. A few weeks later Betty met with another group member, Bob, and reported that she was going to insist that Doris see Bob in treatment. She alleged that Doris's daughter had reported some instances in which Doris had been rather abusive to her. In other separate meetings, other group members

expressed the concern that Betty was trying to turn the peer group into an incestuous melange in which everyone was going to be treated by someone else in the group. Doris refused to see Bob in therapy and dropped out of the group. The others, in separate conversations, spoke of wanting to reconvene as a supervisory group without Doris, but never did.

Each group member should make a personal commitment to the group not to be party to conversations about other group members that are not (ultimately) shared with the whole group.

6. *Rotating leaders.* All leaderless peer supervision groups with which I am familiar have at some point in their development either discussed or actually adopted a rotating leader format. Nobler (1980) discusses the evolution of this format in the peer supervision group of which she is a member. All of the participants in this group have had at least 20 years of professional experience, are within a ten-year age range, are in private practice, and come from a background of psychoanalytic orientation. Nobler reports:

> In a discussion concerning various ways of intensifying our level of involvement in this experience, we decided to try having each member take turns leading the group for a session, saving the last few minutes of each session for a critique of both the session and of the style of the leader, the idea that two years earlier we had discussed and dismissed without trying. We had not anticipated the immediate change that this brought about in the climate of the group. There was an emotionally charged atmosphere in the room, a tension and anxiety in the air. The tone and interaction now had the quality of a therapy group, and the therapeutic potential of this peer group was apparent to all. The content of the sessions quickly moved from outside issues to our own individual and interpersonal relations in the group session. During the critique part of the sessions the emphasis also quickly shifted from examining the leader's style to looking at the emotional dimension of the experience and examining our own group process. In the following two and a half months, each member led the group session, and then we discontinued alternating leaders. We all agreed that these sessions led by our members were the most intense and valuable that we had in our peer group experience, yet by mutual agreement we returned to the leaderless format.

The use of rotating leaders reflected an evolution in the colleagues' willingness to deepen their personal involvement with one another and, as Nobler wrote, "to risk more intimacy by sharing our reactions to each other, including competitive feelings, anger, irritation, and boredom. We agreed to focus on our personal as well as professional selves."

Evidently, as a result of changing the structure of a peer group, members are faced with a choice of reconstituting the peer group into a therapeutic modality, as did the group described by Hunt and Issacharoff (1975; 1977), or of utilizing the therapeutic potential evoked in the new structure to dissolve isolation and enhance professional growth, as did Nobler's (1980) group. The use of the rotating leader format may be appropriate for the former but not for the latter, as a rotating leadership structure often militates against concerns about intimacy without openly exploring these concerns. In a group with a manifest therapeutic aim this is less likely to happen.

Nora, a colleague in a peer group, was simultaneously in the process of terminating with her therapist, finding another therapist, and ending a long and stormy affair. Not surprisingly, she was also an unhappy group member. She usually waited until the last few moments of the session to indicate that she felt unfairly maligned and misunderstood by her colleagues. She requested that they employ a rotating leader structure so that there would be someone in the group who would prevent pathological involvements in the group. The format wasn't accepted, and Nora both changed therapists and left the group.

There are circumstances in which rotating leadership may be useful. A group of very experienced practitioners in Philadelphia, all of whom have had considerable personal therapy experience, successfully employs a unique leadership format. This group meets leaderless every week, except for one session a month, in which they invite a guest leader to meet with them. They believe that in this way they can continue to get objective assessment of issues in the group without the magical investment in leadership. They have continued to meet this way for several years.

7. *Composition.* A certain latitude of differences in experience, treatment philosophy and personal style among the members of a peer supervision group may invigorate and proffer a rich arena for professional growth. Too similar treatment philosophy and clinical experience may incur the problem of Kline's (1972, 1974) peer group of male psychoanalysts: "[an] unwillingness to expose and share their fears and feelings was reinforced by their professional training and practice."

On the other hand, too great a difference and training may defeat the very purpose of the supervisory group—peer interchanges. If some of the participants have considerably more experience than others, they may be bestowed with the role of experts, while their less experienced colleagues are relegated to the status of students. In a leaderless peer supervision group in which I participated, several of the psychiatrists had never had their own personal psychotherapy. Discussions in the group were formal and, in my view, superficial. The participants seemed intent on having a pleasant lunch, getting continuing education credits, and exchanging referrals rather than meaningfully reviewing their clinical work with colleagues. Other than myself, they all seemed in close concordance with these themes.

8. *Personal attributes.* It would, of course, be impossible to ascertain what specific personal attributes contribute to desirable peer membership. The personal chemistry between people defies a simple, straightforward delineation. Nonetheless, we can state certain basic personal attributes that participants must demonstrate to integrate smoothly in a peer group. Those who express no concern, support, or warmth for others in the group and withhold participation in sessions, no matter what their reputations are as practitioners, and regardless of their willingness to refer clients, will have a detrimental impact on the intimacy, disclosure and sharing of the other participants. The prime attribute for membership in a peer group is the capacity for equity, that is to say, the ability and willingness to give and receive sentiments and ideas in interchange with colleagues. Those who drop out frequently do because they experience considerable discrepancy in equating what they are able to give and receive in peer exchange.

A word about criticalness: Criticism in a peer supervision setting is double-edged. Colleagues join peer groups purportedly for candid exchanges of how they are experienced by colleagues and how they experience themselves as practitioners. Yet, if these candid interchanges are not informed by personal concern, warmth, and support, hurt and defensiveness may be engendered. In my experience, angry outbursts and expressions of hurt and disappointment are usually directed at a colleague's criticalness. Colleagues are generally able to listen to and integrate criticism and confrontation, as I discussed in Chapter 11, if they are expressed as "personal-I" statements rather than "you" statements. It is useful, therefore, to ask confronting group members to make personal statements and express criticisms in terms of their own feelings rather than intimating they are objective statements of reality.

9. *Sharing intimacy with peers and clients.* Leaderless peer supervision groups, perhaps more than any other professional endeavor, require a considerable degree of psychological maturity. With rare exception, colleagues who have not had sufficient personal therapy (regardless of their professional training and experience) will pose difficulties for the others in a group in which intimate and candid interchange is normative. Moreover, peers who have had individual psychotherapy, particularly more traditional approaches, but have had no group experience, whether in therapy, supervision or in some other group training experience, may also experience considerable difficulty in a leaderless group, in which the examination of group process is encouraged.

Each of us must choose how much of ourselves we are willing to experience deeply. Experiencing the deeper recesses of one's self is frequently painful because it reveals unbuttressed the loneliness and dread that result from our existential responsibility—our having to make our own choices—in a world of uncertainty. The defenses we erect provide a respite from pain inasmuch as the probe of our deeper concerns is averted. Our basic choice is in how we wish to experience our own lives (Goldberg, 1973). It seems to me that it is the practitioner's task to help clients discover how they have chosen to experience the world and the impelling motives behind their choices. This endeavor may require a considerable amount of courage from client and therapist.

In the throes of my own existential malaise I spoke of in Chapter 2, I was seriously considering leaving the practice of psychotherapy. As it happened, a psychiatrist friend invited me to join a peer group of colleagues that he was organizing. This group would be comprised of five psychiatrists and myself. All of us practiced group psychotherapy and were interested in sharing our feelings and problems about our work with some supportive colleagues. The group met every two weeks for luncheon. Each of us took turns hosting and paying the tab for the whole group. There was a covert, but intense, competition among the group members as to who could find the restaurant with the best food and, at the same time, the best prices.

In one of these crowded restaurants, with each of us leaning forward to hear, one of the group members disclosed a series of incidents that has had a lasting effect on me. The practitioner, an experienced and well-respected psychiatrist, demonstrated what I regarded as a peculiar kind of courage. He told us that he conducted a therapy group in his home. For more than a year, his wife lay upstairs dying of cancer. He kept this information and his agitated feelings from his patients. He reported that, to the best of his knowledge, none of his patients was aware that his wife was painfully dying just above them as they discussed the various—one must imagine, at times, the trivial—vicissitudes of their lives. In short, he claimed that he had no countertransferential reactions to working for over a year in this way.

On the surface, I had to admire the great valor and composure this physician applied to his emotions, which the others in the peer group regarded as expected and proper professional behavior toward his patients. But I also felt uneasy about his display of "proper courage." I was not entirely sure why at the time. I was weary of the unexamined attidues of the other therapists in the supervision group, all physicians, who expressed admiration and strong concordance with the therapist's behavior. They indicated that their Hippocratic oath ethically necessitated that they keep their own personal struggles and concerns from their patients so as not to constrain them by having them feel guilty about burdening their doctor with their problems when he harbored a serious one of his own. One of the others in the group maintained that for a therapist to allow patients to know that the practitioner has conflicts was like a surgeon with a shaky hand saying to his patients, "I am not sure I can operate properly." I was asked how I might feel about such a situation if I were the patient.

I had trouble knowing why, at the time, but I kept feeling that the issue was, for this psychiatrist, not a matter of proper ethical behavior toward patients, but something far more disturbing. He was demonstrating a peculiar kind of courage—although it was a courage that was professionally and socially acceptable. I have described elsewhere how displays of courage may mask even greater fears than those addressed in the ostensible act of courage (Goldberg & Simon, 1982). Purported self-honesty and courage may be masochistic ploys to cover and protect the person from more painful truths about him/herself.

My colleague had made the absolute assumption that the awful situation he was in would not adversely affect his patients as long as he did not speak about it and did his job dutifully. It has occurred to me more recently that my colleague was acting courageously in order not to allow his clients to act caringly toward him. Intimacy implies a caring awareness and concern about one's own needs. My colleague's courage was an expression of lofty ideals about protecting others, which, simultaneously, cemented privacy and aloneness for himself.

Emotional intimacy involves the striving to become real. The advent of intimacy is only possible between people who recognize and respond to the humanity of the other. In psychotherapy it occurs when the therapist is an agent of the client, not of the theoretical position or professional code that denies some of his/her important human qualities. The above psychiatrist's professional training and his intense immediate psychic pain apparently precluded the opportunity to experience meaningful intimacy with his patients. It required him to be their guardian and surrogate parent; when, in fact, he was, perhaps, at the time, the most hurt and needy person in the therapy group he conducted. His actions evinced contempt for his patients. A person cannot be emotionally intimate with those whom he regards as contemptible. As such, his courageous display was a tragic and unfortunate model, which I regard as a massive but unrecognized investment in keeping his clients "innocent" and, as such, "victims." If the therapist won't share intimacy with his/her clients, then who will?

10. *Existential concerns.* Private practitioners may be deprived of opportunities to examine openly their own and their colleagues' personal values and existential concerns. The practitioner needs the opportunity to represent him/herself in all aspects of self, rather than be confined to a few aspects of circumscribed, professional attributes (Goldberg, 1977; 1980a). A leaderless peer supervision group may serve as a propitious occasion for a meaningful review of the values that inform the practitioner's therapeutic encounters. Peer groups in which these reviews are restricted offer their group members a more limited potential for personal and professional growth. I found the others in the group of psychiatrists unwilling to examine this possibility. My colleagues attempted to invalidate the existential concerns I had by patronizingly indicating that, because I was not a physician, I had unrealistic notions about clinical responsibility. This was clearly the wrong peer group for me.

11. *Process.* Nobler (1980) has reported the group process of her peer group:

During a session the discussion shifts between content, the issues brought in by group members, and process, the examination of our group interactions, and individual reactions to the member presenting. We discuss a wide range of individual and group therapeutic situations as they may affect our ability to function as therapists. It is increasingly apparent that we do not want to talk about patients primarily, but about ourselves in relation to patients, our feelings about them, about our work and personal life.

In the course of this process, group members may share personal feelings and reactions or suggest what they have done in similar situations or in their own personal lives. They may role-play or simulate various clinical situations being explored in the supervision group. They may even respond to the complexities of the situations being addressed by induced statements of feelings (e.g., paradoxical response to the presenter, which may be very helpful in learning about the therapeutic use of self [Goldberg, 1980b]).

12. *Presentation*. Whether presentation concerns clinical cases or the exploration of personal concerns, peer supervision groups generally develop a normative format. Colleagues may present in turn (of course, with the provision that "crises" are given priority), or the presentations may be left to the spontaneous enjoinder of the participants. In groups in which presentations are conducted systematically, there should be some agreement about how formally these presentations are to be made. Overly elaborate presentation may stifle spontaneous expressions of the other colleagues. Moreover, it frequently connotes a feeling that less-than-perfect therapeutic work and consideration are not tolerated by this group. "Success" stories and insignificant problems may be presented as a result of this agenda.

The procedure in Nobler's (1980) group is rather typical of the groups I have attended:

> In any session precedence is given to any member who indicates a disturbance. The disturbance may be a personal one, or between two members, or relating to therapeutic impasse. Group process is inevitably impeded if one member is preoccupied and burdened by an unshared problem.

This procedure parallels the clinical orientation found in therapeutic groups and is, generally, advisable. Nonetheless, as a clinical model it emphasizes conflict, crisis, and disrepair. In my view, peer supervision should also encourage growth by encouraging the discussion of therapeutic encounters and personal life experiences that have brought joy and enrichment to the practitioner's being. Colleagues would be wise to seek a balance among the concerns to which they attend in a peer group.

13. *Attention.* As in a therapeutic group, it is prudent that the members of a peer group attend the manifestations of group process—both inside and outside the group meetings. Concerns that are not openly acknowledged in sessions may foster an overintellectual climate in the group or may even result in serious risk to the participants' health. One participant in a peer supervision group, who had appeared to be unable to hear fairly gentle but direct questions from the peer group members about his need for controlling his clients, reported the occurrence of a bleeding ulcer. Of course, I cannot attest to the direct causal relationship of these events. Such occurrences, nonetheless, should be examined to protect members from additional insult from group conflict.

14. *Development of trust.* We are willing to share uncomfortable feelings about our practices to the degree that we trust the peer group as a safe place to present personal vulnerabilities and self-doubts. One cannot fault practitioners for exercising judgment in assessing the safety of intimate disclosure in a peer group. Moreover, a demonstration of patience, acceptance, and confidence that trust and good-will will eventually emerge and will be worth waiting for does much toward fostering that trust. The sense of trust as a backdrop for interchanges in a peer supervision group may take six months, a year, or longer. But, on the other hand, the kind of commitment to risk any group member makes decisively influences the commitment others will make. For trust to develop, someone must take a chance and risk more personal disclosure. Existentially, each participant is responsible for what happens or fails to happen in the group (Goldberg, 1973). No less than in a therapeutic group, the seductiveness and dangers of intimacy that come from the fear that repressed wishes will be activated is an underlying theme in leaderless peer groups.

15. *Sharing.* Clinical research has indicated that experienced psychotherapists tend to ask significantly fewer questions and to make significantly more direct, personal statements than do inexperienced psychotherapists. Correspondingly, extensive appeals for information frequently connote a cautious

group in which insufficient trust is experienced for members to be open and direct with each other. Moreover, extensive questions lead to greater intellectual processing than does a spontaneous and direct interchange. I would recommend the approach utilized by psychodramatists called "sharing," especially for clinical presentation. No discussion of a clinical case, no matter how thoroughly examined, should be ended until each of the participants has shared his/her personal feelings about the material presented. This kind of sharing may be a healthy antidote to sessions in which colleagues inordinately employ theoretical systems to supervise one another. Colleagues can, perhaps, best enable each other to achieve meaning in their work by their personal concern—caring that their colleagues' struggles to examine the assumptions they each make about their therapeutic encounters as statements of their being in the world will be worthy of them. This will enable each to present him/herself as each intends, rather than trying to fulfill a metapsychological theory.

16. *Protectiveness.* Nobler (1980) reports that in the peer group of which she was a member, during the second year there was still: "an unspoken agreement to avoid harsh criticism. This was a model of relating that none of us as therapists would have allowed to continue in our own groups."

I have found it remarkable, not only in leaderless peer supervision but also in groups conducted by experienced practitioners I have supervised, that these therapists appear to ask more of their clients in terms of openness and examination of their motives than they ask of themselves. In peer supervision groups where the need to keep one's professional reputation intact at all costs is paramount, very little meaningful learning will take place.

The protectiveness of professional integrity is based often on questionable normative considerations which contradict the open examination of psychological motives. In a peer supervision group, a psychiatrist referred to a group colleague a couple whom he had seen individually for a couple of years. He indicated their current need for marital psychotherapy. In the second session of marital therapy, the couple was 15 minutes late due to an accident on the highway involving two other cars. They were furious that the therapist didn't give them extra time, despite the therapist's explanation that another client was scheduled right after them. When the practitioner confronted their narcissistic involvement in the time issue, they complained to the referring psychiatrist. The psychiatrist vowed never to refer another patient to his colleague. He expressed concern about his reputation being endangered by his referral to a colleague who was not "polite" to his clients.

17. *Primal organizer(s).* Those colleagues who originally form a peer group are frequently invested with a progenitor role. This role may remain suppressed during much of the life of the group, but may be openly reinvoked by projective identifications during strains in the group process. These primal organizers may be sharply questioned about why they gave life to the group, why particular group members were admitted and why they have allowed the group to fall into disrepair. The participants involved in this projection may entirely ignore that they, themselves, have been party to the transactions and vicissitudes of the group for most or all of this time period. Peer group organizers should be aware that the price they may have to pay for the satisfaction of forming a peer group will be occasional, pointed criticism.

18. *Handling dissonance.* One of the most crucial issues a peer supervision group will face is how to handle conflict in sessions. The concept of peer supervision brings to mind a group of colleagues who examine issues, reason and decide together in an egalitarian manner. However, there are always some disagreements in the group, and there have to be some decisions made about how to resolve conflict. The group members must consider whether this will be by democratic vote or some other way. A voting procedure would probably be as ineffective for a peer supervision group as it would be for a therapeutic one. But at least the therapeutic group generally has reason to believe that the therapist will be the ultimate authority. When a leaderless peer supervision group reaches an insoluble impasse, outside consultation may be valuable. But careful consideration of who does the consultation, his/her relationship to group members, and specifically which issues the group members wish the consultant to address should be examined prior to the consultation.

19. *Sexual issues.* The sexual composition of the group will heavily influence the particular issues and the manner in which they are explored in a peer supervision group. If sexual agendas are not aired in the group, they may cause considerable conflict. After two members of a peer supervision group discussed, in a private conversation, starting a sexual relationship, the married

male practitioner sharply attacked his female colleague in the next session for her insensitivity to other group members' feelings. She was shocked and immobilized by the attack which, in her perception, "came out of the blue." She stayed away from the group for several weeks. In another peer supervisory group, the participants were aware that a rather narcissistic female psychologist was trying to seduce another psychologist in the group, although this issue was not openly discussed. After a brief relationship, the woman angrily snapped at the others in the group, "Don't you see he won't even make eye contact with me!" "Yes, we do, but what do you want from us?" they responded. This was a group that didn't wish to deal with the sexual tensions operating in the group, despite the fact that it was of considerable concern to one of its members.

20. *Legal ramifications.* I have never heard of members of peer supervision groups becoming involved in legal proceedings as a result of their peer supervisory experience. Nonetheless, in these days of rampant litigation and professional accountability, it is quite conceivable that such may occur. The crucial question is that, as peer supervisors, is each member responsible for overseeing the clinical work of every other colleague in the group? If they are, they may be held ethically and legally responsible, as would an administrative or clinical supervisor, for the conduct of a group member who they are aware (or perhaps even unaware) is in violation of a professional statute. It may be advisable that there be some early discussion of the statutes governing each of the professions represented in the group that bear on issues attended to in the group.

In addition to an organized peer group, there are other means of support for the practitioner.

Peer/Colleague Support

Collegial interaction is a very important source of support regardless of whether or not one returns to personal therapy. Peers, colleagues, and friends are people with whom one can share one's concerns with, who provide the caring and recognition the practitioner desires. This may be in a formalized peer group, as I have just described or more informally. Haveliwala and his associates (1979) have strongly emphasized, in a guide for mental health practitioners, that our training prepares us for a considerable amount of private work—the one-to-one therapy model. But professionally and personally we require collaboration and support from other people. There are numerous clinical problems that we do not have to, and sometimes should not, deal with without assistance. Too often, our pride and our training may prevent us from asking for the help we require. Emergencies are almost always times when we require other professional help. Haveliwala and his associates (1979) cogently indicate that:

> Emergencies demand the response of others better equipped than the mental health worker. Such agencies as the police, emergency wards, or the fire department have both the resources and the expertise to handle emergencies. Mental health workers do not. We can assist a person in obtaining proper help and we can later pick up the case and thereby bring the expertise of mental health to the scene.
>
> Threats of suicide, homicide, or other forms of violence, as well as sickness or accidents, demand action, but not that of psychotherapy. The police, courts, fire department, ambulance, medical hospital, etc., are the appropriate institutions to meet the non-mental health emergency.
>
> The second type of emergency...is the psychiatric emergency. At this moment, this type of situation requires resources beyond the reach of most mental health workers. Hospitalization may be repugnant to some mental health workers, but there are clearly those instances when the mental hospital is best equipped to tackle the immediate problem. Later, as the emergency is cooled down, the mental health worker can enter the scene to assist in the process of returning the individual to a healthier life-style. (pp. 6–7)

Support from Family and Friends

Many of the practitioners in Burton's book went out of their way to indicate how essential their spouses were to them in handling life's crises, as well as providing a positive emotional current in their lives, which enabled them to obtain sufficient gratification amidst frequent self-doubt. It should be noted that this is one area in which Burton and Henry's findings greatly differ. The impression one is left with in reading the autobiographical accounts of famous therapists is that their marital relationships were for most (but, hardly, all) unusually blissful relationships. In contrast, Henry's respondents report that their marriages were generally satisfying, but temperate. Their experiences of intimacy came largely from their offices rather than their homes. Common sense tells us that a good personal life outside the office is an essential requirement to maintain the practitioner's well-being. One well-known practitioner indicates that for him: "Loving kindness is the only goal of life that has absolute value and represents a true affirmation of human free will" (Chessick, 1969). He tells us that the ability to sustain this loving kindness comes from his extreme fortune to have a wife and children with an unusual capacity for expressing and receiving love.

There are times, Ralph Greenson (1966) has told us, when the practitioner must be allowed to be an ordinary person, who has:

> the opportunity to stop being a psychoanalyst when he comes home. He should feel free to react as a spontaneous, wholehearted, whole person when he leaves the office. If he has to be right and rational in the analytic hours, he needs a place to be wrong and to be irrational at times. He needs a place where he can expose his frailties.

Other Considerations

Taking Time Off

Another way of obtaining support is to take breaks from a busy practice. The therapist is wise to build in breaks within any daily schedule as well as to take breaks between ongoing treatment appointments, so that he/she does not become exhausted but can find new energy from outside interests to bring in to enrich and invigorate his/her work.

Time Management

Time management is also important. On the one hand, the therapist is concerned about utilizing clinical time in order to best provide services for all clients treated and sufficient income to meet ongoing needs. On the other hand, the therapist also needs to find nonremunerable times to get resources for him/herself and must balance out clinical hours with other kinds of professional activities.

Scheduling Sessions

Psychotherapists have been criticized in recent years for utilizing an "assembly-line" scheduling of sessions. The impact of Jacques Lacan's ideas have provoked a number of practitioners in the United States and abroad to question the wisdom of fixed length of sessions. Some practitioners believe that following the clock serves to reinforce the obsessive traits of both therapist and client. They maintain that the client's time to be understood is not measured by a chronological clock. Those following Lacan's concepts end a session in such a way as to punctuate the client's speech in an active way, in effect, to say, "Let's end here because what has just been said would be diminished by further declarative in the session" (Muller and Richardson, 1983).

Some practitioners find it convenient to schedule some appointments back-to-back. These are clients with whom they don't have to struggle arduously. At the same time, there are clients with whom one works who create such stress that it is necessary to take a break between such a client's appointment and the next. For still others, practitioners schedule appointments so that they can extend the session for as long as two or more hours, especially in the cases of emergencies and of certain families who are difficult to work with. This practice recognizes Greenson's (1974) sharp criticism of "assembly-line practice" of psychotherapy in recent years.

The notion of the "50-minute hour" (now, generally, 45 minutes) was designed by Freud and the early psychoanalytic practitioners to allow about 50 minutes or so of time and might exceed this allotment if necessary to permit a catharsis of agitated affect which had, in the analyst's view, not been sufficiently discharged during the session or for the analyst to complete an interpretation or some such matter. The approximate ten minutes between sessions allowed the analyst, in Greenson's words:

> to recall the fragments of the incoming patient's previous hour, or at least offers you a chance to recharge your internal empathically constructed model of the new patient. If you work with patients "back to back," the moment the buzzer or light indicates the next patient has arrived, you have to shut off your analytic involvement with the patient on the couch and plan how to stop

the session. To put it succinctly, if you work without an interval, the patient starts and ends the hour without you.

Greenson attributes the practice of scheduling clients back to back as a continuation of how the practitioner was him/herself scheduled by a personal analyst or in supervisory sessions. The primary cause, however, is monetary. Greenson writes that this practice is rarely done to accommodate the suffering of more clients or for acquiring more clinical experience. He claims it is almost always a matter of financial considerations. It is also an act of bad faith. Greenson writes:

> It is obvious that taking on patient after patient on an assembly-line schedule is an act of hostility, subtle and unconscious though it might be. There is a degree of hurtfulness in ending every hour, but the assembly-line method adds an unnecessary element of degradation of the patient. It will also produce more fatigue and interfere with the relaxed, accepting atmosphere necessary for even-hovering attention.

Therefore, taking a ten- or 15-minute break for reflection after a session to think about what you learned is a gesture of good will toward the client whether or not he/she is aware of this.

There is still another important reason for taking breaks. Each of us, undoubtedly, has experienced times in practice when we were able to be a marathon man or woman who could see client after client with no apparent breach in our effectiveness. When we are in good spirits, we may be able to do this day after day, and it will work out fine. However, when we are not in good spirits, even if this is due to a cold or some other simple physical discomfort, even two sessions back to back may seem too long. In that we see clients over time and our schedules may continue for many months (for some practitioners, even years), we need to take into consideration our own state-of-being over time. On those occasions when we are not feeling buoyant, breaks are welcome, and we should provide them in our clinical schedule.

Handling Between-session Time

The fact that the practitioner has time between sessions suggests that common sense and compassion for self dictate that seeing client after client in an assembly-line fashion is not prudent; or it may suggest that there are hours that the practitioner has not been able to fill. The latter is an issue discussed in Chapter 8. We will confine ourselves to the former consideration here.

The practitioner must balance relaxation and necessary clinical and administrative considerations with the clinical schedule. Reviewing notes and impressions about a difficult or puzzling client and trying to understand what might be interfering with their work together may be appropriate before or after a session.

Learning to relax also helps improve the practitioner's perceptual sensitivity and ability to concentrate. Some practitioners are devout advocates of meditation. Others find going to a health spa, playing tennis, swimming, going to a museum, or simply taking a nap at some point during the day is extremely helpful. If the time between sessions is limited, free-floating thought, listening to music in the office, or doing some physical exercises may be relaxing.

Breaks are also times when practitioners check their phone messages or answering machines or service and return calls. If some of these calls are potentially stressful, it may be better that the practitioner call back at a time when he/she is feeling less pressured.

Combining Professional Activities

I have found it very useful in my own practice to work in a number of different settings where I can take what I have learned from one setting and use it in another. Even those years in which I worked full-time in private practice, I still found time to teach in several psychotherapy institutes and/or medical and graduate schools, and to consult in hospitals, counseling centers, mental health associations, and free clinics. I also conducted supervision groups in private for colleagues. This variety of experience was challenging as well as emotionally and intellectually gratifying. In this way, I didn't feel the staleness of any one circumscribed endeavor. Instead, I felt—and feel—the new challenges of each of the different activities in which I was—and am—involved.

The Question of Publication

Is it useful for the practitioner to publish? It can be! It depends on the kinds of practice and the reputation sought. Certainly, if the therapist publishes in popular journals and magazines, he/she is more likely to reach clients. If the therapist publishes in more scholarly journals and books, other practitioners are the audience. Which kind of writing he/she does is dependent upon what he/she wants to say, and where it will be best said.

How does one go about publishing? I suppose it is a truism to state that one should start by believing that one has something to say, something of interest and/or value to the lives and work of others. I will confine my discussion only to professional journal publications, while recognizing and appreciating that there are a number of practitioners who write and derive considerable enjoyment from being fiction writers, poets, and other types of writers on subjects other than psychotherapy.

The sources for inspiration are manifold. As I have discussed earlier, the practitioner is both witness to and often participant in a living drama. Undoubtedly he/she has innumerable ideas about these events and his/her role in them. The practitioner may choose to write about them from a theoretical, clinical, or personal perspective. Whatever perspective is taken, he/she needs to feel that what he/she says is a contribution. This may be because of some particular insight about these events, such that he/she has seen things somewhat differently from the way others have. It may be because the practitioner has put together ideas, impressions, and reactions in a new synthesis or may feel simply that what he/she has seen needs to be reported because many others are not sufficiently aware of its occurence or the intricacies of its process.

Having written something that the practitioner feels is a contribution to the field, he/she next seeks a journal that will be most responsive to the article. The practitioner should objectively try to assess the merits and limitations of the article or book. If he/she feels unable to be objective, the practitioner should ask a published colleague to look over the manuscript. If the paper is of considerable merit, it should be sent to the journal with the best reputation, with the size of its circulation of secondary consideration. Of course, such journals have significant rejection rates and, generally, long periods for review. Even after acceptance, publication might take a long while. Delays up to a year and more for reviewing a manuscript and up to two years or more for publication are no longer uncommon in professional journal publication. I suggest that the practitioner/writer check this information before selecting a journal to which to send the manuscript. There are a number of books in university and medical school libraries which list circulation, rejection rates, publishing delays, and topics of interest for journals in the fields of psychology, psychiatry, and psychoanalysis.

If the practitioner is planning to send a manuscript to a journal with a long delay for review, I suggest that he/she submit simultaneously to about three journals. In the face of long review periods, I believe this to be an acceptable practice. It is not usually, on the other hand, if a manuscript is to be reviewed within a reasonable time period. Three to four weeks is a reasonable amount of time for review and up to three months is generally acceptable. Under these circumstances, simultaneous submission is not usually advisable.

If the editor accepts your manuscript and will publish it in less than six months, you probably happened upon a journal that was planning an issue or special edition into which your paper fits. I would say that nine to 12 months is generally acceptable for publication.

Need for Additional Training

What does the practitioner do when he/she feels that training has been inadequate? Different types of supervision and training are available for different phases of a practitioner's career. First, he/she has to assess realistically where his/her training and preparation are limited. Does he/she lack theoretical knowledge? Current information? Or research information in some specific clinical areas? If so, devoting time to the library and using some excellent audiotapes can be helpful. Moreover, if the practitioner has sufficient time, he/she may wish to attend graduate courses or seminars taught at the better psychotherapy institutes. If the limitation is in clinical skills for client populations with which he/she intends to work but has not heretofore, some work experience with close supervision should meet these needs. A good workshop or two may also be helpful. On the other hand, if the problem is due to a lack of clinical skills with clients he/she is already working with, the clinician needs first to assess whether his/her own psyche is being threatened by clinical work or whether it has more to do with lack of sufficient clinical preparation. In either case, consultation with a senior practitioner is recommended. Consultation should help determine whether the problem would best be dealt with in personal therapy and supervision or could be sufficiently improved by good supervision alone.

For the practitioner who requires intensive, ongoing training, a good psychotherapy training institute is recommended. The practitioner should be cautious in choosing an institute, however. There are advanced training institutes in psychotherapy at all levels of sophistication and given to all theoretical persuasions. Some are considerably better run and provide far better training and clinical services than do others. Whereas there may be a number of them in large urban centers, many are simply private-outpatient clinics that give some supervision and offer some courses on matters pertaining to psychotherapy. Moreover, most are devoted to promoting a particular school of psychoanalytic or other psychotherapeutic treatment. Some, as Phillip Rieff (1968) has indicated, are essentially trade schools, preparing candidates for an affluent life in the suburbs. Often, the institute has been founded by a practitioner whose theory is exclusively promoted by the staff and the institute alumni. Too often, despite the theoretical and academic trappings, the actual reason for providing supervision and course work is the pretense of training neophyte practitioners in order to secure psychotherapists who will accept a low fee for treating clinic patients. In fact, many of these institutes are little more than assembly-line operations in which the administrative staff practitioners "cream" the clinic referrals, taking the more desirable clients who can afford their fees and relegating the less desirable clients to the inexperienced psychotherapists who are paid a few dollars a session. The minimal supervision these neophytes receive is supposedly compensation for their clinical work. There are better institutes available, of course. Generally, in these institutes, supervision is paid out-of-pocket by the trainees. Because of the extreme variation in quality among these institutes, the practitioner is prudent to investigate carefully who is on the faculty, who actually supervises and teaches courses and what type and how much supervision trainees receive.

In the better institutes, completion of an advanced (graduate) academic education is required. These institutes may admit only M.D.'s (psychiatrists with at least two years of residency) and Ph.D. and Psy.D. clinical psychologists. A few of the better institutes also admit psychiatric social workers and psychiatric nurses. In fact, until very recently, some of the psychoanalytic institutes barred all but physicians. It is a better measure of the quality of an institute to ascertain what constitutes the disciplines of the candidates of an institute than how restrictive the entrance requirements are. In that qualified psychiatrists and psychologists can choose whatever institutes they wish, those that have few or no psychiatrists and/or psychologists should be suspect.

Costs vary greatly among these institutes, depending on the amount of supervision and training analysis or personal psychotherapy required in addition to course work. A prospective candidate who is already in personal therapy must check to see if his/her current therapist is acceptable for the personal therapy requirements of the institute. If not, the practitioner will have to choose whether to terminate with the present therapist. In that this may be a very painful decision, the prospective candidate needs to be certain of the requirements prior to making a decision about a particular institute. For these reasons and because the quality of advanced training varies so greatly, practitioners should be cautioned from choosing a program solely on the basis of convenience.

For practitioners who are already graduates of institutes and would like other avenues of continuing professional growth, I recommend the peer group, discussed earlier. Finally, some professional organizations are known for providing generally excellent training during their yearly or biyearly conferences. The American Academy of Psychotherapy and the Institutes of the American Group Psychotherapy Association are highly regarded in this area.

In summary, we have been oriented as practitioner—through our training, if not our own character—to handle life's most excruciating problems and suffering alone in private. Common sense dictates that we are not *always* sufficient unto ourselves. Compassion for ourselves dictates that we need not be alone in dealing with difficult human issues. As we try to persuade our clients of this simple human reality, so we must persuade ourselves! I have tried to show that we can share the most agonizing moments of our practice with trusted colleagues—whether this be a private consultation, in a peer group, or in collaborative clinical endeavors. This is true whether the concern is one of self-doubt, an error or omission—or even of commission, such as rageful or sexual indiscretion toward a client. Of course, we can handle many of these things by returning to the couch. The usefulness of the couch, however, is often not immediate. In the meantime, we can turn to colleagues for assistance.

NOTES

1. The concepts for the co-therapy partnership model are taken from Goldberg (1977), Chapter 9.

2. I would appreciate hearing from any reader who has had direct experience with or knowledge of this type of consultation.

PART III

Epilogue

Chapter 15
Careers After Practice

The practitioner's knowledge, skills, and experience can be effectively utilized for ventures other than psychotherapy. Psychotherapy need not be a terminal career! Notwithstanding, many practitioners hold on to the saddle to the very end. There is nothing else they want to do or believe that they can do well enough to pursue as a second career. There are others who retire to fish, take the boat out, play tennis or golf, visit the grandchildren, or travel around the globe. Many of them feel that, after so many years spent as a psychotherapist, it is too late to learn new skills and pursue another field of endeavor.

I spoke recently with a senior psychoanalyst, a man close to sixty. I have known him for a number of years. He had spoken in the past of being ready to retire. He had complained that the winters in the Midwestern city in which he practices were getting more unbearable each year. Where he is in life, he doesn't need to practice for financial reasons. When I saw him at a conference, I asked if he was planning to retire to Florida as he had previously told me. He looked at me sideways and asked, "And do what?" I indicated that I knew that he had interests other than analysis.

"I've been a card-carrying member of an archeology association for 25 years," he said. "I once taught ancient history at the university."

We spoke about our mutual interest in archeology and classical studies. I asked if he ever gets the opportunity to go on excavations.

"No," he said, sadly. "My wife can't take the extreme heat you find in the desert."

I indicated that, since he had taught ancient history and was interested in Israel, perhaps he had thought of teaching there or some other place.

"No," he said. "I would have to start all over again from the bottom. After where I've reached (he has been a president of a psychoanalytic association) in this field, I'm too old to do that."

This friend echoes the sentiments of many psychotherapists. Still other practitioners feel that they would like to pursue another field, but to do so would be tantamount to admitting to themselves and to others that they have failed in their careers as healers. In order to protect their integrity, they look upon their psychotherapeutic practice as necessarily final.

Yet, what many of us tell our clients is that psychotherapeutic experience should open a world of possibilities for them. This should be valid for ourselves as well. To pursue an allied or even a distant field after years as a psychotherapist is hardly a statement of failure. It is no more a failure to move on to other pursuits after being a therapist than it is a failure to terminate a marriage, not because it wasn't once enriching for both, but because one or both have matured over the years and have moved in different directions, requiring different kinds of experience for increasing their capacity for intimacy and self-development. There are some people who are "born" therapists. In keeping with the thesis of this book, I mean by this that their programmed needs are continuously throughout life satisfied by working as therapists. There are many other practitioners, however, whose maturation is different. They have achieved for themselves, after a number of years of practice, the most they can achieve or derive from practice. They experience the felt need to move in different directions to relate to and be in the world with others. I have written this chapter in the belief that turning to other fields is not necessarily a sign of failure and because I hold that the seasoned practitioner has much to offer society in taking new and expanded ventures.

In that the psychotherapist treats the whole person, his/her experiences as a therapist over the years should provide a variegated range of knowledge, experience, and skill. If an effective practitioner, he/she must have been at various moments a mentor, a problem-solver, a spiritual counselor, a practical business-person, an intimate sojourner and fellow traveler, a social philosopher, a creative artist, an astute psychologist of societal events, as well as a healer. These are aptitudes and skills that can enhance our society. Such life experiences enable a practitioner to go into business, teaching, consultation, or a career in the arts. They speak to the question whether there is life after practice.

I offer this belief supportively. Each particular practitioner for whom this issue is relevant needs, of course, to decide for him/herself what specific direction, and what particular time, is best for using his/her life skills and experiences in other ways than as a psychotherapy practitioner. The psychiatrist Werner Mendel describes in his autobiography the issues which enabled him to know when to leave practice.

> Nothing should be done any longer than it is fun. At first the fun of therapy came in the mastery of the art, then the fun came in the results I achieved, then the fun was to have the secondary benefit of earning high fees and much fame. Finally, it was no longer fun. Then one has the choice of letting go and going on or becoming a conservator. To be conservative is doing something because I do it well and because I am successful and I try to do it as long as possible. That is not for me.
>
> If I look at the stages of my sources of pleasure doing psychotherapy, I can see how these have changed over the years. At the beginning it was exciting to discover the patient, to understand what was going on, and then eventually to learn not only what was happening in the patient but also what was happening in me and what was going on between us. The next stage was the pleasure in mastering and learning the techniques of intervention, of seeing how I could influence the transaction, and how I could make things happen. The next stage was one in which I was comfortable enough with my own feelings and with the mastery of the techniques to be able to really listen to the patient and to hear the many fascinating 'war stories.' Then after I had heard all the stories came the pleasure of the results, the ability to help people change their situations for the better...In the next stage of my twenty-two years of existing as a psychotherapist, I became interested in further refinement of

technique, handling more difficult cases, doing it faster, doing it with more skill and with more finesse . . .

But when all of these stages were past there was only one real gratification, one real pleasure remaining from the difficult, arduous task of psychotherapy. From each human contact I grew . . . At this stage of my development, I do psychotherapy . . . for the pleasure of the human transaction . . . However, I have also realized that most people who identify themselves as patients tend to lead constricted, limited lives, tend to be rather boring, and not able to be able to give a great deal to human transaction. For this reason the time has come for me to move on to another kind of human transaction. The expanded hearing, expanded vision, and expanded feeling which I derived from the reflective self [practicing as a psychotherapist] can apply to nontherapeutic relationships and yield more of a growth experience for me at this time (Burton, 1972, pp. 287–289).

Conclusion

I have attempted to describe in this volume who the psychotherapist is in terms of his/her background—family of origin, values, and ways of handling conflict that derive from this background. Background shapes the practitioner in particular ways. I have contended that we cannot successfully understand the satisfactions the practitioner seeks and the impediments to these goals unless we are well acquainted with the ways the practitioner tries to make sense of his/her experiences. The conflicts the practitioner carries from his/her background and the sensitivity about these conflicts shape the way the therapist views others who are suffering and in distress. Vulnerability emanates from a subjective repository of carried-over conflict. This condition of being, I have maintained, is not necessarily a disability in practicing psychotherapy. Indeed, it is one of the prerequisites for effective, meaningful rapprochement between practitioner and client. Therapy is the most human of the arts and sciences. A responsive vulnerability is the basis of the practitioner's sensitivity, compassion, and responsiveness to others' suffering. But, as such, it is, by necessity, a double-edged instrument. It is potentially his/her most sensitive tool for responsively attending human suffering, while at the same time, potentially a wound which may become exacerbated by excessive, painful stress and self-doubt.

I have recommended that the practitioner may best maximize the advantages of this highly attuned responsiveness by treating him/herself and clients with liberal amounts of compassion and common sense. Whatever the practitioner does, it must make sense to him/her and to those with whom he/she works. Clients, whatever their specific symptoms, all undoubtedly suffer from lives that were bereft of sufficient common sense and compassion. If the practitioner does no more than offer clients both sincere compassion and common sense, he/she can do no harm; indeed, the practitioner will more likely serve as a meaningful human bridge to the world they both share. The competent practitioner well knows this in terms of his/her clients. The common sense and compassion of which I speak are, therefore, in the treatment of oneself. One needs to take seriously one's own humanity and must sensibly be cognizant of what is and is not possible to accomplish as a practitioner, without unreasonable risk to health and well-being. One needs to use common sense to provide—in one's practice and in one's personal life—those satisfactions, securities, and provisions of well-being necessary to apply oneself meaningfully and energetically to this important and difficult human task.

In a word, this book has attempted to help the practitioner deal with the strain of being an idealized person during those moments and periods of life when the practitioner experiences him/herself as merely human—all too human. For no matter how intelligent, well-trained, experienced, caring, and well-meaning we are as professionals, we are, at the same time host to the same fears, ambitions, and temptations as those we treat. We can be no more than that and no less if we are to treat meaningfully those who petition us with their suffering. Burton (1975) points out that psychotherapy is a business but it takes a more or less vulnerable person to do it well. This is to say, the practitioner must remain vulnerable and, at the same time, professional and skillful. We must be openly human, which means being less than the ideal for which we strive, without regarding our limitations as weaknesses or our efforts as failures. To believe otherwise is nothing less than to regard ourselves as superordinary beings who should be the fulfillment of our ego-ideal at all times. Our vulnerabilities are the bridges to our clients. If we carry out this complex task without pretense or apology, we cannot fail.

Selected
Bibliography

Bernstein, A. The fear of compassion. In B. B. Wolman (Ed.), *Success and failure in psychoanalysis and psychotherapy*. New York: Macmillan, 1972, 160–176.

Examines Freud's statements about the therapeutic relationship. Contends that the analyst's unwillingness to offer simple, human feelings to the suffering analysand is a misunderstanding and a rigid interpretation of Freud's original proposals.

Book, H. E. On maybe becoming a psychotherapist, perhaps. *Canadian Psychiatric Association Journal, 18* (1973), 487–493.

Identifies basic anxieties that interfere with trying to become a medical psychotherapist. The practitioner must give up the relatively simple and clear-cut medical model of illness and acquire skill in a more complex system.

Buckley, P., T. B. Karasu, & E. Charles. Common mistakes in psychotherapy. *American Journal of Psychiatry, 136* (1979), 1578–1580.

Based on an examination of patient and beginning-psychotherapist interactions, this article discusses the most common and least common therapist errors.

Burton, A. The adoration of the patient and its disillusionment. *American Journal of Psychoanalysis, 29* (1970), 194–204.

Examines factors in the disillusioning process that precedes the therapeutic maturation of the practitioner. Burton contends that these factors are attempts by the practitioner to come to terms with unfinished aspects of self.

Burton, A. Therapist satisfaction. *American Journal of Psychoanalysis, 35* (1975), 115–122.

"There is almost a silent conspiracy in the refusal to look at the treatment needs of the psychotherapist." Burton contends that if these needs are not met, treatment will be sabotaged.

Burton, A. *Twelve therapists: How they live and actualize themselves.* San Francisco: Jossey-Bass, 1972.

These literate, provocative, and revealing autobiographical accounts of eminent psychotherapists enable the reader to follow their significant development issues in becoming the types of practitioners they are.

Farber, B. A., & L. J. Heifetz. The satisfactions and stresses of psychotherapeutic work: A factor analytic study. *Professional Psychology, 12* (1981), 621–630.

One of the few comprehensive, empirical studies of the working conditions and experiences of practitioners of psychotherapy.

Farber, B. A., & L. J. Heifetz. The process and dimensions of burnout in psychotherapists. *Professional Psychology, 13* (1982), 293–301.

A second analysis of Farber and Heifetz's (1981) study. "The primary source of stress for therapists is lack of therapeutic success. . . [and] the nonreciprocated attentiveness and giving that are inherent within the therapeutic relationship."

Freud, S. *Analysis terminable and interminable.* Chapter 30, pp. 316–357. Standard Edition of the Complete Works of Sigmund Freud. London: Hogarth Press, 1955 [1937].

One of Freud's most famous and, perhaps, most enduring papers. Freud indicates that the analyst's self-examination of his own neurosis and resistances toward his work is a ceaseless endeavor.

Freud, S. *Further recommendations in the technique of psychoanalysis: Observations on transference-love,* Chapter 33, pp.377–391. Standard Edition of the Complete Works of Sigmund Freud. London: Hogarth Press, 1955 [1915].

Freud examines the countertransferential reactions of the analyst, which induce him to believe that the patient is actually in love with him.

Freudenberger, H. J. The staff burnout syndrome in alternative institutions. *Psychotherapy: Theory, Research and Practice, 12* (1975), 73–82.

Examines the causes of disillusionment among practitioners of mental health. Makes some useful distinctions among the meanings and activities of commitment, overcommitment, involvement, and dedication, and in assessing the lack of support and satisfaction in the practitioner's personal life.

Freudenberger, H. J., & A. Robbins. The hazards of being a psychoanalyst. *Psychoanalytic Review, 66* (1979), 275–296.

A rather comprehensive view of the types of people who become analysts and how their character, training, and world view contribute to the disillusionment of practice.

Goldberg, C. Existentially oriented training for mental health practitioners. *Journal of Contemporary Psychotherapy, 8* (1976), 57–68.

Conventionally trained practitioners are poorly prepared to deal with certain existential concerns. Specific types of structural existential situations and exercises and the philosophical issues involved in these situations are explored.

Goldberg, C. *Therapeutic partnership: Ethical concerns in psychotherapy.* New York: Springer, 1977.

Examines the negotiating and contracting of roles, tasks, and responsibilities necessary for fostering meaningful therapeutic work.

Goldberg, C. *In defense of narcissism: The creative self in search of meaning.* New York: Gardner Press, 1980.

Demonstrates the importance of passion, courage, and commitment in psychotherapy and human development.

Greben, S. Some difficulties and satisfactions inherent in the practice of psychoanalysis. *International Journal of Psychoanalysis, 56* (1975), 427–434.

A rather comprehensive account of the concerns and satisfactions of practicing psychoanalysis and psychotherapy. Attempts to balance these considerations so that psychotherapy remains "the most human of all human endeavors."

Greenson, R. R. That "impossible" profession. *Journal of the American Psychoanalytic Association, 14* (1966), 9–27.

A now classic article, which empathically examines the skills, traits, and motivations required of the analyst. Discusses the conditions in the analyst's personal life necessary to function fully.

Groesbeck, C. J., & B. Taylor. The psychiatrist as wounded physician. *American Journal of Psychoanalysis, 37* (1977), 131–139.

The client in psychotherapy has a healer within himself, and the therapist, a patient. The therapist, in this sense, must be prepared to have his own inner wounds activated in therapy in order to heal the client and give meaning to the practitioner's own distress.

Haveliwala, Y. A., A. Scheflen, & N. Ashcroft. *Common sense in therapy.* New York: Brunner/Mazel, 1979.

A very practical, sensible, empathic guide for mental health practitioners. It also contains some strong indictments against conventional psychiatry.

Henry, W. E. Some observations on the lives of healers. *Human Development, 9* (1966), 47–56.

Compares modern psychotherapists with traditional shaman healers. Indicates similar rituals and mysteries entered by both and the privileged status accorded each.

Henry, W. E., J. H. Sims, & S. L. Spray. *The fifth profession: Becoming a psychotherapist.* San Francisco: Jossey-Bass, 1971.

The first of two volumes based upon the most comprehensive nationwide study of psychotherapists ever conducted. On the basis of data from over 4,000 practitioners, the authors present detailed information about the personal and professional lives of psychotherapists.

Henry, W. E., J. H. Sims, & S. L. Spray. *Public and private lives of psychotherapists.* San Francisco: Jossey-Bass, 1973.

The second volume, examining the backgrounds, training, and belief systems of psychotherapists.

Kovacs, A. L. The emotional hazards of teaching psychotherapy. *Psychotherapy: Theory, research and practice. 13* (1976), 321–334.

Examines the developmental crises in human growth, which being a psychotherapist reactivates.

Luborsky, L. The personality of the psychotherapist. *Menninger Quarterly, 6* (4) (1952), 1–6.

Examines the personal qualities that make a good psychiatric psychotherapist, according to supervisors' impressions at the Menninger Foundation.

Marmor, J. The feeling of superiority: An occupational hazard in the practice of psychotherapy. *American Journal of Psychiatry, 110* (1953), 370–376.

There is no single type of motivation for, or personality drawn to, practicing psychotherapy, but there are inherent factors in practice that adversely affect all practitioners, if not carefully attended.

Marston, A. R. What makes therapists run? A model for analysis of motivational styles. *Psychotherapy: Theory, Research and Practice, 21* (1984), 456–459.

An analysis of the motivation of practitioners for doing psychotherapy, based on the empirical studies of Farber and Heifetz (1981; 1982). Posits eight basic motives for doing psychotherapy, with discovery and healing at the core of these motives.

Spensley, J., & K. H. Blacker. Feelings of the psychotherapist. *American Journal of Orthopsychiatry, 46* (1976), 542–545.

Persuasively evinces that there are inherent stresses in the practice of psychotherapy not based upon the practitioner's countertransference or neurosis.

Viscott, D. *The making of a psychiatrist.* New York: Fawcett, 1973.

A highly readable, and often insightful, autobiographical account of Viscott's experience as a psychiatric resident in a large teaching hospital.

Wheelis, A. The vocational hazards of psycho-analysis. *International Journal of Psycho-Analysis, 37* (1956), 171–184.

Wheelis, in his poetic and profound style, describes psychoanalysis as a profession understood only by those who practice it and only after many years of experience. The actual reasons for entering practice may be incidental to analytic work.

Winnicott, D. W. Countertransference. *British Journal of Medical Psychology, 33* (1960), 17–21.

This now classic paper indicates our professional demeanor is actually an idealized version of the ordinary person. Personal analysis frees practitioners from excessive neurosis, but cannot remove human vulnerabilities. Indeed, vulnerability is essential to effective therapeutic sensitivity.

References

Aaron, R. The analyst's emotional life during work. *Journal of the American Psychoanalytic Association, 22* (1974), 160–170.

Adams, S., & M. Orgel. *Through the mental health maze.* Washington, D.C.: Health Research Group, 1975.

Adler, J., & I. R. Berman. Multiple leadership in group treatment of delinquent adolescents. *International Journal of Group Psychotherapy, 10* (1960), 213–225.

Ajaya, S. *Psychology East and West.* Honesdale, PA.: The Himalayan International Institute of Yoga Science and Philosophy, 1978.

Ames, E. What your shrink really thinks of you. *Reflections* (Merck, Sharp & Dohme Publ.), 15 (1980), 19–31.

Bach, G. The marathon group: Intensive practice of intimate interaction. *Psychology Reports, 18* (1968), 995–1002.

Bailis, S. S., & G. Adler. Co-therapy issues in a collaborative setting. *American Journal of Psychotherapy, 28* (1974), 559–606.

Bandura, A. Psychotherapist's anxiety level, self-insight, and psychotherapy competence. *Journal of Abnormal Social Psychology, 52* (1956), 333–337.

Benoit, H. *The supreme doctrine.* New York: Viking, 1955.

Bergantino, L. Human relationships are destined to failure. *Psychotherapy: Theory, Research and Practice, 12* (1975), 42–43.

Bermak, G. E. Do psychiatrists have special emotional problems? *American Journal of Psychoanalysis, 37* (1977), 141–146.

Berne, E. *Games people play.* New York: Grove Press, 1964.

Bernstein, A. The fear of compassion, pp. 160–176. In B. B. Wolman (Ed.) *Success and failure in psychoanalysis and psychotherapy.* New York: Macmillan, 1972.

Bion, W. H. *Learning from experience.* London: Heinemann, 1962.

Blatte, H. Evaluating psychotherapies. *Hastings Center Report,* 1973 (Sept.), 4–6.

Book, H. E. On maybe becoming a psychotherapist, perhaps. *Canadian Psychiatric Association Journal, 18* (1973), 487–493.

Bookbinder, L., R., Fox, & V. Rosenthal. *Minimal standards for psychotherapy education in psychology doctoral programs.* Unpublished report, American Psychological Association, Washington, D.C., Oct. 12, 1969.

Bromberg, W. *From shaman to psychotherapist.* Chicago: H. Regnery, 1975.

Brown, G. S. *Laws of form.* New York: Julian Press, 1972.

Buber, M. *I and thou.* New York: Scribner, 1970.

Buckley, P., T. B., Karasu, & E. Charles. Common mistakes in psychotherapy. *American Journal of Psychiatry, 136* (1979), 1578–1580.

Burton, A. Beyond the transference. *Psychotherapy: Theory, Research and Practice, 1* (1964), 49–53.

Burton, A. The adoration of the patient and its disillusionment. *American Journal of Psychoanalysis, 29* (1970), 194–204.

Burton, A. The mentoring dynamic in a therapeutic transformation. *American Journal of Psychoanalysis, 37* (1977), 115–122.

Burton, A. Therapist satisfaction. *American Journal of Psychoanalysis, 35* (1975), 115–122.

Burton, A. To seek and encounter critical people. *Voices, 5* (1969), 26–28.

Burton, A. *Twelve therapists: How they live and actualize themselves.* San Francisco: Jossey-Bass, 1972.

Campbell, J. *The Hero with a thousand faces.* Bollinger series. Princeton, N.J.: Princeton University Press, 1968.

Castaneda, C. *A separate reality.* New York: Pocket Books, 1976.

Chessick, R. P. Socrates: First psychotherapist. *American Journal of Psychoanalysis, 42* (1982), 71–83.

Chessick, R. P. The tremendous interaction with my wife and children. *Voices, 5* (1969), 28–29.

Chodoff, P. The effect of third-party payment on the practice of psychotherapy. *American Journal of Psychotherapy, 20* (1972), 122–123.

Clark, T. *Going into therapy.* New York: Harper, 1975.

Clement, C. Misusing psychiatric models: The culture of narcissism. *Psychoanalytic Review, 69* (1982), 283–295.

Cooley, C. H. *Human nature and the social order.* New York: Scribner, 1900.

Colony, J. Hers. *New York Times,* Sept. 23, 1982.

Daniels, A. K. What troubles the trouble shooters. In P. M. Roman & H. M. Trice (Eds.), *The sociology of psychotherapy.* New York: Jason Aronson, 1974.

Demarest, E. W., & A. Teicher. Transference in group therapy: Its use by co-therapists of opposite sexes. *Psychiatry, 17* (1954), 187–202.

Dreikurs, R. The techniques and dynamics of multiple psychotherapy. *Psychiatric Quarterly, 24* (1950), 785–799.

Dublin, J. E. A further motive for psychotherapists: Communication intimacy. *Psychiatry, 34* (1971), 401–409.

Dymond, R. F. Personality and empathy. *Journal of Consulting Psychology, 14* (1950), 343–350.

Enelow, M. L. Discussion of papers of Gadpaille and Gelb. In J. H. Masserman (Ed.), *The dynamics of power.* New York: Grune and Stratton, 1972.

Erikson, E. *Childhood and society.* New York: Norton, 1963.

Evans, R. I. *Dialogue with Erik Erikson.* New York: Dutton, 1967.

Farber, B. A., & L. J. Heifetz. The process and dimensions of burnout in psychotherapists. *Professional Psychology, 13* (1982), 293–301.

Farber, B. A., & L. J. Heifetz. The stresses and satisfactions of psychotherapeutic work: A factor analytic study. *Professional Psychology, 12* (1981), 621–630.

Fenichel, O. The scopophic instinct and identification. *International Journal of Psycho-Analysis, 18* (1937), 6–34.

Fiske, D. W., & S. P. Maddi (Eds.), *Functions of varied experience.* Homewood, Ill.: Dorsey, 1961.

Fliess, R. The metapsychology of the analyst. *Psychoanalytic Quarterly, 13* (1944), 211–227.

Foulkes, S. H., & E. Anthony. *Group psychotherapy.* Baltimore: Penguin, 1957.

Frank, J. *Persuasion and healing.* Baltimore: Johns Hopkins University Press, 1961.

Freud, S. *Analysis terminable and interminable.* Standard edition of the complete works of Sigmund Freud. London: Hogarth Press, 1955 [1937].

Freud, S. *Further recommendations in the technique of psy-*

choanalysis: Observations of transference love. Standard edition of the complete works of Sigmund Freud. London: Hogarth Press, 1955 [1915].

Freud, S. Group psychology and the analysis of the ego. New York: Bantam, 1960 [1921].

Freud, S. Lines of advance to psychoanalytic therapy. Standard edition of the complete works of Sigmund Freud. London: Hogarth Press, 1955 [1919].

Freud, S. Psychopathology of everyday life. New York: Norton, 1952 [1914].

Freud, S. Recommendations for physicians on the psychoanalytic method of treatment. Standard edition of the complete works of Sigmund Freud. London: Hogarth Press, 1955 [1912].

Freud, S. The economic problem of masochism. Standard edition of the complete works of Sigmund Freud. London: Hogarth Press, 1955 [1924].

Freud, S. The ego and the id. Standard edition of the complete works of Sigmund Freud. London: Hogarth Press, 1955 [1923].

Freudenberger, H. J. The staff burnout syndrome in alternate institutions. Psychotherapy: Theory, Research and Practice, 12 (1975), 73–82.

Freudenberger, H. J., & A. Robbins. The hazards of being a psychoanalyst. Psychoanalytic Review, 66 (1979), 275–296.

Friedman, L. The struggle in psychotherapy: Its influence on some theories. Psychoanalytic Review, 62 (1975), 453–462.

Friedson, E. Profession of medicine: A study of the sociology of applied knowledge. New York: Dodd, Mead, 1976.

Gaddini, E. Discussion of "the role of family life in child development": On "father formation" in early child development. International Journal of Psycho-Analysis, 51 (1976), 397–401.

Gadpaille, W. J. The uses of power: A particular impasse in psychoanalysis, pp. 173–183. In J. H. Masserman (Ed.), The dynamics of power. New York: Grune and Stratton, 1972.

Gans, R. W. Group co-therapists and the therapeutic situation: A critical evaluation. International Journal of Group Psychotherapy, 12 (1962), 82–88.

Gelb, l. A. Psychotherapy as a redistribution of power, pp. 184–195. In J. H. Masserman (Ed.), The dynamics of power. New York: Grune and Stratton, 1972.

Gillis, J. S. Social influence therapy: The therapist as manipulator. Psychology Today, 8 (1974), 90–95.

Glasser, W. *Reality Therapy.* New York: Harper, 1965.

Glover, E. The theory of the therapeutic results of psychoanalysis: A symposium. *International Journal of Psycho-Analysis, 18* (1937), 125–189.

Goldberg, C. Courage and fanaticism: The charismatic leader and modern religious cults, pp. 163–185. In D. A. Halperin (Ed.), *Psychodynamic perspectives on religion: Sect and cult.* Boston: John Wright, 1983b.

Goldberg, C. Courtship contract in marital psychotherapy. *Journal of Family Counseling, 3* (1975a), 40–45.

Goldberg, C. *Encounter: Group sensitivity training experience.* New York: Science House, 1970.

Goldberg, C. Existentially oriented training for mental health practitioners. *Journal of Contemporary Psychotherapy, 8* (1976), 57–68.

Goldberg, C. *In defense of narcissism: The creative self in search of meaning.* New York: Gardner Press, 1980a.

Goldberg, C. Review: A. Rothstein, The narcissistic pursuit of perfection. *Group, 8* (1984b), 52–55.

Goldberg, C. Termination: A meaningful pseudodilemma in psychotherapy. *Psychotherapy Theory, Research and Practice, 12* (1975b), 341–343.

Goldberg, C. The function of the therapist's affect in therapeutic conflict. *Group, 7* (1983a), 3–18.

Goldberg, C. *The human circle: An existential approach to the new group therapies.* Chicago: Nelson-Hall, 1973.

Goldberg, C. *Therapeutic partnership: Ethical concerns in psychotherapy.* New York: Springer, 1977.

Goldberg, C. The peer supervision group: An examination of its purpose and process. *Group, 5* (1981), 27–40.

Goldberg, C. The role of the mirror in human suffering and in intimacy. *Journal of the American Academy of Psychoanalysis, 12* (1984a), 511–528.

Goldberg, C. Utilization and limitation of paradoxical intervention in group psychotherapy. *International Journal of Group Psychotherapy, 30* (1980b), 287–297.

Goldberg, C. What ails Antonio? The role of evil in human suffering. *Journal of Psychology and Judaism 9* (1985).

Goldberg, C., & J. Kane. A missing component in mental health services to the urban poor: Services-in-kind to others, pp. 91–110. In D. A. Evans & W. L. Claiborn (Eds.), *Mental health issues and the urban poor.* New York: Pergamon, 1974b.

Goldberg, C., & J. Kane. Services-in-Kind: A form of compensation for mental health services. *Hospital and Community Psychiatry, 25* (1974a), 161–164.

Goldberg, C., & J. Simon. Towards a psychology of courage: Implications for the healing process. *Journal of Contemporary Psychotherapy, 13* (1982), 107–128.

Goldberg, C., & M. Goldberg. Encounter group experience workshop. pp. 663–667. In *Proceedings of the International Group Psychotherapy Congress.* Zurich: H. Huber, 1975.

Greben, S. *Love's labor: My twenty-five years in psychotherapy.* New York: Schocken, 1984.

Greben, S. Some difficulties and satisfactions inherent in the practice of psychoanalysis. *International Journal of Psycho-Analysis, 56* (1975), 427–434.

Greenberg, R. P., & J. Staller. Personal therapy for therapists. *American Journal of Psychiatry, 138* (1981), 1467–1471.

Greenson, R. R. That "impossible profession." *Journal of the American Psychoanalytic Association, 14* (1966), 9–27.

Greenson, R. R. The decline and fall of the 50-minute hour. *Journal of the American Psychoanalytic Association, 22* (1974), 785–791.

Groesbeck, C. J. The archetypal image of the wounded healer. *Journal of Analytic Psychology, 20* (1975), 122–145.

Groesbeck, C. J., & B. Taylor. The psychiatrist as wounded physician. *American Journal of Psychoanalysis, 37* (1977), 131–139.

Grunebaum, H. A study of therapists' choice of a therapist. *American Journal of Psychiatry, 140* (1983), 1336–1339.

Gussow, M. Theatre: Richard III at the Riverside. *New York Times,* Nov. 26, 1982.

Haigh, G. The residential basic encounter group. In H. A. Otto & J. Mann (Eds.), *Ways of growth.* New York: Viking Press, 1968.

Haley, J. *The power tactics of Jesus Christ.* New York: Avon, 1969.

Halifax, J. *Shaman voices.* New York: Dutton, 1979.

Halleck, S. *The politics of therapy.* New York: Harper, 1971.

Halpert, E. The effect of insurance on psychoanalytic treatment. *Journal of the American Psychoanalytic Association, 20* (1972), 122–133.

Haveliwala, Y. A., A. Scheflin & N. Ashcroft, *Common sense in therapy.* New York: Brunner/Mazel, 1979.

Hart, H. H. The eye in symbol and system. *Psychoanalytic Review, 36* (1949), 1–21.

Havighurst, H. C. *The nature of private contract.* Evanston, Ill.: Northwest University Press, 1961.

Heidegger, M. *Discourse on thinking.* New York: Harper, 1966.

Heider, F. *The psychology of interpersonal relations.* New York: John Wiley, 1957.

Hellwig, K., & R. J. Memmott. Co-therapy: The balance act. *Small Group Behavior, 5* (1974), 175–181.

Henry, W. E. Some observations on the lives of healers. *Human Development, 9* (1966), 47–56.

Henry, W. E., J. H. Sims, & S. L. Spray. *Public and private lives of psychotherapists.* San Francisco: Jossey-Bass, 1973.

Henry, W. E., J. H. Sims & S. L. Spray. *The fifth profession: Becoming a psychotherapist.* San Francisco: Jossey-Bass, 1971.

Hetherington, R. Communication between doctors and psychologists. *British Journal of Medical Psychology, 29* (1983), 99–104.

Hinde, R. A. Interpersonal relationships: In quest of a science. *Psychological Medicine, 8* (1978), 373–386.

Holt, R. Editor's foreword, pp.1–43. In D. Rapaport, M. M. Gil, & R. Schafer, *Diagnostic psychological testing.* New York: International Universities Press, 1981.

Homans, G. *The human group.* New York: Harcourt, 1950.

Horney, K. The problem of the negative therapeutic reaction. *Psychoanalytic Quarterly, 5* (1936), 29–44.

Hunt, W., & A. Issacharoff. History and analysis of a leaderless group of professional therapists. *American Journal of Psychiatry, 132* (1975), 1164–1167.

Hunt, W., & A. Issacharoff. Observations on group process in a leaderless group of professional therapists. *Group, 1* (1977), 162–171.

Jacoby, S. Hers. *New York Times,* April 21, 1983.

Jones, E. *The life and work of Sigmund Freud.* New York: Basic Books, 1957.

Jordan, M. Behavioral forces that are a function of attitudes and of cognitive organization. *Human Relations, 6* (1953), 273–287.

Jourard, S. I-thou relationship versus manipulation in counseling and psychotherapy. *Journal of Individual Psychology, 15,* 1959, 174–179.

Jourard, S. *The transparent self.* Princeton, N.J.: Nostrand, 1964.

Jung, C. *Analytical psychology: Its theory and practice.* New York: Vintage, 1968.

Kernberg, O. Some effects of social pressures on the psychiatrist as a clinician. *Bulletin of the Menninger Clinic, 32* (1968), 144–159.

Kierkegaard, S. *Fear and trembling and sickness unto death.* New York: Doubleday, 1954.

Kline, F. M. Dynamics of a leaderless group. *International Journal of Group Psychotherapy, 22* (1972), 234–242.

Kline, F. M. Terminating a leaderless group. *International Journal of Group Psychotherapy, 24* (1974), 452–459.

Kohut, H. *The restoration of the self.* New York: International Universities Press, 1977.

Kohut, H., & E. Wolf. Disorders of the self and their treatment: An outline. *International Journal of Psycho-Analysis, 59* (1978), 413–424.

Kopp, S. B. *If you meet the Buddha on the road, kill him!* New York: Bantam, 1976.

Kovacs, A. L. The emotional hazards of teaching psychotherapy, *Psychotherapy: Theory, Research and Practice, 13* (1976), 321–334.

Kozrelecki, J. Suffering and human values. *Dialectics and humanism, 4* (1978), 115–127.

Krishnamurti, J. *You are the world.* New York: Perennial Library, 1972.

La Barre, W. *Culture in context: Selected writings of Weston La Barre.* Durham, N.C.: Duke University Press, 1980.

Lacan, J. *The language of the self.* Baltimore: Johns Hopkins University Press, 1977.

Langer, S. *Philosophy in a new key: A study in the symbolism of reason, rite and art.* Boston: Harvard University Press, 1957.

Le Shan, L. Editorial. *Association for Humanistic Psychology Perspective,* 1984 (October).

Levinson, D. J. *The seasons of a man's life.* New York: Ballantine, 1978.

Lewis, J. M. *To be a therapist.* New York: Brunner/Mazel, 1978.

Loeffler, F. J., & H. M. Weinstein. The co-therapist method: Special problems and advantages. *Group Psychotherapy, 6* (1953–1954), 189–192.

London, P. The psychotherapy boom: From the long couch for the sick to the push button for the bored. *Psychology Today, 8* (1974), 62–68.

Luborsky, L. The personality of the psychotherapist. *Menninger Quarterly, 6* (1952), 1–6.

Lundin, W. H., & B. M. Aronov. The use of co-therapists in group psychotherapy. *Journal of Consulting Psychology, 16* (1952), 76–80.

MaCiver, J., & F. Redlich. Patterns of psychiatric practice. *American Journal of Psychiatry, 115* (1959), 692–697.

MacLennan, B. W. Co-therapy. *International Journal of Group Psychotherapy, 15* (1965), 154–166.

Madden, D. J., J. R. Lion, & M. W. Penna. Assaults on psychiatrists by patients. *American Journal of Psychiatry, 133* (1976), 422–425.

Mahrer, A. R. Some known effects of psychotherapy and a reinterpretation. *Psychotherapy: Theory, Research and Practice, 7* (1970), 186–191.

Marmor, J. The feeling of superiority: An occupational hazard in the practice of psychotherapy. *American Journal in Psychiatry, 110* (1953), 370–376.

Marston, A. R. What makes therapists run? A model for analysis of motivational styles. *Psychotherapy: Theory, Research and Practice, 21* (1984), 456–459.

May, R. The emergence of existential psychology, pp. 11–51. In R. May (Ed.), *Existential psychology.* New York: Random House, 1961.

Marziali, E., C. Marmar, & J. Kiupnick. Therapeutic alliance scales: Development and relationship to psychotherapeutic outcome. *American Journal of Psychiatry, 138* (1981), 361–364.

Mead, G. H. *Mind, self and society.* Chicago: University of Chicago Press, 1934.

Meerloo, J. A. Father Time. *Psychiatric Quarterly, 22* (1948), 587–608.

Meltzer, M. L. Insurance reimbursement: A mixed blessing. *American Psychologist, 30* (1975), 1150–1156.

Michaels, R. Ethical issues of psychological and psychotherapeutic means of behavior control. *Hastings Center Report, 1973* (April).

Mintz, E. E. Special values of co-therapists in group psychotherapy. *International Journal of Group Psychotherapy, 13*

(1963a), 64–74.

Mintz, E. E. Transference in co-therapy groups. *Journal of Consulting Psychology, 17* (163b), 34–39.

Mintz, E. E. Male-Female co-therapists. *American Journal of Psychotherapy, 19* (1965), 293–301.

Mullan, H. Transference and countertransference: New horizons. *International Journal of Group Psychotherapy, 5* (1955), 169–180.

Muller, J. P., & W. J. Richardson. Jacques LaCan: Letter to the editor. *New York Times Book Review,* May 15, 1983.

Natanson, M. An editorial fragment. *Journal of Medicine and Philosophy, 6* (1983), 3.

Nobler, H. A. A peer group for the therapists. *International Journal of Group Psychotherapy, 30* (1980), 51–61.

Older, J. Four taboos that may limit the success of psychotherapy. *Psychiatry, 40* (1977), 197–204.

Ormont, L. The treatment of preoedipal resistances in the group setting. *Psychoanalytic Review, 61* (1974), 429–441.

Ormont, L. Training group therapists through the study of countertransferences. *Group, 4* (1980), 17–26.

Parson, T. *Social structure and personality.* New York: Free Press, 1964.

Paulson, I., J. C. Burroughs, & C. B. Gelb. Co-therapy: What is the crux of the relationship? *International Journal of Group Psychotherapy, 27* (1976), 213–224.

Pennebaker, J. W., & R. C. O'Heeron. Confiding in others and illness rates among spouses of suicide and accidental death. *Journal of Abnormal Psychology, 93* (1984), 473–476.

Pfeiffer, E. (Ed.) *Sigmund Freud and Lou Andreas-Salomé letters.* New York: Harcourt, 1972.

Pine, I., W. E. Todd, & C. Boenheim. Special problems of resistance in co-therapy groups. *International Journal of Group Psychotherapy, 13* (1963), 354–362.

Pines, M. Group therapy with "difficult" patients. In L. R. Wolberg & M. L. Aronson (Eds.), *Group therapy 1975.* New York: Stratton Intercontinental Medical Books, 1975.

Pirandello, L. Six characters in search of an author, pp.211–278. In E. Bentley (Ed.), *Naked masks: Five plays by Luigi Pirandello.* New York: Dutton, 1952.

Polsky, H. W., D. S., Claster, & C. Goldberg, *Dynamics of residential treatment.* Chapel Hill, N.C.: North Carolina University Press, 1968.

Polsky, H. W., D. S. Claster, & C. Goldberg, *Social system perspectives in residential institutions.* East Lansing, Mich. Michigan State University Press, 1970.

Pratt, S., & J. Tooley, Contract psychology and the actualizing transactional field. *International Journal of Social Psychiatry*, Congress issue (1964), 51–59.

Rabin, H. M. How does co-therapy compare with regular group therapy? *American Journal of Psychotherapy, 21* (1967), 244–255.

Racker, H. The meanings and uses of countertransference. *Psychoanalytic Quarterly, 26* (1957), 303–357.

Redlich, F., & R. F. Mollica, Overview: Ethical issues in contemporary psychiatry. *American Journal of Psychiatry, 133* (1976), 125–136.

Reik, T. *Compulsions to confess: On the psychoanalysis of crime and punishment.* Salem, N.Y.: Ayer, 1959.

Reik, T. *Listening with the third ear.* New York: Farrar, Straus & Giroux, 1948.

Rieff, P. *Triumph of the therapeutic: Uses of faith after Freud.* New York: Harper, 1968.

Riegel, K. F. The dialectics of human development. *American Psychologist, 31* (1976), 689–700.

Roe, A. Personality structure and occupational behavior. In H. Borow (Ed.), *Man in a world at work.* Boston: Houghton Mifflin, 1964.

Rogers, C. *Becoming a person.* Boston: Houghton Mifflin, 1961a.

Rogers, C. The loneliness of contemporary man. *Review of Existential Psychology and Psychiatry, 1* (1961b), 94–101.

Rogers, C. The attitude and orientation of the counselor. *Journal of Consulting Psychology, 13* (1949), 82–94.

Rogers, S. L. *The shaman: His symbols and his healing power.* Springfield, Ill: C. C. Thomas, 1982.

Rogow, A. *The psychiatrists.* New York: Putnam, 1970.

Rosenhan, D. On being sane in insane places. *Science, 179* (1973), 250–258.

Rosenman, D., J. Karylowski, & K. Hargis. Emotion and altruism. In J. P. Rushton & R. M. Sorrentino (Eds.), *Altruism and helping behavior.* Hillsdale, N.J.: Erlbaum Press, 1981.

Rosenthal, D. *Experimenter effects in behavior research.* New York: Halsted Press, 1976.

Rychlak, J. F. The motives to psychotherapy. *Psychotherapy: Theory, Research and Practice, 2* (1965), 151–157.

Sager, C. J., H. S. Kaplan, R. H., Gundlach, M. Kremer, R. Lenz, & J. R. Royce. The marriage contract, pp. 483–497. In C. J. Sager & H. S. Kaplan (Eds.), *Progress in group and family therapy*. New York: Brunner/Mazel, 1972.

Salzman, L. Will and the therapeutic process. *American Journal of Psychoanalysis, 34* (1974), 277–290.

Sandler, J., A. Holder, & C. Dave. Basic psychoanalytic concepts: 7. The negative therapeutic reaction. *British Journal of Psychiatry, 117* (1970), 431–435.

Satow, R. Response to Collen Clement's "Misusing psychiatric models: The culture of narcissism." *Psychoanalytic Review, 69* (1982), 296–302.

Schafer, R. Talking to patients in psychotherapy. *Bulletin of the Menninger Clinic, 38* (1974), 503–515.

Schofield, W. *Psychotherapy: The purchase of friendship.* Englewood Cliffs, N.J.: Prentice-Hall, 1964.

Schopenhauer, A. *The world as will and idea.* New York: Dover Press, 1966 [1818].

Schwartz, T. The making of a psychiatrist. *New York Magazine,* Feb. 27, 1984 (pp. 32–43), and March 5, 1984 (pp. 75–92).

Schwitzgebel, R. K. A conceptual model for the protection of the rights of institutional mental patients. *American Psychologist, 30* (1975), 815–820.

Seabury, B. A. The contract: Uses, abuses and limitations. *Social Work, 21* (1976), 16–21.

Searles, H. *Countertransference and related subjects.* New York: International Universities Press, 1977.

Shaffer, P. *Equus: A play.* New York: Avon, 1975.

Shapiro, D. The analyst's own analysis. *Journal of the American Psychoanalytic Association, 24* (1976), 5–42.

Sharpe, E. The psychoanalyst. *International Journal of Psycho-Analysis, 28* (1947), 1–6.

Shepard, M. *Marathon 16.* New York: Pocket Books, 1971.

Shore, M. F. Introduction. In M. F. Shore & S. E. Golman (Eds.), *Current ethical issues in mental health.* Publication No. (HSM) 73–9029. Washington, D.C.: Dept. of Health, Education and Welfare, 1973.

Simon, J., & C. Goldberg. The role of the double in the creative process and psychoanalysis. *Journal of the American Academy of Psychoanalysis, 12* (1984), 341–361.

Small, L. *The briefer psychotherapies.* New York: Brunner/Mazel, 1971.

Sobel, D. Freud's fragmented legacy. *New York Times Magazine*, Oct. 26, 1980.

Solomon, A. F., J. Loeffler, & G. H. Frank. An analysis of co-therapist interaction in group psychotherapy. *International Journal of Group Psychotherapy, 3* (1953), 171–180.

Spensley, J., & K. H. Blacker. Feelings of the psychotherapist. *American Journal of Orthopsychiatry, 46* (1976), 542–545.

Spruiell, V. The analyst at work. *International Journal of Psycho-Analysis, 65* (1984), 13–30.

Steinzor, B. *The healing partnership.* New York: Harper, 1967.

Storr, A. An unlikely analyst: Marie Bonaparte. *New York Times Book Review*, Feb. 6, 1983.

Strachey, J. The nature of the therapeutic action of psychoanalysts. *International Journal of Psychoanalysts, 15* (1934), 122–159.

Strunk, O. Training of empathic abilities: A note. *Journal of Pastoral Care, 11* (1957), 222–225.

Strupp, H. H., R. E. Fox, & K. Lessler. *Patients view their psychotherapy.* Baltimore: Johns Hopkins University Press, 1969.

Sullivan, H. S. *The interpersonal theory of psychiatry.* New York: Norton, 1953.

Szalita, A. B. The use and misuse of empathy in psychoanalysis and psychotherapy. *Psychoanalytic Review, 68* (1981), 3–21.

Szasz, T. *The ethics of psychoanalysis.* New York: Dell, 1969.

Szasz, T. & M. H. Hollender, The basic models of the doctor-patient relationships. *Archives of Internal Medicine, 97* (1956), 585-592.

Thibaut, J. W., & H. H. Kelley. The social psychology of groups. New York: Wiley, 1959.

Thomas, H. F. An existential attitude in working with individuals and groups, pp. 227–232. In J. F. Bugenthal (Ed.), *Challenges of humanistic psychology.* New York: McGraw-Hill, 1967.

Thomas, L. *The lives of a cell: Notes on a biology watcher.* New York: Viking Press, 1974.

Tillich, P. *The courage to be.* New Haven, Conn.: Yale University Press, 1952.

Torrey, E. F. Plumbers and psychiatrists: A consumer's view of mandatory evaluation. Presented at the meeting of the American Psychiatric Assn., Detroit, May 8, 1974.

Trotter, S. Nader group releases first consumer guide to psychotherapists. *American Psychological Association Monitor*, 6 (1975), 11.

Viscott, D. *The making of a psychiatrist*. New York: Fawcett, 1973.

Walster, E., & G. W. Walster. Equity and social justice. *Journal of Social Issues*, 31 (1975), 21–43.

Warkentin, J., N. L. Johnson, & C. Whitaker. A comparison of individual and multiple psychotherapy. *Psychiatry*, 14 (1951), 415–418.

Watts, A. *Psychotherapy: East and West*. New York: Ballantine, 1961.

Weigert, E. Contribution to the problem of terminating psychoanalysis. *Psychoanalytic Quarterly*, 21 (1952), 465–480.

Weinberg, G. *The heart of psychotherapy*. New York: St. Martin's Press, 1984.

Wheelis, A. The vocational hazards of psycho-analysis. *International Journal of Psycho-Analysis*, 37 (1957), 171–184.

Whitaker, C. A. My philosophy of psychotherapy. *Journal of Contemporary Psychotherapy*, 6 (1973), 49–53.

Wilber, K. Psychologia perennis: The spectrum of consciousness, pp. 7–28. In J. Welwood (Ed.), *The meeting of the ways: Explorations in East/West Psychology*. New York: Schocken, 1979.

Wilde, O. The picture of Dorian Gray. In Richard Aldington & Stanley Weintraub (Eds.), *The portable Oscar Wilde*. New York: Penguin, 1982.

Winnicott, D. W. *Collected papers*. New York: Basic Books, 1958.

Winnicott, D. W. Counter-transference. *British Journal of Medical Psychology*, 33 (1960), 17–21.

Winnicott, D. W. The development of the capacity for concern. *Bulletin of the Menninger Clinic*, 27 (1963), 167–176.

Woods, T. L. The study group: A mechanism for continuing education and professional self-development. *Clinical Social Work Journal* 2 (1974), 120–126.

Yalom, I. *The theory and practice of group psychotherapy*. New York: Basic Books, 1970.

Author Index

Aaron, R., 257
Adams, S., 34, 178, 182
Adler, A., 316
Adler, G., 316
Adler, J., 317
Ajaya, S., 304
Ames, E., 104
Anthony, E., 124
Aronov, B.M., 320
Bach, G., 176
Bailis, S.S., 316
Bandura, A., 120
Benoit, H., 306
Bergantino, L., 103
Berkow, I., 41
Bermak, G.E., 65, 66
Berman, I.R., 317
Berne, E., 170, 176
Bernstein, A., 72, 294
Bion, W.H., 121, 218
Blacker, K.H., 80-82
Blatte, H., 170
Boenheim, C., 320
Bonaparte, M., 81
Bookbinder, L., 127, 129
Bromberg, W., 7
Brown, G.S., 305
Buber, M., 234
Burroughs, J.C., 317
Burton, A., 10, 46, 47, 52-60,
    62, 66, 76, 90, 104, 113,
    116, 118, 119, 120, 128,
    132, 133, 284, 299-301,
    346, 362, 364

Campbell, J., 8, 11, 13, 14, 306
Camus, A., 208
Casteneda, C., 9, 12
Chessick, R.P., 126, 347
Chodoff, P., 167
Churchill, W., 288
Claiborne, C., 108
Clark, T., 180, 184, 312, 315
Clement, C., 216
Claster, D.S., 319
Colony, J., 233
Cooley, C.H., 211
Daniels, A.K., 106
Dave, C., 250
De Marest, E.W., 316, 320
Dreikurs, R., 316
Dublin, J.E., 172
Dullea, G., 164
Dymond, R.F., 130
Eisenreich, J., 41
Ekstein, R., 58
Ellis, A., 58
Enelow, M.L., 196
English, O.S., 58, 104, 133
Erikson, E., 33, 163, 257, 282
Evans, R.I., 257, 282
Farber, B.A., 61, 106, 107, 110,
    161
Fay, T.H., 164
Fenichel, O., 43
Fine, R., 56, 57
Fiske, D.W., 191
Foulkes, S.H., 124
Fox, R., 127, 250

Frank, G.H., 316
Frank, J., 41, 277, 301
Freud, S., 9, 31, 36, 38, 39,52,
    54, 63, 81, 86, 90, 91, 100,
    101, 109, 113, 125, 132,
    176, 188, 204, 214, 215,
    216, 250-252, 282, 294-296,
    308, 324, 348
Freudenberger, H.J., 61, 68, 72,
    87
Friedman, L., 97
Friedson, E., 35, 36, 168
Frost, R., 288
Gadini, E., 30
Gadpaille, W.J., 196
Gans, R.W., 316
Gelb, I., 191, 196, 317
Gillis, J.S., 199
Glasser, W., 170
Glover, E., 4
Goldberg, C., 6, 10, 20, 28, 32,
    35, 40, 43, 51, 63, 70, 71,
    73, 76, 85, 90, 97, 98, 109,
    111, 115, 166, 181, 189,
    191, 195, 204, 205, 214,
    216, 226, 232, 237, 238,
    246-249, 254-256, 264-267,
    271, 274, 285, 293, 295,
    297, 300, 318, 319, 321-
    323, 328, 334, 339-342, 355
Goldberg, M., 318
Granet, R.B., 164
Greben, S., 69, 294
Greenberg, R.P., 131
Greenson, R.R., 69, 104, 111,
    289, 293, 347, 349
Groesbeck, C.J., 12, 84
Grunebaum, H., 120, 121
Gussow, M., 211
Haigh, G., 285
Haley, J., 198
Halifax, J., 6, 12, 13
Halleck, S., 170
Halperin, D.A., 14
Halpert, E., 167
Hargis, K., 27
Hart, H.H., 42

Haveliwala, Y.A., 104, 345, 346
Havighurst, H.C., 175, 176
Heidegger, M., 231
Heider, F., 191
Heifetz, L.J., 61, 106, 107, 110,
    161
Hellwig, K., 316
Henry, W.E., 36, 52-54, 56-60,
    63, 65, 84, 97, 100, 113,
    115, 133, 154, 289, 346
Heraclitus, 12
Herzberg, A., 109
Herzl, T., 109
Hetherington, R., 152
Hinde, R.A., 33
Holder, A., 250
Hollender, M.H., 177
Holt, R., 73
Homans, G., 193, 194
Horney, K., 32, 251
Huessy, H., 202
Hunt, W., 336
Issacharoff, A., 336
Ivy, A.O., 170
Jacoby, S., 209, 210
Johnson, N.L., 325
Jones, E., 86, 100
Jordan, M., 191
Jourard, S., 130, 294
Jung, C., 11, 13, 32, 52, 54
Kafka, F., 109, 212
Kane, J., 97, 98
Kaplan, H.S., 19
Karylowski, J., 27
Kelley, H.H., 200
Kernberg, O., 96, 216
Kernberg, P., 24
Kierkegaard, S., 208
Kipling, R., 121
Kiupnick, J., 250
Klein, M., 261
Kline, F.M., 329, 336
Kohut, H., 26, 31, 32, 122, 216
Kopp, S.B., 11, 13, 78
Kovacs, A.L., 5
Kozrelecki, J., 211
Kris, E., 127

Krishnamurti, J., 303
Kunitz, S., 11, 14
La Barre, W., 40, 258
Lacan, J., 24, 121, 348
Langer, S., 11
Lawrence, D.H., 323
Le Shan, E., 125
Lessler, K., 250
Levinson, D.J., 10
Lion, J., 82, 82
Loeffler, J., 316
London, P., 170
Longfellow, II.W., 11
Lundin, W.H., 320
MaCiver, J., 106
MacLennan, B.W., 320
Madden, D.J., 83
Maddi, S.P., 191
Mahrer, A.R., 129
Marmar, C., 250
Marmor, J., 43, 86, 87, 101, 112
Marston, A.R., 61, 107, 108, 161
Marziali, E., 250
Maugham, S., 228
May, R., 204
Mead, G.H., 211
Meerloo, J.A., 30
Meltzer, M.L., 72, 167
Memmott, R.J., 316
Mendel, W., 76, 261
Michaels, R., 186
Michener, J., 228
Milton, J., 59, 233
Mintz, E.E., 316, 317
Mollica, R.F., 177
Mullan, H., 271
Muller, J.P., 348
Nader, R., 34
Natanson, M., 208
Nietzsche, F.W., 25, 109
Nobler, H.A., 329, 335, 336,
    340, 341, 343
O'Heeron, R.C., 89
Older, J., 272, 273
Orgel, M., 34, 178, 182
Ormont, L., 268, 269, 328
Orwell, G., 197

Parson, T., 174
Paulson, I., 317
Penna, M.W., 83
Pennebaker, J.W., 89
Pfeiffer, E., 176
Piaget, J., 63
Pine, I., 320
Pines, M., 249
Pirandello, L., 17
Plato, 228
Polsky, H.W., 319
Pratt, S., 175
Rabin, H.M., 317
Racker, H., 252-254, 268
Redlich, F., 106, 177
Reik, T., 89, 252
Reinhardt, A., 234
Richardson, W.J., 348
Rleff, P., 124, 125
Riegel, K.F., 239
Rivere, J., 251
Robbins, A., 61, 68, 72, 87
Roe, A., 55
Rogers, C., 54, 115, 235, 236,
    298, 299
Rogers, S.L., 6, 50, 51
Rogow, A., 106
Rosenhan, D., 109, 110
Rosenman, D., 27
Rosenthal, D., 303
Rosenthal, V., 127
Rychlak, J.F., 112, 113, 115,
    119
Sachs, H., 4
Sager, C.J., 190
Salzman, L., 214
Sandler, J., 250-252
Satow, R., 215
Schafer, R., 121, 203, 252
Schaffer, P., 287
Schofield, W., 98
Schopenhauer, A., 226
Schwartz, T., 93
Schwitzgebel, R.K., 170
Seabury, B.A., 181
Searles, H., 234, 291
Shakespeare, W., 43

Shapiro, D., 131

Sharpe, E., 70, 112, 113, 119

Shepard, M., 169

Shore, M.F., 206

Simon, J., 20, 28, 32, 63, 214, 232, 339

Sims, J.H., 36

Small, L., 36

Sobel, D., 37, 137

Socrates, 126

Solomon, A.F., 316, 320

Spensley, J., 80-82

Spray, S.L., 36

Spruiell, V., 68

Staller, J., 131

Steinzor, B., 57, 180

Stierlin, H., 47, 48, 58

Storr, A., 81

Strachey, J., 298

Strunk, O., 130

Strupp, H., 249, 250

Sullivan, H.S., 33, 63, 289, 296

Szalita, A.B., 26

Szasz, T., 51, 177, 180, 205, 296

Taylor, B., 12, 84

Teicher, A., 316, 320

Tennyson, A., 9

Thibault, J.W., 200

Thomas, H.F., 205

Thomas, L., 90

Tillich, P., 231, 236

Todd, W.E., 320

Tooley, J., 175

Torrey, E.F., 34

Trotter, S., 35

Viscott, D., 184

Walster, E., 194

Walster, G.W., 194

Warkentin, J., 58, 59, 120, 325

Watts, A., 115, 301, 302, 305

Wiegert, E., 70, 188

Weinberg, G., 73, 74, 151, 157, 161

Weinstein, H.M., 316

Wheelis, A., 95, 96, 99-101

Whitaker, C., 60, 325

Wilber, K., 304-306

Wilde, O., 233

Winnicott, D.W., 115, 218, 309

Wolf, E., 29

Woods, T.L., 329, 330

Yalom, I., 277

Subject Index

Alcohol, 22, 23, 233
  alcoholism, 181, 247
Alcoholics Anonymous, 236
American Academy of Psychotherapy, 354
American Board of Professional Psychology, 45
American Journal of Orthopsychiatry, 80
American Medical Association, Judicial Council of, 170
American Psychoanalytic Association, 257
American Psychological Association, 35, 167
Analyst,
  as teacher, 9
Animal Farm, 197
Basic Emotional Communication (BEC), 238-247
  twenty-five principles, 239-247
Bonding, 15, 16
  mother-child, 15, 20, 21, 26, 30, 32
  father-child, 31
Buddhism, 301
Cocaine, 23
Columbia Presbyterian Medical Center, 164
Consultation,
  conjoint with clients and colleagues, 325, 326

to assess progress and impasse, 326-328
Consumer Reports, 160
Contractual psychotherapy, 175-177
  elements of contract, 182
  equity and balance in, 191-194
  for difficult patients, 194, 195
  negotiation for, 190
  outline for, 184-190
  phase in, 181, 182
  power, 196-202
  relationship in, 177-180
Cooper Union, 14
Cornell Medical College, 164
Co-Therapy, 155
  advantages and limitations, 318-320
  as personal psychotherapy, 324, 325
  model for, 320-323
Countertransference, 80-82, 85, 130, 197, 200, 252, 253, 257, 258, 262, 263, 268-270, 316
  problem of, 284-286
Courage, 214, 215, 219-221, 231
Crises,
  developmental, 163
  emergencies-in-living, 163
  identity, 163

Dartmouth College v. New
  Hampshire, 206
Development,
  mirror phase, 24, 26
  personality, 24
Dialectics, 126
Difficult clients, 248-278
  negative therapeutic reaction,
    250-252
  therapeutic impasse, 265
Don Juan, 9, 12
Don Quixote, 227
Drugs,
  hardcore, 181
  psychopharmacological, 209
Electric shock, 169, 188, 209
Equus, 18, 287
"Eriksonian therapist," 151
Evil Eye, 42, 43
Games People Play, 170
"Gestalt practitioner," 151
Group Psychology and the
  Analysis of the Ego, 31
Harvard Medical School, 120
Haworth Press, 164
Health Research Group, 34
Holocaust, 58
Hinduism, 301
In Defense of Narcissism, 99
Institutes of the American Group
  Psychotherapy Association,
  354
Insurance,
  for practitioners, 141
  liability, 142
  national health, 166, 168
  paid fees, 150
  third party, 137, 150, 167
International Journal of Psy-
  choanalysis, 104
Intimacy, 19-21, 23-25,
  abuses of therapeutic, 230
  Basic Emotional Communica-
    tion, 238-247
  caring, 221
  definition, 25

developing, 237-247
father's role, 30
mother's role, 26-30, 32
role in psychotherapy,
  207-232
sexual, 29
therapeutic, 20
  breach of, 20
Jewish,
  culture, Freud's view, 109,
  113
  mothers, 57, 117
  practitioners, 55-57
  tradition, 113, 114
Joanne Little trial, 38
LSD, 23
Landau v. Werner, 169
Leaders,
  charismatic, 10
  false messiahs, 10
Loneliness, 208, 209, 212-214
Man of La Mancha, 227
Mandrax, 23
Marathon 16, 169
Mental Health Study Group, 182
Metaphor, 265, 266
Minnesota State Senate, 42
Mirroring, 218
Mitchell-Stans trial, 38
Myth, 11, 44, 45
Narcissism, 16, 29, 32
  contemporary view of, 215,
    216
Neanderthal, 7
"Neurolinguistic practitioner,"
  151
New School for Social Research,
  14
New York Times, 41, 42, 66,
  108, 164, 209, 210
New York University, 168
New Yorker, 34
One Flew Over the Cuckoo's
  Nest, 110
Paradise Lost, 233
Peer supervision groups, 328

guidelines for forming,
    330-345
hidden agendas, 329, 330
why formed, 329
Philosophy,
    Western and Eastern con-
    trasted, 302-307
Placidyl, 23
Power,
    denial of, 196-198
    suicide threat, 198-202
    therapist-client, 196-198
Prado, 228
Private practice, 137
    business aspects, 144-146
    collaborative, 155
    collecting fees,161
    crisis management, 162
    family, 154, 155
    fear of compassion, 294
    fees, 149
    follow up, 162
    group, 153
    home vs. office, 158, 159
    limits to involvement with
        clients, 299, 300
    office, 157
    promoting, 146
    referrals, 147, 148
    risk and reward, 142, 143
    scheduling, 156, 157
    starting, 137-164
    termination of treatment, 161
        162
Profession of Medicine, 168
Projective identification, 261
Psychoanalysis,
    Adlerian, 124
    difficult clients, 250-252
    distinction from psychother-
        apy, 45, 46
    Freud's view, 39, 52, 124, 178
    Horney position, 178
    Jungian, 124
    Kohutian, 178
Psychopathology of Everyday

Life, 91
Psychosurgery, 169
Psycotherapist,
    additional training, 352-354
    ambiguity of field, 65
    backgrounds of, 53-55
    certification of, 45
    clinical responsibility of, 102,
        103
    difficult clients, dealing with,
        248-280
    distinction from psy-
        choanalyst, 45, 46
    education of, 124-128
    emotional control, 64, 65
    forensic, 149
    goals, 282, 283
    group/family practice, 154,
        155
    hazards of, 78-110, 309-317
    identification denial, 84, 85
    identity,47, 48
    institutional practice, 139, 140
    interdisciplinary work, 152,
        153
    isolation of, 64
    Jewish values, 55
    loneliness and boredom, 289,
        290
    media image, 37
    motivations of 111-120
        creative, 117-122
        ethical, 115-117
        scholarly, 113-115
    omnipotent wishes, 65
    power of, 68, 69, 196-202
    public's view, 34-36
    qualities of, 111-132
    satisfaction of practice, 67-73,
        84
    supervision of, 128, 129
    voyeurism, 287, 288
Psychotherapy Finances, 164
Psychotherapy in Private Prac-
    tice, 164
Reality Therapy, 170

Reductionism, 100
Rites of Spring, 228
Roosevelt-St. Lukes Hospital, 33
Saint Elizabeths Hospital, 170
Sexual Problems, 290
  attraction, 291
  exploitation, 201, 202
Shaman, 6, 12, 13, 76
  anthropological significance, 7
  as psychotherapist, 41
  healers, 12, 13, 106, 301
  history of, 7
  psychic structures, 258
  therapy, 50
Six Characters in Search of an Author, 17
Social workers,
  as psychotherapists, 61
Stanford University, 27, 109
Symposium, 228
Taoism, 301
The Courage to Be, 236
The God Complex, 86
The Impossible Profession, 104
The Lives of a Cell, 90

The Razor's Edge, 228
The Secret of the Sea, 11
The World as Will and Idea, 226
Therapeutic Partnership, 192, 195, 206, 247, 322
Transference, 167, 252, 253, 257, 258, 297, 316
Twelve Psychotherapists, 55, 56, 58
Ulysses, 9
University of Chicago, 52
Valium, 22, 23
Vedanta, 301
Veterans Administration, hospitals, 138
Washington Post, 170
Washington School of Psychiatry, 162
Whitney Museum, 236
Women in Love, 323
Wounded Knee Indian trial, 38
Yale University, 38
Young Coyote, 74, 75

ABOUT THE AUTHOR

Carl Goldberg, Ph.D., is in private practice in New York City. He also is an Associate Clinical Professor of Psychiatry at Albert Einstein College of Medicine. A fellow of both the American Psychological Association and the American Group Psychotherapy Association, he is a member of the latter's Standards and Ethics Committee and has been a master instructor in its annual institutes. Dr. Goldberg is a former Director of Group Psychotherapy Training, Department of Psychiatry, City Hospital at Elmhurst, and a former faculty member and supervisor at the National Institute for the Psychotherapies, the Greenwich Institute for Psychoanalysis, the Training Institute for Mental Health Practitioners, and the Nondeterministic Center (all in New York City).

Previously, Dr. Goldberg served as Director of the Laurel Comprehensive Community Health Center and the Northern Mental Health Team, Prince George's County, Maryland. He was an Associate Professor in Psychiatry at George Washington University Medical School and Consultant in Psychotherapy at Saint Elizabeth's Hospital CNIMH, Washington, D.C. He has also taught at The University of Virginia, Antioch College, The Virginia Institute for Group Psychotherapy in Richmond, and the Washington School for Psychiatry.

He is the author of some 60 publications. Dr. Goldberg's previously published books include *Therapeutic Partnership, In Defense of Narcissism, The Human Circle, Encounter*, and two co-authored books on residential treatment and social systems theory.